# Foundations of Intercultural Communication

**Guo-Ming Chen**
*University of Rhode Island*

**William J. Starosta**
*Howard University*

**Allyn and Bacon**
*Boston • London • Toronto • Sydney • Tokyo • Singapore*

*Vice President, Editor in Chief:* Paul Smith
*Series Editor:* Karon Bowers
*Series Editorial Assistant:* Kathy Rubino
*Marketing Manager:* Kris Farnsworth
*Production Administrator:* Susan Brown
*Editorial-Production Service:* Matrix Productions Inc.
*Cover Designer:* Jennifer Hart
*Composition Buyer:* Linda Cox
*Manufacturing Buyer:* Suzanne Lareau

Copyright © 1998 by Allyn & Bacon
A Viacom Company
160 Gould St.
Needham Height, Mass. 02194
www.abacon.com

### *Library of Congress Cataloging-in-Publication Data*

Chen, Guo-Ming.
    Foundations of intercultural communication / Guo-Ming Chen,
William J. Starosta.
        p.    cm.
    Includes bibliographical references and index.
    ISBN 0–205–17529–5
    1. Intercultural communication.   2. Communication and culture.
3. Language and culture.   4. Nonverbal communication.   5. Cultural
relations.   6. Conflict management.   I. Title.
HM258.C465   1997
302.2—dc21                                                      97–18261
                                                                    CIP

Printed in the United States of America

10  9  8  7  6  5  4  3  2  1        01  00  99  98  97

# Contents

# Preface

The progress of communication and transportation technology has made McLuhan's prophecy of a "global village" a reality. Internationally, people from different cultures increasingly and inevitably encounter each other during travel, study, and business interaction. Especially in the United States, the movement toward multiculturalism, or cultural diversity, has become a cascade, with the daily influx of immigrants and the growing expectations of co-cultural groups for equitable treatment.

Knowledge and skill in intercultural communication are critical in meeting the demands of an integrated society and world. More and more colleges require students to take intercultural communication or related courses, and business has now begun to diversify its workforce as never before. Our book presents a comprehensive overview of intercultural communication that explains the need to understand communication among culturally diverse persons at a theoretical level, while simultaneously addressing the need for application of theoretical principles by contemporary students, instructors, businesspersons, and professionals.

Our book differs from other intercultural communication texts in four important ways. First, our text represents a dialogue among scholars of differing perspectives—a social-science and historical-interpretive perspective; an international and domestic outlook; and a research-based and experience-based orientation—and discusses key topics as they relate to the past, the present, and the future of the field. Second, the book adopts a thematic approach to address subjects ranging from the history of the field and traditional topics to multicuturalism, training, listening across cultures, and ethical issues of intercultural communication studies. In addition, *Foundations of Intercultural Communication*, the most comprehensive book of its kind, analyzes topics that cannot be found in other works. Chapter 1 provides a concise history of intercultural communication study that is unavailable elsewhere. Whereas this chapter helps students understand the nature of the field, Chapter 12, on training, explains its practical application and career orientation. Throughout, the text also makes unique contributions in its discussions of ethics, listening across cultures, and the building of intercultural relationships. Third, our book provides a highly readable introduction to intercultural communication, while advancing a more sophisticated theoretical position. Comprehensive and research-based, the book is definitely a unique resource work. It is an ideal textbook for students taking intercultural communication and related courses. Finally, our book urges students to "rethink" the work in each chapter and to confront unanswered questions. A "rethink" section can be found in no other intercultural communication textbook. This section and the authors' commentaries portray intercultural communication as a boundless discipline. Our approach not only invites students to think critically about issues but asks them personally to shape the future of the field.

Many persons helped to make this book possible. Our families, friends, students, and the Department of Communication Studies at the University of Rhode Island and of Human Communication Studies at Howard University provided more support than we can possibly acknowledge. We are also indebted to reviewers who contributed insightful comments on the manuscript: Janice W. Anderson, S.U.N.Y. at New Paltz; John R. Baldwin, Illinois State University; Dolores Cathcart, retired; Hsiu-Jung Chang, University of Richmond; Melbourne S. Cummings, Howard University; Janie Harden Fritz, Duquesne University; Thurmon Garner, University of Georgia; Nemi C. Jain, Arizona State University; Mark L. McPhail, University of Utah; and Armeda C. Reitzel, Humbolt State University. The staff at Allyn and Bacon have been encouraging and helpful. Among them, we especially give credit to Paul Smith, Andrea Geanacopolous, Carla Daves, and Joseph Opiela.

Finally, we owe a tribute to members of the Association for Chinese Communication Studies. Through regular discussions and debates by computer, we were alternately challenged and supported, queried, and corrected. The "rethinking" that was provoked by ACCS members moved us beyond what we would have accomplished on our own.

# ▶ Part I

## Foundation

# ► Chapter 1

## Introduction to Intercultural Communication

### Objectives

Upon completion of this chapter, you will

- Understand why we need to study intercultural communication.
- Understand the chronological development of the field of intercultural communication.
- Understand the content of intercultural communication study.
- Understand the structure of this book.

> *Let there be a small country with few people. . . .*
> *Though neighboring communities overlook one another*
> *and the crowing of cocks and barking of dogs can*
> *be heard, yet the people there may grow old and*
> *die without ever visiting one another.—LAO TZE*

From Lao Tze's ideal, stated two millennia ago, to the global village forecast by Marshall McLuhan, the wheel of human history has moved us inexorably forward from isolation to integration. As our world shrinks and its inhabitants become interdependent, people from remote cultures increasingly come into contact on a daily basis. Always, intercultural communication operates at the hub of the wheel, directing the change, critiquing the change, even resisting the change to an emergent worldview.

3

# WHY STUDY INTERCULTURAL COMMUNICATION?

As the world populace grows more aware of its interdependence, it confronts the ever-shifting cultural, ecological, economic, and technological realities that define modern life. The utopias of Lao Tze or of Mahatma Gandhi, who prepared for a society of self-sufficient villages, have been replaced by newer ways of living in the world together that require our seeing things through the eyes of others and adding the knowledge of others to our personal repertoire. The development of a global mind-set has become pivotal for further human progress. This mind-set can only result from intercommunication among diverse peoples.

Four trends combine to usher in a more interdependent future that shapes our differences into a set of shared concerns and a common agenda: (1) technological development, (2) globalization of the economy, (3) widespread population migration, and (4) the development of multiculturalism. Taken together, these dynamics argue eloquently for the development of more proficient intercultural communicators.

## *Technological Development*

The development of new transportation and information technologies has connected all nations in ways that were possible before this century only in the imagination. Suddenly moon walks, the Chernoble nuclear reactor accident, and the death of a leader half a world away share space with local stories in our newscasts. Supersonic transports carry passengers from continent to continent in a matter of hours, in time for them to conduct business, attend conferences, or to meet friends and associates face-to-face. The continent of Australia that once stood geographically apart from the Northern Hemisphere now talks with its European and North American neighbors just as easily as it does with its Indonesian, New Zealand, or Japanese neighbors.

Communication technologies, including the Internet computer network, facsimiles, the cellular telephone, interactive cable TV systems, and the anticipated information superhighway, permit us instantaneous oral and written interchange at any hour to most locations in our own country and around the world. Porter and Samovar (1994) indicate that the improvement of information technology has greatly reshaped intercultural communication, creating common meanings and a reliance on persons we may or may not meet face-to-face at some future date in our lives. Government is no longer the only disseminator of information across cultural boundaries; indeed, common people talk and type their way daily into a web of mediated intercultural interactions.

As we learn instantaneously about South African elections, a World Cup match, or a Palestinian peace accord, our separateness starts to dissolve. We begin to desire information about other places and to cultivate contacts with people we have met along the information highway. We ride the wave of information that surges about the globe. We sit in our living rooms but feel connections to events that happen elsewhere in the world. The immediacy of our new technology involves us with persons of widely varying regions and ethnicity and builds in us a new sense of national and global commonality. We find ourselves moving from uncertainty, to curiosity, to an active need to improve our understanding of persons and groups from outside our immediate circle.

## Globalization of the Economy

The progress of communication and transportation technology has made markets more accessible and the world of business more globally interreliant in past decades. The trend toward a global economy brings people and products together from around the world.

In the face of economic globalization nations must determine how to remain competitive in the presence of new trade communities and must find ways to promote products and services in places where they have not historically existed. Such interdependence among national economies hinges on effective intercultural communication and calls for ever more skillful interaction in the future across linguistic and national boundaries. Greater cultural and ethnic understanding becomes necessary both to carry out world business and to preserve threatened cultural diversity.

Although globalization of the economy leads to a more uniform way of conducting business, Harris and Moran (1989) note that even decreasing differences among people will require of them intercultural knowledge and skills. Five attitudinal imperatives, described by Harris and Moran, will be needed in an age of economic interdependence:

1. Possessing a cosmopolitan mind with a sensitive, innovative, and participative ability to operate comfortably in a global or pluralistic environment.
2. Acknowledging the importance of intercultural communication by recognizing cultural influences on personal needs, values, expectations, and sense of self.
3. Becoming culturally sensitive by integrating the understanding of culture in general with insights gained from service in multicultural organizations or from activities that bring us into contact with ethnically and culturally different persons.
4. Adjusting to the norms of a new culture, whether that be a domestic coculture or another national culture.
5. Building upon similarities and common concerns while integrating and understanding differences, to further our personal growth and to aid us in our dealings with other cultures that are, as yet, unfamiliar to us.

Clearly, the attitudes requisite for a global economy force us to reexamine our isolation and to prepare to deal with a wide variety of persons from a broad range of cultural backgrounds. The search for mutually acceptable guidelines for conducting economic exchange as trade barriers are lowered entails frequent intercultural communication.

## Widespread Population Migrations

With the cultural interconnectedness that accompanies technological development comes the influence of cultural migration between nations. Conditions at home and abroad push or pull persons to leave their country to find peace, employment, learning, or a new start. Canada and the United States have been the destination of choice for generations of refugees, job seekers, and others seeking a change in political climate.

The 1990 U.S. census reveals that nearly 20 million persons residing within U.S. borders are of recent foreign extraction. About 8.7 million of these arrived between 1980 and 1990. Some 32 million Americans speak a mother tongue besides English, and 14 million are not very fluent in English. Although various legislative initiatives have been made to declare English the official language at the state (Peterson, 1988) and national level (Short, 1988), as many as one American in nine speaks black English vernacular (Ebonics) as a mother tongue, 17 million Americans speak Cuban, Mexican, Puerto Rican, or South American varieties of Spanish, and 4.5 million Americans first speak a language from Asia or the Pacific Islands. Some 91,000 Americans originate from the Philippines; 75,000 come from Canada (including French bilinguals); 74,000 have arrived from Cuba; 71,000 are German; 58,000 are Italian; and 56,000 originate from Korea. Since 1980, the average age of immigrants has dropped from 46.3 to 28.

Earlier immigrants to the United States considered the United States to be a "melting pot" of ethnicities; more recently, this image has been replaced by that of the "tossed salad," in which each ethnic group retains its own "flavor." Be their result a melting pot or tossed salad, successive waves of immigration have rewoven the fabric of American and Canadian society, turning North America into a continent of persons of recent foreign ethnic origin.

This multiethnic composition makes contact among North American cocultures inevitable. Children in multicultural classrooms and workers in multinational corporations look for ways to learn and work efficiently in settings that are no longer defined exclusively by mainstream norms and rules. The quest for more productive interaction in international and domestic settings calls for a detailed understanding of the dynamics of communication among persons of diverse national and ethnic origin. Intercultural communication as a field of study investigates the dynamics of interaction among persons of differing ethnic or national origin.

## Development of Multiculturalism

Changing North American demographics now affect every aspect of life. Johnston and Packer (1987) report five demographic trends in the United States that will affect organizational life in the twenty-first century:

1. The population and the workforce will grow more slowly.
2. The average age of the population and the workforce will decline.
3. More women will enter the workforce.
4. More nonmainstream workers will enter the workforce.
5. Immigrants will make up the largest share of the workforce since the 1920s.

These demographic trends will produce classrooms and workplaces that are defined by no predominant ethnic culture or gender. The tributaries of different ethnicities, nations, genders, ages, tribes, and languages will flow into the mainstream of the classroom and workplace. Cultural diversity, or multiculturalism, will become the norm, not the exception. Intercultural communication scholars will be needed to smooth the transition to bicultural, bidialectal classrooms, to multinational boardrooms, to multiethnic neighborhoods, and to gender and ethnic sensitivity on the part of professionals and service providers.

The public must acknowledge and adjust to difference but build on commonality. It must begin to recognize the culturally defined qualities in all persons but not elevate one set of qualities above any other. It must understand that competency in a culture is a learned process and that understanding resides in persons, not in words. Such adjustments, though critical for the smooth functioning of society, do not always come easily; they are accompanied by the attempts of some persons to keep their position of privilege.

The field of intercultural communication will play a vital part in teaching new ways of interacting, in helping to negotiate multicultural understandings, in dealing with the frictions that accompany the adjustment to new cultural realities, and in educating citizens to a greater global awareness. Whereas multiethnic societies have been the rule rather than the exception in Europe, Africa, Asia, Canada, and the Caribbean, it is in the United States that intercultural communication first evolved as a formal field of study. Therefore, it is instructive to trace the development of this field from its origins within the past fifty years.

## A SHORT HISTORY OF INTERCULTURAL COMMUNICATION

Intercultural communication is one of the younger academic fields in the United States. In relating the history of intercultural communication study, we separate our analysis into two parts: the chronological development and the content of intercultural communication study.

# The Chronological Development of Intercultural Communication Study

Although the beginnings of the field of intercultural communication as a field can be traced back to the 1920s in the teaching of linguistics and in various academic and youth-oriented programs, communication scholars commonly recognize E. T. Hall as the father of the field of intercultural communication study (Condon, 1981; Dodd, 1982; Gudykunst, 1985; Singer, 1987). Hall introduced terms such as "intercultural tensions" and "intercultural problems" in 1950.

## The Burgeoning Period

In 1958, Lederer and Burdick's *The Ugly American* first raised mass awareness of intercultural issues, but the term "intercultural communication" itself did not appear until Hall's *The Silent Language* was published in 1959. The same book paved the way for the study of intercultural communication. According to Leeds-Hurwitz (1990), Hall made at least eight contributions to the study of intercultural communication:

1. Hall extends the single-culture focus of traditional anthropology study to comparative culture study, with a new focus on the interaction of people from different cultures. This focus continues to be central to the present time.
2. Hall shifts the study of culture from a macro perspective to a micro analysis. This shift encourages the study of intercultural communication in terms of the practical needs of the interactants in communication.
3. Hall extends the study of culture to the field of communication. His extension gradually develops a link between anthropology and communication studies and changes the emphasis from the qualitative methods of anthropology to the quantitative methods of communication research.
4. Hall treats communication as a rule-governed, analyzable, and learned variable, a practice that permits communication researchers to theorize about cultural patterns of interaction.
5. Hall proposes that a holistic understanding of a counterpart's culture is not necessary to intercultural communication. He enumerates several items that can be used to understand another culture, including the use of voice, gestures, time, and space. To this day these concerns remain important, notably to students of nonverbal communication as well, in such areas as kinesics, proxemics, paralanguage, and chronemics.
6. The training methods developed by Hall at the Foreign Service Institute are still applied to the intercultural communication training. Hall, for instance,

advocated using the student's field experience in foreign countries as part of the teaching materials, and he encouraged students to interact with foreign sojourners in the United States to better understand a foreign culture.

7. Hall's use of descriptive linguistics as the model of intercultural communication research at the Foreign Service Institute continues to be the cornerstone of contemporary intercultural communication study. Current "etic" (from a generalizable perspective) and "emic" (from the culture's own perspective) research methods are derived from Hall's model.

8. Hall not only applied intercultural communication training to foreign service officers but also introduced it to international business. Today, training people in intercultural business has become one of the major activities of intercultural communication specialists.

Hall continued his theorizing about intercultural communication in other books, including *The Hidden Dimension* (1966), *Beyond Culture* (1976), *The Dance of Life* (1984), and *Understanding Cultural Differences* (Hall & Hall, 1989). His works continue to influence the development of the field of intercultural communication.

## From 1960 to 1970

Hall's influence on the study of intercultural communication is far-reaching. His writings have attracted numerous scholars to the study of intercultural communication. In addition to Kluckhohn and Strodtbeck's (1961) discourse on cultural value orientations, which provides an important conceptual contribution to the field, two representative books reflect the continuous efforts made by scholars in the field in the 1960s: Oliver's *Culture and Communication* (1962) and Smith's *Communication and Culture* (1966). Oliver's study focuses on Asian philosophy and communication behaviors, especially from a rhetorical perspective. His book establishes a model for the comparative study of communication behaviors between cultures.

Smith's book is a collection of essays on human communication covering thirteen types of communication studies. Although only four articles on intercultural communication are included in the book, their presence confirms the status of intercultural communication as a field of study. The first college class in this field taught in 1966 at the University of Pittsburgh.

## From 1971 to 1980

The 1970s witnessed rapid development in the field of intercultural communication. In 1972, after three years of refining his model of intercultural communication, Stewart published his *American Cultural Patterns*. In 1973, Samovar and Porter published *Intercultural Communication: A Reader*, and Indiana University awarded the first doctoral degree in intercultural communication. Many books on intercultural communication became available in the years that followed, the most influential including Prosser's *Intercommunication among Nations and People* (1973) and *Cultural Dialogue* (1978), Smith's *Transracial Communication* (1973), Condon and Yousef's *Introduction to Intercultural Communication* (1975), Barnlund's *Public and Private Self in Japan and United States* (1975), Sitaram and Cogdell's *Foundations of Intercultural Communication* (1976), Fischer and Merrill's *International and Intercultural Communication* (1976), Dodd's *Perspectives on Cross-Cultural Communication* (1977), Weaver's *Crossing Cultural Barriers* (1978), and Kohls' *Survival Kit for Overseas Living* (1979). The publication of Asante, Blake, and Newmark's *The Handbook of Intercultural Communication* in 1979 highlighted the achievements of intercultural communication scholars in the 1970s.

In addition to these books, *The International Journal of Intercultural Relations* began publication in 1977. The journal influenced research in the field of intercultural communication in the years that followed.

Disorder characterizes the initial development of the field. Intercultural communication scholars pursued their own directions and definitions, with few attempts at integration. It was not until the 1980s that the field began to move from disarray to a more coherent focus.

### From 1981 to the Present Time

Condon and Yousef's *Introduction to Intercultural Communication* (1975) and Samovar and Porter's *Intercultural Communication: A Reader* (1973) are two major forces from the early 1970s in the integration of the study of intercultural communication in the 1980s. Its seventh edition published in 1994, Samovar and Porter's work offers theoretical and practical perspectives, and especially emphasizes the relationship between culture and communication. Condon and Yousef's book is also an outstanding textbook. The authors approach the study of intercultural communication using a linguistic and rhetorical perspective by combining research done in anthropology and communication.

Condon and Yousef's stress on cultural value orientations and communication behaviors parallels Hofstede's (1984) later work on cultural values and Hall's writing on high-context and low-context cultures in *Beyond Culture* (1977). Their writing on the relationship of culture and verbal and nonverbal communication are still important to contemporary intercultural communication study. In addition, their discussion of the interaction between language, thinking patterns, and culture drew from Oliver's method of comparative cultural study. In the 1980s, Starosta (1984) continued to draw upon this line of research.

Scholars who received formal academic training in intercultural communication in the late 1960s and the early 1970s began to make their contributions in research and teaching by the 1980s. Many of their mentors had been trained in rhetoric, including John Condon, Michael Prosser, William Howell, and Arthur Smith (a.k.a. Molefi Asante), whose students defined the course of intercultural

---

**Research Highlight 1–1**

Who:　　Starosta, W. J.

What:　　"On Intercultural Rhetoric."

Where:　　In W. B. Gudykunst & Y. Y. Kim (Eds.) (1984), *Methods for Intercultural Communication Research* (pp. 229–238). Beverly Hills, CA: Sage.

The author bases the analysis on the assumption that rhetoric is divisive and that intercultural exchanges to not necessarily achieve mutual satisfaction. The stated premise—that cultures promote their own existence because they allow their supporters to survive in a difficult world—is supported and clarified by eleven propositions. The first three propositions concern intercultural rhetoric:

Proposition 1: The cultural is the incompletely understood.

Proposition 2: The province of intercultural rhetoric is externalities.

Proposition 3: Intercultural rhetoric redefines "need" in terms of an external exigence.

The next five propositions spell out the implications of the premise for the intercultural rhetorician:

Proposition 4: Intercultural rhetoric is extractionist.

Proposition 5: Intercultural rhetoric substitutes intercultural worldviews for intracultural ones.

Proposition 6: Success reinforces the rhetor.

Proposition 7: Distinctions of materiality and nonmateriality become meaningless.

Proposition 8: The intercultural inherently exploits.

The final three propositions reveal the consequences of intercultural rhetoric that evolve from the practice of it:

Proposition 9: Extractionist rhetoric breeds cultural disharmony.

Proposition 10: Intercultural rhetoric erodes diversity.

Proposition 11: Intercultural rhetoric stresses the here-and-now.

A full understanding of these propositions reveals the author's challenge to and deconstruction of several of the accepted assumptions of Marshall McLuhan's "global village" from the perspective of intercultural rhetoric. However, the essay does not make a negative portrayal of nor take a position against intercultural rhetoric. Rather, it exemplifies how intercultural rhetoric's philosophical underpinnings encourage self-reflexive critique by its practitioners.

---

communication in the 1980s and 1990s. Five volumes published in the 1980s advanced an agenda for the study of intercultural communication: Gudykunst's *Intercultural Communication Theory: Current Perspectives* (1983), Gudykunst and Kim's *Methods of Intercultural Research* (1984), Kincaid's *Communication Theory: Eastern and Western Perspectives*, Kim and Gudykunst's *Theories in Intercultural Communication* (1988), and Asante and Gudykunst's *Handbook of*

*International and Intercultural Communication* (1989). Theory building and methodological refinement characterize intercultural communication study during this decade. This effort at self-definition enlivened numerous sessions at professional communication conferences and at syllabus-building conferences sponsored by the University of Virginia under a USOE (United States Office of Education) grant. The result was a more focused and mature discipline in the 1990s in which rhetoric became a secondary concern, behind that of interpersonal communication, and in which mass media issues were all but neglected. The Society for Intercultural Education, Training, and Research (SIETAR) took up consideration of intercultural training issues.

The book *Theories in Intercultural Communication* by Kim and Gudykunst (1988) features two approaches to theory building. First, the study of intercultural communication draws from existing communication theories in constructivism, coordinated management of meaning, uncertainty reduction theory, communication accommodation theory, network theory, and convergence theory. Second, most intercultural communication theories focus on the interpersonal communication level with a brief mention of rhetoric. These two characteristics served to define the mainstream study of intercultural communication in the 1980s. The shift in focus can be seen by noting of the eclectic contents of *Smith's Culture and Communication* in 1966, the emphasis on international communication in Fischer and Merrill's *International and Intercultural Communication* in 1975, and the largely interpersonal, intercultural perspective of Asante and Gudykunst's *Handbook of International and Intercultural Communication* in 1989.

Methodologically, the traditional quantitative and rhetorical-interpretive research methods used in the communication discipline were also applied to the study of intercultural communication. Gudykunst and Kim's *Methods of Intercultural Communication Research* (1984), composed of six articles, each on quantitative and qualitative research, describes a number of methodological possibilities, although, in reality, quantitative research methods dominated intercultural communication study in the 1980s. Fortunately, scholars resumed work in rhetorical, semiotic, linguistic, and ethnographic methods of intercultural communication research by the early 1990s.

We can foresee that in the next decade the two research orientations will coexist, sometimes in the form of triangulation, wherein one form of study supplements the other, and sometimes in direct competition. Further, both of these orientations will be challenged by critical scholars who focus on correcting historical patterns of domination and oppression.

From the 1970s to the present time the direction for the study of intercultural communication has been determined mainly by three influences: (1) the International and Intercultural Communication Annual (IICA), (2) the Speech Communication Association (SCA), and (3) the International Communication Association (ICA). Early volumes of IICA were edited by Casmir and Jain. Beginning in 1983, each volume of IICA focused on one specific topic. *Inter-*

*cultural Communication Theory: Current Perspectives* (Gudykunst, 1983) and *Theories in Intercultural Communication* (Kim and Gudykunst, 1988) are two of the IICA volumes. The editorial direction of IICA was strongly oriented toward quantitative research in the 1980s and early 1990s. This trend is reversing in the mid-1990s because of calls for methodological pluralism, a renewed place for rhetorical study, the rise of interpretivist and critical methods in the communication discipline, and a concern for coverage of domestic co-cultures.

SCA and ICA are the two major professional associations for communication study. Both associations have a division promoting research and study of intercultural communication, the International and Intercultural Communication Division of the SCA, and Intercultural/Development Communication Division of the ICA. In addition to SCA and ICA, other associations, including SIETAR, Eastern Communication Association (ECA), Western Communication Association (WCA), Southern States Communication Association (SSCA), Central States Communication Association (CSCA), and journals sponsored by these associations also make significant contributions to the development of the field of intercultural communication.

Recently, three additional journals, *The Howard Journal of Communications, Intercultural Communication Studies*, and *World Communication*, a publication of the World Communication Association, have begun to specialize exclusively in the cultural issues of communication research.

## The Content of Intercultural Communication Study

Four decades after Hall's emphasis on the study of nonverbal messages in different cultural settings, the study of intercultural communication has expanded to cover a diverse set of variables deriving from the concepts of "communication," "culture," and the combination of communication and culture. As is the case for the communication discipline itself, the study of intercultural communication is influenced by traditional disciplines such as anthropology, linguistics, philosophy, psychology, and sociology. Since the 1970s, scholars have been trying to clarify the parameters of intercultural communication study. In addition to efforts made by Saral (1977, 1979), Prosser (1978), and Asante (1980), who set boundaries for intercultural communication study in the first four volumes of *The Communication Yearbook*, works by Rich (1974), Stewart (1978), and Gudykunst (1987) also represent scholars' attempts to enumerate the core contents of the field.

According to Rich (1974), intercultural communication is an ambiguous concept. For the purpose of her study, Rich argues that the content of intercultural communication can be classified into five forms. First, *intercultural communication* focuses on the study of interaction between people from different cultural backgrounds, such as interactions between people from America and China. Second, *international communication* focuses on the study of interaction between representatives of different nations, such as the interaction

---

**Research Highlight 1–2**

Who:      Asante, M. K.

What:     "Intercultural Communica-
          tion: An Inquiry into Re-
          search Directions."

Where:    *Communication Yearbook, 4,*
          1980, 401–411.

This essay deals with intellectual communication and its Eurocentric bias as
well as other alternative perspectives.
The author starts with the discussion of
two prevalent schools of thought in
contemporary intercultural communication scholarship: cultural dialogue
and cultural critics. The cultural dialogue school argues that its theories
can be utilized to promote world understanding and believes that people
from different cultures could and
should communicate with others. The
cultural critics try to pose researchable
questions by isolating the conflict
found in cross-cultural communication
and attempt to seek ways of improving
interaction among people across cultures by eliminating barriers through
classificatory, analytic, and applicative
steps.

The author indicates that three
worldviews of cultural reality affect
the study of intercultural communication: Afrocentric, Eurocentric, and Asio-
centric. However, most theories of

intercultural communication have a
Eurocentric bias. After discussing the
Eurocentric bias in the study of intercultural communication, the author explicates some alternative perspectives,
including the Afrocentric model, in
which the personal value of situation is
emphasized.

Finally, two significant intercultural communication situations that
may lead to misunderstanding among
people are identified: temporary communication estrangement and historical
cultural cleavage. Temporary communication estrangement impairs communication because through it we allow
the incorrect view to persist for the
sake of achieving overall acceptance of
a proposal even if we know a certain
view of history is incorrect. Historical
cultural cleavage occurs when we
know our history and our points of
view, but for the sake of an argument
we change them because we do not
want to get into a long discussion
about another culture's points of view.
The author also indicates four factors
that may constrain intercultural interaction: (1) the political consciousness of
colonized people, (2) mythology,
(3) creative motif—the guiding symbolic modality that is present in every
cultural group, and (4) ethos—the collective image of the culture group.

---

between representatives in the United Nations. Third, *interracial communication* focuses on the study of interaction between members of the numerically
or politically dominant culture and co-culture in the same nation, such as the
interaction between whites and African Americans. Fourth, *interethnic or minority communication* focuses on the study of interaction among co-cultures
in the same nation, such as the interaction between Hispanic and Japanese
Americans. Lastly, *contracultural communication* focuses on the study of the

developmental process linking intercultural communication to interracial communication, such as the developmental process that led from the interaction between Columbus and Native Americans to the interaction between First Nation tribes and Canadians. Rich considered that the study of intercultural communication should include all these five areas. Rich's classification clearly shows that intercultural communication study should be approached from an interpersonal or rhetorical level. Except for contracultural communication, Rich's categories remain visible today.

In his *Outline of Intercultural Communication* (1978), Stewart pointed out that the study of intercultural communication should lead to application in real-life situations. Stewart emphasized intercultural training programs similar to those from his experience as a Peace Corps trainer, and based on a comparative culture model of cognition. He emphasized that intercultural communication training should lead trainees through nine stages of gradual change, enabling them to

1. select information among alternative facts they already possess.
2. understand the goal of training and apply it in their decision making.
3. identify or recognize generalizations and concepts to modify their perception of events and guide their performance at a general level.
4. master the content of the training.
5. sensitize them to cultural concepts that will assist them in their interaction with people from other cultures.
6. change aspects of their conscious attitudes, such as cultural self-perception and certain emotional and cognitive perceptions, to reach a higher level of empathy.
7. govern their behavior and emotions in working and in living with people from other cultures by increasing their adaptability.
8. adopt a changed way of perceiving and behaving so that they can improve their social performance in other cultures.
9. integrate the emotional and perceptual change which govern their actions prior to the training.

Gudykunst (1987) classified the contents of intercultural communication study by using interactive-comparative and mediated-interpersonal dimensions to divide the realm of the inquiry into four categories: (1) intercultural communication, (2) cross-cultural communication, (3) international communication, and (4) comparative mass communication. According to Gudykunst, intercultural communication includes a focus on both the "interactive" and the "interpersonal." It deals with interpersonal communication between people from different cultures or co-cultures, such as that among Chinese and Americans, or between whites and African Americans, and encompasses the areas of intercultural, interracial, and interethnic communication identified by Rich.

Cross-cultural communication focuses on the concepts of "interpersonal" and "comparative" and deals with the differences in communication behaviors between people of different cultures, such as the differences in negotiation strategies between Swazis and South Africans. International communication stresses the concepts of "interactive" and "mediated." It mainly deals with media communication in another countries, exploring, for example, the role media play in Korean society. Finally, comparative mass communication focuses on the concepts of "mediated" and "comparative." It deals with the differences and similarities of media systems in different countries, as in China and Russia. Gudykunst further delineated five subareas of intercultural communication study based on the concepts of "interactive," "comparative," "interpersonal," and "mediated."

In sum, in four decades of theorizing and research in intercultural communication advances occurred on several fronts. More and more intercultural communication training programs developed, including long-term and short-term workshops and seminars in the tradition of the University of Minnesota's, Intercultural Communication Workshops of the 1970s. While the content of intercultural communication has been classified by scholars into different categories, it maintains its historical focus on intercultural, cross-cultural, interracial, and interethnic communication that was developed by Condon, Gudykunst, Hall, Oliver, Rich, and Smith.

## OUTLINE OF THE TEXTBOOK

To fully reflect the field of intercultural communication this book is divided into five parts. Part I, with three chapters, serves as a basic introduction to the field. As we have seen, Chapter 1 seeks to describe the rationale for studying intercultural communication and introduces the history of intercultural communication as a field of study. Chapter 2 examines three basic concepts of intercultural communication: communication, culture, and intercultural communication. Chapter 3 deals with cultural perceptions and values and how stereotypes and prejudice impede understanding and cooperation in human communication. To reach a point where we can see how intercultural communication can be successful, we need to know how it fails.

Part II, comprised of Chapters 4 and 5, examines the context of human communication—the relationship between human language and cultures. Human language is made up of verbal and nonverbal codes, which are the most basic and necessary tools human beings have to communicate with each other. Both chapters examine symbolic systems in some depth.

Part III, consisting of four chapters, describes the process of intercultural interaction. Chapter 6, which explores how people develop a relationship in intercultural settings, focuses on human relationships and explains the connection between their development and culture. Chapter 7 discusses intercultural conflict management by considering causes of intercultural conflict, including differences in thinking patterns and language barriers. Chapter 8 concentrates on intercultural adjustment; cultural shock and the stages of intercultural adaptation are examined in this chapter. Chapter 9 deals with listening across co-cultures.

Part IV, with three chapters, concerns the practical application of intercultural communication study. Chapter 10 examines cultural diversity, using organizational and educational perspectives, and management of the culturally diverse workforce. Chapter 11 discusses intercultural communication competence and presents a model of intercultural communication. Chapter 12 deals with intercultural training and delineates the goals and methods of intercultural training.

Part V, the final section, composed of Chapter 13, ponders ethical issues and the future of the field of intercultural communication.


## RECAP

Four trends of the modern world make intercultural communication inevitable: (1) technological development, (2) globalization of the economy, (3) widespread population migrations, and (4) development of multiculturalism. Only through the understanding of intercultural communication can people develop a global mind-set in the interdependent global village that is our world today and live more harmoniously and productively with one another.

Intercultural communication as a field began in the 1950s, burgeoning as a result of the work of E. T. Hall. Each decade afterward marks a specific contribution to the development of intercultural communication study. The 1960s was the period of conceptualization of the field by communication scholars. The 1970s showed rapid development, reflected in the publication of numerous studies. During the 1980s the field moved toward integration and a clearer identity. The 1990s, stressing diversification of methods and displaying increased concern with domestic co-cultures, has also witnessed efforts to redress historical and colonial imbalances.

In forty years the field of intercultural communication has developed both theoretical and applied perspectives. Theoretically, the study of intercultural communication focuses on more or less purposive interaction between people of different cultures and different racial and ethnic groups. Practically, intercultural communication is applied in different kinds of intercultural and interethnic training programs to help people of different backgrounds understand and accept each other in academic, business, government, and other settings.

## Research Highlight 1–3

Who:    Belay, G.

What:   "Toward a Paradigm Shift for Intercultural and International Communication: New Research Direction."

Where:  *Communication Yearbook, 19*, 1993, 437–457.

This articles looks at the study of intercultural communication from a fresh point of view. The discussion is divided into three sections: (1) The first uses the *third-culture-building* model to explain how intercultural communication has been dealt with in the past; (2) the second reframes the discourse by indicating that the world has changed, but the study of intercultural communication remains static; and (3) the third proposes the model of *interactive-multiculture building* as an alternative approach for the study of intercultural communication.

In the first section the author evaluates and critiques Casmir's *third-culture-building* model. He raises four points:

1. To treat third-culture building as an ethically motivated alternative to asymmetries and conflicts in intercultural or international relationships is not a new idea.
2. The model of third-culture building does not provide a consistent conceptual framework for understanding and resolving intercultural discords.
3. The attempt at giving the third-culture-building model a social and historical legitimacy reflects the lack of understanding of the complexity of interactional interdependence.
4. Third-culture building ignores discussions of the relational factors of power, which play an especially important role in intercultural communication.

In the second section the author describes the impact of civilization, nation, and modernity on research paradigms of intercultural and international communication. The discussion includes three parts: (1) three philosophical outlooks, (2) international communication: nationalhood and modernity, and (3) intercultural communication: cultures and differences. The theme is that the world has changed, the study of intercultural communication should follow the change theoretically and methodologically.

In the last section the author proposes *interactive-multiculture-building* model as an alternative approach for the study of intercultural communication. The model is based on the challenges and opportunities of the contemporary realities of intercultural and international communicational study, including (1) instability of the state, (2) erosion of the state, (3) multiplicity of cultural identity, (4) end of ideologies, and (5) the human challenge. As an ideal, interactive-multiculture building denounces all forms of authoritarian and liberal efforts to defuse cultural heterogeneity. It aims to promote mutual respect and tolerance of cultural differences. As a research theory, it provides six levels of analysis for the study of intercultural communication: (1) intrapersonal analysis, (2) interpersonal analysis, (3) intraorganizational analysis, (4) interorganizational analysis, (5) intergroup (intercommunity) analysis, and (6) cross-national analysis.

## RETHINK

**1.** The development of communication technology will continue to make a remarkable impact on the study of intercultural communication. One of the most significant developments at the beginning of the twenty-first century will be the technological superhighway. The influence of this system will be revolutionary in the way human beings communicate with each other. Will the expansion of this superhighway greatly change the structure of the field of intercultural communication? Will the superhighway reach some groups and not others? These are worthwhile questions for consideration by intercultural communication students, scholars, and practitioners.

**2.** Methodological and cultural pluralism should inform the study of intercultural communication. The history of the intercultural communication study demonstrates the incompleteness of any single methodological or theoretical orientation. To date, the mainstream theories in the field of intercultural communication have been Western-oriented. Both in method and content, researchers have looked for universal "laws" and for comparisons and contrasts defined by instruments created in North America. Non-Western theories have yet to be developed. Methodologically, quantitative methods have dominated the field since the inception period of the 1950s, although qualitative-interpretive studies have emerged in the 1990s. This development will lead to both competition and cooperation among the two camps of scholars, quantitative and qualitative, and among critical theorists. We propose that the field of intercultural communication depends on triangulation among various methods of intercultural inquiry, in which multiple methods are used to compensate for the others' limitations. We hope that the major camps of methodological orientation can peacefully coexist and avoid the pitfall of unfriendly competition.

## QUESTIONS FOR DISCUSSION

**1.** Discuss the four trends that make our world more interdependent.
**2.** What are the contributions of E. T. Hall to the study of intercultural communication?
**3.** Discuss the key scholars and their works in the development of the field of intercultural communication.
**4.** Compare the core content of intercultural communication study, as proposed by Rich, Stewart, and Gudykunst.
**5.** Discuss the relationship between the technological superhighway and the study of intercultural communication.
**6.** Why should methodological and cultural pluralism inform the study of intercultural communication?

# ▶ Chapter 2

## Communication and Culture

### *Objectives*

Upon completion of this chapter, you will

- Be able to define such terms as *communication, culture,* and *intercultural communication.*
- Understand the characteristics and the model of communication.
- Understand the functions and characteristics of culture.
- Understand the forms of intercultural communication.

> *To be human is to be in communication in some human culture, and to be in some human culture is to see and know the world—to communicate—in a way which daily recreates that particular culture. . . . But the sufficient condition of that which constitutes human reality is the way in which a people construct and maintain that reality in communication.—L. THAYER*

Culture and communication mutually influence one another, producing different behavioral patterns in different contexts. Culture not only conditions our perceptions of reality but also programs our language patterns. What, where, and how we should talk are regulated by culture (Becker, 1986; Oliver, 1962). Culture not only shapes our communication patterns, but communication in turn influences the structure of our culture. Indeed, the two are inseparable. In order to study intercultural communication we must understand communication and culture and explore their relationship. In this chapter we separate our discussion into three parts: (1) the process of communication, (2) the nature of culture, and (3) intercultural communication.

# THE COMMUNICATION PROCESS

As indicated in Chapter 1, the formal study of communication can be traced back to Aristotle's *Rhetoric* of 2,000 years ago. Early views of human communication tended to embrace a mechanistic perspective of the communication process. This perspective regards communication as a unidirectional process in which the receivers are passively influenced or victimized by powerful sources. Recently, more and more scholars have treated human communication as a process in which our behaviors can be explained by referring to our intentions, reasons, and goals. In other words, we are active agents, possessing the ability to choose actions in the interactional process rather than being driven by external factors that determine our behaviors. Based on this actional view, the following section examines the definition and characteristics of communication and provides a model to explain the nature of human communication.

## Communication Defined

It is a great challenge trying to search for a universal definition of communication. *Communication* is a term that has been used in many ways, for diverse purposes. For the purpose of this chapter we define communication as "an interdetermining process in which we develop a mutually dependent relationship by exchanging symbols." Through the participation in this symbol-exchanging process we begin to establish a world of "communicational reality" (Thayer, 1987). This communicational reality assists us to learn a particular way of coding the world and to form a community in which we organize ourselves socially and culturally. From this definition we can generate several characteristics and a model of human communication.

## Characteristics of Communication

Our definition of communication includes four components. First, communication is a *holistic phenomenon*. The holistic principle of human communication asserts that interactants belong to a whole in which they cannot be understood without reference to each other and to the whole system. In other words, communication is itself a network of relations that gives interactants an identity by granting them unique qualities or characteristics. Thus, in communication the interactants cannot be understood unless we understand their net-

**Research Highlight 2–1**

Who:     Thayer, L.

What:    "On Communication: Essays in Understanding."

Where:   Norwood, NJ: Ablex, 1987.

Thayer defines "communicational realities"—a concept fundamental to this book—as "those ideas, beliefs, preferences, qualities, evils, and ideals which exist for us essentially because they can be and are talked about" (p. 172). It is these self-created realities that allow "intercommunication" between and among people. Communicational realities represent the consciousness of all that we speak of and relate to in our humanity. Thus, communicational realities function to organize us socially through different channels, including friendships, conversation, political or aesthetic affairs, and our groups or institutions. They determine what is possible in our daily lives.

Two categories of communicational realities have significant consequences for the human condition. First, through the metaphors we use to create ourselves, to define why we are a particular kind of human in a given culture or society, we develop our human potential and our social possibilities.

Second, the beliefs and values that characterize a given community at a given time are essential components of our identity. In a provisional, dialectical, and evolutionary sense, our communication realities order and vitalize our minds and our social relations. Thus, people who hold similar communicational realities naturally form an "epistemic community" that is not defined by their racial, political, or geographic boundary but by common beliefs, values, and symbolic schemas.

The most basic communicational reality is "I," but the indispensable communicational realities of human association are "I" and "you." We all need to relate each other. Communicational realities establish not only our conscious identities but also the total social environment in which we exist and rationalize our actions. In other words, communicational realities enable us to control and manipulate, or to inform and in-form each other. Thayer concludes, therefore, that the criterion used to assess communicational realities is whether they can enable us to achieve our goals through intercommunicating with one another or with our environments, rather than whether they are identical with what exists.

work of relations, and we cannot understand their network of relations unless we understand the interactants (Cheng, 1987).

Second, communication is a *social reality*. Like social phenomena that are created by consensus of people who collectively agree that those phenomena exist, human communication phenomena are social realities. The socially created nature of human communication is based on the common meanings people symbolically assign to verbal and nonverbal behaviors. Thus, in different contexts the same message can be interpreted in different ways. For example, the statement, "You're lovely," could be interpreted as a "compliment" or a "caring" gesture. However, if the statement were uttered by an employer to a

**Research Highlight 2–2**

Who:  Cheng, C. Y.

What:  "Chinese Philosophy and Contemporary Human Communication Theory."

Where:  In D. L. Kincaid (Ed.) (1987), *Communication Theory: Eastern and Western Perspectives* (pp. 23–44). New York: Academic Press.

In this insightful essay the author discusses contemporary human communication theory from the perspective of Chinese philosophy and provides an alternative view for the understanding of human communication, the study of which has been traditionally dominated by Western thought.

The author first points out the three kinds of relationships between communication and philosophy: (1) philosophy can be the content of communication (i.e., philosophical communication); (2) as a system of basic beliefs and inceptive orientations, philosophy can serve as a context for communication; and (3) philosophy can provide a method of communication, because it communicates the most fundamental aspirations, values, beliefs, thoughts, and perceptions of a person, a society, and a culture.

The author indicates that Chinese philosophy, with its rich background

and insights into human nature and human understanding, can make significant contributions to contemporary communication theory. Three reasons support this claim. First, Chinese philosophy provides a comprehensive framework to anticipate and reevaluate communication problems and to locate a new focus for the process of communication. Second, with its holistic orientation to human existence and its emphasis on the integration of theory and practice, Chinese philosophy underscores the human context of communication and its incorporation with practical goals. Finally, Chinese philosophy, especially Taoism and Zen Buddhism, can provide a method for communication study by enlarging and emancipating the mechanistic models of communication theory with new conceptual tools.

In the last part of the essay the author provides a detailed explanation of the six principles of Chinese philosophy that are closely related to contemporary communication theory: (1) the principle of the embodiment of reason in experience, (2) the principle of epistemological-pragmatic unity, (3) the principle of part-whole interdetermination, (4) the principle of dialectical completion of relative polarities, (5) the principle of infinite interpretation, and (6) the principle of symbolic reference.

newly hired employee, it might be interpreted as an inappropriate message or as sexual harassment.

Third, communication is a *developmental process*. This process implies that the content and social realities communication creates evolve and change over time. Human communication is ever in a state of change and transformation, with no fixed substance. Thus, human communication is never absolutely complete or finished. In this transforming and endless process the role of interactants is vital, because only through mutual enlightenment and influence can a mutual and interdependent interaction be produced.

Lastly, communication is an *orderly process.* Although human communication is an ever-changing process, it is changing like the succession of day and night and the periodical ebb and flow of the tide. In other words, human communication behaviors are orderly and patterned rather than unpredictable and chaotic. The consensus of shared meanings and action of communicators through the use of symbols consistently follows a set of consensual rules of interaction. These rules of creating shared meaning and action promote the achievement of personal and collective goals in communication process.

## A Model of Communication

A dialectical model can be used to delineate the dynamic and mutually dependent feature of human communication. In Figure 2–1 A and B represent the interactants as the two mutually dependent and penetrating forces. Each force is a self-changing system that itself develops an internal transforming process. However, it is the interaction and connection of these forces that forms a com-

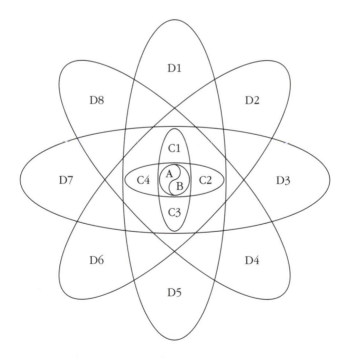

**FIGURE 2–1**   **A Model of Human Communication**

plete and holistic system of human communication. Contradictions and conflicts may appear in the interactional process, but the success of communication depends on the ability of the interactants to keep a dynamic balance.

The model emphasizes the holistic orientation to human communication that represents a structure of dynamic and dialectical balance between the interactants. The process of connecting two individual systems defines understanding in communication. C1, C2, C3, and C4 represent the outcomes of the interaction between A and B. The continuation of production from the interaction of A and B is represented by D1 to D8. Two elements account for this endless transforming and reproducing process toward the achievement of individual and collective goals of human communication: temporal contingencies and spatial contingencies. Temporal contingencies require the interactants to know when it is appropriate to initiate, maintain, and terminate an interaction verbally and nonverbally. Spatial contingencies refer to static attributes such as one's position, status, and the communication environment. They all affect the dynamic balance of interaction between A and B.

## THE NATURE OF CULTURE

An analogy with electronic computers is one way to introduce the concept of culture. In order to make computers do what they should do we must program them first. Likewise, we are programmed by our culture to do what we do and to be what we are. In other words, culture is the software of the human mind that provides an operating environment for human behaviors. Although individual behaviors may be varied, all members within the same operating environment share important characteristics of the culture. Unlike computers, of course, persons may reach idiosyncratic conclusions and carry out irrational and unexpected actions. In not every action is cultural "programming" evident. In this section we discuss the definition of culture, functions of culture, and characteristics of culture.

### Culture Defined

The word *culture* has numerous meanings. An early definition was provided by E. B. Tylor (1967), who treated culture as a complex whole of our social traditions and as prerequisite for us to be a member of the society. Culture can be a set of fundamental ideas, practices, and experiences of a group of people that are symbolically transmitted generation to generation through a learning process. Culture may as well refer to beliefs, norms, and attitudes that are used to guide our behaviors and to solve human problems. Moreover, we can look at culture from an interpretive and performance perspective by viewing it as a system of expressive practices and mutual meanings associated with our behaviors. Our concern in this chapter is to present a particular definition of culture to explain the close relationship between culture and communication. Thus, we define culture as "a negotiated set of shared symbolic systems that guide individuals' behaviors and incline them to function as a group."

## Functions of Culture

As the software of human mind, culture, in addition to allowing our participation in a specific group, serves two major functions. First, culture provides a context in which three aspects of human society are embedded: linguistic, physical, and psychological (Borden, 1991). Language allows us to communicate with people who have similar value and belief systems. Physical aspects supply an environment of activities and permit what we do within the culture. Finally, the psychological aspect is related to our mental activities, including what we believe and what we have learned.

Second, culture functions to provide structure, stability, and security that are used by the group and members to maintain themselves as a healthy system. For some persons, "structure and stability" may indicate subordinate status. For others, such stability is welcomed. For example, according to traditional Chinese custom, the marriage of young people had to be arranged by their parents. A matchmaker was used to introduce the two parties. If the parents of the male were interested in seeing the lady, the matchmaker would plan an arranged meeting for both sides to meet and observe each other. If the male family was pleased with the lady, the matchmaker would be sent to the female family to formally propose a marriage. A payment made by the groom's family to the family of the bride would be made when the couple married. Dowry, including money, jewelry, or other gifts, from the bride's family usually accompanied the bride. The structural process of this matching process for the young people in traditional Chinese society clearly reflects the functions of culture. This practice not only maintained the stability of the Chinese society for many hundred years but also ensured the financial security of the female family after a daughter moved out to stay with the other family.

## Characteristics of Culture

From the definition of culture given above we can generate four basic characteristics of culture: it is holistic, learned, dynamic, and pervasive.

First, culture is holistic. This characteristic underscores the complex nature of culture. As a holistic system, culture can be broken down into several subsystems, including a kinship system, an educational system, a religious system, an association system, a political system, and so on, but the various aspects of culture are closely interrelated. In other words, any change in a subsystem will affect the whole system. For example, as Samovar and Porter (1995) indicated, the American Civil Rights Movement brought about changes in different facets of American culture and altered American attitudes, values, and behaviors.

Second, culture is learned. Because culture is a shared symbolic system within a relatively large group of people, the only way for group members to integrate into, reinforce, and co-create this shared symbolic system is through a learning process. We begin to consciously and unconsciously learn our culture in our early life through the process of socialization or enculturation. Interaction with family members and friends is the most common way for us to learn about our culture. Other sources for learning our culture are schools, church, media, folk tales, and art. The process of learning our own culture will inevitably foster a phenomenon called *ethnocentrism*. Ethnocentrism leads group members to tie themselves tightly together and to be proud of their own heritages by subjectively using their cultural standards as criteria for interpretations and judgments in intercultural communication.

Third, culture is dynamic. Cultures are constantly changing over time. Some cultures are more open and accepting of change, others tend to resist it. Cultures change in the process of transmission from generation to generation, group to group, and place to place. Four major mechanisms account for the change of cultures: technological invention, disasters, cultural contact, and environmental factors. Technological invention, such as the discovery of communication and transportation tools referred to in Chapter 1, normally elicits a different set of social habits and behaviors that eventually alter the pattern of a culture. Disasters include natural and human calamities. The American Civil War and China's Opium War brought great social and cultural changes to both societies. Likewise, the vanishing of the city of Pompeii in Italy was due to the eruption of the Vesuvius volcano. Cultural contact gives each culture a chance to borrow things from other cultures. For instance, Italian pizzas and Chinese egg rolls have become staple dishes in America, while American fast foods and pop culture have greatly changed the way Asian people live. As for environmental factors, a notable example is that of increasing population, which has expanded the size of cities and reduced the size of farmlands. The result is that an industrial lifestyle has replaced the traditional agricultural living pattern. The change completely alters the way people initiate, maintain, and terminate interpersonal relationships.

Finally, culture is pervasive. Like the ubiquitous air we breathe, culture penetrates into every aspect of our life and influences the way we think, the way we talk, and the way we behave. Culture combines visible and invisible things around us. Kohls (1984) pointed out that culture pervades all these areas: arts and artifacts, beliefs, behaviors, ceremonies, concept of self, customs, ideas and thought patterns, ideals, knowledge, laws, language, manners, morals, myths and legends, religion, rituals, social institutions, tools, and values. Culture is the sum total of human society and its meanings.

# INTERCULTURAL COMMUNICATION

Once we understand the meanings of communication and culture it becomes clear that intercultural communication refers to the communication between people from two different cultures. If, in Figure 2–1, A is an Afghan and B is a Brazilian, the interaction between the two persons is intercultural communication. However, because we are destined to carry our cultural baggage whenever and wherever we go, when A and B are from two different nations rather than from the same national culture, communication is often more complicated. (However, two groups from a single national culture, such as Israeli Jews and Arabs, Indian Hindus and Muslims, or African and European Americans, can also experience major difficulties in communication.) The potential for miscommunication and disagreement is great because of cultural differences. Thus, the study of intercultural communication aims to understand the influence of culture on our attitudes, beliefs, and behaviors in order to reduce misunderstandings that result from cultural variations. According to Dodd (1991), successful intercultural communication is based on three factors: (1) the positive feeling we possess at the affective level, including affirmation, self-esteem, comfort, trust, and safety; (2) the beliefs we bring into the intercultural encounter at the cognitive level, including expectations, stereotypes, uncertainties, and misunderstanding of rules or procedures; and (3) the action or skills we possess at the behavioral level, including verbal and nonverbal communication skills in intercultural settings. Mini Case 2–1 illustrates the potential for misunderstanding due to cultural differences. Read it to see whether you can answer the question at the end, taking such differences into account.

## *Forms of Intercultural Communication*

Chapter 1 introduced the forms and content of intercultural communication delineated by Rich (1974) and Gudykunst (1987). Here we consider the forms of intercultural communication from another perspective. According to Guan (1995), three potential forms of intercultural communication can take place, depending on the interactants' intentions: self-centered dialogue, dominant dialogue, or equal dialogue. The self-centered intercultural communication takes the form of ethnocentrism. In this form of intercultural communication A and B in Figure 2–1 completely use their own cultural standards to judge and interact with each other. The outcomes of this type of intercultural communication always lead to misunderstandings. A main reason for this kind of problem is the lack of cultural understanding between A and B.

In dominant intercultural communication, A is well aware of B's cultural traits and differences, and uses this advantage to control B to achieve his or her personal goals. This problem may happen at the interpersonal or international communication level, as illustrated, for example, by the colonization and cul-

**Mini Case 2–1**

Kenneth, an American student, met Vernon, a student recently arrived from Malaysia, and they decided to have dinner together at the university cafeteria. In the cafeteria, Kenneth ordered a pizza and some other food for their dinner. When the food was sent to them, Kenneth tore the pizza into pieces and handed one piece to Vernon, using his left hand. Vernon took that piece of pizza and put it on his plate without eating it. Kenneth was quite confused about what had gone wrong, so he asked Vernon, "Are you all right?" "Yes, I'm fine," Vernon replied. Kenneth kept on asking, "Why don't you eat the pizza?" Vernon said nothing but began to eat the other food, ignoring the pizza. Kenneth was confused but he ceased his questioning. And the two just kept on eating without much conversation.

How would you help explain Vernon's behavior?

(*Source:* Lai Suet Ying, Hong Kong Baptist University)

tural imperialism imposed by Western cultures on the remaining nations in contemporary times. Further, within a single nation, patterns of gender and ethnic domination may proliferate.

Finally, equal dialogue between A and B represents an ideal form of intercultural communication. This type of intercultural communication is based on mutual understanding of cultural similarities and differences. Both parties make sincere and empathic efforts to overcome their differences on an equal basis.

# RECAP

Culture and communication act on each other. As the carrier of culture, communication influences the structure of a culture, and culture is necessarily manifested in our communication patterns by teaching us how we should talk and behave. This chapter has focused on the explanation of the three basic concepts of intercultural communication study: communication, culture, and intercultural communication.

Communication is defined as "an interdetermining process in which we develop a mutually dependent relationship by exchanging symbols." Four characteristics of communication are discussed: (1) communication as a holistic phenomenon, (2) communication as a social reality, (3) communication as a developmental process, and (4) communication as an orderly process. A dialectic model of communication is also illustrated to delineate the dynamic and mutually dependent feature of human communication.

Culture is defined as "a negotiated set of shared symbolic systems that guide individuals' behaviors and incline them to function as a group." Culture serves two functions. First, it provides a context in which three aspects of human society are embedded: linguistic, physical, and psychological. Second, it functions to provide the structure, stability, and security that are required for the group and its members to maintain themselves as a healthy system. Four basic characteristics of culture include the following: (1) culture is holistic, (2) culture is learned, (3) culture is dynamic, and (4) culture is pervasive.

Intercultural communication is communication among people from two or more cultures. Successful intercultural communication is based on the positive feeling and beliefs we bring to the intercultural encounter and on the behavioral skills we possess. Finally, three potential forms of intercultural communication can take place, based on the interactants' intentions: self-centered dialogue, dominant dialogue, and equal dialogue.

## RETHINK

In this chapter we take a nontraditional view of the concept of communication. Instead of treating communication as a linear and mechanical process in which control and power play the key role, we conceptualize it as a more dynamic, interactive, and responsive process. Human communication is a holistic system by which people develop and maintain harmonious relationships in a continuously transforming process of mutual dependency. This model of communication, which is clearly embedded in Eastern thought, especially in Chinese philosophy, is essentially different from common Western approaches because it holds that harmony is the end rather than the means of human communication. While many scholars treat communication as a process in which people strive to direct the interaction in their own favor, we view it as a process of adapting and relocating ourselves in the dynamics of interdependence and cooperation. Thus, communication should include a kind of ethical appeal that can induce a sense of duty for cooperation with the other party, not by the communicator's strategic words or behaviors but by the sincere display of whole-hearted concern for the other. A question can be raised by this difference in approach for future research consideration: If it is culture that dictates the perception of difference in communication, then how will perceived differences affect interaction when people of diverse cultural backgrounds meet?

## QUESTIONS FOR DISCUSSION

1. Describe the characteristics of communication.
2. Compare the model of communication in this chapter with any other communication model you know.

3. Could you provide one or two examples to illustrate the functions of culture?
4. Explain the characteristics of culture.
5. What is the key to the successful intercultural communication?
6. Give an example of each form of intercultural communication.
7. How does the perception of communication due to cultural differences affect intercultural communication?

# ▶ Chapter 3

## Cultural Perception and Values

### *Objectives*

Upon completion of this chapter, you will

- Be able to define such terms as *perception, stereotypes, prejudice,* and *cultural value orientations.*
- Understand the stages of the process of perception.
- Understand how culture influences perception.
- Gain insight into the origins and impact of stereotypes and prejudice.
- Increase your understanding of the nature of values.
- Know the four models of cultural value orientations.

> *In the quest for good food in China, the most useful quality may be a spirit of adventure. Many foods considered delicacies by the Chinese cause Westerners to shudder. Among such exotica are snakes, sea slugs, turtles, bird's nests formed of swallows' saliva, dried jellyfish, and webs of duck feet. Though a bit startling to the eye, thick, dark, firmly gelatinous sea slugs are delicious cooked in a velvety, dark sauce that is mellow with wine and fragrant with star anise. This is a sauce that would make even paper towels palatable."*
> —TIME, OCTOBER 5, 1987

Before discussing cultural perception in his intercultural communication class, one of the authors of this text used to observe his students' reactions when he told them that people in some Asian countries eat pig ears, chicken feet, fish innards, and the meat of dogs and snakes. As expected, the most common reaction was, "Yuck! It's disgusting," accompanied by a look of stunned disbelief on their faces. Why do the students feel this way, and what makes them produce this kind of reaction? This chapter answers the question by examining cultural perception and cultural values.

# THE NATURE OF PERCEPTION

Since the way we behave is dictated by the way we perceive the world, it is important for us to understand the nature of perception and how our perception depends on our cultural experiences. This section defines perception, describes the process of perceiving, and delineates some cultural influences on perception.

## Perception Defined

Human *perception* is an active process by which we use our sensory organs to sense the world. Using the nervous system and our brains, the process allows us to recognize and identify the existence of all kinds of stimuli and then evaluate and interpret what we identify. In other words, perception is a process by which we make what we sense into a meaningful experience by selecting, categorizing, and interpreting internal and external stimuli to form our view of world. Internal stimuli include our nervous system, desires, interests, and motivations. External stimuli are the sensations that come from the way we see, smell, touch, hear, and taste.

## Stages of the Perception Process

The process of perception is thus composed of three stages: selection, categorization, and interpretation.

### Selection
*Selection* is a major part of the process of converting the environment stimuli into meaningful experience. As we face a large variety of stimuli every day, we are only capable of perceiving part of them through a selective process. For example, simply ask yourself what you see when you enter the classroom every day? You may see John or Mary are there, you may see the board, the chairs, and the light. But do you see other things such as the dress your classmates wear, the hair style they have, and those different kinds of posters on the

wall? Do you see that your classmate is of African or of European lineage? Obviously, we can only perceive parts of the things that surround us. The partiality of our perception is the origin of misunderstanding in interactions, especially when people are from different cultural backgrounds with diverse perception systems.

Selective perception involves three steps: selective exposure, selective attention, and selective retention (Klopf, 1995). First, we usually selectively expose ourselves to certain kinds of information that will reinforce the decision we are making. Of course, selective exposure also refers to our avoidance of other kinds of information that is not consistent with our intention. For example, when we plan to buy a car, we naturally expose ourselves to the automobile section when we open the morning newspaper.

Second, selective attention dictates that we can only pay attention to one piece of our environment. If our budget and preference only allow us to purchase an American-made car, when we examine the automobile section in the newspaper, we do not pay attention to cars made by Sweden or Yugoslavia. As students, if we are worried about our grade and an exam, we will be inclined to read those materials relating to the subject area that will be tested in class. Selective exposure and attention are influenced by our needs, training, expectations, and attitudes. For example, a hungry person will seek exposure and pay attention to food-related messages to satisfy his or her need. A communication major will be exposed and pay more attention to information about media. If we expect human nature is good, we will focus on the positive attributes of our acquaintances. Or, if we believe in social Darwinism (the "survival of the fittest"), we will try to find ways to gain advantage over others. Moreover, we tend to focus on events that reinforce our existing attitudes.

Third, because of selective retention, we can only retain some of the stimuli we perceive. Most of them are perceived, processed, and then forgotten. Basically, we tend to remember messages that are pleasant and favorable to our own image; that are consistent with our beliefs, attitudes, and values; and that are likely to be used in the future.

### Categorization

When we selectively perceive stimuli from the external environment, we must arrange them into meaningful patterns. In the categorization stage of perception the social and physical events or objects we encounter immediately have shape, color, texture, size, and intensity. For example, when people are asked what a human being is, some may describe it from the perspective of skin color, others from that of race or nationality. If we close our eyes and think what our university library is like, we experience an organized environment with an internal and external structure.

Two characteristics of human perception emerge at this stage. First, the categorization process gives human perception *structure*. We always translate the raw stimuli of the external world into structured experience. Second, the process shows that human perception is *stable*. After we organize the stimuli into patterns they become durable. For example, the height of a person will not shrink two or three feet because of variation in distance.

### Interpretation

Once we have selectively organized our perceptions into structured and stable patterns, we try to make sense of the patterns by assigning meaning to them. The interpretation process plays a very important role in intercultural interactions. An American audience may interpret the smiles on the face of Japanese athletes after being terribly defeated by their opponents as indicating that Japanese athletes don't care about their losing the game. From the Japanese perspective, the same smile is interpreted as a painful expression that is used to cover the embarrassment of being defeated. A kiss in the public may just represent a way of saying hello in the West, but viewed as "lovemaking" in Sri Lanka, the same sort of kiss caused two German tourists to be expelled from the country.

Interpretation is the third characteristic of human perception. That is, human perception possesses meanings. Our structured and stable perceptions are not isolated from others. When we organize a library into an environment with an internal and external structure, we attach a set of meanings to it. For example, a library is a place for us to study and collect information but not a place to have a nice nap or dinner with our friends. Moreover, we usually use—words such as *place, book, study*, and *catalog*—to define and name the categories of our perception of a library in order to produce meanings. It is important to note that although we treat the three stages of perception separately, in reality they are an integrated process with no clear boundary between them.

## Cultural Influence on Perception

Although our physical makeup and social roles affect the way we perceive external stimuli, both are essentially conditioned by our culture. As mentioned previously, a person's culture has a strong impact on the perception process. Culture not only provides the foundation for the meanings we give to our perceptions, it also directs us to word specific kinds of messages and events. Bagby (1957) best describes the influence of culture on our perception. In the study, a dozen of participants from the United States and Mexico were asked to view separately ten pairs of photographs in a special bifocal viewer. Each pair of photographs contained a picture from each culture (e.g., a bullfight represented Mexican culture, and a baseball game represented U.S. culture). After reviewing all the photographs the participants were asked what they had seen. The results show that participants tended to report only those pictures representing their culture.

The perceived meanings of different colors also show the influence of culture. A group of American students were asked to write down their perceptions of different colors. Following are the meanings they attached to the colors:

- Black—death, evil, mourning, sexy.
- Blue—cold, masculine, sad, sky.
- Green—envy, greed, money.
- Pink—feminine, shy, softness, sweet.
- Red—anger, hot, love, sex.
- White—good, innocent, peaceful, pure.
- Yellow—caution, happy, sunshine, warm.

Students from different cultural backgrounds would assign a totally different set of meanings to each color. For instance, to the Chinese, Japanese, and Koreans red represents a color of longevity, splendor, and wealth; the color black is very much welcome in the Caribbean and Africa; green is a holy color to Moslems but means adultery to the Chinese; and yellow is a noble color for the Chinese and Indians. White is a wedding color in the United States, but a funeral color in India; by contrast, red is a wedding color in parts of India, but suggests sexual impurity (i.e., a "scarlet woman") in a U.S. wedding.

The influence of culture on perception is often reflected in the attributional process. *Attribution* means that we interpret the meaning of other's behaviors based on our past experience or history. Culture provides an environment for us to develop all the meanings we possess. Thus, people from different cultures will perceive and interpret others' behaviors in different ways. For instance, Smith and Whitehead (1984) found that Asian Indians, compared to Northern Americans, have a tendency to refer to contextual factors more than dispositional factors in interpreting others' behaviors. Similarly, the Chinese and Japanese, as opposed to Americans, tend to attribute success to group action rather than individual effort.

The different attributional process may cause serious misunderstandings in communication. Consider the example of a colleague. On his first day when in the United States, he and a friend made a trip to Olympic National Park in Washington State. When they finished their lunch and came out of the restaurant, a young American woman approached him and asked, "Do you have time?" My friend said that he was shocked by the question, because from his own perspective the question meant that the lady wanted to do something sexually with him. In other words, the question was interpreted by my friend as "Are your free now? If yes, let's walk together." When our colleague answered the lady, clearly the meaning of the question was, "What time it is now?" To avoid this kind of misunderstanding we must try to make an "isomorphic attribution" of the situation that requires us to better understand the other's culture

## Research Highlight 3–1

Who:     Okabe, R.

What:    "Cultural Assumptions of East and West: Japan and the United States."

Where:   In W. B. Gudykunst (Ed.) (1983), *Intercultural Communication Theory* (pp. 21–44). Beverly Hills, CA: Sage.

Although most studies regarding human communication originate in the United States, this essay presents a Japanese perspective on the subject and compares and contrasts the differences between the two cultures.

The first section of the essay deals with cultural values in Japan and the United States. In terms of communication substance (what enables the speaker to link his or her values to those of his or her listeners), several differences in cultural values are identified by the author.

1. Values concerning the nature of society and culture.

   a. Japan—homogeneity and verticality.
   b. United States—heterogeneity and horizontality.

2. Attitudes toward nature.

   a. Japan—to adapt to nature.
   b. United States—to confront and exploit nature.

3. Values concerning interpersonal relationships.

   a. Japan—interdependence.
   b. United States—independence.

4. Values concerning thinking patterns.

   a. Japan—synthetic tendency, relativism, idealism, point/dot/space.
   b. United States—analytical tendency, absolutism, realism, line.

In terms of form of communication (that is, the problem of ordering and organizing a discourse), there are four differences in respect to

1. The speaker's perspective.

   a. Japan—cautious, tentative, complementary.
   b. United States—polarized, dichotomous, confrontational.

2. Logic and rhetoric.

   a. Japan—dotted, pointlike, no sense of rigidity or logicality.
   b. United States—step-by-step, chainlike.

3. Composition.

   a. Japan—heavy reliance either on the general or on the specific.
   b. United States—construction of a coherent and unified paragraph, emphasis on a harmonious balance between the theme and the details.

4. Language usage.

   a. Japan—reliance on product.
   b. United States—reliance on process.

In terms of communication strategy (which refers to the instruments of rhetoric that the speaker uses for elicit-

*Continued*

**Research Highlight 3–1**   *Continued*

ing the intended response from the listeners), there are two differences in respect to

1. Rhetorical proof.

   a. Japan—tendancy to accept constituents of ethos as seniority, sex, and family background; tend to value the assumptions of subjectivity and ambiguity that avoid using specific facts, figures, and quotations from authority.

   b. United States—tendancy to accept constituents of ethos as intelligence, competence, and character as potent in communication; tend to value specificity, objectivity, and precision by relying on logical proof facts, figures, and quotations from authority.

2. Decision-making strategy.

   a. Japan—consensus.
   b. United States—majority votes.

   In terms of communication style (which refers to the way in which language works to embody the user's communicative intentions), the rhetorical canon is influenced by cultural values and assumptions. Three differences between the two cultures are identified:

1. Because of their cultural values of precision, Americans tend to use explicit words, whereas the Japanese, because of their cultural assumptions of interdependence and harmony, tend to use implicit and even ambiguous words.

2. Because of their doing/making orientation, Americans tend to be informal, spontaneous, and free from adherence to strict stylistic patterns, whereas the Japanese, because of their orientation, tend to be conscious more about the form than about the content of communication.

3. Because of their low-context orientation, Americans tend to verbalize their messages to make their intentions clear and explicit, whereas the Japanese, because of their high-context orientation, establish and preserve a great number of specific rules of conduct and forms of expression.

   Finally, in terms of tone of communication (which refers to the speaker's attitude toward his or her listeners), Americans clearly differentiate between the roles of speaker and listener. Americans tend to view the speaker as an agent of change who can manipulate and persuade the listener in a confrontational setting. In contrast, Japanese rhetoric emphasizes the importance of the perceiver. A speaker always adjusts himself or herself to the listeners.

and put ourselves to another's shoes in the process of interaction (Harris & Moran, 1989).

   The subjective nature of perceptual frameworks arising from our culture indicates that our perceptions are often partial and inaccurate. The problem can be explained by considering stereotyping and prejudice.

# STEREOTYPES

*Stereotypes* are those overgeneralized and oversimplified beliefs we use to categorize a group of people (Allport, 1958). We have a tendency to make a claim that often goes beyond the facts, with no valid basis. Stereotypes may be based on the truth, but they are exaggerated statements regarding our belief about what a group of people are or should be. For example, imagine that your wallet was stolen by "a" Korean when you were traveling in Korea last summer. The incident ruined your whole trip there. When you came back, your friends asked how your trip to Korea was. You might have said, "Those Koreans are thieves. They stole my wallet." This is an example of stereotyping.

We form stereotypes in three ways. First, we may categorize people or things by the most obvious characteristics they possess. For example, I asked a Japanese student about her first impression of the United States of America. She said, "Wow! Everything is big here." Following are the first impressions of the United States of a group of Japanese visitors:

- Americans walk very fast.
- Americans are always in a hurry.
- American are wasteful in utilizing space.
- Americans always try to talk everything out.
- Americans are very straightforward in talking.
- American students ask too many questions in the classroom and don't respect professors.

Second, we may apply a set of characteristics to a whole group of people. For example, you may hear someone say that Americans eat hotdogs and wear cowboy boots. The following is a complaint from an Asian undergraduate student enrolled in an American college:

> *Another nasty event was with the Financial Aid Office. When they learned that I have an above-average perfect GPA of 4.0 on a 4.0 scale for my major and a 3.95 GPA for my cumulative, I was told publicly that I must be a math major. What a faulty assumption! Asians are always associated with the sciences and math. They are never linked to the humanities or social sciences. I am a speech communication major. I know that I do not fit the norm of an Asian. So, don't put me into your narrow category. I am who I am and I do extremely well in what I do.*

Third, we may give the same treatment to each member of the group. "You are a Chinese, you must be smart" is stereotyping. The following are common stereotypes of Americans:

- Americans are rich.
- Americans drive big cars.
- Americans talk a lot but say little.
- Americans have superficial relationships.
- Americans do not care about old people.
- Americans think only about money.
- Americans are outgoing and friendly.
- Americans lack discipline.
- Americans are disrespectful of age and status.
- Americans are ignorant of other countries.
- Americans are extravagant and wasteful.
- Americans are loud, rude, boastful, and immature.
- Americans are always in a hurry.

A pervasive stereotype in the United States is that ours is a white, English-speaking culture. At an academic conference attended by the present authors, a doctoral student from a prestigious university revealingly divided subjects in a U.S organization into the two groups "Japanese Americans" and "Americans." It did not strike the researcher that "Japanese Americans" are also "Americans."

## Dimensions of Stereotypes

Stereotypes may vary along four dimensions: direction, intensity, accuracy, and content. The direction of stereotypes refers to the positive/favorable and negative/unfavorable aspects of statements. We might say that Americans are honest, friendly, hardworking, and ambitious. We might also say that Americans are aggressive, lacking discipline, or don't care about old people. The intensity of a stereotype indicates the strength of a belief about a group of people. "African Americans are very musical" is an example of an intense stereotype. Stereotypes also vary in their accuracy. Although stereotypes are exaggerated and overgeneralized beliefs, they are not always false. Some of them may be half-truths, and others may be partially inaccurate. Finally, stereotypes may vary in their specific content, for example, in the specific traits attributed to a group of people. For example, some African Americans may view white Americans according to a range of traits: aggressive, biased, cold, or evasive. Could you classify the common stereotypes toward Americans listed above into each dimension of stereotypes?

## PREJUDICE

Stereotypes naturally develop from a set of oversimplified beliefs into a rigid attitude toward a group of people. Such an attitude based on erroneous beliefs or preconceptions is called *prejudice*. Stereotypes and prejudice often occur together. In other words, when we hold beliefs (stereotypes), for example, about Italians, we also tend to have prejudice toward them. While beliefs refer to the likelihood that a group of people possesses certain characteristics, they contribute to the formation of attitude systems that directly affect to the way we treat the group of people. Thus, prejudice is a learned tendency by which we respond to a given group of people or event in a consistent (usually negative) way. When cognitions (stereotypes) are assigned values (prejudice), we may enact biased action (e.g., discrimination).

## Forms of Prejudice

Prejudice varies principally along the dimension of intensity. Five common forms of prejudice can be identified in terms of intensity: verbal abuse, physical avoidance, discrimination, physical attack, and massacre (Brislin, 1981; Klopf, 1995).

Verbal abuse is often accompanied by ethnic jokes and name-labeling. Examples of the latter include the following:

- Dead Indians are good Indians.
- Chinese = Chinks.
- Japanese = Japs.
- Blacks = Negroes.
- Polish = Polacks.

Moreover, a controversy over spearfishing by Sioux tribes in the U.S. Midwest elicited the comment, "Save a walleye. Spear a pregnant squaw." And French Canadians in Quebec were said by Mohawks to commonly call them "savages."

Physical avoidance occurs when we dislike a group of people. Because of different religious beliefs, language systems, and behavioral patterns, we may intentionally avoid making friends, going out, studying, or working with certain people. For instance, some Irish Catholics and Protestants have been outcast for dating one another.

Discrimination refers to the denial of equal opportunities to outgroup members. When the British posted the sign "Dogs and the Chinese can't enter" at the front gate of the Chinese park in the colonial area, they performed discrimination. Discrimination often occurs in the areas of employment, residential housing, political rights, educational and recreational opportunities, and other social privileges. Historically, some black and white Americans determined who could join a political party by judging whether a person' skin tone was lighter than the color of a paper bag that hung at the door.

As the degree of discrimination intensifies, physically punishing the group of people who are disliked becomes inevitable. In an eighteen-month period some fifty African American churches were burned down, mainly from arson. At the same time, African Americans in New York City tried to drive Korean merchants from black neighborhoods by means of intimidation. Finally, the worst result of prejudice is massacre. The genocidal slaughter by Hitler of the Jewish people and the burning of women as witches in colonial America are two examples. Recent conflicts in Bosnia and Rwanda also reflect the tendency of ethnic groups to exterminate each other because of different beliefs.

## ORIGINS AND IMPACT OF STEREOTYPES AND PREJUDICE

As we mentioned above, stereotypes and prejudice do not suddenly appear when we are born. We gradually develop our stereotypes and prejudices through the process of learning and socialization. As children, we learn stereotypes from our parents and friends. As we grow up, we learn them from our schools, churches, friends, and significant others. We also develop stereotypes from our personal experiences, especially through the interactions with people who had visible and distinct traits such as impairment, physical appearance, and skin color. Finally, mass media also play an important role in the development of stereotypes and prejudice. For example, television, radio, books, newspapers, magazines, and films often portray most groups in our society with an overgeneralized and oversimplified view that directly fosters certain kinds of images we form of a group of people.

Because stereotypes and prejudice are based on our belief and attitude systems, they affect the way we communicate in intercultural encounters. They may prevent us from interacting with people of different backgrounds; they tend to produce negative feelings during the interactions; and they can lead to unnecessary conflicts when they are intense. To improve the problems of stereotypes and prejudice, we suggest that empathy is the main communication skill we should learn. Empathic persons know how to show understanding by projecting themselves into their partner's position. This means that to be empathic in intercultural interactions we need to be open-minded in terms of information sharings, to be imaginative in correctly drawing the picture of other's situation, and to show a commitment or strong willingness to understand our culturally different partners in any kind of situation.

While cultural perception dictates the development of a belief system, which helps us see something as what it is or what it should be, it also helps to establish the value system by which we can judge what is good or bad, right or wrong, or what we ought to be. The next section discusses cultural values.

# THE NATURE OF VALUES

Values fundamentally influence our behavior in society. They do not describe how we act in a culture but dictate what we ought or ought not to do. Values tend to be the basis of all the decisions we make and provide standards for us to evaluate our own and others' actions. Thus, a value can be defined as "a conception, explicit or implicit, distinctive of an individual or characteristic of a group, of the desirable which influences the selection from available modes, means, and ends of action" (Kluckhohn, 1951, p. 395). The definition implies that values are guiding forces of human behavior. It also shows the close relationship between the values we hold and the way we communicate.

# VALUES AND COMMUNICATION

Sitaram and Haapanen (1979) summarized the relationship between values and human communication as follows. First, values are communicated, both explicitly and implicitly, through symbolic behavior. Although what we say and what we do may reflect our personal motives or are constrained by the context of a situation, most of our speech and actions symbolically reflect the values embedded in our mind that have been learned through the socialization process. Values are normally expressed through verbal and nonverbal behaviors. Verbal expressions are used to highlight the importance of specific values to individuals or groups. For example, Jacob, Teune, and Watts (1968) found that the intensity of the language and the frequency and duration of time we consciously or unconsciously invest in expressing values are the indicators of the importance of the values to us. Proverbs demonstrate how verbal expressions are used to underscore values. For example, certain cultural values are expressed in the proverbs used by North Americans:

- Time and action: "Time is money," and "A stitch in time saves nine."
- Practicality: "A bird in the hand is worth two in the bush," "Don't cry over the spilt milk," and "Don't count your chickens before they are hatched."
- Privacy: "A man's home is his castle."
- Cleanliness: "Cleanliness is next to godliness."
- Future orientation: "Take care of today, and tomorrow will take care of itself."

Nonverbally, we tend to communicate our values through social rituals. For example, the custom of exchanging gifts in China and Japan reflects the cultural values of reciprocity, generosity, and friendship.

---

**Research Highlight 3–2**

Who:   Sitaram, K. S., & Haapanen, L. W.

What:   "The Role of Values in Intercultural Communication."

Where:   In M. K. Asante & C. A. Blake (Eds.) (1979), *The Handbook of Intercultural Communication* (pp. 147–160). Beverly Hills, CA: Sage.

This essay summarizes some of the studies about cultural values and discusses the relationship between cultural values and intercultural communication.

To the authors, values guide human behavior toward ourselves, our culture, and others. They are the basis of all decisions we make, including how something ought to be, what is worth living, fighting, and dying for in our life. Studies investigating the relationship between values and human behavior have supported two general propositions:

1. Values are communicated, both explicitly and implicitly, through symbolic behavior.
2. The way in which people communicate is influenced by the values they hold.

Values cannot be measured by scientists, because they are not accessible to clinical experimentation. Instead, in order to understand cultural values we can observe and measure "customs" people practice (e.g., marriage), "expectations" (that are the basis of customs), and "beliefs" (that are the basis of expectations). Values seldom change, whereas customs, expectations, and beliefs based on the values might change. In addition, a value cannot be isolated from the overall value system of a culture.

The authors emphasize that values are the most important variables in the process of intercultural communication. Problems and misunderstanding occur when we judge others by using our own values as the standard. The best example is "ethnocentrism." "Cultural relativism," which refers to the study of others' cultural values within the framework of that culture rather than in comparison with our own values, is a good way to solve the problem of ethnocentrism.

Finally, to reach understanding in intercultural communication, we should follow two rules: (1) understand each other's values, and (2) adapt our communication to each other's values.

---

Second, the way in which people communicate is influenced by the values they hold. Just as communication is a mediator of values, communication is shaped by our value system. Because values determine what is desirable and what is undesirable, they dictate the way we choose to act in the process of communication. For example, *harmony* as a key Chinese cultural value leads the Chinese to avoid saying "no," to speak admiringly and respectfully of others, and to avoid expressing aggressive behaviors in social interactions. In

**Mini Case 3–1**

Jane, an American, had a very good Japanese friend Suki living in Japan. Suki was a talented designer working for a famous company. Suki decided to get married and invited Jane to her wedding. Thus, Jane flew to Japan to meet Suki. Suki wanted to introduce her fiancé to Jane, so they all had dinner together. During dinner, they began a pleasant conversation, and Suki's fiancé was nice and polite to Jane. Then Suki told Jane that she would quit her job and be a housewife after marriage. Jane was surprised. She told Suki that she should not waste her talent and that she still should continue to work even after marriage. Suki said that as a housewife she would be very busy and that there would be no time for work. Besides, they had decided to have a baby, and this would increase the workload for Suki. Jane suggested that Suki could share the housework with her husband so she could have time to develop her career. Suki seemed embarrassed, while her fiancé remained silent for the rest of the evening. Jane felt that his attitude toward her became cold.

Why there was a change in the attitude of Suki's fiancé toward Jane?

*Source:* Ng Ka Yung, Hong Kong Baptist University

other words, the values we hold influence our preference in selecting communication channels and sources that symbolize our value system. Thus, the relationship that exists between communication and values is both mutual and reciprocal. Mini Case 3–1 illustrates the influence of values on communication.

## CULTURAL VALUE ORIENTATIONS

To study the relationship between cultural values and communication behaviors more systematically, Kluckhohn and Strodbeck (1961) introduced the concept of *value orientations*. According to the authors, value orientations are the means society uses to solve the universal problems of daily life. The concept implies four assumptions. First, all human societies will face the same problems; second, they use different means to solve universal problems; third, the means to address universal problems are limited; and, fourth, value orientations are behaviorably observable through empirical study (Condon & Yousef, 1975). Cultural value orientations are often used to develop a cultural assimilator that enables people to understand their own and others' cultures in intercultural training programs (see Chapter 11). The following section is devoted to discussing models used to study cultural value orientations.

## MODELS FOR THE STUDY OF CULTURAL VALUE ORIENTATIONS

The four most common models for the study of cultural values orientations were developed by Kluckhohn and Strodbeck (1961), Condon and Yousef (1975), Hall (1976), and Hofstede (1980, 1983, 1984).

### *Kluckhohn and Strodbeck's Model*

Kluckhohn and Strodbeck (1961) were pioneers in the study of cultural value orientations. They singled out five universal problems faced by all human societies and the cultural value orientations they represent:

1. What is the character of innate human nature? (the human nature orientation)
2. What is the relationship of people to nature (and supernature). (the man–nature orientation)
3. What is the temporal focus of human life? (the time orientation)
4. What is the modality of human activity? (the activity orientation)
5. What is the modality of a person's relationship to other persons? (the relational orientation)

   Each orientation represents a universal problem all human actors and societies need to face. Kluckhohn and Strodbeck provided three possible variations of the solution for each problem:

a. Human nature—evil, mixture of good and evil, and good.
b. Human–nature relationship—subjugation to nature, harmony with nature, and mastery over nature.
c. Time—past, present, and future.
d. Activity—being, being-in-becoming, and doing.
e. Relational—lineality, collaternity, and individualism.

### *Condon and Yousef's Model*

Condon and Yousef (1975) revised and extended Kluckhohn and Strodbeck's five categories to include six spheres of universal problems all human societies must face: the self, the family, society, human nature, nature, and the supernatural. The six spheres intersect each other and are interdependent. Under each sphere the authors added three to five orientations with three variations of the solution for each one. Figure 3–1 illustrates a total of twenty-five value orientations encompassed by the six spheres of universal problems.

The model offers a comprehensive list of cultural value orientations. According to Condon and Yousef, all the variations may exist in any one society at the same time, but the degree of preference for choosing a given response to the problem differs. The variations in the left column tend to be the ways in which Northern Americans solve universal problems. Instead of explaining the meanings of all the variations of the six spheres, let us use examples to delineate some of them.

The following chart compares the different orientations of the Chinese and Northern Americans toward family.

| **Family** | **China** | **United States** |
|---|---|---|
| Relational orientation | Lineal orientation—Characterized by a highly developed historical consciousness and a close association with extended families. Wife tends to be subordinate to husband and to parents in the family. | Individualistic orientation—Older and younger members of the family always share the same values. Wife and children are more equal to husband, and children must be obedient to parents. |
| Authority | Authoritarian orientation—Reflects a strong orientation toward paternal authority. | Democratic orientation—Reflects a more even balance between paternal and maternal authority. The family is child-centered. |
| Positional role behavior | Specific orientation—Generation, age, and sex hierarchy is very strong; i.e., the older generation, elders, and male are superior. | Open orientation—Obligations are open to negotiation. |
| Mobility | Low-mobility orientation—The family structure and an agricultural society made the Chinese settle in a fixed place and cultivate the land in an orderly fashion. | High-mobility orientation—Conjugal family structure, no kinship bondage and high degree of technology and transportation have produced a highly mobile society. |

Finally, the "jigoku no kuren" (hell camp) held in Malibu, California, is another example showing that Japanese cultural values are highly group- and formality-oriented in the social and organizational life. The "hell camp" is a thirteen-day training program designed to teach Americans about the Japanese

SELF

*Individualism—interdependence*

| | | |
|---|---|---|
| 1. individualism | 2. individuality | 3. interdependence |

*Age*

| | | |
|---|---|---|
| 1. youth | 2. the middle years | 3. old age |

*Sex*

| | | |
|---|---|---|
| 1. equality of sexes | 2. female superiority | 3. male superiority |

*Activity*

| | | |
|---|---|---|
| 1. doing | 2. being-in-becoming | 3. being |

THE FAMILY

*Relational orientations*

| | | |
|---|---|---|
| 1. individualistic | 2. collateral | 3. lineal |

*Authority*

| | | |
|---|---|---|
| 1. democratic | 2. authority-centered | 3. authoritarian |

*Positional role behavior*

| | | |
|---|---|---|
| 1. open | 2. general | 3. specific |

*Mobility*

| | | |
|---|---|---|
| 1. high mobility | 2. phasic mobility | 3. low mobility, stasis |

SOCIETY

*Social reciprocity*

| | | |
|---|---|---|
| 1. independence | 2. symmetrical-obligatory | 3. complementary-obligatory |

*Group membership*

| | | |
|---|---|---|
| 1. many groups, brief identification, sub-ordination of group to individual | 2. balance of nos. 1 and 3 | 3. few groups, prolonged identification, sub-ordination of the member to the group |

*Intermediaries*

| | | |
|---|---|---|
| 1. no intermediaries (directness) | 2. specialist inter-mediaries only | 3. essential intermediaries |

*Formality*

| | | |
|---|---|---|
| 1. informality | 2. selective formality | 3. pervasive formality |

*Property*

| | | |
|---|---|---|
| 1. private | 2. utilitarian | 3. community |

**FIGURE 3–1    Condon and Yousef's Model of Value Orientations**

HUMAN NATURE

*Rationality*

| | | |
|---|---|---|
| 1. rational | 2. intuitive | 3. irrational |

*Good and evil*

| | | |
|---|---|---|
| 1. good | 2. mixture of good and evil | 3. evil |

*Happiness, pleasure*

| | | |
|---|---|---|
| 1. happiness as goal | 2. inextricable bond of happiness and sadness | 3. life is mostly sadness |

*Mutability*

| | | |
|---|---|---|
| 1. change, growth, learning | 2. some change | 3. unchanging |

NATURE

*Relationship of man and nature*

| | | |
|---|---|---|
| 1. man dominating nature | 2. man in harmony with nature | 3. nature dominating man |

*Ways of knowing nature*

| | | |
|---|---|---|
| 1. abstract | 2. circle of induction-deduction | 3. specific |

*Structure of nature*

| | | |
|---|---|---|
| 1. mechanistic | 2. spiritual | 3. organic |

*Concept of time*

| | | |
|---|---|---|
| 1. future | 2. present | 3. past |

THE SUPERNATURAL

*Relationship of man and the supernatural*

| | | |
|---|---|---|
| 1. man as god | 2. pantheism | 3. man controlled by the supernatural |

*Meaning of life*

| | | |
|---|---|---|
| 1. physical, material goals | 2. intellectual goals | 3. spiritual goals |

*Providence*

| | | |
|---|---|---|
| 1. good in life is unlimited | 2. balance of good and misfortune | 3. good in life is limited |

*Knowledge of the cosmic order*

| | | |
|---|---|---|
| 1. order is comprehensible | 2. faith and reason | 3. mysterious and unknowable |

*Source:* From John C. Condon & F. Yousef, *An Introduction to Intercultural Communication.* Copyright © 1975 by Bobbs-Merrill. Reprinted/Adapted by permission.

management style, in which participants are taught to bow like the Japanese, loudly announce their return from a walk, hike twenty-five miles at night, and shout a song in a suburban shopping mall.

## Hall's Culture Context Model

Hall (1976) divided cultural differences into two categories: low-context culture and high-context culture. The two cultural contexts form a continuum in which some cultures, such as China, England, France, Ghana, Japan, Korea, and Vietnam, orient to the high-context culture, and other cultures, such as Germany, those in Scandinavia, Switzerland, and the United States, orient mainly to the low-context culture (of course, any nation may contain communities whose orientation differs from that of the national norm). According to Hall and Hall (1987), low context and high context

> *refers . . . to the fact that when people communicate, they take for granted how much the listener knows about the subject under discussion. In low-context communication, the listener knows very little and must be told practically everything. In high-context communication the listener is already "contexted" and does not need to be given much background information. (pp. 183–184)*

One of the major differences in terms of communication between low-context and high-context cultures is in verbal expression. People from low-context cultures tend to use a direct verbal-expression style, and people from high-context cultures tend to use indirect verbal-expression style. The direct verbal-expression style consists of four features: (1) the situational context is not emphasized; (2) important information is usually carried in explicit verbal messages; (3) self-expression, verbal fluency, and eloquent speech are valued; and (4) people tend to directly express their opinions and intend to persuade others to accept their viewpoints. The indirect verbal-expression styles also consist of four features: (1) Explicit verbal messages are not emphasized; (2) important information is usually carried in contextual cues (e.g., place, time, situation, and relationship); (3) harmony is highly valued, with a tendency toward using ambiguous language and keeping silent in interactions; and (4) people tend to talk around the point, and to avoid saying "no" directly to others (Hall, 1976).

In sum, whereas the direct verbal-expression style refers to verbal messages we use to show our intentions in the process of conversations, the indirect verbal-expression style refers to verbal messages we use to camouflage and conceal our true intentions (Gudykunst & Ting-Toomey, 1988).

Other differences that distinguish between low-context and high-context cultures have been succinctly summarized by Chung (1992):

| Low-Context Culture | High-Context Culture |
| --- | --- |
| 1. Overtly displays meanings through direct communication forms. | 1. Implicitly embeds meanings at different levels of the sociocultural context. |
| 2. Values individualism. | 2. Values group sense. |
| 3. Tends to develop transitory personal relationship. | 3. Tends to take time to cultivate and establish a permanent personal relationship. |
| 4. Emphasizes linear logic. | 4. Emphasizes spiral logic. |
| 5. Values direct verbal interaction and is less able to read nonverbal expressions. | 5. Values indirect verbal interaction and is more able to read nonverbal expressions. |
| 6. Tends to use "logic" to present ideas. | 6. Tends to use more "feeling" in expression. |
| 7. Tends to emphasize highly structured messages, give details, and place great stress on words and technical signs. | 7. Tends to give simple, ambiguous, noncontexting messages. |

## Hofstede's Cultural Dimensions

Hofstede (1980, 1983, 1984) compared work-related attitudes across over forty different cultures and found four consistent dimensions of cultural values held by over 160,000 managers and employees: individualism/collectivism, power distance, uncertainty avoidance, and masculinity/femininity. While Hofstede's work has been criticized for understating domestic cultural and gender variability, it offers a good starting point for thinking about values.

The dimension of individualism and collectivism describes the relationship between the individual and the group to which the person belongs. Individualistic cultures stress the self and personal achievement. People in an individualistic culture tend to emphasize their self-concept in terms of self-esteem, self-identity, self-awareness, self-image, and self-expression. In other words, the individual is treated as the most important element in any social setting. Personal goals supercede group goals, and competition is often encouraged in this culture. Moreover, in individualistic cultures people tend to emphasize more affiliativeness, dating, flirting, and small talk in social interactions (Andersen, 1994). Hofstede's findings indicate that the United States, Australia, Great Britain, Canada, the Netherlands, New Zealand, Italy, Belgium, and Denmark belong to this group.

By contrast, collectivistic cultures are characterized by a more rigid social framework in which self-concept plays a less significant role in social interactions. Ingroup (e.g., immediate and extended families) and outgroup members are clearly distinguished, and only ingroup views and needs are emphasized. In these cultures people are also expected to be interdependent and show conformity to the group's norms and values. In other words, the social networks are much more fixed and less reliant on individual initiative (Andersen, 1994). Columbia, Venezuela, Pakistan, Peru, Taiwan, Thailand, Singapore, Chile, and Hong Kong are the top nine collectivistic cultures specified in Hofstede's studies. If we compare them with Hall's high- and low-context cultures, we can see that individualistic cultures tend to be similar to low-context cultures and collectivistic cultures to high-context cultures.

The dimension of power distance specifies to what extent a culture adapts to inequalities of power distribution in relationships and organizations. High-power-distance cultures tend to orient to authoritarianism, which dictates a hierarchical or vertical structure of social relationships. In these cultures people are assumed to be unequal and complementary in social interactions. The differences of age, sex, generation, and status are usually maximized. Thus, people in high-power-distance cultures develop relationships with others based on various levels of hierarchy. The Philippines, Mexico, Venezuela, India, Singapore, Brazil, Hong Kong, France, and Columbia represent the high-power-distance cultures in Hofstede's studies.

Low-power-distance cultures are more horizontal in terms of social relationships. People in these cultures tend to minimize differences of age, sex, status, and roles. Instead, individual differences are encouraged. Thus, they tend to be less formal and more direct in social interactions. Australia, Israel, Denmark, New Zealand, Ireland, Sweden, Norway, Finland, and Switzerland are those countries that scored low in power distance scales. Info 3–1 shows how different high- and low-power-distance cultures can be in terms of management styles.

The dimension of uncertainty avoidance measures the extent to which a culture can accept ambiguous situations and tolerate uncertainty about the future. Members of high-uncertainty-avoidance cultures always try to reduce the level of ambiguity and uncertainty in social and organizational life. They pursue job and life security, avoid risk taking, resist changes, fear failure, and seek behavioral rules that can be followed in interactions. As a result, high-uncertainty-avoidance cultures tend to use fewer oral cues and are more able to predict others' behaviors. Such cultures are found in Greece, Portugal, Belgium, Japan, Peru, France, Chile, Spain, and Argentina.

However, other cultures, including Denmark, Sweden, Norway, Finland, Ireland, Great Britain, the Netherlands, the Philippines, and the United States, are oriented to cope with the stress and anxiety caused by ambiguous and uncertain situations. Members of these low-uncertainty-avoidance cultures tend to better tolerate the deviant behaviors and unusual stress connected with the uncertainty and ambiguity. As a result, they take more initiative, show greater flexibility, and feel more relaxed in interactions.

**Info 3–1**

Power Distance

*The Chinese Dinner Party*

One of Canada's leading banks invited a Chinese delegation for dinner. The Canadian host chose to share his hosting responsibilities with a colleague.

The dinner was not a success. Both the Chinese and the Canadians remained relatively uneasy throughout the meal. During the dinner, no welcoming speeches or toasts to mutual good health were made. At the end of the meal, the Chinese stood up, thanked the bank officials, declined a ride back to their hotel, and left feeling slighted.

The Canadians also felt upset. They found the departure of the Chinese to be very abrupt, yet they did not know what they had done wrong. Despite planning the menu carefully (avoiding such foods as beef and dairy products), providing excellent translation services, and extending normal Canadian courtesies, the Canadians knew something had gone wrong; they were worried and somewhat hurt by the lack of rapport.

When the situation was analyzed, it was clear that the Chinese expectations had not been fulfilled. First, having two people share hosting responsibilities was confusing to the hierarchically minded Chinese. Second, because age is viewed as an indication of seniority, the Chinese considered the youth of their Canadian hosts as a slight to their own status. Third, in China, it is traditional for the host to offer a welcoming toast at the beginning of the meal, which is then reciprocated by the guests; by not doing so, the Canadians were thought rude.

The specific incident that upset the Canadians—the abrupt departure of the Chinese following the banquet—was, in fact, neither unusual nor a problem: the Chinese retire early and it was getting late.

The Canadians' lack of understanding of the hierarchical nature of Chinese society and the Chinese ways of communicating respect clearly cost them in their business dealings with the visiting delegation.

*Source:* From G. Hofstede, *Culture's Consequences,* copyright © 1983 by Sage Publications. Reprinted by permission of Sage Publications.

Finally, the dimension of masculinity and femininity refers to the extent to which stereotypically masculine and feminine traits prevail in the culture. In masculine cultures men are expected to be dominant in the society and to show quality of ambition, assertiveness, achievement, strength, competitiveness, and material acquisition; thus, the communication styles are more aggressive. In male-dominated cultures women are expected to play the nurturing role. Hofstede's studies indicate that Japan is the best example of a masculine culture. Other nations in this category include Australia, Venezuela, Switzerland, Mexico, Ireland, Great Britain, and Germany.

Members of feminine cultures tend to emphasize the quality of affection, compassion, emotion, nurturing, and sensitivity. Men in these cultures are not expected to be assertive. Thus, gender roles are more equal and people are more capable of reading nonverbal cues and tolerating ambiguous situations. Sweden, Norway, the Netherlands, Denmark, Finland, Chile, Portugal, and Thailand represent feminine cultures, according to Hofstede.

## RECAP

This chapter discusses two fundamental concepts of intercultural communication: cultural perception and cultural values. Perception is a process by which we turn external stimuli into meaningful experiences. The process of perception includes three stages: selection, organization, and interpretation. Because perception is selective, we can only partially perceive the things that surround us. It usually follows three steps: selective exposure, selective attention, and selective retention. Organization refers to the way we arrange what we perceive into meaningful patterns, based on their shape, color, texture, size, and intensity. Interpretation is the process whereby we assign meanings to what we perceive.

Culture has a major impact on the perception process. It not only provides the foundation for the meanings we assign to our perceptions, it also determines how we choose to expose ourselves to and direct our attention toward specific kinds of messages and events. The influence of culture on perception is often reflected in the attributional process. Attribution involves interpreting the meaning of others' behaviors based on our past experience or history. Culture provides an environment that allows us to develop all the meanings we possess. Thus, people from different cultures will perceive and interpret others' behaviors in different ways.

The subjective nature of the perceptual framework arising from our culture indicates that our perception is often partial and inaccurate. The insufficiency manifests as stereotyping, prejudice, and discrimination. Stereotypes are those overgeneralized and oversimplified beliefs we use to categorize a group of people, and prejudice is a rigid attitude based on erroneous beliefs or preconceptions. Discrimination is the acting out of prejudicial attitudes. Stereotypes may vary along four dimensions: direction, intensity, accuracy, and content. Prejudice especially varies along the dimension of intensity. Five common types of prejudice differ in intensity: verbal abuse, physical avoidance, discrimination, physical attack, and massacre.

Stereotypes and prejudice do not suddenly appear when we are born. They are gradually developed from the process of learning and socialization, and from exposure to mass media images. Finally, in striving to solve the problems of stereotypes and prejudice, we suggest that empathy is the most important communication skill we should learn.

The second part of the chapter focuses on cultural values and the close relationship existing between values and communication. "Value orientation" is the concept used to study systematically the relationship between cultural values and communication behaviors. Value orientations are the means societies tend to use to solve the universal problems of daily life. This chapter describes four models for the study of cultural value orientations, including Kluckhohn and Strodbeck's model, Condon and Yousef's model, Hall's high-context and low-context cultures, and Hofstede's four dimensions of cultural values.

## RETHINK

Three key issues inform the study of cultural values. First, the four models specified in this chapter represent only the common ones used in the discipline. They are neither exhaustive nor perfect, and each model has its strength and weakness. Kluckhohn and Strodbeck's model serves as a classic example. Though it is precise and heuristic, the five categories of value orientations are far too simple to describe complex human society. Condon and Yousef's model makes an effort to refine Kluckhohn and Strodbeck's model, but the huge list of cultural value orientations makes it impossible for any communication scholar to completely monitor each item in the space of a lifetime. Hall's model has been a major influence on the study of intercultural communication. Nevertheless, the dichotomous classification of high-context and low-context cultures not only oversimplifies the complex nature of culture but also misleads students of intercultural communication to believe that the two cultural schemes are in polar opposition to each other. In fact, as Schwartz (1990) argued, many universal values such as achievement, security, and hedonism are emphasized in high-context and low-context cultures. The similarities found between the two groups indicates that people of different cultures may share similar values. In other words, all variations of cultural values may exist in any one society. Hofstede's model is especially applicable to the understanding of cultural values in social and organizational settings. The weaknesses of the model are threefold:

**1.** Because the questionnaire respondents were middle managers in multinational companies, the dimensions Hofstede identified are work-related values.

**2.** Among the four dimensions only individualism/collectivism has been widely studied and validated. However, research has documented that some persons in individualistic societies are collectively oriented, and the reverse is true as well. The other three dimensions have yet to be validated.

**3.** The concepts of nation and culture are not clearly differentiated (Mead, 1990; Samovar & Porter, 1995).

Second, the cultural value orientations specified by Kluchhohn and Strodbeck and by Condon and Yousef are meaningful only in combination, not in isolation (Condon & Yousef, 1975). We may treat each category individually for

---

**Research Highlight 3–3**

Who:    Schwartz, S. H., & Sagiv, L.

What:   "Identifying Culture-Specifics in the Content and Structure of Values."

Where:  *Journal of Cross-Cultural Psychology, 26,* 1993, 92–116.

One of the main purposes of this article is to test the propositions of the theory of universals of human values across cultures. The theory derives ten motivationally distinct types of values that are universal in all cultures and delineates the interrelations of conflict and compatibility among the ten types of values that give structure to value systems. Previous research by Schwartz (1992) supports the near universality of the value types and their structure. In this study the authors extend the research by analyzing data from eighty samples from forty countries to reevaluate the universal principle of values types and provide criteria that can be used to identify what is culture-specific in the meanings and structure of values. The ten motivational types of values that are tested in this study include power, achievement, hedonism, stimulation, self-direction, universalism, benevolence, tradition, conformity, and security. These ten value types are comprised of fifty-six core values.

In addition to discussing deviations due to the unique, culture-specific expressions of values and unreliable measurement deriving from the prototypical structure and meanings of values in specific samples, the authors report three findings:

**1.** The results further support the findings of earlier research that the ten motivationally distinct value types can be recognized across cultures and can be used to express value priorities.

**2.** The ten value types can be arrayed on a motivational continuum in most cultures. These value types can be classified into two dimensions across cultures: (1) "Openness to change" (self-direction and stimulation) versus "conservation" (security, conformity, and tradition) and "self-enhancement" (universalism and benevolence) versus "self-transcendence" (power and achievement) (*Note:* Hedonism is related both to "openness to change" and to "self-enhancement").

**3.** Forty-four out of fifty-six core values under the ten value types show highly consistent meanings across cultures. A cross-culturally comparable index of the importance attributed to each value type can be devised, based on these consistent meanings.

the convenience of study, but to more completely understand a culture we need to integrate all the categories into a whole picture. In other words, a change in any category influences the other categories.

Finally, Condon and Yousef (1975) emphasized that it is important to apply the knowledge of cultural values to real communication settings. They raised a provocative research question concerning the relationship between cultural values and communication behaviors: What communication patterns do interactants adopt when they are from two different cultures? Does communication follow the cultural pattern of either interactant? Or will a synthetic pattern of the two interactants' cultures emerge? These questions invite empirical testing in this line of research.

## QUESTIONS FOR DISCUSSION

1. Describe the stages of the perception process.
2. Compare your perception of the meanings of the following colors with those of a friend from another culture: black, blue, green, pink, red, white, yellow.
3. Discuss the stereotypes on Americans listed in the chapter and indicate whether you agree with them.
4. Give an example of each form of prejudice.
5. Compare and contrast the models of cultural value orientations developed by Kluckhohn and Strodbeck, Condon and Yousef, Hall, and Hofstede.
6. What are the limitations of the models used for the study of cultural value orientations?
7. Discuss how cultural value orientations affect human communication.

# ▶ Part II

## Context

# ▶ Chapter 4

## Language and Culture

### *Objectives*

Upon completion of this chapter, you will

- Be able to define such terms as morphology, phonology, syntax, semantics, and pragmatics.
- Understand the structure of human language.
- Understand the characteristics of language.
- Be able to distinguish the variations of human language.
- See the relationship between language and culture.
- See the relationship between cultural value orientations and language expressions.

*"Hey blood, when it is? Ah, Man, ain't notin to it but to do it."*

*"Huney, I done told ya', God, be don't lak ugly."*

*"Look-a-there. I ain't seen nothin like these economic indicators."*

The above remarks were recorded by Weber (1994) to show the variations of black language used everywhere. The variations of human language are, in fact, as complex as human faces. And human language is at once verbal and nonverbal. Nonverbal language will be discussed in the next chapter. In this chapter we discuss several aspects of verbal language: linguistics; the structure, characteristics, and variations of human language; and the relationship between language and culture.

# LINGUISTICS

*Linguistics* is the scientific study of human language. The field generally examines how human beings use language as symbols in the communication process. In other words, linguistics deals with the relationship between language and communication.

Nevertheless, human beings are not the only creatures using symbols for communication purposes. Scientists have found that other animals also have their own communication systems by which they are able to send out signals in different kinds of situations to warn or instruct others of their species to get help, search for food, or avoid danger. For example, bees use a round dance to indicate that there is a food source within 10 meters of the hive. Italian honeybees also use a sickle dance to instruct their companions to seek a food source between 10 and 100 meters of the hive by following the bisector of the pattern of the dance. Moreover, bees even use a tail-wagging dance to tell others to seek a food source at a distance of $x$ by flying at $y$ degrees with respect to the sun. Scientists have long been surprised by the accuracy of the instructions bees give by the three kinds of dances.

The bird is another kind of animal having a communication system in which three signals are commonly found. When seeing a predator overhead, the bird will make an aerial predator call, and the receivers of the warning call will take cover in bushes and remain motionless. A mobbing call, indicating a stationary predator nearby, invites other birds to surround and attack the predator. A territorial song is used to warn other male birds to keep out of the territory of the message sender and beckons female birds to come there.

Finally, dolphins also communicate among themselves. A sick bottle-nosed dolphin may send out a distress whistle to request help. When other nearby dolphins receive the message they, for example, come to the distressed one and raise it to the surface of the water.

Is there any difference between human beings and animals in their use of symbols as a communication system? Obviously, we can easily figure out the difference from the ability of handling the symbol. There are four steps for processing the symbol: receiving, storing, manipulating, and generating. Scientists found that some kind of animals are able to receive symbols and a few, e.g., chimpanzees, can store small numbers of symbols, but no nonhuman animal is able to manipulate and generate symbols. Manipulation of symbols refers to the ability to articulate one's intentions in different situations, and generation of symbols refers to the ability to continuously produce new messages in interactions. Only human beings possess the ability to manipulate and generate symbols, which makes human communication a very dynamic process.

# THE STRUCTURE OF HUMAN LANGUAGE

Linguistics is comprised of five areas of study: morphology, phonology, syntax, semantics, and pragmatics. Among them, semantics and pragmatics have special importance for intercultural communication.

## Morphology

*Morphology* is the study of words and word building. For example, "love" has been coined to represent the internal passion we have toward others. The verb "love" can become "lovable," which is an adjective; "lover," a noun; or "lovably," an adverb. It is said that the Chinese characters are based on six morphological categories: (1) the pictograph—which consists of greatly simplified drawings of the objects the characters denote; (2) the indirect symbol—which takes the form of various kinds of substitutions, such as parts standing for wholes, attributes for things, effects for causes, instruments for activities, or gestures for actions—in a metaphorical way; (3) the determinative-phonetic—which is formed by a radical (i.e., the determinative) and a phonetic, with the former element indicating the category within which the meaning of the word is to be sought, while the latter indicates the pronunciation; (4) the associative compound—which is formed by the significant combination of two or more pictographs; (5) the mutually interpretative symbol—which is formed by different characters or phonetics that can be used to represent the same meaning; and (6) the phonetic loan character—which is formed by a character the sense of which properly belongs to another character having the same sound but a different form (Lin, 1984).

## Phonology

*Phonology* is the study of the sounds of human language and their patterns. Two branches of this study include phonetics and phonology. Phonetics focuses on the study of the articulatory and acoustic properties of sounds. It deals with how to pronounce a word. Phonology focuses on the study of the principles and abstract rules that govern the distinction of sounds in human languages. It deals with why the word should be pronounced in the way we pronounce it.

## Syntax

Syntax is the study of the structure of sentences and phrases. For instance, to change the expression "I know her" into an interrogative sentence, we need to add "do" before "I," to give, "Do I know her?" If, however, we have a root verb in the expression, then we simply move the root verb in front of the subject instead of adding a verb. For example, "I am a happy person" becomes "Am I a happy person?"

## Semantics

*Semantics* is the study of meaning and reference in human language. In human language systems, a word may have several meanings, and many words may have the same meaning. For example, as a noun, the word "present" can mean "gift." As a verb, it can be used in many ways, such as "I present myself to the president," "I present a speech," and "The situation presents numerous problems."

In human language, two types of meaning have been identified: linguistic meaning and the speaker's meaning. Linguistic meaning is the dictionary meaning or the meaning or meanings of an expression in the language. It is the literal meaning of the expression without any reference to the feeling of the speaker. The speaker's meaning depends on the intention of the speaker. It can be literal or nonliteral. Thus, if we express ourselves in a literal way, our meaning is no different from the linguistic meaning. However, if we use irony, sarcasm, or metaphor, we may not mean to be understood by the surface meaning of the expression. For example, a student comes to the class ten minutes late. When he enters the classroom, the instructor says to him, "Good morning, sir." This expression, ostensibly a greeting to the student, in fact delivers the message, "You are late! Try to be here on time next time." Such nonliteral meaning often causes misunderstandings among people, especially in intercultural communication, in which interactants have different native languages.

## Pragmatics

*Pragmatics* is the study of the effect of language on human behavior. It is human nature to like to hear positive words or expressions such as "honey," "dear," "you are pretty," and "you are great!" In many cultures such expressions lead to a good mood and pleasant interactions. Conversely, to be called "savage," "nigger," "bitch," or "hey seed" may cause deep anger, lasting many days. Worse, such negative expressions also cause unnecessary confrontations among people. Thus, the words speakers choose tend to evoke various reactions that often produce an impact on the subsequent behavior of the listeners.

The five structural levels of human language comprise the content of linguistics. In linguistic analysis, an expression is generally broken down at each level into a set of discrete units by following the rules and principles that govern the combining or ordering of the discrete units. We now turn to a discussion of the characteristics of human language.

# CHARACTERISTICS OF LANGUAGE

Human language has four characteristics: it is symbolic, rule-governed, subjective, and dynamic. First, language is symbolic; it stands in place of "reality." For example, we use the symbol "hatred" to represent our internal negative feelings toward others. The reality is the "bad feeling" within our heart. In other words, a symbol is never equal to the reality to which it refers. To use another example, we use the symbol "rice" to represent something that can satisfy physical hunger. When we are really hungry, of course we don't eat the symbol "r-i-c-e" but the real steamed or boiled grain. Finally, the same reality can be represented by different symbols. Different language systems use different symbols to stand for the same reality.

Second, language is rule-governed. Every structural level of human language is regulated by its own grammatical rules and principles. Subject (I) + Verb (love) + Object (you) is the most basic pattern of English structure. You will definitely confuse the listener if you say "love I you" instead of "I love you." The rules or principles of human language are not universal. Different language systems to regulate their structures in different ways. We will inevitably encounter problems of language rules when we are learning a second language, as did some American students who went to Taiwan in summer to make their living and who created many jokes when they tried to use Mandarin to communicate with Chinese people there. For example, in Chinese the "you" in the expression of "How are you" should be put at the beginning of the sentence. Confusion about the language rule in this sentence can make the greeting in Mandarin sound like "Hi, mom, how are you," or "How's your mom?"

Third, language is subjective. Meanings of the language reside in people, not in words. Asking students to define "capitalism," "pregnancy," "love," or "happiness," we may produce twenty different meanings for each term from the students. Likewise, it is not surprising that students from mainland China or Russia claim that their country is a "democratic" one. According to communist doctrines, their political system is a people's "democracy." But American students may vehemently argue that only Western democracy is a real democracy. No matter who is right or wrong, the meanings of a language are dependent on cultural experience rather than on the words themselves.

Fourth, like human life, language is dynamic and has its own life cycle. No language is fixed or unvarying; in order to survive, all languages must constantly undergo changes and variations. Change in a language is based on the concept of time. When time changes, language also changes. For example, we have old, medieval, and modern English. When we read Shakespeare's *Hamlet,* we still see expressions such as "hath," "thy," "thee," and "thou." Nowadays, instead of using "hath" we change it to "have," and "thy," "thee," and "thou" to "you" or "your." Variations refer to the differences in the pronunciation, spelling, or

usage of the same language by different groups of people. For example, the following list shows some variations in British and American English:

| American English | British English |
| --- | --- |
| apartment | flat |
| eggplant | auberg |
| cleaning lady | charwoman |
| elevator | lift |
| first floor | ground level |
| long-distance call | trunk call |
| organization | organisation |
| pharmacist | chemist |
| rare | underdone |
| roast | joint |
| string bean | French bean |
| sweater | pullover |

# VARIATIONS OF HUMAN LANGUAGE

Many kinds of language variations have been identified by scholars. In this section we focus the discussion on seven of them: dialects, lingua franca, pidgins,
creole, jargon, argot, and taboo.

## Dialects

When groups of people speak the same language system differently, they may
be said to speak different *dialects* of the language. In other words, dialect is a
form of language peculiar to a group of people, as distinguished from the literary language of the whole people (Gleason, 1989). Three common kinds of
dialects include regional, social, and ethnic dialects. A regional dialect is usually developed in a certain geographic area. Examples of regionally different
dialects can be seen around the world. The Italian spoken in Rome sounds
totally different from the Italian that is spoken in Sicily. Parisian French and
Canadian French also sound like two different languages. It is said that India
has over 800 regional dialects. China is no exception. Each province in China
has its own dialect. Moreover, every African nation exhibits significant linguistic variety.

Social dialect is a distinct form of a language spoken by people belonging
to a specific socioeconomic class. The English spoken in poor black neigh-

borhoods differs from the English spoken in a historically black college. The English spoken by the working class in England is also very different from that of the middle and upper classes. Campus language is another example of social dialect. Most college students on U.S. campuses use expressions such as the following that may be not known by the general public:

Bomb the exam

Do Bong

Get laid

Get stoned

Get hammered

Get pounded

Get pie-eyed

Hit the book

Nerd

Ethnic dialect is a distinct form of a language spoken by members of a specific ethnic group. A good example is Yiddish English, which is historically associated with speakers of Eastern European Jewish ancestry. The following table illustrates the ethnic dialect spoken by the Amish:

| Amish English | American English |
| --- | --- |
| Balledicks | Politics |
| Bortsch | Porch |
| Budder | Butter |
| Chob | Job |
| Choose | Juice |
| Hungerich | Hungry |
| Leifinshurings | Life insurance |
| Mit choy | With joy |
| Powider | Provider |
| Sinterklaas | Santa Claus |
| Smearkase | Cottage cheese |
| Zucker | Sugar |

A controversy surrounding dialects is that we have a tendency to define one dialect as the formal or standard form of a language in a society. For example, black English in the United States is sometimes treated as "nonstandard" English. Yet, the mixing of English with various African languages has produced a language of its own, one with a distinctive grammar. The term *Ebonics* has been coined to describe this distinctive language. Because language will naturally show variations, showing respect and open-mindedness for language diversity is more important than arguing which dialect should be pure, formal, or standard. Today's preferred dialect may be tomorrow's relic.

## Pidgins

*Pidgin* languages, also called contact or marginal languages, have most often developed as a result of colonialization in military-occupied areas. Because of the desire on the part of the dominant group to communicate or trade with the subordinate group, pidgin naturally emerges. When there is no longer a need for the groups to communicate, the pidgin language may disappear. For example, some pidgin language is still spoken in Hong Kong, which was colonized by Great Britain over 150 years ago. Although Cantonese is the native language in Hong Kong, a mixture of Cantonese and British English is very common. However, the phenomenon may disappear now that China has reclaimed the sovereignty over the island.

Pidgin languages possess two properties. First, they have no native speakers. Pidgins serve basically as a means of communication between native and nonnative speakers. Second, the linguistic and grammatical structure of pidgin languages is always simple and based on one or two other languages. For example, "sex wonderful" is an expression used by prostitutes in Taiwan in soliciting American GIs to vacation there during the period of the Vietnam War. "Long time no see" is an example of a pidgin expression coined by early Chinese immigrants in the United States.

## Creole

When a pidgin language begins to acquire native speakers and becomes the permanent language of a region, it is called a *creole*. The origins of Creole (with a capital "C"), which is related to French-African speech, can be traced to the slave trade. Slaves brought from Africa had to communicate not only with each other in diverse tongues but also with their white masters. Because they were forbidden to speak their native languages, creole developed as the only language they could use. Other creoles include Gullah, which is an English creole spoken by the descendants of African slaves on the islands off the coast of Georgia and South Carolina, and Haitian creole which is based on French and Louisiana creole.

Because people tend to believe that both pidgin and creole languages lack cultural potential, they are undervalued and inadequately understood. As a result, the social status of creole speakers, in all but a few instances, tends to be low even today.

## Lingua Franca

*Lingua franca* is a compound language. According to Fromkin and Rodman (1978), "Frankish language" is the original term for lingua franca, the trade language used in the Mediterranean ports, admixed with French, Spanish, Greek, and Arabic. Lingua franca often develops in an area where groups of people speak diverse languages. When a given language known to all the participants is used by common agreement for the purpose of communication, this language is called lingua franca: Hindustani mixes Hindi, Urdu, Persian, Punjabi, and Arabic, and is used as a market language in Northern India. Swahili is used as a lingua franca in Africa to conduct business. Yiddish can be considered a lingua franca that is used by Jewish people to bind them together. Moreover, English and French have been called the "lingua franca of the whole world" and "lingua franca of diplomacy" separately (Fromkin & Rodman, 1978). Adler (1977) indicated also that English is a first or second language for 54 percent of the business world. For instance, English is the language of choice of most international airlines.

## Jargon

*Jargon* refers to the special or technical vocabularies developed to meet the special needs of particular professions such as medicine and law. Medical professionals tend to communicate with other professionals using technical terms but address patients in lay terms. Legal jargon is used everywhere. Note the complicated terminology on the back of the warranty or guarantee of any product. "CD-rom," "megabyte," and "default" are jargon in the computer field. As a communication major, we may understand better than others the terms "coding," "feedback," and "noise." And, unless we are pilots, we might not understand the real meaning of "touch-and-go."

Jargon may change over time. For example, in a gambling casino "stiff" is now used to replace "Tom" to describe a poor tipper, and "live one" rather than "George" is used to describe a good tipper (Fromkin & Rodman, 1978).

## Argot

*Argot* is a language that is peculiar to itself. It is a language in which the meaning of a word is changed or reversed. It is a more or less secret or unique series of vocabulary words and tends to be used by nondominant groups or co-cultures such as gays, prostitutes, prisoners, gang members, and the drug community. For example, a "claim" is an area that gangs have staked out as their turf, and "buster" is a gang member who does not stand up for his gang. Gang members also call a gun a "gat" or a "strap." A prostitute uses "trick" or "john" to describe a male customer and "steak" for the customer who will pay

$50 to be with her for one night; a "roast beef" pays $75, a "lobster" $150, and "champagne" $300 (Samovar & Sanders, 1978). Gays use the word "queen" to describe another male who appears in personal attire or in conversation to be especially effeminate and the terms "card-carrying member" or "stock broker" to identify each other so that no one else around them will know what they are talking about. In addition, members of the gay community use "Bill" to describe a masculine homosexual, "Black Widow" a gay who steals another gay's mate, and "chicken" a young male gay (Irwin, 1972).

Samovar and Porter (1995) pointed out that argot is used by nondominant groups or co-cultures for four purposes. First, it helps protect them from their enemies. If prostitutes can conceal their occupation from the law by using argot, they will avoid being arrested. Second, argot allows the nondominant groups to express frustration and hatred without risk of revenge. Third, it is used to bind groups together. Using argot provides group members with a sense of identity and pride. Finally, it gives group members a social identity by distinguishing them from the other social groups.

## Taboo

Fromkin and Rodman (1978) indicated that the term *taboo* was borrowed from the Polynesian word *Tongan,* which refers to behaviors that are forbidden or that should be avoided. Thus, words that are not polite for a society are considered taboo. Because the use of words varies from culture to culture, the customs and perceptions of the society play an important role as to what is taboo or not. For example, words that have to do with bodily functions are considered taboo in the United States. In Quebec, this is also true, but in many other societies it doesn't seem to matter. Likewise to the Chinese, the number *4* is taboo because it sounds like the word for "death." Cultural reality can never be fully explained to those of another culture using only language.

## LANGUAGE AND CULTURE

The relationship between culture and language has been studied for many decades, but scholars from different disciplines still have not reached consensus on the degree to which culture and language are related to each other. The argument proposes that language either determines or only reflects our attitude, beliefs, or culture.

## Language Determines Our Culture

Scholars who assert that language determines culture are proponents of the "Sapir-Whorf Hypothesis," which postulates that language not only transmits but also shapes our thinking, beliefs, and attitudes. In other words, language is a guide to culture—a major tenet of the writings of Edward Sapir. (see Mandelbaum, 1949). According to Sapir, language is the medium of expression for human society, and it conditions our thinking about social problems and processes. Language habits usually unconsciously form the "real world" of the group. Because each culture possesses a unique lexicon and grammar, no cultural reality can ever be fully explained by members of one culture to those of another.

After a series of studies on American Indian languages (Hoijer, 1994), Sapir systematically discussed the idea of language as a "guide of social reality," later elaborated by Boas in 1911. This line of research was continued by Benjamin Lee Whorf and reached its climax in the 1950s. According to Whorf (1952), the linguistic system of each language is itself the shaper of ideas. Language not only programs our mental activity but also guides our analysis of impressions. Whorf considered language the originator of culture. Language controls the human beings' cognitive system in the process of interaction, and this, in turn, systematically patterns the human beings' experience.

Whorf (1952) further showed that a people's cultural background can be easily recognized by the language they use. Because individuals are unable to totally acknowledge their own culture, they can neither consciously nor completely control their own language. This is a major reason why communication problems often occur in the intercultural setting.

Some scholars feel that Sapir and Whorf exaggerated the role language plays in the human society. Hoijer (1994), for example, pointed out that the Sapir-Whorf Hypothesis overemphasizes the linguistic differences that cause communication barriers, arguing instead that no culture can be completely self-contained or isolated. Important similarities exist among cultures in the real world. These similarities may stem "in part from diffusion and in part from the fact that all cultures are built around biological, psychological, and social characteristics common to all mankind" (p. 227). Accordingly, language is not a necessary presupposition of an individual's experience or cognitive activity, and the intercultural communication barriers mentioned by Sapir and Whorf are in fact surmountable.

## Language Reflects Our Attitude

Other scholars argue that language merely reflects—rather than shapes—our thinking, beliefs, and attitudes. Erickson, Lind, Johnson, and O'Barr (1978), for instance, claimed that language reflects the degree of power one can wield. And just as language exerts control, it can reflect lack of control. The authors cite as examples of powerless language the following expressions: "I guess I'd like to . . . ," "I think I should . . . ," "Well, we could try this idea . . . ," "So that's how I feel . . . ," "Excuse me sir . . . ," "It's about time we got started, isn't it?"

## Research Highlight 4–1

Who:       Hoijer, H.

What:      "The Sapir-Whorf Hypothesis."

Where:     L. A. Samovar & R. E. Porter (Eds.) (1994), *Intercultural Communication: A Reader* (pp. 194–200). Belmont, CA: Wadsworth.

In this article Hoijer attempts to review, clarify, and illustrate the Sapir-Whorf Hypothesis through reference to his own work on the Navajo language.

First, as mentioned in this chapter, the Sapir-Whorf Hypothesis holds that language plays a very important role in the totality of culture. In addition to being a communication tool, language directs the speaker's perceptions and gives the speaker a habitual mode with which to analyze experience into significant categories. Thus, because human languages differ remarkably from each other, it will be difficult for us to overcome the barriers of intercultural communication. Hoijer considers that the Sapir-Whorf Hypothesis exaggerates linguistic differences of this nature and the consequent barriers of intercultural communication. He argues that existing cultures resemble each other because of their diffusion about the globe and the biological, psychological, and social characteristics common to all mankind. The view of language determinism reflected by the Sapir-Whorf Hypothesis seems to be pessimistic about the possibility of intercultural understanding.

Second, the Sapir-Whorf Hypothesis considers language in both its structural and its semantic aspects and concludes that both aspects of the language are inseparable. Hoijer asserts that not all the structural-semantic patterns of a language are equally important to its speakers in observing, analyzing, and categorizing their experience. In other words, based on the study of the Navaho language, not all the structural patterns of common speech have the same degree of semantic importance. Thus, Hoijer suggests that ethnolinguistic research needs to follow four steps: (1) determine the structural patterns of a language as completely as possible, (2) determine those semantic patterns that attach to structural patterns as accurately as possibly, (3) distinguish between structural categories that are active in the language and therefore have definable semantic correlates, and those that are not, and (4) determine and compare the active structural-semantic patterns of the language and draw from them the manner of speech evidenced there.

Finally, the Sapir-Whorf Hypothesis specifies that the manner of speech found in a language provide a partial description of the speakers' thought world and can be used to measure and understand what we can of the macrocosm. Hoijer states that the connection between language and the rest of culture is not direct, because in certain patterns of nonlinguistic behavior the same meaningful modes found in a language can also be found. Navaho religious behaviors are used to illustrate the point.

"I'm not really sure, but . . . ," and so on. Wiener and Mehrabian (1968) proposed that the way one uses language reflects one's (1) liking or disliking, through one's choice of demonstrative pronouns, sequential placement of words, and negation and frequency in using certain words; (2) degree of intimacy with someone, through words such as "baby," "honey," "buddy," and "dear"; and (3) willingness to take or not take responsibility through the use of "it," "we," "you," and "but" statements.

Thus every culture, by means of its own language system, expresses universal human feelings and attitudes. This common characteristic of language demonstrates the similarities among cultures mentioned by Hoijer. Although they have not reached final agreement about the degree to which language determines or reflects culture, scholars all agree that a close relationship exists between language and culture. The following section uses China as an example to illustrate the relationship between cultural value orientations and language expressions.

## CULTURAL VALUE ORIENTATIONS AND LANGUAGE EXPRESSIONS

As mentioned in Chapter 3, Kluckhohn and Strodbeck (1961) claimed that every society finds a distinctive way to solve societal problems and that value orientations are possible solutions for the universal problems faced by all societies. They proposed five sets of cultural value orientations. Condon and Yousef (1975) then added an additional twenty, for a total of twenty-five sets, and further classified the twenty-five sets of cultural value orientation into six categories: the self, the family, society, human nature, nature, and the supernatural. Here we use three family value orientations proposed by Condon and Yousef to demonstrate the relationship between culture and language: relational orientations, positional role behavior, and ancestor worship.

### *Relational Orientations*

According to Condon and Yousef (1975), relational orientations in a family can be classified according to three dimensions: the individualistic orientation, the collateral orientation, and the lineal orientation. Using this distinction, a Chinese family can be characterized as having a lineal orientation that is based on a highly developed historical consciousness. The Chinese inherently believe that they should look after their parents and elderly persons. They not only take care of their ancestors' graves but also obey the wishes of deceased parents. A very close association exists among extended families. All these familial traits and beliefs are expected to continue from one generation to the next (Baker,

1979; Chen, 1992). Two basic relationship ties are illustrated below: husband and wife and parents and children.

## Husband and Wife

"Follow the man you marry, be he a fool or a crook" and "The husband sings, the wife accompanies" show the typical relationship between a husband and wife in the traditional Chinese family. The wife's status is subordinate to her husband. The household is the wife's domain, and she actually manages the family business only when her husband is weak and incapable.

The Chinese believe that there should be no public expression of affection between a husband and wife. In public they are to appear indifferent toward each other, as in the saying: "In bed, husband and wife, out of bed, guests." Ideally, the most important duty for the wife is to "bear children for the family in order to extend the generations." Practically, the wife's main duties are to take care of her husband's parents and her husband. The wife is expected to submit to her husband just as she submits to her parents-in-law and her own father. When the husband's parents die, she is expected to show deep sorrow. When his wife dies, however, the husband is only expected to show a little grief (Chen, 1990). A series of words and phrases embedded in the daily social interaction reflect the unequal relationship between the husband and wife in Chinese family and society. In marriage, for example, a man "marries" a woman, but a woman "is being married to" a man. After marriage the husband names his wife "inside person," and the wife names her husband "outside man." In addition, "Follow her father before she marries; follow her husband after she marries; follow her son after her husband dies" mirrors the wife's subordinate status in the Chinese family.

Female subordination has given rise, further, to a set of linguistic expressions that devalue the status of women in Chinese society, for example: "wicked" (*chien*), "weird" (*yao*), "slave" (*nu*), "ignorant" (*wang*), "prostitute" (*chi*), "prostitute" (*biao*), "whore" (*chang*), "to patronize whorehouses" (*piao*), "illicit intercourse" (*pin*), "a female slave" (*pi*), "ugly" (*chih*), "minion" (*pi*), "frivolous" (*shuan*), "to flirt with" (*niao*), "to ridicule" (*shan*), "jealousy" (*tu*), "hinder" (*fang*), "adultery" (*chien*), "greedy" (*lan*), "flattering" (*mei*), "detesting" (*shien*), and "envious" (*chi*). The structure of this vocabulary is based on the character "nu" (women), the basis of hundreds of negative phrases in the Chinese language system. Although other expressions based on the character "nu" reflect positive meanings, they are far fewer in number than those with negative meanings (Lu & Chen, 1995).

## Parents and Children

Traditionally, Chinese parents have enjoyed the freedom to decide their children's future. Hsu (1981) pointed out that the basic difference in the relationship between parents and children in Chinese and American families is that the

---

**Research Highlight 4–2**

Who: Lu, X., & Chen, G. M.

What: "Language Change and Value Orientations in Chinese Culture."

Where: Paper presented at the 5th International Conference on Cross-Cultural Communication: East and West. August, 1995, Harbin, China.

The paper aims to investigate how language change reflects, facilitates, and perpetuates cultural change. The authors argue that linguistic change not only reflects cultural change but it also provides the impetus for cultural change. Moreover, change in language and culture renews and creates infinite discursive possibilities as well as multidimensional human experiences.

To support their argument the authors examine the change of value systems in Chinese culture as reflected and facilitated by the change in vocabulary inventory. Three traditional Chinese value orientations, including ethical idealism, hierarchy in family relationship, and kinship, that were reflected and shaped by the use of vocabulary, sayings, proverbs, and aphorisms, are illustrated.

These traditional cultural values began to change when the communists came to power and adopted a Marxist ideology in 1949; later, the economic reforms of the 1980s also bespoke monumental upheaval. The authors provide many examples of the official language imposed by the government and the common language invented by ordinary people to show the shift in traditional cultural value orientations from (1) ethical idealism to materialism, (2) from hierarchy to equality in family relationships, and (3) from kinship to "guanxi" (interrelations).

Two implications are generated from this paper. First, the study shows that language, especially the lexical items, serves as a bridge and mirror for people to learn about or understand cultural values. It shows that the sound and structure of language are relatively stable, whereas the vocabulary of language is ever-changing and reflects cultural dynamics and diversified cultural experiences. Second, understanding culture from the linguistic perspective can help us establish shared meanings and minimize misunderstanding in intercultural communication. The interplay between language and culture creates infinite discursive possibilities that can enrich our human experience, expand our vision of the universe, and promote understanding among people with different language and cultural systems.

---

Chinese ask what children should do for their parents, and Americans ask what parents should do for their children. The communication between Chinese parents and children is one-way—from parents to children. The children are said to "have ears but no mouth." An interruption in the adult's conversation usually brings severe punishment upon the children.

The children are fully expected to fulfill their parents' wishes of whether they seem reasonable or not, as illustrated in the tales from Chinese literature called *The Twenty-Four Examples of Filial Piety*. The sentiment of Chinese children toward their parents is called *filial piety (shiao)*, which requires unconditional sacrifice to parents in any situation. Thus, "Filial piety is the chief of the hundred virtues." The statement "Parents are always right" reflects the absolute respect children pay to their parents.

Because the family is the basic unit of Chinese society, filial piety in the family system translates to *chung* in the social group. *Chung* is similar to "commitment" and "loyalty" in English. However, the concept of *chung* implies "sacrifice" whenever necessary in fulfilling the group's needs. The discrepancy of meaning between *chung* and "commitment" or "loyalty" shows that understanding the cultural value orientations implied by the terms would be key to effective intercultural communication.

## Positional Role Behavior

Condon and Yousef (1975) categorized positional role behavior within the family into three patterns: open, general, and specific. There is no role behavior appropriate in terms of age and sex in the open orientation, but, in the specific orientation, positional role behavior is chiefly determined by sex and relative age. In the general orientation a balance exists—role behavior is neither completely fixed nor completely free. The Chinese family holds a specific orientation.

Positional role behavior within the Chinese family is decided by three factors: in order of priority, generation, age, and sex. Three features characterize the family structure: (1) in the sex hierarchy, the maternal system is subordinate to the paternal line; (2) age is the locus of power; and (3) males are superior to females. The three features represent the three kinds of human relationship delineated by Confucius in the *Five Code of Ethics* (Chen & Chung, 1994). Common expressions of these cultural values in the daily life include "A boy is better than two girls," "An elderly man at home is like jade in the hand," "Men rear sons to provide for old age," "A married daughter is like water bursting its banks," "Daughters must not be kept at home unmarried; if they are forcibly kept in this condition, it is sure to breed enmity," "A virtuous woman cannot marry two husbands," "Ignoring the old man's advice makes one stupid," "A grown daughter cannot be kept unmarried for long," "A girl will doll herself up for him who loves her," and "It is a virtue for women to be without talent."

Based on the positional role structure a complete Chinese kinship system was developed. The system is comprised of four categories:

1. One's own family (*pen-chia*)—which includes all relatives with the same surname as "ego" (oneself), such as father, mother, brother, unmarried sis-

ters, husband, wife, sons, unmarried daughters, father's brothers with their wives, sons, and unmarried daughter.

2. Relatives outside the household (*wai-chin*)—which include all *pen-chia* relatives together with all relatives they may acquire by their marriage, such as ego's married sisters and daughters together with their husbands and their children and the other "in-laws" generated by the marriage.

3. Wife's relatives (*nei-chi*)—which include relatives of ego's wife that would be her *pen-chia* relatives had she not married. When a woman marries, this group of relatives becomes her *chin-chi,* and her husband's *pen-chia* relatives are the only *pen-chia* relatives she has thereafter.

4. Relatives of different surname (*chin-chi*)—which include any relatives excluding not listed in categories 1, 2 and 3. One has the same *chin-chi* as one's father and mother. When a woman marries, all relatives who belong to categories 1 and 2 before marriage become her *chin-chi*. When a man marries, all his wife's *chin-chi,* other than his *nei-chin,* become his own *chin-chi* as well.

The kinship structure shows a complex but orderly communication system in which a clear terminology describes each positional role and a set of appropriate behaviors is assigned to each role. The linguistic expressions used to specify the kinship system reveal its cultural value orientations as distinct from those of other cultures.

The three basic characteristics of the Chinese kinship structure can be illustrated linguistically and by linguistic comparison to American culture. First, the age hierarchy is shown in the terms designating the relationship among siblings. The Chinese use "ko" (older brother), "di" (younger brother), "chieh" (older sister), and "mei" (younger sister) to represent the age hierarchy among siblings. In addition, numbers are used to indicate the order of age, which in turn distinguish each person's obligation in the family system. In English, "brothers" and "sisters" are used to include all the children in the family. Although "older" and "younger" are occasionally used to refer to the order of age, no sense of obligation is attached (Chen, 1992)

Second, sex distinction is shown in the terms designating the children of ego's brothers and sisters. In the Chinese family "chih erh" is used to represent the sons of ego's brothers and "chih nui" the daughters of ego's brothers; "shen erh" is used to represent the sons of ego's sisters and "shen nui" the daughters of ego's sisters. In English, "nephew" is used to describe the sons of ego's brothers and sisters, and "niece" the daughters of ego's brothers and sisters.

Third, the generation hierarchy is shown in the naming of the brothers and sisters of ego's parents. The Chinese use "bo" to name the older brothers of ego's father and "shu" the younger brothers of ego's father. In addition, "ku" is used for mother's older and younger brothers and "yi" for mother's older and younger sisters. In English, however, "uncle" is used to indicate all of the father's and mother's brothers, and "aunt" all of the father's and mother's sisters. Obviously, these Chinese and English expressions usually cause misunderstandings when used in intercultural encounters, for their meanings aren't clear unless the cultural value orientations behind them are understood(Chen, 1992).

Within this collectivistic family system one becomes only a member of a family in which one must learn to restrain oneself and to subdue one's individuality in order to maintain the harmony in the family (Hofstede & Bond, 1988). "Harmony" (*Ho*) therefore becomes the cultural value to keeping the key Chinese family system functioning smoothly. It is believed that "Harmony is the first virtue," "If the family lives in harmony, all affairs will prosper," and "Domestic scandals should not be publicized." The ideal structure of the family is thus to have "five generations live under the same roof." Moreover, the Western concepts of "individualism" and "privacy" do not exist linguistically in Chinese because of the collectivistic family orientation.

## Ancestor Worship

*Ancestor worship* is one of the most distinctive features of the Chinese family system. It is one of the main components of Chinese family life. Hsu (1981) claimed that ancestor worship is literally China's universal religion. It is the central link between the world of humans and the world of the supernatural. Ancestor worship is a cardinal ingredient in every aspect of Chinese life.

In the Chinese family, ancestor worship implies that the physical bodies of ancestors die, but their souls continue to live and watch over the life of their descendants with a supernatural power, as in the saying, "You may hide a thing from a man; from the spirits you cannot hide it." In China, the function of ancestor worship is to reinforce the unity of the family and to enhance the generation-age-sex scheme of authority in the family (Baker, 1979).

There are two places where the Chinese worship their ancestors: home and the graveyard. Most Chinese families have a shrine in their house for worshipping ancestors. Inside the shrine, the ancestral tablets are placed so that they are able to "overlook" the life going on there. This is the way "to have the divine help" or "to have divine assistance from the ancestors." Incense and tea are offered to the ancestors every day. On the first and fifteenth days of the Chinese lunar month, in addition to incense and tea, foods, fruits, and paper money are offered.

The lunar New Year's Day is the most active time for worshipping ancestors with more elaborate offerings. Ancestors are remembered again on the anniversaries of their birth and death. The practice of "continuously offering sacrifices to ancestors" functions to fulfill the virtue of "carefully attending to the funeral rites of parents and following them when done with due sacrifices."

The ancestor's grave, which resembles a house, is always built as elaborately as possible. Normally ancestors are worshipped one or two times per

---

**Research Highlight 4–3**

Who:    Keesing, R. M.

What:    "Linguistic Knowledge and Cultural Knowledge: Some Doubts and Speculations"

Where:    *American Anthropologist, 81,* 1975, 14–35.

In this article, using the language of the Kwaio of Malaita, Solomon Islands, as an example, the author criticizes the contemporary Western grammatical theory that suggests human language is a culture-free phenomenon. The author investigates human language from a cultural point of view. He argues that human language is like a mirror that reflects the speakers' cultural background. In other words, a language (which includes the meanings of lexical items, the pragmatic conventions of speaking, and the social uses of speech) always presupposes and is infused by cultural assumptions about the thinking of a community.

Based on this point, the author further distinguishes linguistic knowledge from cultural knowledge, insisting that to communicate effectively and competently across cultures we have to possess both linguistic and cultural knowledge at the same time. This is also the reason why the author declares that contemporary linguistic study should position cultural knowledge and linguistic grammars as complementary elements of a single enterprise.

Using the data from the Kwaio (a language spoken by about 6,000 people who mainly live in Malaita Island in the Solomons) as an example, the analysis is divided into four parts: (1) how speakers' knowledge of their language is contingent on and takes for granted a culturally defined model of the universe, (2) how the meanings of lexical items are subtly but crucially connected with cultural assumptions and symbolic structures, (3) how linguists have little knowledge about how cultural models of the universe in which speech takes place infuse and support language when they explore the "pragmatic" aspects of using and understanding sentences, and (4) how insufficient appreciation of the range of cultural variation in the uses of speech prevents incorporation of the illocutionary force of language into syntactic theory in attempts to extend the philosophical theory of speech acts.

---

year at the graveyard. The principal one is the "Chin Ming Day" (April 5) of the Chinese lunar month. This day is called the "grave-sweeping festival." On that day, the grave site must be cleaned, swept and seeded, and repaired by the living offspring, and the ancestors are worshipped by the whole family. Some families repeat the ceremony on "Tsuon Yiang Day" (September 9) of the Chinese lunar month.

The practice of ancestor worship in the Chinese family system is extended to a holistic value system connecting human nature, nature, and the supernatural. Examples of the many phrases developed to describe these value orientations include "to live is to suffer," "tao," "chi," "shui," "tai chi," and "yin and yang." All these phrases are very culture bound, and it is difficult to find equivalent concepts in other language systems.

The examples discussed above indicate the close relationship between cultural values and language expressions. We may conclude that language is a bridge people can use to learn or understand cultural values, and it is necessary to comprehend cultural values in order to acquire the language used to portray them. This corresponds to the argument by Keesing (1975) following his study of the Kwaio language, that human language is a mirror that reflects the speakers' cultural background. A language, which includes meanings of lexical items, pragmatic conventions of speaking, and the social users of speech, always presupposes and is infused by cultural assumptions about the thinking of a group. Therefore, to communicate effectively and appropriately with people from different cultures, we must possess both cultural and linguistic knowledge.

## RECAP

Linguistics is the scientific study of human language. It consists of five areas of study: morphology, phonology, syntax, semantics, and pragmatics. Semantics and pragmatics directly affect the process of intercultural communication.

Human language has four characteristics: (1) it is symbolic, (2) it is rule-governed, (3) it is subjective, and (4) it often shows change and variation. This chapter discusses six types of language variation: dialects, pidgins, creole, lingua franca, argot, and taboo.

The relationship between language and culture is also discussed. Although no agreement among scholars has been reached about whether language determines or only reflects culture, the close relationship between the two concepts is recognized. The last part of this chapter uses Chinese family value orientations to illustrate the relationship between language expressions and cultural values. It is concluded that language is a bridge people can use to learn or understand cultural values, and it is necessary to comprehend cultural values to acquire the language used to portray them. In other words, to be competent in intercultural communication we need to be aware of both the cultural values and the language expressions of our cultural counterparts.

## RETHINK

From an intercultural communication perspective a fundamental question regarding human language that deserves further research is whether there is a universal principle of linguistic assumption toward languages. In other words, can one language accommodate expressions from another language? This is especially a concern in the process of translation and interpretation, and it arises repeatedly when in the attempt to translate humor. Can a language be translated into another one without losing its original meaning? The Ethiopian proverb, "After the jackal leaves, the dog barks," reminds American students of "When the cat's away, the mice will play." Ethiopian students are likely to explain, however, that "Jackals eat all the food, so that dogs starve." Could we find matching concepts or directly translate terms such as "filial piety," "yin and yang," "chi," "tao," "democracy," and "privacy" into another language system? Although some scholars argue that we can translate these concepts by using a larger number of expressions, would this be suitable in different kinds of communication situations? If no, how can we solve this problem? Family planners have found difficulty locating a word for "family" in nations with joint or extended families. Could they actually be asking citizens to plan their parents, aunts, uncles, and grandparents? All such questions demand further exploration.

Another problem concerns whether language determines or reflects our culture. As indicated in this chapter, no agreement has been reached among scholars. The argument has become a chicken-and-egg problem. Because it is almost impossible to resolve the problem from the standpoint of human cognition, we suggest that future research should focus on the study of the interdependent relationship of the two concepts rather than attempt to decide whether language controls or reflects culture.

Finally, because both language and culture are changing over time, would language change reflect, facilitate, and perpetuate culture change? The study of change in language and culture may help us understand the creation and renewal of infinite discursive possibilities and multidimensional human experiences (Lu & Chen, 1995).

## QUESTIONS FOR DISCUSSION

1. Explain the difference between human beings and animals in terms of communication system.
2. Give examples of linguistic meanings and speaker's meanings.
3. Give an example of each of the variations of language.
4. Give examples student dialect used on your campus.
5. Compare and contrast the two arguments regarding the relationship between language and culture.
6. Critique the Chinese family value orientations used to demonstrate the relationship between culture and language in this chapter.
7. How would the change of language over time reflect, facilitate, and perpetuate cultural change?

# ▶ Chapter 5

## Nonverbal Communication and Culture

### *Objectives*

Upon completion of this chapter, you will

- Be able to distinguish the similarities and differences between verbal and nonverbal communication.
- Understand the functions and characteristics of nonverbal communication.
- Understand the structure of nonverbal communication.
- Be able to define such terms as *kinesics, proxemics, paralanguage,* and *chronemics*.
- Understand the relationship between nonverbal communication and culture.
- Be able to identify the skills necessary to effective intercultural nonverbal communication.

> *"As Macbeth and his wife plan the murder of their guest King Duncan in the first act of William Shakespeare's great play, Lady Macbeth warns her reluctant husband to take care to hide the uneasiness his nonverbal actions betray. "Your face, my thane," she warns him, "is a book where men may read strange matters."—DAVID A. VICTOR*

Long before communication scholars dug into the meanings of nonverbal behaviors, Shakespeare keenly observed the unspoken aspect of human action.
Our face or eyes can talk. Although in their book *How to Read a Person like a
Book* Gerard I. Nierenberg and Henry H. Calero (1971) oversimplified the
analysis of nonverbal behaviors, there is no question that the nonverbal aspect
of human interaction has become an indispensable part of communication
study. In this chapter we divide the discussion of nonverbal communication
into four parts: (1) the nature of nonverbal communication, (2) the structure of
nonverbal communication, (3) nonverbal communication and culture, and (4)
intercultural skills in nonverbal communication.

## THE NATURE OF NONVERBAL COMMUNICATION

All intentional and unintentional stimuli between communicating parties, other
than the spoken word, are considered to be nonverbal communication. More
specifically, nonverbal communication involves those humanly and environ-
mentally generated stimuli in a communication setting that convey potential
nonlinguistic message values to the interactants (Samovar & Porter, 1995).
Without the company of nonverbal cues in communication, human words
would be like listening to a boring, inhuman, and meaningless monotone
recording. Thus, successful interaction in intercultural settings requires not only
the understanding of verbal messages but of nonverbal messages as well. To
understand the nature of nonverbal communication, we need to examine its relationship to verbal communication and its functions and characteristics.

## NONVERBAL AND VERBAL COMMUNICATION

Although Mehrabian (1972) argued that in face-to-face communication nonverbal cues convey about 93 percent of the meanings and Birdwhistell (1970)
also indicated that 65 percent of human communication is nonverbal, this
doesn't mean that nonverbal messages are more important than verbal messages in the efforts people make to understand each other. The entire process
of human communication must be viewed as a whole that combines verbal and
nonverbal messages. In addition, both verbal and nonverbal systems require a
sender and a receiver to make the communication complete.

Both verbal and nonverbal communication use symbols to represent something. "I love you" is a statement you use to show caring and passion. Or, instead of saying, "I love you," you might give your friend a kiss or a hug. In this
case, the gesture represents the same feeling as the statement.

While the two systems show similarities, they also are distinguishable in
five ways. First, we can consciously control the flow of our verbal messages,

but not so easily the incidence of our nonverbal messages. Our nonverbal behaviors in large part are controlled by biological necessity. For example, the blinking of our eyes, the blushing of our face in an embarrassing situation, and the shivering of our hands when we are scared are all biological reactions that are not in our conscious control.

Second, verbally we express ourselves word by word and sentence by sentence; nonverbally several communications may happen at once. For example, in the public speaking class we are required to make a speech in front of classmates. The speaker may be so nervous that her hands may be shivering, her face may blush, and her heart may beat more rapidly, but at the same time she tries to keep smiling. All these nonverbal cues happening simultaneously indicate stage fright.

Third, only part of nonverbal communication is available as an international or interracial language. Unless we spend many years among Italians, for example, we won't understand Italian nonverbal cues. However, when we see a **V** sign, we know it means peace or victory; when we see someone is laughing, we know he or she must be happy; and when we see a burning cross, we recognize a message of hatred. These nonverbal cues tend to be widely recognized.

Fourth, as human beings we begin to learn how to talk when we are one and a half or two years old because of the gradual development of our physical structure. Does this mean that at an earlier age we are unable to communicate with people around us? Obviously, no. A baby will begin to communicate with her mother when she is born, if not before. She will cry when she is hungry or feel uncomfortable; she will smile when she is satisfied and happy; and she will figure out the meanings of facial expressions, gestures, and vocal signs from interactions with her parents or siblings. In other words, we learn nonverbal communication much earlier in our life than verbal communication.

Finally, nonverbal communication can be more emotional than verbal communication. We may say, "I'm very angry," but without our raising our voice or displaying our wide-open eyes and red face, people may not know how angry we are. A good example is the TV commercial several years ago in which a gentleman shouted at a garage cashier, "I am not going to pay a lot for this muffler." You can only know how emotional he is by seeing his nonverbal cues on the screen. Nonverbal messages also serve a set of functions that are different from verbal messages in the process of communication. The following section discusses those functions.

## FUNCTIONS OF NONVERBAL COMMUNICATION

In addition to the transmission of our feelings and emotions, nonverbal messages also serve five major functions in the communication process: repetition, replacement, emphasis, contradiction, and regulation.

## Repetition

We can use nonverbal cues to repeat what we say orally. For example, if someone asks you where the city library is located, you can explain that it is at the corner of the second block on the left, and you can use your finger to point in the direction of the library to repeat what you just said.

## Replacement

We can use nonverbal messages to substitute for verbal messages. Instead of raising your voice by shouting "bravo" after a great performance of the orchestra, you may silently sit there with an awed expression. Your expression automatically indicates that the performance is excellent and that you are moved by the experience.

## Emphasis

Nonverbal messages can emphasize or accent the feelings or emotions conveyed by verbal messages by adding more information to the expressions. For example, an extra-firm handshake can complement the expression "I am so glad to see you" and simultaneously transmit a message to the receiver that you are a confident person. Moreover, turning one's back on a conversation partner may emphasize that the person has nothing more to say, or, within an African American setting, that a joke was thoroughly enjoyed.

## Contradiction

Nonverbal messages often contradict the meanings of verbal messages. For example, when you are sick and a friend asks you how you feel, you may say, "I am fine" in a weak voice and with a slouchy posture. Nonverbally, you are telling your friend that you are not fine, but, verbally, you give your friend an opposite answer.

## Regulation

We use nonverbal messages to tell someone to do or not to do something. In other words, nonverbal messages can be used to control other persons' behaviors. For instance, stern eye contact from parents can stop the naughty behavior of children while guests are in the house; hand clapping by the instructor in a classroom demands the attention of the students. Nonverbal messages can be as effective as verbal messages in conveying orders.

Analysis of the functions of nonverbal communication shows that in most communication settings both verbal and nonverbal communication are working in combination rather than in isolation. This tendency reinforces the premise that a holistic framework encompassing both verbal and nonverbal systems is necessary to fully understand the process of human communication.

## CHARACTERISTICS OF NONVERBAL COMMUNICATION

We send and receive nonverbal messages every day because nonverbal communication exists no matter whether we speak or not. Without being able to use words, our bodies generally express our feelings and attitudes. In other words, we cannot not communicate in terms of nonverbal messages. Nonverbal communication possesses three more characteristics: it is less systematized than verbal communication; it is culture-bound; and it is ambiguous.

### Nonverbal Communication is Less Systematized than Verbal Communication

Unlike verbal language that is grounded on a set of systematized and comprehensible rules, nonverbal communication is so complicated that scholars still have never been able to devise a set of rules that would govern it. According to Condon and Yousef (1975), although scholars tend to assume that nonverbal behaviors conform to some system that is similar to a grammar, syntax, or vocabulary, little is in fact known about nonverbal communication in different societies.

### Nonverbal Communication is Culture-Bound

Although certain nonverbal messages, such as the **V** sign and the laugh mentioned above, can be used as interculturally and interracially, nonverbal cues are not universal. No single culture gives significance to much over half of all possible cues, and the same cue may carry various meanings across cultures. Even if some expressions of nonverbal behaviors are universal and governed by biological necessity, the meanings attached to these expressions show great variety across culture. For example, while physical contact between a male and a female is a common practice of social greeting in Western society, it is a taboo in some Asian cultures. Moreover, gender also plays an important role in nonverbal communication. Gender differences in regard to nonverbal communication have been identified. For example, compared to men, women claim less territory, maintain closer distance from each other in conversation, use more eye contact, are more expressive, use more facial expressions, smile more, take up less space (e.g., holding legs more together), use fewer gestures (but use more when they are seeking approval), have less negative reactions to crowd-

**Research Highlight 5–1**

Who:     Eakins, B. W., & Eakins, R. G.

What:    "Sex Differences in Nonverbal Communication."

Where:   In L. A. Samovar & R. E. Porter (Eds.) (1991), *Intercultural Communication: A Reader* (pp. 297–315). Belmont, CA: Wadsworth.

This article discusses some significant sex differences in nonverbal communication patterns. In general, females are more responsive than men to nonverbal cues, read more accurately nonverbal cues, and are more able to pick up small nonverbal cues. More specifically, differences in the nonverbal communication style of men and women are discussed in relation to the following factors: eye contact, facial expression, posture, gesture, use of space, touch, and status.

**1.** Eye contact—Women look more at their counterparts in interaction, hold longer with each other in eye contact, look at each other more while speaking, are more willing to establish and maintain eye contact, and tend to tilt their head while looking at a man.

**2.** Facial expressions—Women are more likely to reveal emotions in facial expressions. They tend to smile more than men.

**3.** Posture/bearing—In their arm-body carriage, women tend to keep their upper arms close to the trunk, whereas men move the arms 5 to 10 degrees away from the body; women tend to assume more tense posture; men's leg positions tend to be more asymmetric, and they assume more reclining pos-

tures; women tend to display less arm openness with high-status persons than with low-status persons; and in general people of both genders feel more relaxed when communicating with women than with men.

**4.** Gesture—Women tend to put both hands down on chair arms, arrange or play with their hair or ornamentation, put their hands in their laps, tap their hands, cross their legs at the knees, and cross their ankles with their knees slightly apart. Men tend to use more sweeping gestures, use their arms more in lifting or in moving the body, use closed fists more, stroke their chin more, sit with their ankle of one leg crossing the knee of the other, exhibit a greater amount of leg and foot movement, stretch hands and crack knuckles, point, put both feet on floor with their legs apart, stretch their legs out, cross their ankles, and spread their knees apart when sitting.

**5.** Use of space—Women tend to be approached more closely than men by both men and women, tend to stand more closely to good friends but farther away from other people, are more cautious in terms of space before a close relationship is developed, feel more comfortable than men in crowds, and take up less space in an office.

**6.** Touch—Women tend to be touched by others more often; mothers tend to touch their sons more, and fathers tend to touch their daughters more; men's touch tends to have a connotation of sexual interest; and women are not as likely to touch a man as a man is to touch a woman.

*Continued*

---

**Research Highlight 5–1**    *Continued*

7. Status—Compared to a female superior, a male superior tends to look
aggressive, to smile less, to be more
impassive, to be more relaxed, to
have larger and more sweeping gestures, to use more touches, to use
more space, to walk into another's
path, and to wear loose and more
comfortable clothing.

---

ing, and tend to keep their hands on the arms of a chair when sitting down
(Burgoon, Buller, & Woodall, 1989; Eakins & Eakins, 1991).

## Nonverbal Communication is Ambiguous

We cannot read nonverbal behaviors like reading a book. Nonverbal communication is dominated by ambiguity. In addition to being culture bound, the
context in which the communication occurs, the relationship between the interactants, and the mood or feeling of the sender and receiver will affect the
interpretation of the nonverbal behaviors. Thus, to make sense of ambiguous
nonverbal behaviors, all these factors must be considered.

## THE STRUCTURE OF NONVERBAL COMMUNICATION

The elements of nonverbal messages include hand gestures, eye contact, posture and stance, facial expressions, odors, clothing, hair style, walking behavior, interpersonal distance, touching, architecture, artifacts, graphic symbols,
preference for specific tastes, arts and rhetorical forms, somatypes of bodies,
vocal signs, color symbolism, synchronization of speech and movement, ther-
mal influences, cosmetics, drum signals, vocal inflections, smoke signals, fac-
tory whistles, police sirens, time symbolism, timing and pose, and silence
(Condon & Yousef, 1975). For the purposes of study, we classify these elements
into four categories: kinesics, proxemics, paralanguage, and chronemics.

## Kinesics

*Kinesics* is the study of body movements and activities in human communication. It is also called body language. Based on the function of each body
movement, kinesics can be classified into five categories: emblems, illustrators,
regulators, affect displays, and adaptors (Ekman & Friesen, 1969, 1972). This
classification may vary across cultures.

   *Emblems* are kinesic cues that have direct verbal counterparts. They are
used to replace verbal messages. In other words, emblems can directly substi-

tute for words and have precise verbal meanings. For example, the thumb and forefinger touch to form a circle sign can clearly represent an oral consent meaning "okay" in the United States. Of course, the same sign can have another meaning in other cultures such as China and Japan. We will discuss this further in the section on hand gestures.

*Illustrators* are nonverbal messages that are directly tied to speech and that are used to describe, reinforce, or supplement what is said verbally. Although very much culturally bound, illustrators tend to be more universal than emblems. For example, in most cultures people will use fingers to point at the direction of the target and verbally repeat the message "it's over there." Despite the universality of illustrators, their use varies across cultures. "Come here" may be expressed by moving the fingers with the palm upward in some cultures, and with the palm downward in others. Morain's (1987) study of the use of illustrators by a New York mayor who was brought up in the United States with an Italian-speaking father and a Yiddish-speaking mother, indicates that when he speaks in English, he uses fewer gestures, when he speaks Yiddish, his gestures are choppy, one-handed, and kept close to the body; when he speaks in Italian, he uses more gestures and they tend to be symmetrical.

*Regulators* are nonverbal messages used to influence or control other's behaviors. For example, as a listener of a speech, we may constantly use head nodding or eye contact to monitor what the speaker says. These nonverbal cues enable the speaker to know whether we are paying attention to his or her speech, that we want him or her to continue what he or she is saying, or that we would like to raise a question. Culture influences how frequently regulators are used. For instance, Vagas (1986) reported that African Americans tend to use more subtle regulators than white Americans. The difference frequently leads to misunderstanding on the part of American students of African descent, who complain that they feel insulted because white American teachers often talk down to them.

*Affect displays* are bodily and facial expressions that convey our feelings and emotions. Smiling, laughing, and crying help to transmit a person's feeling and emotion cross-culturally. While showing emotions in a certain manner has become somewhat standardized in our era of mass communication, culture dictates the degree to which affect is displayed. For example, people in Middle Eastern cultures and Latin America are more free to express their emotions than are northern European, white northern Americans, and most Asians. In North America, women are likely to be more expressive of their emotions than men, whereas in West Asia the reverse holds.

Finally, *adaptors* are body movements that usually occur when we are in anxious situations. The appearance of adaptors in the process of communication is often unconscious. We tend to develop adaptors early in our life and remain relatively unaware of them. For example, one may bite fingernails or chew a pencil to release nervous feelings. Knapp (1980) pointed out that we usually have no intention of using adaptors in communication, but they may be triggered by our verbal messages that are associated with the adaptive habit we learned in early life. Interculturally, as Victor (1992) indicated, certain adaptors without specific meanings in one culture may hold highly offensive emblematic significance in others. For example, the gesture of the middle finger carries little meaning in China but is highly obscene in English-speaking North America, just as the "a-okay" symbol could offend in Latin America.

The following section discusses the four most common body activities: facial expressions, eye contact, hand gestures, and touch.

## Facial Expressions

Facial expressions are the most obvious and important source of nonverbal communication. The Chinese people have always said that a person's character is clearly written on his or her face. This belief is reflected in Chinese operas in which face paintings are used to indicate the personalities and dispositions of the characters. In communication we constantly observe and interpret the meanings of expressions from another's face. Ekman and Friesen (1975, 1982) indicated that six basic human emotions can be easily reflected on our face: surprise, fear, anger, disgust, happiness, and sadness.

Across cultures, the same facial expression may acquire different meanings. For example, we tend to consider smiling as a universal nonverbal cue that symbolizes a happy feeling. In Japan, however, smiling serves another purpose. To the Japanese, the smile not only expresses happiness and affection but is also a way to avoid embarrassment and unpleasantness. For example, the Japanese always smile at the guests no matter how sad the situation is, even when friends come to see the last face of one's deceased husband. An athlete badly defeated in a competition and a student receiving a poor grade in the class will also use smiling to cover their deep-down sorrow and thereby avoid losing face.

## Eye Contact

Shakespeare's "your lips tell me no, but there is yes, yes in your eyes" well describes the function of eye contact in human communication. *Oculesics* is the term used for the study of eye contact in communication process. The way we use eye contact not only transmits messages to others and reflects our personality but also indicates what we are thinking. For example, Leo (1983) reported that neurolinguistic programming therapists believe that when we move our eyes up and to the left we are recalling something we have seen before, and when we move our eyes up and to the right, we try to envision something we never saw before. Madonik (1990) believes that people who are seeking auditory data tend to move their eyes side to side or down to the left, and tend to look upward when accessing a visual system.

The use of eye contact follows some unstated rules. For example, Argyle (1975) indicated that staring at a person at a distance may mean an invitation for interaction, and returning of the gaze is generally interpreted as acceptance of the invitation. In addition, more mutual eye contact appears among friends than others, and persons seeking eye contact while speaking tend to be more believable. However, these rules may vary in different cultures. Cross-culturally, the misinterpretation of the use of eye contact can lead to serious misunderstanding. For example, in North America it is impolite for a man to gaze at women, but Italian men may gaze at women all the time and the women don't feel offended. People in the Middle East, especially Arabs, also consider gazing a way to show respect in communication, because they think one can see a person's soul from the person's eyes. This is why political leaders from that area often wear sun eyeglasses when they are interviewed by reporters. It is difficult to hide information if the reporters can see their eyes directly.

Direct eye contact is a taboo or an insult in many Asian cultures. Cambodians consider direct eye contact as an invasion of one's privacy. In ancient China, only a "bad" girl or a prostitute will look straight into the eyes of males, whereas the English consider such gazing as attentive listening. Some scholars have even claimed that one of the main sources of racial misunderstanding in the United States is differences in the use of eye contact. That is, white Americans tend to look at their communication partner more when they are listening than when they are talking, but African Americans use more eye contact when they are talking than when they are listening. Direct eye contact is also related to age and rank in cultures such as Spain, Latin America, and sub-Saharan Africa. In the United States, however, the use of direct eye contact does not concern such status markers (Beebe, 1974; Vargas, 1986).

### Hand Gestures
Humans are superior to other animals not only because they are capable of using hands to handle tools but also because human beings can use hand gestures as symbols in communication. We use a wide range of hand gestures to "talk" with each other in daily communication. For example, Morris, Colletee, Marsh, and O'Shaughnessy (1979) identified twenty hand gestures commonly used by European people: (1) the fingertips kiss, (2) crossing of the fingers, (3) the nose-tap, (4) the hand purse, (5) the cheek screw, (6) the eyelid pull, (7) the forearm jerk, (8) the flat-hand flick, (9) the ring sign, (10) the vertical horn-sign, (11) the horizontal horn-sign, (12) the fig, (13) the head toss, (14) the chin flick, (15) the cheek stroke, (16) the thumb-up sign, (17) the teeth flick, (18) the ear touch, (19) the nose tap, and (20) the palm-back **V**-sign.

Most of these hand gestures are culturally determined. For example, the ring sign with index finger and thumb in a circle means "A-okay" to North Americans and money to the Chinese and Japanese. Moreover, to the French the ring sign indicates that we think someone is a "zero," and to people in Malta it is an invitation to have homosexual sex. The thumb held upright with a closed fist also has various meanings. To North American it means "Okay" or "right on"; to the Chinese it means "excellent" or "number one"; to the Japanese it represents boss, father, or husband (the little-finger-up sign is used to represent mistress, woman, or wife); and to people in the Middle East it is an obscene gesture.

Hand gestures are often used in social greetings. For example, Westerners shake hands; the Chinese hold hands in their sleeves and bow to each other; Tanzanians clap hands ten times to say hello; the Polish and Romanians kiss the back of the hand; Eskimos use hands to give a friendly punch on the head or shoulder; Thais and Indians put hands together in front of the face and slightly bow; and Swahili language speakers in Eastern Africa shake hands first, then hook each other's thumb, and again shake hands. In many areas, such as Africa, West Asia, India, and Central and South America, people use fingers instead of chopsticks or forks for eating. In addition, Moslems and Hindus only use their right hands to pick up foods or to give an object to someone else. The left hand is considered unclean. Info 5-1 provides information about hand gestures and other components of nonverbal communication.

### Touch

The study of how we use touch in communication is called *haptics*. The area has received increasing attention among students and scholars of nonverbal communication. Argyle (1975) identified many types of touch commonly used in the Western world, including patting, slapping, punching, pinching, stroking, shaking, kissing, licking, holding, guiding, embracing, linking, grooming, and tickling.

Touch is used not only to convey caring and nurturance but also to signify the following events: (1) a professional relationship (in which one is touched by a medical doctor for example); (2) a social relationship (hugging); (3) friendship (holding hands); (4) intimacy (kissing); and (5) sexual arousal (embracing) (Heslin & Alper, 1983). Sexual harassment is also inferred from touching or gazing.

The meaning of a touch is influenced by at least eight factors (Samovar & Porter, 1995):

**1.** Our mood at the time of touch: The meanings will be different when someone touches us at a time of sorrow or happiness.

**2.** Our past history or experience: Touch between males and females is taboo in some areas such as the Middle East and traditional China because it is associated with sexual activities. In Saudi Arabia a brother and sister may not publicly touch, even after a long absence, for fear that society might think the sister a "loose woman." However, in the Arab world or Southeast Asia, males hold forearms, shoulders, or hands as a sign of friendship.

**3.** The perceived relationship between the persons: A touch by your parents, your teacher, or a stranger can lead to different interpretations.

**Info 5-1**

**Crossing cultures—carefully: In other countries, friendly gestures may be misunderstood**

HURLBURT FIELD, Fla. (AP)—The best advice to Americans abroad is to keep your hands in your pockets, lest you be gravely misunderstood.

For instance, a thumbs up might mean "okay" or "right on" to you, but it's an obscene gesture in the Middle East.

And the "A-okay" sign of the forefinger and thumb in a circle can get you into all kinds of trouble. It means money in Japan. But in France it means you think someone is a "zero" and in Malta, heaven forbid, it's an invitation to have homosexual sex.

Goodness knows how they might take a "high five."

That's why Capt. Mike Rafferty has his hands full teaching a cross-cultural communications course at this Air Force base in the Florida Panhandle. He's trying to avoid misunderstandings when American servicemen teach foreign military personnel the intricacies of U.S. military equipment and procedures.

Just when you want to deliver a compliment to a foreign student, you might be picking a fight.

The five-day course is taught at the Air Force Special Operations School. The school also offers more specific courses for personnel being sent to particular parts of the world such as Latin America or Africa, but Rafferty's class gives troops an insight into cultural differences around the world.

For instance, patting children on the head may be a sign of endearment to an American, but in some Asian cultures, where the top of the head is considered the home of the soul, it's an insult.

*Group vs. individual rights*

"In most other cultures the development has been different," Rafferty says, noting many have changed little over thousands of years. "In the United States the emphasis is on individual rights. In other cultures it's the survival of the group that's important."

This difference shows up in the classroom. Individualistic Americans are taught to ask questions, figure things out for themselves and understand that their instructors don't know everything, says Rafferty.

In many non-Western countries, students learn by rote and don't ask questions or admit they failed to understand something because they don't want to be considered different from the rest of the group.

"We have a saying in this country that 'the squeaky wheel gets the grease,'" Rafferty says. "In Asia, the saying is 'The nail that stands up gets hammered down.'"

The individual competitiveness of Americans is one of the first things foreign students notice, Rafferty says. They often see it as a negative factor that takes away from the importance of the group.

Other countries tend to stress group competition, perhaps refined to the ultimate by the Japanese, Rafferty says.

The group emphasis also makes the family more significant in many countries. In the Middle East, for example, elders are respected, revered and sought out for advice.

*Continued*

**Info 5-1**    *Continued*

Time and space are other important differences.

In Arabian, African and Latin American countries, arriving 30 minutes or more after a meeting was scheduled to start may be considered "on time," while in the United States it would be insulting to show up so late, Rafferty says. On the other hand, a Swiss-German would get there early.

While Americans feel uncomfortable when others invade their space, many foreigners, particularly Arabs and Latin Americans, like to get up close and personal.

When that happens to an American at a social function with foreigners he is likely to back away, but the foreigner again will close the gap, Rafferty says.

"There's a little dance that goes on," he says.

Same-sex touching also is common in the Middle East and Asia, where it has none of the sexual connotation it has in America.

Rafferty recalls a personal experience. When attending the squadron Officer School at Maxwell Air Force Base in Montgomery, Ala., he was good friends with an officer from Thailand. They played on the same soccer team.

While dressed in their soccer shorts they were sitting in the stands and talking when the visitor reached over and put his hand on Rafferty's bare thigh.

"That was real uncomfortable for me," Rafferty says. "Everybody in the stands behind me was laughing, but it wasn't a problem."

Americans also don't like too much direct eye contact, particularly between men and women. Hispanics and Arabs, who share some cultural similarities because of the 700-year Moorish occupation of Spain, like eye contact.

*Source:* Used by permission of The Associated Press, 1989.

**4.** The location of the touch: The person who touches you leg, arm, breast, or private part will bring about different reactions from you.

**5.** The relative pressure of touch: For example, is it an emotional hug? A firm handshake? A soft kiss?

**6.** The duration of touch: For example, a long, passionate kiss will not be acceptable for the purpose of a social greeting, but it is perfectly okay for those in love.

**7.** The touch is purposeful or accidental: For example, in China or Japan males and females often avoid touching each other in public, but in the public transportation system, they are accustomed to squeezing against one another.

**8.** The setting for touch: The meanings of touch tend to be different when we touch each other alone inside a room, in a bar, or in a shopping mall.

In addition to facial expressions, eye contact, hand gestures, and touch, kinesics includes many other elements such as body movement or posture, hair style, clothing, and artifacts. Artifacts are things like cosmetics, jewelry, bandages, ribbons, tattoos, glasses, and hair ornaments that we use to adorn ourselves and that can send messages to others. Yawning can transmit the message that we are tired or not interested in a topic. Clothing can communicate our emotion and behavior and can also differentiate us from other people and designate whether a situation is formal or informal. Head nods can denote "yes" or "no". Hair style can distinguish males from females and distinguish one's politics or profession. Lastly, people of different cultures show diverse ways of using body movement or posture. For example, squatting is popular in Japan, India, and China, but is viewed as childish, primitive, and uncomfortable by Northern Americans. In addition, the Japanese like to sit on floor mats with their legs crossed, whereas Westerners prefer to sit in chairs with their feet up on a desk or stool to signify a relaxed or informal attitude. Westerners invite negative judgment when they place their feet up in a multicultural setting, however, since they are pointing the most profane part of their body, their feet, toward the most sacred part of another's body, the head.

## Proxemics

*Proxemics* refers to the study of how human beings and animals use space in communication process. Hall (1966) was the first scholar to systematically study proxemics. According to Hall, there are three kinds of space: fixed-feature space, semifixed feature space, and informal space. Fixed-feature space refers to those unmovable structural arrangements around us. When a house is built, it and the wall around it become *fixed-feature space*. The only way to move the fixed-feature space is to destroy the structure. This kind of space is a dimension, in particular, of architecture, which varies markedly from culture to culture. Note the differences, for example, between the traditional palace or temple structure of the buildings in China or Japan and the ranch, cottage, or Victorian style of buildings in the United States.

*Semifixed feature space* is the arrangement of movable objects that we don't move unless a special need arises. For example, after the furniture at home or the desks in the office have been arranged, they usually stay there for a long period of time until the floor needs to be cleaned, a new mood is being sought, or furnishings themselves are being replaced.

*Informal space* refers to the distance between the interactants in communication. It is the personal territory that travels with us wherever we go. According to Hall (1966), informal space directly affects the way we communicate with others. Hall classified American cultural interpersonal distances into eight categories of interaction: (1) Very close—activities include soft whispering and discussing top secrets. The distance is between 3 and 6 inches. (2) Close—activities include audible whispering and talking in a very confidential way. The distance is between 8 and 12 inches. (3) Near—activities include soft talking indoors and talking in full voice outdoors. The distance is between 12 and 20 inches. (4) Neutral—activities include talking in a soft voice and at low volume and discussing personal matters. The distance is between 20 and 36 inches. (5) Neutral—activities include talking in full voice and discussing nonpersonal matters. The distance is between 4.5 and 5 feet. (6) Public distance—activities include talking in full voice somewhat too loudly and discussing public matter for others to hear. The distance is between 5.5 and 8 feet. (7) Across the room—activities include talking in a loud voice and talking to a group. The distance is between 8 and 12 feet. (8) Stretching the limits of distance—activities include those requiring a distance of 20 to 24 feet indoors and up to 100 feet outdoors.

Hall's eight categories can be further classified into four discernible distances: intimate, personal, social, and public. Intimate space is from 0 to 18 inches. For two persons a close relationship between them is required to occupy intimate space. Hugging, kissing, and holding hands together are included in this category. For human beings or animals, the most intimate space they occupy is when they engage in sex. Personal space, is from 1 or 1.5 feet to 4 feet, is the distance we occupy in interpersonal communication, usually with friends. To North Americans, it is about the distance covered when we stretch out our hands. Social distance, from 4 to 12 feet, most likely characterizes comfortable interactive in the workplace between acquaintances or strangers. Finally, public space is any distance beyond 12 feet. It typically describes a public speaking situation.

The use of informal space varies cross-culturally. For example, while North Americans feel most comfortable an arm's length apart in interactions, Latin Americans tend to keep a much closer distance, and the Japanese and Chinese prefer to keep somewhat greater distance. Research also shows that nonverbal distance varies according to setting, gender, relationship, and topic, among other factors (Matawi, 1995). Differences in using informal space often cause misunderstanding in intercultural communication. North Americans may feel that Arabs from North Africa and from the northern and western Middle East intrude on their personal space. Similarly, Saudi males like to stand close enough to smell each other's breath and may comment on the other's health if the smell is unpleasant. Likewise, Arabs complain that North Americans have an aloof or indifferent attitude in communication. In addition, the traditional concept of "feng shui" (the art of space arrangement) also reflects how the Chinese arrange the space in the design of rooms and the selection of a place for dwelling or burying a dead family member (Chen, 1996).

## Paralanguage

*Paralanguage* refers to the study of voice or the use of vocal signs in communication. Comprised of all the sounds we produce with our voices that are not words, paralanguage forms the border between verbal and nonverbal com-

**Research Highlight 5–2**

Who:    Chen, G. M.

What:   "Feng Shui: The Chinese Art of Space Arrangement."

Where:  Paper presented at the 1996 annual meeting of Speech Communication Association, November, San Diego, California.

*Feng Shui* is a Chinese cultural phenomenon. It is the study of the relationship between humans and environment. With its pervasive, mysterious, utilitarian, and harmonious nature, Feng Shui teaches us how to live in harmony with the environment and to gain maximum benefit, peace, and prosperity from being in the right place at the right time. In this article the author examines the philosophical and cultural bases of Feng Shui and further discusses the impact of Feng Shui on Chinese social life.

Philosophically, the development of Feng Shui is influenced by four concepts of Chinese philosophy: (1) mutual responding between heaven and men—Feng Shui extends the idea to explain that earth and humans are also mutually affecting each other; (2) Yin and Yang, the two opposite but fundamental forces that form the universe—Yin implies the shady north side of a hill and Yang the sunny sides of a river or a hill; the direction and the dynamic and harmonious interaction of Yin and Yang greatly influence Feng Shu; (3) Wu Hsing (the Five Elements)—Wu Hsing are the five basic elements for human life (i.e., water, fire, wood, gold, and earth); their dialectical interaction plays an important role in Feng

Shui; and (4) Chi, the vital energy that forms the essence of all materials—it leads to the dynamic interaction between Yin and Yang and among the Five Elements; Feng Shui uses the concept of Chi to explain the creation of the universe, to develop the theory of "living chi," and to as a general criterion for judging whether a space is appropriate for human purpose.

Culturally, Feng Shui is based on four Chinese cultural values: (1) prosperity—the emphasis makes Feng Shui one of the most attractive aspects of Chinese culture because it can satisfy the psychological needs of the Chinese; (2) harmony—Feng Shui teaches people how to create harmony and avoid conflicts with nature by adapting to the natural environment; (3) moral concern—Feng Shui strongly reflects the moral concern of filial piety in the Chinese family system; and (5) aesthetic views—Feng Shui is concerned with the holistic balance of the Chinese aesthetic view and applies it to architecture.

Feng Shui impacts two aspects of Chinese social life: interpersonal interaction and business life. First, the principles of Feng Shui directly influence Chinese interpersonal communication, not only by suggesting that people should work harmoniously with those around them to promote well-being but also by proposing a pattern of selective communication. Second, to ensure business profits and create a favorable business environment, Feng Shui is applied to four aspects of business life: (1) the name of the company (the name must represent the image of

*Continued*

---

**Research Highlight 5–2** *Continued*

the company and spell luck and confidence), (2) the location of the company (should be in an appropriate place, referred to as "dragon vein"), (3) interior design and setting (including the arrangement of doors, windows, room setting, lighting. mirror, color, plant for creating a comfortable working condition), and (4) organizational behaviors.

Finally, the author emphasizes that the study of Feng Shui should be included in nonverbal communication study, in particular of the emphasis on the arrangement of space and the use of time and color. The author also encourages scholars to use various research methods to validate the assumptions embedded in the theory of Feng Shui.

---

munication. Vocal cues can be used to detect the emotional state of the speaker in communication. They not only reflect the degree of liking communicated but also suggest the personality of the speaker. For example, we tend to think that persons are more dynamic if they increase the rate, loudness, and pitch of their speech. We also tend to think the persons are more persuasive if they are more fluent in their speech, use more volume, higher speech rates, and more intonation (Davitz & Davitz, 1961; Mehrabian & Williams, 1969). According to Trager (1958), paralinguistic cues can be classified into four categories: voice qualities, vocal characterizers, vocal qualifiers, and vocal segregates.

*Voice quality* consists of the recognizable characteristics of our voice that are separated from the actual messages. These paralinguistic cues include pitch range, quality of articulation, rhythm, resonance, and pace. Each individual has a distinctive voice quality. A person's voice may be shrill, muffled, childish, or nasal, and another's can be breathy, resonant, or melodious. Although the study by Beier and Zautra (1972) indicated that culture does not affect the interpretation of voice quality as related to the speaker's emotional state or general attitudes, certain types of voice quality are still affected by cultural stereotypes. For example, North Americans tend to think a woman is discontented when she uses a strident and high-pitched voice, and sexy when she uses a breathy and low-pitched voice (Victor, 1992). In Japan men are considered to be more masculine or authoritarian when they use a low-pitched voice with great volume. Users of American Sign Language may rehearse beautiful, expressive signing for songs, sermons, or literary works, or may add voice to their signing. That voice may or may not sound like "words" to the "speaking" community.

*Vocal characterizers* are nonverbal voices that reveal our physical and emotional state. It is nearly universal for humans to laugh when they are happy; cry when they are in sorrow; yell (or be totally silent) when they are angry at someone; and yawn when they are tired. Vocal characterizers also include cues such as belching, groaning, hiccupping, moaning, sighing, sneezing, snoring, and spitting.

*Vocal qualifiers* are variations of our voice that convey our emotions and personality. They represent the range of volume from soft to loud, low to high pitch, and the extent of our word elongation. In other words, they include the manner in which a word or phrase is uttered—the changes of volume, pitch, and the speech rate used in communication. Every language system possesses its own acceptable range of vocal qualifiers. For example, in the Arab world speaking loudly signifies being strong and sincere (Vagas, 1986), but such behavior may seem irritating and aggressive to North Americans. People in Hong Kong tend to be more expressive, using high-pitched voice in Cantonese, than their counterparts in Canton province, China. Vocal qualifiers are also reflected in the international community. For example, foreign students from different cultures show a distinctive variation in speaking English in the United States. The variations often become a source of distancing when the local population evaluates such differences negatively.

Finally, *vocal segregates* are those voice noises that seem not to serve any function but to interfere with the flow of speech. Examples include "um," "uh," "eh," "I mean," and "you know" in the middle of speaking. Like that of vocal characterizers, the use of vocal segregates is fairly universal. However, the duration, placement, and use of vocal segregates may vary in different cultures. For example, within the Aristotelian rhetorical tradition, Westerners feel it more appropriate to decrease the use of vocal segregates in a speech or conversation, whereas in China their use signals wisdom and attractiveness.

## Chronemics

*Chronemics* is the study of how we use time in communication. Hall (1959) classified the North American conception of time according to three categories: formal time, technical time, and informal time. *Formal time* represents the classification of time into different units that can be used to measure time itself. For example, we can separate time into years, seasons, weeks, days, hours, minutes, and seconds. As measurement units, these time concepts are neutral in meaning. However, the ways of perceiving categories of time will vary because of cultural differences. *Technical time* is useful and meaningful only to those in a specific profession. *Informal time* has a great impact on human communication. When we say "time talks," or "time is money," we are referring to the concept of informal time. In order to grasp the meanings of informal time it is necessary for us to know its context or cultural setting. For example, the Irish statement, "I'll be back in a pint," can have many interpretations depending on the situation and who utters the sentence. To Indians, "in a pint" may have little meaning; to the Irish, it may indicate 15 minutes; while to other cultures, it may denote infinity. While "tomorrow" is a specific designator in North

America, the equivalent word in Arabic, Hindi or Spanish may or may not literally mean the "next day."

There are two ways to study the concept of time. First, as indicated in Chapter 3, we can look at time or a continuum connecting it into the past, the present, and the future (Kluckhohn & Strodbeck, 1961). Second, we can classify it into monochronic time and polychronic time (Hall, 1959, 1989, 1994).

### Present, Past, and Future Time Orientation

Past-oriented cultures emphasize tradition and history. People having this orientation evaluate daily or business plans based on the degree to which their plans fit with customs and traditions. Innovation and change tend to be discouraged. When change is necessary, it should be justified by the past experience (Adler, 1991). China is an example of a past-oriented culture. Historical dramas in television series or movies often produce high box office sales in Chinese societies. Also, in Saudi Arabia, any person who "changes" is presumed to be violating Muslim religion.

Present-oriented cultures consider the present as the only precious moment: "Carpe diem"—seize the day! We should enjoy today and not worry about what may happen tomorrow. Similarly, the "Protestant ethic" advocates, "work for the night cometh." The bus schedules in the Bahamas illustrate a present-time orientation. There the individual drivers set arrival and departure times, taking breaks whenever they feel like it. For example, if a driver feels hungry, he or she may go home directly to have lunch (Adler, 1991).

In contrast, future-oriented cultures emphasize planning in order to achieve goals. Changes and innovations are encouraged in those cultures and are evaluated in terms of future economic payoffs. According to Adler (1991), the United States tends to be present- and near-future-oriented. For instance, in business Americans may have 5 or 10-year plans, but in practice they evaluate the employees' performance on a monthly or quarterly basis. A manager may be fired because of poor performance at the end of first quarter. The Japanese are future-oriented people, as clearly shown by their system of life-long employment.

**Monochronic and Polychronic Time Orientation.**   According to Hall (1994), *monochronic-time-oriented* cultures tend to treat time as something fixed in nature. Time is like the air surrounding us, which we cannot escape. Thus, time is lineal, segmented, and manageable. People in monochronic-time-oriented cultures tend to do one thing at a time and to follow precise scheduling. In social interactions making appointments and meeting deadlines are common practice. Austria, Germany, Switzerland, and the United States are some examples of monochronic-time-oriented cultures.

*Polychronic-time-oriented* cultures do not emphasize scheduling by separating time into discrete, fixed segments. Instead, they treat time as a less tangible medium in which many things can be done simultaneously. Thus, in these cultures, personal interaction and relationship development are far more important than making appointments or meeting deadlines. Africans, Arabs, Greeks, Mexicans, Native Hawaiians, Portuguese, and Spanish are generally included in this category. Misunderstandings or conflicts may occur between people from monochronic- and polychoronic-time-oriented cultures, as Hall (1984) vividly describes, explaining the tendency to view the "different" as "annoying" or "wrong":

> *Particularly distressing to Americans is the way in which appointments are handled by polychronic people. Being on time simply doesn't mean the same thing as it does in the United States. Matters in a polychronic culture seem to be in a constant state of flux. Nothing is solid or firm, particularly plans for the future; even important plans may be changed right up to the minute of execution. (pp. 47)*

Victor (1992) summarized the characteristics of monochronic and polychronic time orientations. According to Victor, in monochronic time-oriented cultures (1) preset schedules dominate interpersonal relations; (2) appointment times are rigid; (3) people handle one task at a time; (4) breaks and personal time dominate personal ties; (5) time is inflexible and tangible; (6) personal time and work time are clearly separated; and (7) organizational tasks are measured by activities per hour or minute. In contrast, in polychronic time-oriented cultures (a) interpersonal relations supercede preset schedules; (b) appointment time is flexible; (c) people handle many tasks simultaneously; (d) personal ties dominate breaks and personal time; (e) time is flexible and fluid; (f) personal time and work time are not clearly separated; and (g) organizational tasks are measured as part of overall organizational goal.

## NONVERBAL COMMUNICATION AND CULTURE

As Hall (1984) mentioned, the primary level of culture is communicated through nonverbal means, because imitation and observation are the two major ways for us to learn aspects of our culture through the socialization process rather than by means of explicit verbal expressions. Nonverbal communication is a subtle and mostly spontaneous and unconscious process in which we are not aware of most of the nonverbal behaviors we enact (Andersen, 1986). Thus, unlike verbal language, it is very difficult for us to master the other culture's nonverbal behaviors. However, the rules that govern verbal and nonverbal communication are similarly subject to the variations of culture.

Significantly, that which is learned by imitation is least within our awareness. Thus, if a person says "1 + 1 = 4," we may correct him or her, and our reaction is probably nonemotional. However, we react emotionally to violations of what seems "natural" to us. When we are left waiting "too long," or "stared at," our reaction may be anger. According to Samovar and Porter (1994), culture and nonverbal behaviors are interrelated in two ways. First, nonverbal behaviors are dictated by the communicator's culture. As noted earlier, a nonverbal symbol possessing a positive meaning may become negative in another culture. Silence as a nonverbal expression also receives an opposite perception in different cultures. People of Western culture strongly perceive silence as a negative attribute (Ishi & Bruneau, 1994). For example, North Americans tend to interpret silence as sorrow, critique, obligation, regret, and embarrassment (Wayne, 1974). Conversely, the Japanese highly value silence. Ishi and Bruneau (1994) reported that a study by Japanese scholars shows that silence is a key to success for Japanese men, and over 60 percent of Japanese businesswomen said that they prefer to marry silent men.

Second, culture determines the appropriate times to display nonverbal behaviors, emotions in particular. For example, the Chinese and Japanese react much less strongly to provocative events compared to their counterparts in Western societies. Uninhibited emotional display is considered by the Chinese and Japanese as being disruptive and dangerous. It not only contradicts cultural values such as hierarchy and harmony but also puts the person in a face-losing and embarrassing situation (Bond, 1991).

To explain differences in nonverbal behaviors in terms of cultural variations, Andersen (1994) distinguished the following dimensions of culture: contact/low contact, individualism/collectivism, masculinity/femininity, power distance, and high/low context. People in contact cultures display immediacy behaviors that express warmth and availability for communication; they emphasize interpersonal closeness. In contrast, people in low-contact cultures use less touch and tend to stand apart in communication. Nations in warm geographic areas, such as those in West Asia and the Mediterranean region, are more likely to exhibit more contact. Nations with cool climates, such as most Northern European countries, tend to be low-contact cultures.

Individualistic and collectivistic cultures show a certain degree of difference in nonverbal behaviors. Andersen (1994) indicated that in terms of using space, people in individualistic cultures tend to be distant and remote, while people in collectivistic cultures are likely to be interdependent and proximically close. Regarding body activities, people from individualistic cultures smile more than people in collectivistic cultures (Tomkins, 1984). One of the explanations for this difference is that emotional displays are more likely to be avoided in collectivistic cultures. Argyle (1975) also pointed out that kinesic behaviors are more synchronized in collectivistic cultures, because working collectively requires that movement and actions be highly coordinated.

The dimensions of masculinity/femininity and power distance also affect kinesic and paralinguistic behaviors. For example, in egalitarian or feminine cultures women tend to have more relaxed vocal patterns and less tension exists between the sexes (Lomax, 1968). In addition, in high-power-distance

## Research Highlight 5–3

Who:    Andersen, P. A.

What:    "Explaining Intercultural Differences in Nonverbal Communication."

Where:    In L. A. Samovar & R. E. Porter (Eds.) (1994), *Intercultural Communication: A Reader* (pp. 229–239). Belmont, CA: Wadsworth.

This article reviews the code of nonverbal communication and the influence of culture on interpersonal behavior, and delineates five main dimensions of cultural variation that affect nonverbal communication.

Six nonverbal codes of intercultural communication are (1) chronemics—the study of meanings, usage, and communication of time, (2) proxemics—the study of space and distance in communication, (3) kinesics—the study of body movements or body activities, including facial expressions, eye contact, gestures, and body posture, (4) physical appearance—the most important element that affects our perception in the initial intercultural encounters, (5) vocalics, or paralanguage—the study of voice or vocal signs, and (6) olfactics—the study of smell in communication.

Culture shapes our behavior in an enduring, powerful, and invisible way. Culture is a critical concept to communication study, because we are a product of our culture. In order to understand cultural differences in nonverbal behavior we can locate cultural variations along five dimensions:

**1.** Immediacy and expressiveness— Immediacy or expressive behaviors refer to actions that communicate warmth, closeness, and availability for communication. High-immediacy cultures are also called *contact cultures,* and low-immediacy cultures *low-contact cultures.* Research shows that contact cultures tend to locate in warm-temperature areas (e.g., most Arab countries) and low-contact cultures in cool climates (e.g., most Northern European countries).

**2.** Individualism versus collectivism— Research has found that people in individualistic cultures tend to be more remote and distant proximically, and more nonverbally affiliative. People in collectivistic cultures tend to work, play, live, and sleep in close proximity to one another, tend to be synchronized in kinesics, tend to suppress extreme emotional display, and tend to stress groupness and cohesion in their singing styles.

**3.** Masculinity—Research indicates that women in low-masculinity cultures show more relaxed vocal patterns, more vocal solidarity and coordination in their songs, and more synchrony in their movement than those in high-masculinity cultures.

**4.** Power distance—Research shows that high-power-distance cultures tend to be more "untouchable" (in terms of tactile communication), tend to be more tense in subordinates' body movement, tend to smile more for subordinates to appease superiors or to be polite, and tend to be more aware that vocal loudness may be offensive to others.

**5.** High and low context—Research finds that in high-context cultures

*Continued*

---

**Research Highlight 5–3**    *Continued*

people tend to be more implicit in verbal codes, tend to perceive highly verbal persons less attractive, tend to be more reliant on and tuned into nonverbal communication, and expect to have more nonverbal codes in communication.

In conclusion, applying cognitive knowledge of cultural variations in actual encounters with people from different cultures is the best way to achieve intercultural communication competence.

---

cultures touch between males and females is discouraged. Body tension in subordinates in high-power-distance cultures is also apparent (Andersen & Bowman, 1985).

Finally, Andersen (1994) indicated that people in high-context cultures are much more sensitive to nonverbal cues. They are much more able to read and perceive nonverbal behaviors than males in low-context cultures. This ability leads them to expect their low-context communication counterparts to understand environmental cues and hidden and subtle gestures and feelings that are not recognizable in the latter's culture. The last section of this chapter will focus on the acquisition of nonverbal skills that can be applied to intercultural communication.

## INTERCULTURAL SKILLS IN NONVERBAL COMMUNICATION

Because nonverbal behaviors are ambiguous and vary across cultures, it is more difficult for us to correctly interpret the meanings of nonverbal cues in intercultural communication. However, like verbal language, we can learn to be effective nonverbally in intercultural communication. For example, as indicated by Victor (1992), in order to accommodate cultural differences in chronemics in intercultural business interactions, learning to be flexible mentally and behaviorally is critical. This section describes a model of nonverbal skill development.

Ricard (1993) proposed five steps for the development of nonverbal skills: (1) assess learning needs, (2) observe similar situations, (3) use appropriate resources, (4) reach tentative conclusions, and (5) reevaluate the conclusions as necessary.

First, to assess learning needs is to identify needs that are related to the area of nonverbal behaviors and to the meanings of those nonverbal behaviors. At the beginning of this step we should examine our degree of awareness of the following items: (1) our own nonverbal behaviors and their meanings, (2) the nonverbal behaviors accepted by people of our own culture and their meanings, and (3) the nonverbal behaviors accepted by people in the culture of our interest and their meanings. After we have become familiar with the accepted nonverbal behaviors in the specific culture, we can then begin to decide which related nonverbal behaviors are most important to know at the present time and which areas should be the focus of our learning. Finally, we start developing skills by selecting an area of focus.

The second step is to observe similar situations by comparing and contrasting daily life events in both cultures. For example, in what ways are nonverbal expressions similar or different in the wedding, dining, or recreational activities of our own and the observed culture?

The third step is to use appropriate resources that enable us to expand our knowledge of the possible meanings of nonverbal behaviors in the specific culture and to evaluate our observations. When direct interactive observations are not possible, the use of carefully selected literature and audiovisual materials is suggested. Our best resource may be cultural informants.

Based on the needs assessment and the information gathered in the first three steps, our fourth step is to reach a set of tentative conclusions regarding our discoveries. These conclusions should serve as tentative findings, rather than being treated as rigid guidelines.

Finally, we should reevaluate the whole process to ensure the usefulness of our learning. A reevaluation should be conducted without fail in the following three cases:

**1.** When resources are unable to provide us enough knowledge to discover the meanings of nonverbal behaviors.

**2.** When the observation process is restricted in any way.

**3.** When our tentative conclusions are in doubt or have proved to be unworkable.

## RECAP

Verbal and nonverbal communication form the two main contexts of human communication. This chapter focuses on nonverbal communication in a four-part discussion of: (1) the nature of nonverbal communication, (2) the structure of nonverbal communication, (3) nonverbal communication and culture, and (4) intercultural skills in nonverbal communication.

In exploring the nature of nonverbal communication, the similarities and differences of verbal and nonverbal communication systems are compared. Nonverbal communication is different from verbal communication in five respects: (1) it is not consciously controllable, (2) it can indicate multiple events simultaneously, (3) it can be used as an intercultural or international language, (4) it is learned earlier in our life, and (5) it is more emotional in expression. Five functions of nonverbal communication are then discussed, including repetition, replacement, emphasis, contradiction, and regulation. The characteristics of nonverbal communication are also delineated. That is, nonverbal communication is less systemized and more culturally bound, and its meanings are always ambiguous.

The structure of nonverbal communication is comprised of four areas of study. First, kinesics is the study of body movements such as facial expressions, eye contact, hand gestures, and touch. Second, proxemics is the study of how human beings and animals use space in communication. Hall classified space into fixed-feature space, semifixed feature space, and informal space. Informal space is further broken into four distinct categories: intimate space, personal space, social space, and public space. Paralanguage refers to how we use voice or vocal signs in communication. Trager grouped paralinguistic cues into four dimensions: voice quality, vocal characterizers, vocal qualifiers, and vocal segregates. Finally, chronemics is the study of how we perceive the concept of time and how that affects our communication. There are two ways to consider time. The first way is separate the concept of time into past, present, and future orientations. The second is to examine time from a monochronic or polychronic time perspective.

Nonverbal behaviors and culture are closely interrelated in two ways. First, our nonverbal behaviors are dictated by our culture; second, culture determines when it is appropriate time for us to display nonverbal behaviors. Finally, we can improve our intercultural skills in nonverbal communication by following Ricard's five-step model for the development of nonverbal skills, whereby we: (1) assess our learning needs, (2) observe similar situations, (3) use appropriate resources, (4) reach tentative conclusions, and (5) reevaluate our conclusions as necessary.

## RETHINK

Nonverbal communication tends to be a much younger field than verbal communication and shows great potential for contributing to the "unspoken world" of human communication. However, in any young field of study confusion is inevitable. To those who are interested in this area we propose several questions for further discussion.

First, as mentioned previously, a large proportion of human interaction is dominated by nonverbal behaviors. Would this indicate that the nonverbal aspect of communication is more important than verbal messages in the process of human understanding? Could we communicate and understand each other without saying anything verbally? Moreover, how do systems of sign language reflect cultural variation? (e.g., Saudi women sign at the level of their side, but Saudi men sign at eye level).

Second, when we are analyzing nonverbal behaviors, should we separate them into distinct categories? For instance, should we single out eye contact for analysis without considering its relationship to facial expressions or other nonverbal behaviors? How important is the holistic view for the study of nonverbal behaviors, especially in combination with the verbal aspects of human communication? Over the last decades nonverbal communication scholars have focused on the study of particular nonverbal behaviors and excluded others. How valid are the research findings of these studies?

Third, should we apply linguistic tools in analyzing nonverbal systems? In other words, are there fundamental differences we should take into account when we analyze verbal and nonverbal systems?

Finally, two questions raised by Condon and Yousef (1975) likewise deserve further discussion. First, in intercultural communication is it more important to speak the host language than to be fluent in nonverbal expressions? Second, what is the relationship between culture shock and nonverbal communication? Is culture shock more attributable to verbal or to nonverbal communication factors?

## QUESTIONS FOR DISCUSSION

1. What are the major differences between verbal and nonverbal communication?
2. Are the functions of nonverbal communication related to verbal communication?
3. Discuss the contents of kinesics, proxemics, paralanguage, and chronemics.
4. Explain how culture and nonverbal behaviors interrelated to each other.
5. Could you describe intercultural skills in nonverbal communication in addition to those mentioned in the chapter?
6. What are those issues raised by the authors concerning the direction of future research in the area of intercultural communication?

# ▶ Part III

## Interaction

# ▶ Chapter 6:

## Intercultural Relationship Development

### *Objectives*

Upon completion of this chapter, you will

- Understand the meaning, characteristics, stages, and theories of relationship development.
- Understand the impact of culture on relationship development.
- Understand the model of third-culture building.

*What an argument in favor of social connections . . .
the observation that by communicating our grief
we have less, and by communicating our
pleasure we have more.—L. GREVILLE*

No matter whether it is grief or pleasure we intend to share with others, we seek to be included in a human relationship network. From the moment we are born we begin to weave a social network through different channels of communication. It is in our nature that we have a strong need to be cared for and loved, and when we are growing, we develop passions for caring and loving others. Through our life we are constantly developing, maintaining, and terminating relationships with persons we know well or do not yet know. We are social creatures, not isolated islands. In this chapter we first discuss the nature of human relationships, consider their meaning and their developmental processes, and explore representative theories about relationships. Then we introduce cultural variability as a factor in relationships. Finally, we offer a model to explain intercultural relationship development.

# THE NATURE OF HUMAN RELATIONSHIP

To understand the process of interpersonal relationship development we need first to know the meaning and characteristics of human relationships.

## *Human Relationship Defined*

*Human relationship* refers to how we deal with one another in daily life. The desire to be attached to others is based on William Schutz's concept of "social needs." According to Schutz (1966), we perpetually strive to fulfill three social needs through communication: inclusion, control, and affection. *Inclusion* is a sense of belonging. Through our life we have a need to be a member of different human groups, including cultural, religious, social, ethnic, academic, and other networks. Maintaining relationships with other persons in different groups is an important way to develop our own personal identity, because in groups our individuality and distinctiveness are recognized (Mader & Mader, 1990).

*Control* is the ability to be in charge of our own life and to influence people around us. We gain control over ourselves and others because of our knowledge, attraction, and authority. Usually, the various behaviors or roles we play in the network of human relationship can satisfy our need for control. These behaviors include initiating a new idea, providing useful information and opinion, energizing actions, supporting another's idea, resolving conflicts, promoting communication, harmonizing relationships, and actively listening to others. In other words, to gain or to show our control over ourselves and others we must know when and how to play an equal, superior, or subordinate role in the process of communication.

*Affection* refers to the desire to show our love and to be loved by other persons. To keep a relationship in satisfactory condition the needs of inclusion and control must be tempered by affection. Affection fosters passion, commitment, and intimate relationships. It is affection that ties persons together physically, emotionally, and intellectually.

The concept of *social needs* provides a starting point for the examination of relationships. Human relationship then can be defined as an interactional process of connecting ourselves with others in the network of social needs. It contains the three ingredients of inclusion, control, and affection. The con-

---

**Mini Case 6–1**

Henry, a sixteen-year-old Philippine, has recently arrived in the United States from his native land with his family, and is about to go out on his first date since the move. He takes his date, an American girl named Mildred, to dinner and a movie. Everything seems to be going very well. Henry is polite, humorous, and the ambience is very casual. After the movie, Henry attempts to open the car door for his date. Mil- dred, however, immediately declines, takes the door from him, closes it, and instructs Henry to go around. For the remainder of the car ride home Henry continually murmurs to himself, and when he is questioned by Mildred, he simply ignores her.

How would you explain Henry's behavior toward Mildred during the car ride home?

---

*Source:* Ryan Angel, University of Rhode Island.

necting process among people may lead to a largely positive or negative re- sult. In addition, the way we perceive and fulfill social needs is conditioned by culture. Thus, persons of different cultural backgrounds vary in the way they try to meet each other's needs for inclusion, control, and affection. Read Mini Case 6–1 and see whether you can answer the question from the perspective of social needs.

## Characteristics of Human Relationship

Besides the elements of human relationships, identified in the previous section, several other characteristics help us understand how human relationships operate. First, human relationships are *dynamic*. They are ever in a state of transformation in the face of on-going and ever-changing activity. In human re- lationships we constantly affect each other through communication. Thus, the development of human relationships through communication is never ab- solutely completed or finished.

Second, human relationships are *hierarchical*. The hierarchy of human re- lationships includes strangers, acquaintances, and intimate friends. Different levels of relationship ask of us different degrees of involvement in terms of in- clusion, control, and affection.

Third, human relationships are *reciprocal*. A reciprocal relationship exists when members in the relationship network can satisfy each other's needs of inclusion, control, and affection to a certain degree. A prolonged reciprocal in- compatibility usually leads to the breakdown of the relationship.

Fourth, human relationships are *unique*. The bonding of human relationships demands a special set of interactional rules that distinguishes them from more impersonal relationships in which interactions are governed by social norms or standardized rules.

Finally, human relationships are *interdependent and irreplaceable*. In the network of human relationships the fate of members is associated, connected, and inseparable. When we form an interpersonal bond, we begin to affect and depend on each other. For example, while our partner is depressed, excited, angry, or rejoicing, we inevitably share his or her emotions. The change of our feelings in different stages of relationship development, especially when a person we love dies, also demonstrates the feature of irreplaceability.

## STAGES OF RELATIONSHIP DEVELOPMENT

Human relationships develop in stages. We don't build an intimate relationship suddenly. Berger and Calabrese (1975) found that based on the communication transaction, human relationship develops in three phases. In the *entry phase* communication is governed by a set of communication rules or social norms. Thus, communication patterns in this stage tend to be structured, and the contents mostly focus on the demographic information. Interactions with strangers typify this phase. When an interaction proceeds to the latter phases of this stage, a personal association emerges and the interactants begin to solicit information about each other's attitudes and opinions. As a result of growing rapport, strangers gradually become acquaintances. If the interactants decide to further develop their relationship, they will enter the second stage of relationship development.

The second stage is called the *personal phase*. Information on personal problems, liking and disliking, and central attitudinal and personality issues is exchanged in this stage. Communication becomes more informal, spontaneous, and less regulated by the social norms. An intimate relationship then develops at this stage.

The last stage of relationship development is called the *exit phase*, in which the relationship begins to deteriorate. The frequency of interaction decreases; the desirability of future interaction is discussed; and the interactants tend to avoid facing each other. If the interactants can't work out their problems together, the relationship will be terminated through separation or divorce.

Although Berger and Calabrese's model oversimplifies the complexity of human relationship, it represents a fundamental description of relationship development and provides a foundation on which scholars such as Chen (1995), Devito (1992), Knapp and Vangelisti (1992), Krug (1982), Levinger (1983), and Wood (1982) have based further study of the topic. We delineate the models developed by Chen, Devito, and Knapp and Vangelisti in the following section.

## Devito's Model

Devito (1992) specified a five-stage model of human relationship development: contact, involvement, intimacy, deterioration, and dissolution. Each stage of this model is divided into an initial and a final phase. In the perceptual contact phase of the contact stage we concentrate our attention on our partner's physical appearance. Then we enter the interactional contact phase, in which we exchange the superficial and impersonal information. If we like the person, we then proceed to the involvement stage.

In the involvement stage we proceed to connect one to the other by developing an association. At the initial phase of this stage we begin to test whether the judgments made in the contact phase are reasonable or acceptable. We ask different questions to verify our judgments and continue to intensify interactions to increase the degree of involvement in the final phase of this stage. An early intimate relationship is developed in this stage.

In the intimacy stage we continue to show commitment to each other and become best friends or lovers. The initial phase of this stage is characterized by interpersonal commitment in which we commit to each other in a private way. In the final phase, social bonds, we make our relationship public.

The deterioration and dissolution stages represent the weakening and downgrading of the relationship. Intrapersonal dissatisfaction symbolizes the first phase of the deterioration stage. The dissatisfactory interaction appearing in this phase makes us doubt the importance of the relationship and the necessity to continue to keep the relationship going. If the negative feelings continue to increase, we will enter the second phase of the stage, interpersonal deterioration. We feel awkward to be together and begin to withdraw from each other. Verbal and nonverbal interactions decrease. Not sincerely caring for each other in this context may cause serious conflicts that will destroy the intimate relationship.

Finally, if we decide to cut off the connection, reach the stage of dissolution. At the beginning of this stage we realize interpersonal separation by not seeing each other or by living apart from each other. If the deteriorating relationship is not fixed, public separation will replace interpersonal separation. Our partner becomes ex-wife, ex-husband, or ex-lover. (Note that, in some societies, an ascriptive relationship defined by birth can neither be conveniently ended nor publicly questioned. A maternal uncle cannot be disavowed or disowned the way one might divorce a marital partner. Indeed, similarly, marital partners cannot be disavowed in some societies and religious communities.)

## Knapp and Vangelisti's Model

Knapp and Vangelisti (1992) divided the process of relationship development into two parts: coming together and coming apart. *Coming together* describes the developing process of human relationship and *coming apart* describes the terminating process. Each part is comprised of five stages of movement. The five stages of coming together are initiating, experimenting, intensifying, integrating, and bonding. The five stages of coming apart are differentiating, circumscribing, stagnating, avoiding, and terminating. The ten stages represent a systematic continuum of human relationship development. Although some relationships may skip stages, most move from one stage to the next.

Let us examine the stages of coming together. The first time we meet a person, we tend to initiate a relationship. Knapp and Vangelistic indicated that at this stage, we try to present a positive image following, scripts predetermined by social norms in the interaction. The initiating stage of interaction brings about an opportunity for interactants to make an overall judgment about each other's competence or ability.

Based on the initial judgment of each other, in the experimenting stage we begin to make an effort to reduce ambiguity by inducing superficial and conventional conversations that tend to cover a wide variety of topics. Through this we begin to identify similarities between each other and develop a casual relationship without making any specific commitment.

In the intensifying stage the amount of personal and psychological information increases. As in the second phase of Devito's involvement stage, in this stage here we feel a need to move the relationship to an intimate level. We begin to intensify our interactions by creating more informal codes. The topics of interaction in this stage are wide-ranging, and the information disclosed gets deeper. Personal uniqueness is clearly displayed in this stage.

When we enter the integrating stage, we begin to develop a physical and social closeness. We arrange our life pace to match each other's pattern. We spend much time together and appear in each other's social network. A romantic picture is drawn and intimate interaction and relationship develop. In this stage we are well prepared to form a world with our partner. The frequency, depth, and exclusiveness of interaction between ourselves and our partner leads to the emergence of personal bonding.

Bonding—the blossom of the romantic relationship—highlights the coming-together part of the relationship. Through a public ritual, such as engagement or marriage, we announce a formal commitment to each other. This stage of the relationship is characterized by stability and security because the commitment is bound by a viable social contract. However, human relationships are inherently transformational by nature. The impact of internal and external factors constantly challenge the social bond. If the couple is unable to cope with environmental changes, increasing conflicts may loosen the bonds of the relationship and push it onto the slope of disintegration. The process of coming apart begins at this moment.

The first stage of coming apart is differentiating. This is the stage at which we begin to find out that we are actually different from each other. The focus of difference widens the personal distance between us and our partner. We reorient ourselves from the bonding relationship to individual emphasis. Knapp and Vangelisti (1992) maintained that the development of differentiation in the relationship often causes conflict or fighting.

The second stage of coming apart, circumscribing, is characterized by the desire to limit mutual communication. In this stage we try to avoid exchanging information about sensitive and intimate topics. The frequency and depth of interaction between us decreases. We begin to feel more comfortable by keeping silent. If we have to talk with each other, we prefer to keep the interaction at a superficial level.

In the stagnating stage we not only feel more comfortable to keep silent but think that there is no need to talk to each other because we think we have already known what the outcome is going to be. As in interactions with strangers, at this stage we feel the communication between us become awkward. We begin to avoid facing each other.

At the avoiding stage we reestablish a lifestyle by which we can avoid interacting with our partners. We begin to find excuses to avoid talking or seeing each other. Moreover, according to Gudykunst, Ting-Toomey, Sudweeks, and Stewart (1995), we tend to interpret our partner's messages as unfriendliness and antagonism. The deteriorating situation signals that it is time to end the relationship.

The final stage of coming apart is the termination of the relationship. Psychological and physical connections between us and our partners are disassociated in this stage. We stop contacting each other. Separation or divorce finalizes the relationship. The reluctant communication already between us regresses to the prerelationship stage, with feelings of embarrassment, difficulty, hesitation, awkwardness, and ineptitude.

## Chen's Model

Chen's (1995) model of human relationship development is based on the interaction of eight trigrams delineated in the *Book of Changes* (I Ching), a classic Chinese text completed in the Chou Dynasty (1150–248 B.C.). Chen argued that the development of human relationship is a dialectical process built on three ontological assumptions. First, the universe is a great whole in which all is nothing more than a transitional process, with no fixed substance for its substratum. Thus, human relationship is ever in a state of change and transformation. Second, the transforming process of the universe does not proceed onward but revolves in an endless cycle. Human relationship then changes according to this cycle of the universe, like the succession of day and night and the periodical ebb and flow of the tide. Finally, there is no ending for the transforming process of the universe. The development of human relationship is never absolutely complete or finished.

Based on these assumptions, the movement of the eight trigrams from the *Book of Changes* can be used to delineate the developmental process of human relationship. The eight trigrams symbolize eight attributes of human nature, each associated with a portion of the 24-hour day. In other words, they represent the eight stages of human relationship development. In addition, each stage of this model is both an effect of the previous stage and a cause of the next stage. Figure 6–1 illustrates the model.

The first stage is symbolized by "Chen" (thunder—the arousing), paralleling 4:30–7:30 of the morning hours, which signifies the power for developing a relationship with others. It is the birth stage of human relationship. Like the sun preparing to rise, this stage represents the internal process of our psychological need or motivation to develop an association by emotionally attaching ourselves to someone else. The movement of this stage is characterized by an intrapersonal process in which the movement is dominated by personality factors. When the motivation for associating with others is externalized, we enter the second stage.

The second stage, symbolized by "sun" (breeze—the penetrating), represents the continuation of relationship development by a gently penetrating ef-

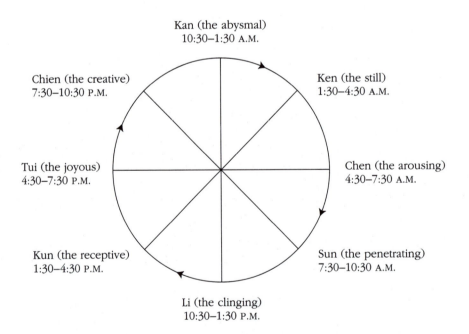

Kan (the abysmal)
10:30–1:30 A.M.

Chien (the creative)
7:30–10:30 P.M.

Ken (the still)
1:30–4:30 A.M.

Tui (the joyous)
4:30–7:30 P.M.

Chen (the arousing)
4:30–7:30 A.M.

Kun (the receptive)
1:30–4:30 P.M.

Sun (the penetrating)
7:30–10:30 A.M.

Li (the clinging)
10:30–1:30 P.M.

**FIGURE 6–1   Chen's Model of Relationship Development**

fort. It parallels the morning hours of 7:30–10:30. Just as the breeze and the rising sun gently penetrate everywhere and attach to everything, bringing up the life-sap from the earth (Wilhelm, 1979), we begin to contact the person with whom we intend to develop a connection. Gathering information unforcefully to reduce the uncertainty level characterizes this stage. By increasingly understanding each other in the latter phase of this stage, we develop the confidence to disclose our passion and enthusiasm for further attachment.

"Li" (fire—the clinging) symbolizes the third stage, which parallels 10:30 A.M.–1:30 P.M. The components of our passion and enthusiasm burst into the flame like the thriving sun at noon, bright, blazing, and vigorous. We openly express our desire to emotionally and psychologically cling to each other. Because the occurrence of fire must rely on its relationship with the other elements (e.g., the flame exists because wood is present), a successful clinging is decided by the response from our partner. If we receive positive feedback from our partner, we continue to move forward to the next stage.

The fourth stage, symbolized by "Kun" (earth—the receptive) and paralleling 1:30–4:30 in the afternoon, represents the reception of each other's relationship. The sun is moving to the west; the evening hours are arriving for the time of resting. It is the preparing time for reaping the consequences of our action and behavior. Our mind is open like the earth, which is considered to be vast, spatial, and receptive. Thus, the relationship in this stage is in bud. The flower is ready to bloom.

The fifth stage is "Tui" (lake—the joyous) and is parallel with the time period of 4:30–7:30 P.M. The lake is considered as a smiling mouth and symbolizes the enjoyment of the harvest. With a joyful feeling to each other an interpersonal bond is built. The relationship in this stage is like the shining, transparent water of the lake in which both parties are clearly mirrored.

The sixth stage, symbolized by "Chien" (heaven—the creative) and paralleling 7:30–10:30 at night, represents the sublimity of the intimate relationship. The heaven is strong, creative, and moves forward like one-dimensional time. This stage is characterized by the purity of the relationship, which leads to the state of acme. However, a certain severity is concealed in this apex stage because the tranformational law dictates that as soon as the relationship reaches its extremity, it will reverse its course. The inability to sustain the pure state of the relationship at this moment begins to develop the deteriorating elements in the interpersonal bonding.

The deteriorating relationship leads to the seventh stage which is symbolized by "Kan" (water—the abysmal) and parallels 10:30–1:30 at night. Like the water in motion, this stage is the waterfall that "rushes downward, is pulverized, rises high above again as clouds, and descends once more as rain;" it is the abysmal that "knows no limitations and unhesitatingly plunges into the depths" (Wilhelm, 1979, p. 9). The relationship at this stage has lost its way, and we are entangled abysmally in misfortune. The harmonious relationship is disturbed. Without patience, perseverance, sincerity, and lasting virtue the relationship is doomed to transform into a motionless state.

The last stage is symbolized by "Ken" (mountain—keeping still) and parallels 1:30 A.M.–4:30 A.M. Endeavoring to continue the old relationship ceases. Like a mountain keeping still, the relationship enters a state of rest because the interactional movement has come to an end. On the one hand, we first keep our toes still, then our calves, our hips, our trunk, our jaw, and our heart. The lack of desire to move toward our partner marks the consummation of the effort to attain individual solitude and tranquillity. However, the time is moving on despite the physical and psychological stagnation. It will move again to the stage of "Chen" to form a cyclic process of human relationship development. This implies two possible consequences: the redevelopment of the old relationship or the germination of a new relationship with another person.

# THEORIES OF RELATIONSHIP DEVELOPMENT

Scholars from different disciplines have provided a number of theories to examine the development of human relationships. Here we discuss four of the theories that can be applied to intercultural relationship development: social exchange theory, social penetration theory, uncertainty reduction theory, and communication accommodation theory.

## Social Exchange Theory

Social exchange theory is based on two economic concepts: rewards and costs. Rewards are what we gain for the amount of cost we pay. The theory indicates that we constantly measure the difference between rewards and costs in order to maximize the positive outcome. When we see the rewards are greater than the costs in the transaction, we purchase the goods. But if the costs are greater than the rewards, we reject the offer.

By the same token, in the process of human relationship development we often seek to reach the greatest rewards in order to minimize the negative outcomes (Kelly & Thibaut, 1978; Roloff, 1981; Thibaut & Kelly, 1959). The rewards from human relationship can include affection, love, happiness, face giving, companionship, gifts, status, acceptance, respect, seniority, or friendship; the costs can include time, money, unhappiness, dissatisfaction, losing face, physical and psychological energy, or the performance of anything one is reluctant to do. According to Devito (1992), when we enter a relationship, we usually carry a certain comparison stick with us by which we can clearly measure the weight of the rewards and costs we are willing to gain and to pay. If we calculate and find the relationship is beyond the comparison level (i.e., the rewards are bigger than the costs), we will feel satisfied with the association and continue to develop the relationship. If not, we might leave the current relationship and begin to seek a new one.

## Social Penetration Theory

Developed by Altman and Taylor (1973), social penetration theory holds that the development of human relationships is determined by the information we disclose to our partner. The information can be categorized into two dimensions: depth and width. The depth of information represents the hierarchical structure of the messages we exchange in an interaction. It ranges from clichés, facts, opinions, and feelings that illustrate the four stages of relationship development: orientation, exploratory affective exchange, affective exchange, and stable exchange (Altman & Taylor, 1973; Adler & Towne, 1990).

The orientation stage is characterized by clichés that contain stereotypical and superficial information (e.g., expressions such as "how are you?" and "the weather is great today"). This is similar to "cultural information" described by Miller and Sunnafrank (1982). The stage of exploratory affective exchange is characterized by facts and cues from the periphery of our personality (Gudykunst & Ting-Toomey, 1988) (e.g., "I am an international student at this university," and "I am not such a smart person as you think, I just study harder"). A more friendly and relaxed relationship appears in this stage. In the affective exchange stage we begin to feel more comfortable to express our personal opinions (e.g., "I used to think that the Chinese have a funny look, now I have changed my impression after traveling to China last month," and "I really don't like to be with Sato").

Information about central areas of our personality emerges in this stage. Our degree of commitment to the relationship increases. Information disclosed in the exploratory affective and affective exchange stages parallels Miller and Sunnafrank's "sociological information." Finally, an intimate relationship is characterized by the stable exchange stage in which we are freely and fully expressing our feelings (e.g., "I feel very unhappy when I know you are not telling me the truth," and "It is disgusting to see Asians eat the innards of chickens"). Through the disclosure of this "psychological information" we know our partner's traits, feelings, attitudes, and other aspects of personality (Miller & Steinberg, 1975).

The four stages of relationship development explicated by the social penetration model exhibit three characteristics: (1) the relationship is developing from a casual/superficial level to a personal/intimate level; intimacy can't be reached overnight; (2) the movement of the relationship is determined by the degree of self-disclosure; and (3) messages exchanged in the casual/superficial mode have a low degree of depth, but the topics may be broad. However, both depth and width are high in the personal/intimate level of relationship.

## Uncertainty Reduction Theory

Berger (1979) and Berger and Calabrese (1975) developed uncertainty reduction theory to examine the ways we come to know each other in the initial stage of relationship development. Uncertainty refers to our cognitive inability to explain our own or other's feelings and behaviors in interactions because of an ambiguous situation that evokes anxiety. The theory posits that interpersonal relationships develop and progress when we are able to reduce our uncertainty about each other. Therefore, we are constantly seeking to reduce the uncertainty level by exchanging information in the process of relationship development. Berger and Calabrese (1975) proposed seven axioms of uncertainty reduction:

**1.** Given the high level of uncertainty present at the onset of the entry phase, as the amount of verbal communication between strangers increases, the level of uncertainty for each interactant in the relationship will decrease. As uncertainty is further reduced, the amount of verbal communication will increase (pp. 101–102).

**2.** As nonverbal affiliative expressiveness increases, uncertainty levels will decrease in an initial interaction situation. In addition, decreases in uncertainty level will cause increases in nonverbal affiliative expressiveness (p. 103).

**3.** High levels of uncertainty cause increases in information-seeking behavior. As uncertainty levels decline, information-seeking behavior decreases (p. 103).

**4.** High levels of uncertainty in a relationship cause decreases in the intimacy level of communication content. Low levels of uncertainty produce high levels of intimacy (p. 103).

**5.** High levels of uncertainty produce high rates of reciprocity. Low levels of uncertainty produce low reciprocity rates (p. 105).

**6.** Similarities between persons reduce uncertainty, while dissimilarities produce increases in uncertainty (p. 106).

**7.** Increases in the uncertainty level produce decreases in liking; decreases in the uncertainty level produce increases in liking (p. 107).

Three general strategies are used to reduce the uncertainty level in interactions: passive, active, and interactive strategies (Berger, 1979). Passive strategies involve no direct communication between us and those persons who are attractive to us. By using passive strategies we unobtrusively observe the person's behaviors in different situations and collect information that can be used to further know the person. The uncertainty level is then reduced through this indirect strategy. Active strategies do not involve direct interaction with the person with whom we may develop a relationship. Rather, by using active strategies of uncertainty reduction, we begin to more actively gather information about our counterpart by asking persons who know him or her. Neither passive nor active strategies guarantee that the information we gather about our counterparts will be accurate, because we do not directly communicate with them. Finally, interactive strategies involve two activities. First, we directly gather information through verbal interrogation or by asking our counterparts questions about themselves. Second, we open ourselves to our counterparts by disclosing personal information that they do not know. Through asking questions and self-disclosing processes, our counterparts usually feel obliged to reveal something equally important about themselves to us. Information gathered from active strategies tends to be more accurate than from indirect ones.

Lastly, the level of uncertainty is measurable. Gudykunst (1994) developed an instrument that is used to assess the amount of uncertainty we experience when we are communicating with strangers. You can use the questionnaire to asses the amount of uncertainty you generally experience when you communicate with others. Table 6–1 contains the questionnaire.

## TABLE 6–1 Questionnaire for the Assessment of Uncertainty

The purpose of this questionnaire is to help you assess the amount of uncertainty you generally experience when you communicate with strangers. (*Note:* You can determine the amount of uncertainty you experience communicating with a specific person by substituting the person's name for "strangers" in each of the statements.) Respond to each statement by indicating the degree to which the adjectives are applicable when you interact with strangers. If you never have the experience, answer 1 in the space provided; if you almost never have the experience, answer 2; if you sometimes have the experience and sometimes do not, answer 3; if you almost always have the experience, answer 4; if you always have the experience, answer 5.

_____ 1. I am not confident when I communicate with strangers.

_____ 2. I can interpret strangers' behavior when we communicate.

_____ 3. I am indecisive when I communicate with strangers.

_____ 4. I can explain strangers' behavior when we communicate.

_____ 5. I am not able to understand strangers when we communicate.

_____ 6. I know what to do when I communicate with strangers.

_____ 7. I am uncertain how to behave when I communicate with strangers.

_____ 8. I can comprehend strangers' behavior when we communicate.

_____ 9. I am not able to predict strangers' behavior when we communicate.

_____ 10. I can describe strangers' behavior when we communicate.

To find your scores, first reverse the responses for the *even-numbered* items (if you wrote 1, make it 5; if you wrote 2, make it 4; if you wrote 3, leave it as 3; if you wrote 4, make it 2; if you wrote 5, make it 1). Next, add the numbers next to each of the items. Scores range from 10 to 50. The higher your score, the more uncertainty you experience when interacting with others.

*Source:* From W. B. Gudykunst, *Bridging Differences,* copyright © 1994 by Sage Publications. Reprinted by permission of Sage Publications.

## Communication Accommodation Theory

Communication accommodation theory (CAT), developed by Gallois, Franklyn-Stikes, Giles, and Coupland (1988), is used to explain the relationship development in the process of intercultural encounters. CAT combines propositions from speech accommodation theory and ethnolinguistic identity theory to examine the communicative moves interactants make in social and psychological contexts and how it is related to personal characteristics.

CAT is based on three cardinal concepts: convergence, divergence, and maintenance (Bourhis, 1979; Giles, 1973). Convergence refers to the change of our language, vocabulary, speech style, speech rate, or tone of voice to become similar to our interactional partner. It functions to show solidarity, enhance understanding, or seek approval. In contrast to convergence, divergence refers to the emphasis of speech differences between us and our interactional partners. Maintenance refers to the continuing use of our own speech style in interaction with or without reference to our partner's style. In intercultural interaction it is argued that convergence tends to increase attraction between the interactant and divergence tends to inhibit it (Giles & Powesland, 1975). Moreover, Giles and Johnson (1981) proposed that if members of a subordinate ethnic group see language as an important asset of the group, they tend to maintain their speech style in interaction.

CAT delineates three principles of intercultural interaction. First, the initial orientation of intercultural encounter is strongly affected by our personal and social identity, which leads us to view the interaction in certain particular way. However, the situational constraints, such as norms, topics, and competitiveness, of each interaction are likely to change the initial orientation of interactants. Second, during the interaction, we begin to employ different strategies to identify ourselves as speakers or to react to our partners. These strategies may include (1) individual factors, such as stating personal goals (e.g., to seek approval or to promote group solidarity) or sociopsychological orientation to each other (e.g., positive or negative), (2) sociolinguistic and behavioral skills (e.g., interactional management and interpersonal control) in encoding process and labeling the speaker's behavior or making attributions about the speaker's effort and intent in the decoding process. Finally, in the last stage of intercultural interaction we evaluate our own and our partner's behavior to judge whether the interaction is viewed in interpersonal or intergroup terms. This, in turn, will change or reinforce our initial orientation in the next interaction.

## RELATIONSHIP DEVELOPMENT AND CULTURE

Although the framework of the four theories previously discussed tend to be universal across cultures, we must understand that the practice of relationship development is regulated by the cultural variability. For instance, Yum (1988) argued that East Asians are influenced by the doctrines of Confucianism that emphasize social relationships. The influence leads East Asians to develop a very different interpersonal relationship pattern as opposed to the individualistic emphasis of North Americans. Yum classified the differences into five categories of relationship pattern: particularism/universalism, long-term/short-term, ingroup/outgroup, formal/informal, and personal/public relationships.

---

### Research Highlight 6–1

Who: Yum, J. O.

What: "The Impact of Confucianism on Interpersonal Relationships and Communication Patterns in East Asia."

Where: *Communication Monographs, 55,* 1988, 374–388.

Based on the argument that communication is a fundamental social process and it is influenced by the philosophical foundations and value systems of its society, this article examines the philosophical roots of the communication patterns in East Asian countries and their differences from those of North Americans.

The author indicates that the major difference between East Asians and North Americans regarding communication is that East Asians emphasize social relationship while North Americans emphasize individualism. This East Asian emphasis is embedded in the doctrines of Confucianism. Confucian philosophy specifies four principles that affect human nature and motivation: *jen* (humanism), *i* (faithfulness, loyalty, or justice), *li* (propriety, rite, or respect for social forms), and *chih* (wisdom or a liberal education).

The four principles have a great impact on two aspects of human communication, leading to major differences between East Asians and North Americans: interpersonal relationship patterns and communication patterns.

**1.** The impact on interpersonal communication patterns:

a. Eastern Asians orient to particularistic relationships, long-term and asymmetrical reciprocity, sharp distinctions between ingroup and outgroup members, informal intermediaries, and overlapping personal and public relationships.

b. North Americans orient to universalistic relationships, short-term and symmetrical reciprocity or contractual reciprocity, less sharp distinctions between ingroup and outgroup members, contractual intermediaries, and separate personal and public relationships.

**2.** The impact on communication patterns:

a. Eastern Asians emphasize process orientation, differentiated linguistic codes, and indirect communication, and are recipient-centered.

b. North Americans emphasize outcome orientation, less differentiated linguistic codes, and direct communication, and are sender-centered.

## Particularism/Universalism

In a society of particularistic relationship, differences in age, sex, role, or status are maximized, and mutuality and interdependency are encouraged (Condon, 1977). Particularistic relationships are governed by a set of specific communication rules and patterns that provide individuals with directions concerning interactions. Individuals know whom to talk to, when, and how in different situations. Thus, particularistic relationships are established based on the levels of hierarchy and are relatively predictable. For example, because of the hierarchical structure of human relationship, in Japan a close relationship is usually established between those of similar rather than different ages, and they tend to associate with those of the same sex (Cronen & Shuter, 1983; Klopf, 1995). Hwang (1988) and Jocobs (1979) indicated that the particularistic relationship practiced in East Asian countries functions to avoid embarrassing encounters or serious conflicts.

In contrast, the universalistic relationship, especially practiced by North Americans, follows general and objective rules that are applied to various relationships. To North Americans the development of an interpersonal relationship is embedded in the principles of fairness and equality. This is why it is so common to see Americans freely say "hi" or "good morning" to strangers they encounter on the street (Yum, 1988).

## Long-Term/Short-Term Relationships

Long-term relationships foster a complementary social reciprocity in which interpersonal relationship is viewed as asymmetrical and reciprocally obligatory. People always feel indebted to others (Chen & Chung, 1994). For example, according to Shiang (1982), the Chinese always show a deep appreciation and heartily try to find an opportunity to return the favor in the social interaction. Applied to the organizational level, the superior-subordinate relationship reflects a complementary interpersonal relationship in which the superiors always show a holistic and fraternalistic concern to the subordinates. For example, Chung (1992) pointed out that in Taiwan and Japan superiors often try to help subordinate solve their family problems. The Korean concept "uye-ri" and the Japanese "giri," both influenced by Confucianism, also dictate that a permanent and obligatory relationship is a norm of interpersonal relationship development (Yum, 1987).

Short-term and symmetrical reciprocity relationships dominate North Americans' behaviors. They do not treat commitments or obligations as important elements in interpersonal relationship development. Instead, they consider complementary relationship a threat to freedom or autonomy. Hence, it is not surprising to see that North Americans split the bill or "go dutch" when having a dinner together with friends.

---

**Research Highlight 6–2**

Who:    Chen, G. M. & Chung, J.

What:   "The Impact of Confucianism on Organizational Communication."

Where:  *Communication Quarterly, 42,* 1994, 93–105

This essay can be treated as an extension of Yum's (1988) "The Impact of Confucianism on Interpersonal Relationships and Communication Patterns in East Asia." The authors investigate the influence of Confucian thought on organizational communication in the Asian Five Dragons (i.e., Hong Kong, Japan, Singapore, South Korea, and Taiwan).

Four principles of Confucianism having an impact on interpersonal communication and organizational lives in the Asian Five Dragons are explicated: (1) hierarchical relationship—which is comprised of five components: particularistic relationship, complementary social reciprocity, ingroup/outgroup distinction, essential intermediary and formality, and overlap of personal and public relationships; (2) family system—which is comprised of five components: private relationship, paternalistic leadership, harmony is the first virtue, distrust of outgroup members, and loyalty and commitment; (3) Jen—which refers to benevolence, self-discipline, filial piety, brotherly love, and trust, and interweaves with Yi (righteousness) and Li (propriety); and (4) emphasis on education—which seeks to provide without discriminating ethical teachings to everyone.

These principles affect organizational communication in two aspects.

First, they influence management principles. For example, the ideal state of management based on these principles is to develop a secure working environment for all employees in the organization. This kind of humanistic management emphasizes that human nature is mutable, a committed employee can adapt to the changing environment, and mutual understanding between superior and subordinate is a key to organizational success. Leaders must correctly perceive their role and their legitimate authority, and they must be honest to themselves and truthful toward employees. Second, the principles influence relationship and communication. For example, in terms of interpersonal relationships, they emphasize explicit communication rules, complementary relationship, ingroup/outgroup distinction, intermediaries, vague boundaries between personal and public relationships, and similar communication contexts. In the area of organizational life several elements are promoted: uncertainty reduction in organization communication, socioemotional and nonconfrontational communication, team building, lifetime employment, conflict avoidance, consensus building, and facilitation of communication and training.

Finally, the authors develop a preventive communication cost and compensation model to describe the characteristics of Confucianism-influenced organizations. The model delineates six elements: (1) the rule-learning cost is compensated by reduced guesswork and uncertainty; (2) the long-

*Continued*

**Research Highlight 6–2**   *Continued*

term interaction cost is compensated by reduced apprehension and increased liking and mutual respect; (3) the outgroup exclusion cost is compensated by greater motivation; (4) the intermediary cost is compensated by reduced conflict; (5) the personal contact cost is compensated by loyalty and commitment; and (6) the education cost is compensated by reduced misunderstanding and effort at clarification.

## Ingroup/Outgroup Relationships

East Asians tend to develop private relationships by clearly distinguishing ingroup from outgroup members. To East Asians ingroup members' ties are the main sources of similarity and affinity that lead to mutual attraction. For example, the Chinese usually develop a relationship with five types of ingroup members: (1) *Shieh Chin* (blood relationships), including one's own family, relatives outside the household, wife's relatives, and relatives of different surnames, (2) *Ton Shiang* (demographic relationships), including persons from the same geographical area, (3) *Ton Shi* (colleague relationships), including persons working in the same organization, (4) *Shi Shen* (teacher-student relationships) and (5) *Ton Shueh* (classmate relationships). In addition, the Japanese concept of *kaisha* strongly displays an ingroup sense in the organizational life. *Kaisha* refers to "my" or "our" company where one belongs to primarily and is deeply involved in establishing relationship networks (Nakane, 1970).

The boundary between ingroup and outgroup members is not as clearly defined for North Americans, the British, and West Europeans, who are used to establishing relationships of the kind that best fits them. They feel comfortable to be affiliated with a relatively large number of groups. Thus, relationship of this kind of affiliation tend to be brief and change frequently (Condon & Yousef, 1975). Stewart and Bennett (1991) further pointed out that the ability to evoke self- rather than group interest is the key to the development of a relationship with Americans.

## Formal/Informal Relationships

In the vertical cultures with obligatory relationships, like those of East Asia, the process of relationship development is much more formal than that of horizontal cultures. The formality renders East Asians more likely to rely on a go-between or mediator to indirectly initiate a new relationship or to resolve a conflict (Ma, 1992). The practice functions to avoid an embarrassing encounter or losing one's face. Therefore, the use of formal codes of conduct, titles, and honorifics are very common in the social interaction, especially in vocal expression. For example, Japanese, Chinese, and Arabic language systems contain many pronouns and honorifics that are used to indicate the degree of formality and relationship intimacy between the interactants (Condon & Yousef, 1975).

---

**Research Highlight 6–3**

Who:   Ma, R.

What:   "The Role of Unofficial Intermediaries in Interpersonal Conflicts in the Chinese Culture."

Where:   *Communication Quarterly, 40,* 1992, 269–278

Previous studies suggest that a major difference between the Chinese and North American cultures is the "indirect" versus "direct" mode of communication. Indirect communication in East Asia prevents the embarrassment of rejection by the other person and maintains interpersonal harmony. Emphasis on individualism in North American cultures, on the other hand, results in more direct communication. Since social harmony and face saving maintenance are crucial in East Asian societies, communication through intermediaries is expected to be especially functional in situations involving interpersonal conflicts. Intermediaries eliminate face-to-face confrontation and, thereby, reduce the risk of mutual attacking and losing face. The purpose of this research was to study the role of unofficial intermediaries in interpersonal conflicts in the Chinese culture.

Based on interviews conducted in informal settings, this study discovered that in the Chinese culture, the fre-quency of unofficial mediation in interpersonal conflicts remains high. Not only are the concepts of "indirect communication" and "mutual- or other-face maintenance" evident in this study, but there is also suggestion of the close association between indirect communication and the existence of intermediaries. The mediator was usually a friend of the two parties in conflict or an elderly person respected by both. He or she intervened on his or her own initiative or in response to a request by a person other than the two in conflict. In addition, impartiality and face maintenance were perceived as two key factors in successful mediation. Like their Western counterpart, Chinese mediators can transmit information, reduce the impact of tactical rigidities, and make the two parties in conflict reconceptualize their relationship. Although no interviewee in this survey mentioned the monitoring of the execution of a reached agreement as being a responsibility of the intermediary, it was assumed that the intermediary would do so under most circumstances.

The study of intermediaries in East Asian cultures is often crucial to understanding how conflicts are resolved in these cultures. The intermediary approach to interpersonal conflicts tends to be as functional in East Asia as is the assertive approach in North America.

Directly initiating a new relationship characterizes the horizontal cultures in which interactions are usually less formal. Like North Americans, persons of such cultures prefer to use first names in addressing each other and avoid using formal codes of conduct, titles, or honorifics. In addition, the languages used in interpersonal relationships tend to equalize the differences caused by age, sex, or status (Javidi & Javidi, 1991).

## Personal/Public Relationships

The overlap of personal and public relationships characterizes East Asian cultures. East Asians feel more comfortable to have an interaction in a personal or human environment. The vague boundary between personal and public relationships usually creates more contacts for members in a group or organization. The frequent contacts in turn provide a great opportunity for members to identify mutual interests and communication contexts that help to build trust and consensus (Chen & Chung, 1994). The principle of mutual reciprocity makes East Asians believe that a good public relationship will be achieved after a warm personal relationship has been developed (Yum, 1988).

In contrast to East Asians, North Americans tend to clearly separate private and public relationships. The emphasis on privacy, individualism, autonomy, and self-reliance underscores North Americans' anxiety about becoming a member of any group in which public relationships are embedded (Stewart & Bennett, 1991).

Differences in cultural values also affect uncertainty reduction and social penetration processes in the formation of interpersonal bondings. As indicated in Chapter 3, Hall's low- and high-context cultures and Hofstede's collectivism-individualism values are related to uncertainty reduction in the process of relationship development. The differences of high-context/collectivistic and low-context/individualistic cultures in terms of uncertainty reduction strategies include the use of verbal and nonverbal means, background and attitude information, and high or low degree of self-disclosure (Javidi & Javidi, 1991).

### Verbal/Nonverbal Differences

Members of high-context cultures tend to use less verbal communication and more nonverbal cues in the process of relationship development. Because, according Gudykunst (1983) and Hall (1976), information is internalized by the members of high-context cultures, they are also more able to read nonverbal cues and expect their counterparts to read their minds. For example, Gudykunst and Nishida (1984) have confirmed Hall's prediction that the Japanese (high-context culture) show a lower level of self-disclosure and interrogation than Americans (low-context culture) in the process of relationship development. The Japanese also display more nonverbal affiliative messages than Americans (Gudykunst & Nishida, 1984; Okabe, 1983).

### Background and Attitude Information
Because the high-context/collectivistic cultures place an emphasis on the concepts of shame, harmony, and face saving, they tend to be more interested in gathering demographic or background information of their counterparts (Adler, 1991; Nakane, 1984). Members of high-context cultures consider that gathering background information enables them to more effectively predict their counterparts' behaviors. This is a way to avoid unpleasant or embarrassing interactions or unnecessary frictions.

Adler (1991) and Gudykunst (1983) also indicated that members of low-context/individualistic cultures are likely to emphasize internal pressures, as in feelings of guilt and self-respect. In addition, they tend to skip background information and directly seek information about their counterparts' attitudes or opinions regarding different issues in order to reduce the uncertainty level.

### Degree of Self-Disclosure
Members of high-context/collectivistic cultures disclose significantly less than those of low-context/individualistic cultures. Barnlund (1974, 1989) explained that the difference is caused by the emphasis on specific cultural values. For example, the Japanese disclose less because they highly value harmony, group interests, formal relationship, private selves, and nonverbal forms of disclosure, while Americans emphasize informal relationship, personal interests, greater social spontaneity, public selves, and direct verbal expressions.

The degree of self-disclosure reflects the difference in the social penetration process between the two cultures. Gudykunst and Nishida (1986) revealed that in the process of social penetration the Japanese disclose significantly less than Americans in terms of brother, mother, acquaintance, coworker, aunt, employer, colleague, lover, sister, roommate, cousin, grandparent, fiancee, classmate, best friend, father, son, uncle, neighbor, and so on. Chen (1995) also found that Chinese students disclose much less than American students on different conversational topics (i.e., opinions, work, finance, personality, and body), and to target persons (i.e., parents, stranger, acquaintance, and intimate friends).

Furthermore, to Asians successful persons refer to those who know what they are talking about and know how to show honest and positive attitudes in self-disclosure, instead of those who talk more or show more feelings. For example, Chen (1995) found that willingness to disclose oneself in depth and breadth is the key to the development of personal relationship for Westerners. Nevertheless, Asian students, including the Chinese, Indians, Malaysians,

---

### Research Highlight 6–4

Who:   Chen, G. M.

What:   "Differences in Self-Disclosure Patterns Among Americans Versus Chinese: A Comparative Study."

Where:   *Journal of Cross-Cultural Psychology, 26,* 1995, 84–91

The purpose of this study is to examine the different patterns of self-disclosure between the Americans and the Chinese. Based on the theories of individualism versus collectivism and high-context versus low-context cultures and using previous research on American and Chinese communication patterns, the author hypothesizes that significant differences of self-disclosure exist between the Americans and the Chinese in the areas of (1) conversational topics, including opinions, interests, work, finances, personality, and the body, and (2) different target persons, including parents, strangers, acquaintances, and intimate friends.

To test his hypotheses the author collects data from 200 American students and 144 Chinese students by using a revised version of Barnlund's Self-Disclosure Scale. The results from

MANOVA confirm both hypotheses. The overall findings suggest that significant differences exist in the verbal styles of the Americans and the Chinese. Americans consistently show higher level self-disclosure than the Chinese in the two areas explored. In addition, females are found to disclose more than males to intimate friends in both cultures.

This study has two major implications. First, the author attributes the differences in self-disclosure between the two nations to differences in cultural values. The Chinese value the "act" rather than the "talk" in the process of relationship development. Articulation and talkativeness are deemphasized in the Chinese society. In contrast, Americans regard speech as the principal vehicle for exchanging personal experiences and developing interpersonal relationships. Second, the results of the study underscore the reciprocal relationship between culture and communication. In other words, culture not only conditions perceptions of reality but also programs language patterns. What, where, and how we should talk are regulated by culture.

---

Pakistanis, and Thais perceive that consciousness, positiveness, and honesty of self-disclosure are much more important than the depth and breadth of the messages. Studies by Nakanishi (1987), Ogawa (1979), and Wolfson & Pierce (1983) also consistently show that the Chinese and Japanese, compared to Americans, are highly reluctant to initiate conversations with strangers, are hesitant to verbally express themselves, and show more self-restraint in interactions. Mini Case 6–2 demonstrates differences of perception in the process of intercultural relationship.

---

**Mini Case 6–2**

Suzanne, an outgoing, overly friendly sophomore at a woman's college in upstate New York meets Max Huong, a Taiwanese student who is in his third year at nearby Cornell University and is living in the Delta Chi fraternity. Max has been in the United States for two years. When not in school, he lives with a nearby aunt and uncle who have not been in the United States for long and speak very little English. Max and Suzanne begin dating seriously, and Suzanne begins to attend all of Max's outside activities at Cornell, which include cultural get-togethers, discussion groups, and forums on the future of China. Max promises to teach Suzanne Chinese. After nine months of dating, Suzanne invites Max to visit her family outside New York city. Max refuses several times but finally reluctantly agrees. Suzanne's family warmly receives Max. Suzanne's father, who is a great cook, makes dinner while Suzanne gets into an active discussion on civil rights with her mother, who is a civil rights leader. Max sits by, quietly listening. Suzanne notes that Max appears depressed and listless on the return to school. A couple of weeks later Suzanne asks Max if she might meet his uncle and aunt. Max keeps refusing. After a while Max stops calling Suzanne, and the relationship ends.

Why was Max reluctant to bring Suzanne home to his aunt and uncle and why did he finally end a relationship that had obviously been an important one to him?

---

*Source:* Susan Kinney Sereni, University of Rhode Island.

# THIRD-CULTURE BUILDING

Given the influence of cultural variability, the development of relationships in the process of intercultural interaction is much more difficult than in intracultural settings. Scholars in different disciplines have endeavored to propose approaches that can be used to develop an effective and satisfactory intercultural relationship. For example, the cultural synergy model asserts that a successful intercultural relationship is based on the effort of culturally different interactants to achieve a common goal. This collaborative effort requires the culturally different persons to recognize and be alert to similarities and differences among their cultures (Adler, 1980; Moran & Harris, 1982). Through the dynamic process of cultural synergy, intercultural interactants can achieve not only the sum but more than the sum of each culture's possibilities (Stauffer, 1982).

The idea of cultural synergy contributes to the development of the third-culture building model. According to Casmir (1993) and Shuter (1993), the third-culture building model assumes that, in the process of intercultural relationship development, participants should and can develop a third culture by mutually negotiating their cultural differences. This negotiating process involves the effort of adapting and converging the different cultural values and the reconfiguration of interactants' cultural identity. The dynamic process of third-culture building is interactive and benefits both parties.

According to Starosta and Olorunnisola (1995), the third-culture development model represents an idealized view of the process of intercultural relationship development which comprises five phases that occur in chronological and cyclic order: intrapersonal intracultural communication, interpersonal intercultural communication, rhetorical intercultural communication, metacultural communication, and intracultural communication.

## Intrapersonal Intracultural Communication

In the phase of intrapersonal intracultural communication all intercultural interactions begin at the *unilateral awareness* stage, which involves persons who are aware of the others' cultural groups and who operate from a motive such as curiosity or need or the wish to influence another person in a way that better serves the mutual interest of the two parties. It follows that an individual may become aware of other persons from educational exchange, a tour of business abroad, a newscast, by greeting a new neighbor, or while preparing a film documentary. Impression formation of persons of other cultures and ethnicities at this stage requires intrapersonal study. At the earliest stages, unilateral awareness is probably an out-of-awareness process, until a general or specific purpose such as information gathering, courtship, or a business transaction begins to take shape.

With the movement of the relationship development toward the stage of *unilateral presentation,* traces of a need or a motive to interact across cultures emerge. This stage involves a telephone call for information, a letter, presentation of credentials, an appointment, catching someone's attention at a gathering, the viewing of a foreign travelogue, or some action that introduces a particular member of one culture to a member of the other. While a face-to-face interaction between two individuals is likely, it is equally possible, for example, that because Bluefield, Nicaragua, or Shanghai, China, is designated a "sister city" to Washington, D.C., a committee from one locale initiates written contact with persons from the other nation.

If the early stages of interaction indicate that the presenter's motive is potentially realistic (friendship, profit, love, peace, more meaningful existence in close geographic proximity, cooperation toward a goal), unilateral presentation inclines the presenter toward further contact. If the contrary proves true, the presenter asks whether the seeming failure resulted from idiosyncrasies of the recipient, some aspect of the message, insensitivity to features of the culture, or other out-of- awareness factors. Since the recipient is viewed as culturally distinct and therefore less known than a member of the presenter's culture, a wider variety of possible explanations confronts the presenter than is the case for interaction with a "known" person, that is, a member of presenter's own culture.

## Interpersonal Intercultural Communication

The interpersonal intercultural communication phase begins at the stage of *inquiry,* when the presenter begins to seek out information about the recipient as a cultural being to assign meanings more accurately between group-based and individual-based meanings. Is there a more favored means to initiate contact than the one chosen? Is business conducted between strangers, or only between persons who have come to know each other in social settings? Is a mediator or a broker needed to "translate" the meanings of the presenter to the recipient of the other culture? How long is "long enough" when an anticipated response has not transpired? Will a certain overture or idea "make sense" within the framework of the recipient's culture?

The *reciprocation* stage occurs when the presenter somehow invites the recipient more fully into a conscious process of interaction. This is done by approaching the recipient in a way that calls attention to itself and asking the recipient to become a message initiator as well. As is true for all communication, offering to involve the other party in interaction places the initiator at risk: The recipient may ignore the request, respond negatively, seek information about the message initiator, make some demands upon the initiator, or may respond more or less positively to the initiator of the message, that is, in a way that is congruent with the wish or expectation of the initiator.

A "positive response" invites further interaction and may have the effect that the second party will move through the three stages already traveled by the originator. All other responses may have at least a temporary cooling effect upon future interaction. They may cause the originator to end the exchange, to take stock, to provide further information about needs or motives, or to devise another avenue of approach. With reciprocation the model moves from a largely intrapersonal level, that is, a phase within which the communication occurs predominantly within a single entity, to an interpersonal level.

By the time of reciprocation, the recipient has used available information to size up motives for contact. During the *mutual adjustment* stage, any appearance of intent on the part of the initiator to exploit, colonize, or to otherwise diminish the recipient may end the progression toward third-culture building and truncate the development of a third culture. Reciprocation at this point does not guarantee the progress of the model/process of third-culture building. It is useful to view reciprocation as a stage in which the recipient of "advances" engages the initiator in a process of imputing of motives other makes the effort to develop a relationship. During the stage of mutual adjustment, a neutral or positive disposition toward the initiator indicates that person B shares the aspirations of person A or sees the possibility of satisfying a separate agenda from that of A. Whether there is a unified agenda or not, the process can comfortably continue, with both parties recognizing that they are in the relationship to satisfy different needs.

Mutual adjustment is thus a stage for identifying a mutual agenda, wherein both parties agree to confer salience on a common slate of concerns. It marks the identification of complementary or identical purposes sufficient to continue to sustain efforts at mutual interaction. Thus, the commencement of mutual adjustment is the genesis of a deliberate attempt by both parties to kindle a relationship.

Essential also to the level of mutual adjustment is a convergence in understanding among participants of the essential aspects of the negotiation. Cultural differences are still strong enough, and the other sufficiently unknown, to lead to variant interpretations of matters of importance such as expected roles. To maximize convergence of meaning requires extensive feedback and a minimal level of mutual disclosure and openness.

## Rhetorical Intercultural Communication

Reaching the phase of *rhetorical intercultural communication,* the two parties have begun to consider not only their own cultural perspective but have also taken steps to render explicit many of the aspects of their respective cultures that will be called into play during this and future deliberations. The awareness of differences has become more conscious, and the parties have accepted that such differences are simply alternative perspectives, not to be judged in terms of their own respective cultures. When two preconditions, namely, a conscious awareness of cultural differences and a willingness to suspend ethnocentric judgments of the other's ways, have been met, some of the values, beliefs, operating assumptions, linguistic preferences, paralinguistic elements, and thinking patterns of each interactant begin to seem preferable to the other. The stage at which the interactants consciously begin to assign positive values to some of the features of each other's cultures is that of Convergence.

*Convergence* is based on information provided by the interactants at the mutual adjustment level. The communicants negotiate the creation of a third perspective that reflects replacements, modifications, adjustments, and abandonment of selected aspects of the original cultures. It is necessary to note the emotional sensitivity of this process and to stress the possibility that interactants will see the cultural indices being negotiated as "ledger items" that have to be "balanced." Yet, the development of a vibrant third culture demands that this level not be reduced to that of enumerating individual gains and losses. What is important is the scrutinizing of all differing tolerances in light of heightened joint awareness. Areas of similarities must likewise be identified during mutual movement toward the end of finding common substance in a third realm. The process of negotiating pragmatic aspects of cultural behavior is necessarily rhetorical, i.e., it provides a conjoint rationale for action.

*Integration* is the level where all patterns of agreement arrived at are integrated into a new body of cultural indices that will embody the third culture. The new cultural indices result from the revised attitudes, mores, and values of the two earlier cultures that become unattractive as behavioral options once third-culture thinking begins to govern patterns of interaction. Above all, the integration level fine-tunes areas of apparent overlap, oversight, and omission that block the evolution of the third culture in a pure state. Because this is still an incompletely informed stage of culture building, further modifications will occur in subsequent stages once abstract formulations undergo practical testing.

## Metacultural Communication

The stages to this point have concentrated on symbolic interchange and reinterpretation and on initial attempts at co-action. At the *readjustment/reinforcement* stage of the phase of metacultural communication, interactants begin to test aspects of the newly negotiated culture for viability. They begin to practice, in behavioral applications, the agreements of role, process, and substance that were mutually adopted, to discover whether these new processes can accomplish what was hoped for them with efficiency and with a certain level of satisfaction. Balance then becomes relevant in this stage because the achievement of a balance will reduce the possibility of deviations from agreed norms and ward off disintegrative tendencies once they are identified.

It is the need for balance that necessitates the suggestion of reinforcement as an added dimension of the third-culture model. The tender nature of the formation at this point requires that permanent features rearing their heads be protected from the contamination of confusion or reversion to any of the cultures on the way to dissipation. Reinforcement here means the restriction of information that may be inconsistent with the beliefs, values, and attitudes that the third culture proposes to maintain.

By the stage of *mutual assimilation,* a section of the renegotiated modality of interaction has become permanent enough to perpetuate itself naturally. What develops from this is the creation of a self-sustaining synthesis that attains its own uniqueness while transcending the differences of the two cultures that have been fused into one. The resulting oneness of the third culture produces a symmetry that is characteristically different.

## Intracultural Communication

The final step is the intracultural phase, which is represented by the stage of *primary culture abandonment.* Here, person A and person B adopt the newly formed meta-identity as a perfected primary culture that will govern subsequent interactions. Whether the relationship is intergroup, intercultural, or international, the primary culture becomes a pattern of interaction, coexistence, living, and/or bilateral negotiations, that governs the patterns of socialization of the interactants. This new pattern then becomes a legacy that is handed down to subsequent generations of participants and marks a new level of intracultural communication.

## RECAP

We develop relationships to meet the social needs of inclusion, control, and affection. The ways to perceive and fulfill social needs vary from culture to culture. This chapter deals with intercultural relationship development. Human relationship has five characteristics: (1) it is dynamic, (2) it is hierarchical, (3) it is reciprocal, (4) it is unique, and (5) it is interdependent and irreplaceable.

This chapter provides three models, developed by Berger and Calabese (1975), Devito (1992), and Chen (1995), to explain the developmental process of human relationship. Four theories of human relationship development are also discussed, including social exchange theory, social penetration theory, uncertainty reduction theory, and communication accommodation theory.

Yum's (1988) five categories of relationship are used to illustrate the impact of cultural variability on relationship development. The five categories are particularism/universalism, long-term/short-term, ingroup/outgroup, formal/informal, and personal/public relationships. The influence of cultural value differences, in terms of high-context/low-context cultures and collectivism/individualism, are also discussed from the following perspectives: verbal/nonverbal differences, background and attitude information, and the degree of self-disclosure.

Finally, based on Starosta and Olorunnisola's (1995) study, a third-culture-building model of intercultural relationship development is delineated, and the five phases of third-culture building are explicated: intrapersonal intracultural communication, interpersonal intercultural communication, rhetorical intercultural communication, metacultural communication, and intracultural communication.

## RETHINK

Scholars in the area of human relationship development face two research problems. First, although research on intracultural relationship development is abundant intercultural studies are scarce. Because of the involvement of culture, the process of intercultural relationship development becomes much more complex. Although the theories discussed in this chapter tend to describe universal characteristics of the process of human relationship development, the behaviors may differ in terms of cultural variability. It is important for scholars to examine cultural impact in each stage of relationship development.

Second, although third-culture building continues to gain popularity in the study of intercultural relationship development, it is conceptually weak in three respects. First, as Belay (1993) points out, the third-culture-building model fails to provide "a consistent conceptual framework for either understanding intercultural discord or designing strategies for its resolution" (p. 440). Future research efforts must try to capture the complexity of the interdependence of intercultural interaction. Second, the third-culture-building model claims to explain relationship development at different interactional levels, including person to person, group to group, organization to organization, and nation to nation. The scope and heuristic power of the model to make this application have yet to be demonstrated. Further conceptual explications are needed to justify the claim. Finally, scholars have yet to show how a third culture is built in a multicultural society.

Significantly, the third-culture model derives from a view of the world according to which interactants produce cultures, whereas other models propose that interactions are determined by the participants' preexisting cultural identities. It is possible that the conflicting notions of "cultural identity" and "third culture" will stand in the way of a unified body of theory explaining relationship development across cultures.

## QUESTIONS FOR DISCUSSION

1. What are the characteristics of human relationship?
2. Compare the relationship development models developed by Devito, Knapp and Vangelisti, and Chen.
3. Compare and critique the following theories of relationship development: social exchange theory, social penetration theory, and uncertainty reduction theory.
4. Discuss the five categories of relationship patterns proposed by Starosta and Olorunnisola.
6. Explain the weakness of the third-culture-building model.

# ▶ Chapter 7

## Intercultural Conflict Management

### *Objectives*

Upon completion of this chapter, you will

- Understand the nature and types of intercultural conflict management.
- Understand the influence of culture on conflict and conflict management.
- Understand the determinants of conflicts.
- Know how to effectively manage intercultural conflicts.

> *Heaven and earth are opposites, but their action is concerted. Man and woman are opposites, but they strive for union. All beings stand in opposition to one another: what they do takes on order thereby. Great indeed is the effect of the time of opposition—BOOK OF CHANGES*

Traditionally, communication scholars have treated conflicts or opposition as an inherent evil. They worry that conflicts or opposition are irrational confrontations that bring only destructiveness and weaken relationships. Our position is based on an understanding of conflict that is grounded in Chinese texts. Our view, however, is that conflict is a practical necessity of intercultural interaction. Conflict and opposition pervade human life. People inevitably encounter the need to manage conflicts and to reconcile oppositions that stem, in part, from cultural differences.

In the spirit of the *Book of Changes,* if we understand the nature of conflicts or opposition, they can be rendered productive for the development of intercultural relationships. As expressed in the *Book of Changes,* the Chinese assume that opposition and fellowship are coproduced by time (Wilhelm, 1979). Because everything we know is moving toward opposites, it is important for us to see the opposites as changing states rather than enduring conditions and to develop a positive attitude toward opposition, or the reconciliation of conflicts. Our task as communicators is to guide ourselves through oppositions to a point of mutually satisfying outcomes. This view is elaborated in Buber's (1958) "dialogic" approach toward human relationship. In his book *I and Thou* Buber stressed the creative bond between person and person. He asserted that an individual attains his or her identity in order to relate to other beings. We exist only inasmuch as we exist with other beings. In other words, through "mutable dialogue" we can go beyond opposition or conflicts and link ourselves to the other.

## THE NATURE OF CONFLICT

Conflict permeates relationship development. It refers to a disagreement between or among persons in an interdependent relationship in which they try to meet each other's social needs while, in many cases, pursuing some instrumental goal. A disagreement can occur when the interdependent parties face incompatible goals, resources, decision making, and behaviors. For example, a group of American students and Chinese students were asked how they perceive the meaning of conflicts (Chen, Ryan, & Chen, 1992). When the key words used to describe conflicts are compared (see Table 7–1), the results show a very similar perception between the two groups. Members of both groups conceive of conflict as a negative phenomenon that affects their internal reactions and their external behaviors. Of the two groups, Chinese subjects put more emphasis on internal reactions and nonverbal cues, choosing terms such as "silence" and "horse face" (i.e., facial expression showing unhappy feeling).

In addition, conflicts usually engender negative feelings in the warring parties. Chen et al. (1992) also describe how the feelings of Americans and Chinese differ when they are in conflict situations. Table 7–2 lists those feelings in the order expressed by the two groups of people. The results strongly suggest that unpleasant feelings are universal in a conflict situation for both groups of people, with only slight differences. That is, Americans feel more challenged in a conflict situation, while the Chinese tend to feel more avoidant.

**TABLE 7-1** **Perceived Meanings of Conflict**

| Americans | Chinese |
|---|---|
| 1. Disagreement | 1. Different Opinion |
| 2. Argument | 2. Fight |
| 3. Different Opinion | 3. Incompatible Goal |
| 4. Dispute | 4. Disagreement |
| 5. Fight | 5. Dispute |
| 6. Incompatible Goal | 6. Silence |
| 7. Discussion/Negotiation | 7. Lack of Communication |
| 8. Confrontation | 8. Stubborn |
| 9. Disruption | 9. Horse Face |
| 10. Friction | 10. Dissatisfaction |
| 11. Stress | 11. Misunderstanding |

Commonly, differences in cultural beliefs and values can lead to a misinterpretation of another's intention or behavior that usually increases the potential for conflict among persons. Thus, to turn conflicts in our favor we have to learn how to convert their negative impact—the feelings of anger, hurt, disappointment, and resentment—into a positive impact. Mini Case 7-1 shows how negative feelings can arise between two people because of different cultural beliefs.

**TABLE 7-2** **American and Chinese Feelings in Conflict Situations**

| Americans | Chinese |
|---|---|
| 1. Angry | 1. Angry |
| 2. Frustrated | 2. Furious |
| 3. Upset | 3. Emotional |
| 4. Irritated | 4. Upset |
| 5. Stressed | 5. Sad |
| 6. Bothered | 6. Unhappy |
| 7. Confused | 7. Stop Contacting |
| 8. Threatened | 8. Try to Solve It |
| 9. Hostile | 9. Try to Calm Down |
| 10. Aggressive | 10. Disappointed |
| 11. Uncomfortable | 11. Disturbance |
| 12. Challenged | 12. Depressed |

**Mini Case 7–1**

An American student from a prominent college wishes to study abroad in France. Part of the exchange program entails living with a French family for two months to learn more about the culture hands-on. The student can speak enough French to communicate fluently. The family does not speak English. She wakes up every morning and showers before going to school. The student begins to sense some tension between her and the family. One morning she overheard them talking about how odd her morning ritual was, but she cannot make out why.

Why does the French family find this so odd?

*Source:* Kimberly Skernich, University of Rhode Island.

## *Types of Conflict*

Conflicts occur at different levels of awareness, and with differing degrees of risk. The simultaneous presence of two or more "incompatible" factors that conflict may be felt at each of several levels: intrapersonal conflict, interpersonal conflict, intergroup conflict, and interorganizational conflict.

*Intrapersonal conflict,* or *intrasubjective conflict,* refers to the different and incompatible or contradictory mental states or needs and desires existing in our mind (Zaharna, 1989, 1991). This sort of conflict may be caused by frustration due to our inability to attain a goal or to "goal conflict," in which we can only attain a single goal with the exclusion of the other possible goals. Andrew and Baird (1989) explored three types of role conflict: (1) approach-approach conflict—in which we must select one of two attractive but mutually exclusive goals, (2) approach-avoidance conflict—in which we must choose a goal that contains both attractive and unattractive characteristics, and (3) avoidance-avoidance—in which we must choose either of two unattractive and mutually exclusive goals.

*Interpersonal conflicts* occur between two persons when they are competing for scarce resources. For example, two persons are vying for the hand of one man or woman in the process of relationship development, competing for the top grade in the class, or pursuing the same position in an organization.

*Intergroup conflicts* occur when two work, cultural, or social groups seek to maximize their own goals without locating perceptual congruities. In the United States, such conflicts may end up being solved by third-party arbitrators or by the courts. To manage intergroup conflicts we must be mindful enough to understand the other's group membership, and to recognize how our expectations for other groups members affect our communication (Gudykunst, Ting-Toomey, Sudweeks, & Stewart, 1995).

While members of organizations often engage in intergroup conflicts, the organizations themselves also may enter such disputes in pursuit of various needs (Folger, Poole, & Strutman, 1993; Putnam & Poole, 1987). For example, organizations like IBM, APPLE, GM, and Toyota may engage in *interorganizational conflict* when they are acting cooperatively to develop new products or are competing for a larger market share.

This chapter considers conflict between two persons from different cultural backgrounds as its focus. The following sections discuss the influence of culture on conflict management and resolution.

## CULTURAL INFLUENCE ON CONFLICT MANAGEMENT

Our discussion of culture's influence on conflict and conflict management focuses on three areas: thinking patterns, language barriers, and cultural context.

### Thinking Patterns

*Thinking patterns* refer to forms of reasoning and approaches to problem solution. Thinking patterns differ from culture to culture. A logical, reasonable argument in one culture may be considered as illogical and undemonstrated in another culture.

In general, for example, many Westerners emphasize logic and rationality. They believe that objective truth exists "out there," waiting to be discovered by us and that our process of discovery must follow a linear sequence. In contrast, some Easterners and many sub-Saharan Africans believe that truth will not be found by following the Western approach. Instead, truth will manifest itself without employing any logical consideration or rationality (Porter & Samovar, 1982), or the way best to construct arguments may be nonlinear. Thinking patterns affect not only the way we communicate in our culture but also the way we interact with people from different cultures.

More specifically, Kaplan (1970) explained the differences of thinking patterns that are reflected in five different language systems: English, Semitic, Oriental, Romance, and Russian. According to Kaplan, the thinking pattern of English speakers is predominantly linear in the language sequence. The linear pattern can take either inductive or deductive reasoning. Inductive reasoning consists of three steps: (1) it starts with a central idea, (2) it relates the central idea to all the other ideas, and (3) it employs the appropriate relationship between the central idea and the other ideas to make an argument or a proof. Deductive reasoning employs a reverse procedure by first stating the various principles and then relating them to cases.

The thinking patterns of the Semitic languages (including Arabic) are characterized by a more intuitive and affective reasoning process. The structure of the Semitic languages is based on a series of positive and negative parallel constructions. This kind of parallel construction embedded in the Semitic languages shows a great degree of flexibility, which is demonstrated by the intensive use of conjunctions and sentence connectors. Degree of coordination then becomes the criterion on which the maturity of style in the Semitic languages is based.

Oriental thinking patterns (especially Chinese and Korean) are marked by an approach of "indirection." The writing style of Oriental languages is characterized by creating the subject with a variety of tangential viewpoints, and creating a cyclical movement in which the subject is never mentioned directly. In other words, the ideas in the writing are developed "in terms of what they are not, rather than in terms of what they are" (p. 10). For example, a reporter for a Western newspaper who was stationed in Japan said if he reported on the Prime Minister's speech so that it read sequentially for a Western reader, then it was no longer faithful to the speech.

Although the sentence arrangement of Romance languages (e.g., French and Spanish) is the same as English, with both following the subject-verb-object order, they allow greater freedom for digression or introduction of extraneous materials into the conversation. This digressing pattern of thought shows that the Romance-language speakers tend to be more inner-oriented than their English-speaking counterparts and to rely more on feelings and expectations in their behavior and judgment.

Finally, the structure of the Russian language is completely different from that of English. Russian is "made up of a series of presumably parallel constructions and a number of subordinate structures" that are often irrelevant to the central statement (p. 13). The reasoning pattern behind the Russian language is similar to the method of deduction (Glenn & Glenn, 1981). According to Glenn, English translations of United Nations speeches inductively mentioned the presenter, whereas Russian speeches deductively stressed the proposition itself. Patience and perseverance become critical in dealing with Russian arguments.

Pribrim (1949) further distinguished four patterns of thinking that prevail in the Western world: universalistic reasoning, nominalistic or hypothetical reasoning, intuitional or organismic reasoning, and dialectical reasoning.

The universalistic reasoning pattern is strongly dominated by the principle of identity of thinking and being. It supposes that a hierarchical system of rigid concepts is inherent in and can be directly proved by the human mind. This pattern is attributed to the French, Mediterraneans, and most of urban Latin America (Condon & Yousef, 1975).

The nominalistic or hypothetical reasoning pattern rejects the principle of identity of thinking and being. Instead, it emphasizes induction and empiricism. Everything is a free creations of the human mind by way of abstraction. In other words, thinking is dominated by hypothetical concepts. Through knowledge based on our sense perceptions and freely formed concepts we are able to discover the general truth. Anglo-Saxon countries are characterized by this pattern.

The intuitional or organismic reasoning pattern blends the universalistic and nominalistic reasoning patterns. It denies the existence of innate ideas but assumes that, with the assistance of the insight of the human mind, we are able to attribute knowledge to the general truth. This pattern places more emphasis on intuition and the unity of the whole and the parts than do the inductive or deductive systems. It is dominant in Germany and Slavic Central European countries and is characteristic of the writing of Max Weber about bureaucracy, for example.

The dialectical reasoning pattern also denies the principle of the existence of innate ideas. Like the universalistic reasoning pattern, it assumes that our mind can fully understand the universe and discover the general truth. However, this pattern dictates that the explanations for all phenomena and events must follow the evolutionary process of thesis, antithesis, and synthesis. Most Marxism-related thinking applies this pattern. A common sub-Saharan African mode of thinking and reasoning recognizes essential similarities in experience by using illustrations and applications that draw an argument forward in spirals, returning again and again to some of the same points, but from different perspectives. These spirals are often anchored in oral traditions, folklore, or personal experience. Some writers propose that the discovery of recurring themes in daily experience through the application of sayings and parables also characterizes the speech of African Americans.

Finally, Ishii (1982) described the reasoning process of Westerners as a line and that of non-Westerners as a progression of dots. In a communication situation, the linear thinking pattern leads people to shift from information already stated to information about to be given in order to let the listener understand the speaker. In contrast, the non-linear thinking pattern leads people, like the Japanese, to jump from idea to idea on the important points without paying attention to details. This happens especially in the communication between persons who know each other well (Klopf, 1995). Thus, we understand that each culture has a characteristic, if not universal, pattern of thought. The learning of cultural differences in terms of thinking patterns helps to avoid many interactional conflicts.

## Language Barriers

Language is one of the main elements that clearly distinguishes one culture from another. It is the most important vehicle we use to encode messages. In the process of communication if we cannot speak another's language, immediately we reach an impasse. All the components of language, including vocabulary, syntax, dialects, slang, argot, and idioms, contribute to difficulties of understanding. As mentioned in Chapter 4, language and culture depend on one another; language depends on culture, and our culture derives from language use. Language affects the way we think, our attitudes, our behavior. Our inability to understand each other verbally may lead us to avoid others or to place a lower value on another's ideas.

In addition to problems derived from differences in linguistic symbols, phonemic structures, and rules that govern the language, we experience three major language barriers in intercultural communication: verbal communication styles, variant meanings, and the adaptive functions of language.

We choose from a repertoire of cultural styles that are commonplace among those of our culture. Through verbal communication styles we express our intentions and wishes to attain the goal we seek to reach. We form our verbal communication styles during the early stages of language acquisition. Thus, our verbal communication styles reflect and embody the beliefs and worldviews of our culture. People from different cultural backgrounds will show diverse styles of verbal expressions. When we try to use our verbal communication styles in another culture, conflicts are likely to occur (Kochman, 1982; Patton, 1986). One way to examine verbal communication styles is to identify direct and indirect patterns.

While the direct verbal communication style refers to verbal messages we use to show our intentions in the process of conversations, the indirect verbal communication style refers to verbal messages we use to camouflage and to conceal our true intentions (Gudykunst & Ting-Toomey, 1988). Persons from low-context cultures may use direct verbal communication style, whereas those from high-context cultures tend to use indirect verbal communication styles.

Four features characterize the direct verbal communication style: (1) The situational context is not emphasized; (2) important information usually occurs in explicit verbal messages; (3) self-expression, verbal fluency, and eloquent speech are valued; and (4) people are likely to express directly their opinions and intentions in persuading others to accept their viewpoints. Indirect verbal communication styles also have four features: (1) Explicit verbal messages are not emphasized; (2) important information is usually carried in contextual cues (e.g., place, time, situation, and relationship); (3) harmony is highly valued, with a tendency to use ambiguous language and keep silent in interactions; and (4) people tend to talk around the point, and to avoid saying "no" directly to others (Hall, 1975).

North Americans typically orient to the direct verbal communication style, and most Asians to the indirect verbal communication style. For example, Okabe (1983) indicated that Americans select explicit words and categorical words such as "certainly," "absolutely," and "positively" in interactions, while Japanese tend to use implicit and ambiguous words and to prefer less assertive expressions such as "maybe," "perhaps," and "somewhat." Hsu (1981) reported that North Americans teach children to be self-expressive. The emphasis leads the children to be more confident in interactions and more independent of the group's restraint. By contrast, Chinese children are taught to deemphasize self-expression, which anchors them more firmly within group patterns. They may suppress their personal desire to achieve an independent goal. Park (1979) likewise pointed out that Koreans tend to use a more indirect communication style in the daily conversation in order to keep group harmony. Compared to Americans, Koreans use fewer negative expressions like "no" and other expressions of disagreement. Mini Case 7-2 illustrates a conflict between people of two different cultures.

## Cultural Context

The two types of cultural contexts described by Hall (1976), high-context and low-context cultures, influence the way people handle conflicts. According to Ting-Toomey (1985), high-context cultures emphasize "we," whereas low-context cultures emphasize "I." Low-context cultures value "individual orientations, overt communication codes, and maintain a heterogeneous normative structure with low cultural demand/low cultural constraint characteristics." High-context cultures value "group-identity orientation, covert communication codes, and maintain a homogeneous normative structure with high cultural demand/high cultural constraint characteristics" (p. 76).

Low-context cultures display several characteristics in a conflict situation: (1) Individuals perceive the causes of conflict as instrumental; (2) conflicts occur when a person's normative expectations of the situation are violated; (3) individuals assume a confrontational, direct attitude toward conflicts; and (4) the persons tend to use factual-inductive or axiomatic-deductive styles of conflict management. In contrast, in high-context cultures: (1) Individuals perceive the causes of conflict as expressive; (2) conflicts occur when collective or cultural normative expectations of the situation are violated; (3) individuals assume a non-confrontational, indirect attitude toward conflicts; and (4) they use an affective-intuitive style of conflict management (Ting-Toomey, 1985).

Culture also affects the selection of a conflict style. Hsu (1953) indicated that the Chinese give more attention to context and less to individual feelings,

---

**Mini Case 7–2**

John, a Korean American, and his American girlfriend, Rachel, decide to marry. When John tells his Korean mother, who is divorced, that he and his future bride will be getting their own place, his mother gets very upset. She is mad and blames Rachel for influencing his decision. Rachel is confused about John's mother's reaction.

Why is John's mother upset over the news that John and Rachel will be getting their own place?

---

*Source:* Heather Heater, University of Rhode Island.

## Research Highlight 7–1

Who:    Ting-Toomey, S.

What:    "Intercultural Conflict Style: A Face-Negotiation Theory."

Where:    In Y. Y, Kim & W. B. Gudykunst (Eds.) (1988), *Theories in Intercultural Communication* (pp. 213–235). Newbury Park, CA: Sage.

The purpose of this article is to examine the impact of culture on the relationship between face maintenance and intercultural conflict styles. The author introduces basic assumption of the face-negotiation process, reviews relevant cross-cultural studies on conflict styles, presents basic axioms of face-negotiation theory, and enumerates twelve theoretical propositions regarding conflict face-negotiation.

In this article face maintenance is illustrated graphically by means of a two-dimensional grid, with the first axis containing positive face and negative face and the second axis containing self-face concern and other-face concern. Applied to individualistic/low-context cultures (I/LC) and. collectivistic/high-context cultures (C/HC), the face-negotiation process of intercultural conflict styles can be summarized as follows:

**1.** In terms of face identity.

   a. I/LC—emphasize "I" identity.
   b. C/HC—emphasize "we" identity.

**2.** In terms of face concern.

   a. I/LC—concern self-face.
   b. C/HC—concern other-face.

**3.** In terms of face-maintenance need.

   a. I/LC—emphasize autonomy, dissociation, and negative-face need.

   b. C/HC—emphasize inclusion, association, positive-face need.

**4.** In terms of suprastrategy of facework.

   a. I/LC—emphasize self-positive-face and self-negative-face.
   b. C/HC—emphasize other-positive-face and other-negative-face.

**5.** In terms of facework mode.

   a. I/LC—orient to direct mode.
   b. C/HC—orient to indirect mode.

**6.** In terms of facework style.

   a. I/LC—orient to controlling, confrontation, and solution styles.
   b. C/HC—orient to obliging, avoidance, and affective styles.

**7.** In terms of facework strategy.

   a. I/LC—tend to use distributive or competitive strategies.
   b. C/HC—tend to use integrative or collaborative strategies.

**8.** In terms of the speech act in the facework process.

   a. I/LC—tend to use direct speech act.
   b. C/HC—tend to use indirect speech act.

**9.** In terms of nonverbal acts in the facework process.

   a. I/LC—tend to employ individualistic nonverbal acts and direct emotional expressions.
   b. C/HC—tend to employ contextualistic nonverbal acts and indirect emotional expressions.

*Continued*

---

**Research Highlight 7–1**  *Continued*

Finally, the author stipulates five implications based on the face-negotiation theory delineated in this article: (1) the theory can be applied to intercultural conflict situations; (2) the theory can be applied to study the uncertainties of facework in intercultural communication situations; (3) the theory can be applied to intercultural communication that demands a high degree of politeness; (4) the theory can be applied to different types of speech acts; and (5) the theory can be associated with other variables, such as compliance-gaining and communication competence.

---

while Americans center more on persons and display more feelings. Nomura and Barnlund (1983) discovered that the Japanese tend to show less dissatisfaction than do Americans in communication. North Americans were also found to be more explicit than the Chinese in conflict situations (Ma 1990, 1991).

Members of low-context cultures tend to adopt direct and confrontational conflict styles, as opposed to the indirect and avoidance styles adopted by high-context members (Chua & Gudykunst, 1987; Ting-Toomey, 1988). A study conducted by Ting-Toomey, Trubisky, and Nishida (1989) also found that Americans use a dominating style, an integrating style, and a compromising style more than the Japanese do, and the Japanese use an avoidance style more than Americans do. Studies from Lindin (1974), Schneider (1985), Wolfson & Norden (1984), and Yang ( 1978) all provided similar findings that the use of a confrontational versus a nonconfrontational conflict style reflects a major difference in communication style between the Chinese and the Americans. The differences between Western and Oriental people in conflict styles are attributed to cultural differences (Becker, 1986; Oliver, 1961; Yum, 1988).

Sometimes, when a communication situation seems to call for a message, differences in directness of style can lead communicators to misinterpret each other's intentions and meanings. Either they may believe a message was sent, when none was intended, or they may give a message a level of meaning that differs from the original intent (Starosta, 1973). It is probable that persons from high- and low-context cultures routinely misunderstand one another's "noncommunication." Info 7–1 illustrates the different conflict styles between high-context (i.e., Japan) and low-context cultures (i.e., the United States).

## DETERMINANT FACTORS OF CONFLICTS

Ten factors more or less affect how we involve, manage, or choose styles of conflicts. Although the degree of emphasis on these factors may vary by culture, we find that they commonly exist in all societies. The ten factors include

## Info 7–1

Norrie Kobayashi and Kentaro Ebiko both grew up in Japan. They came to the United States three years ago, and met while in college. They have been dating for seven months. Norie plans to become a nurse, and Kentaro hopes to begin a business career in the United States and later return to Japan.

*Question:* According to researchers, there are considerable differences between the way conflicts are dealt with in the United States and Japan. Do you agree?

*Kentaro:* Definitely. In the U.S.A. being direct and expressive is very important. In Japan, just the opposite is true. You almost never talk about conflicts there, at least not openly.

*Question:* If people don't talk about conflicts, how do they resolve them?

*Kentaro:* Sometimes they don't. In Japan the tradition is not to show your emotions. Outside appearances are very important. If you're upset, you still act as if everything is okay. So there are lots of times when you might be disappointed or angry with somebody and they would never know it.

*Question:* Do conflicts ever get expressed?

*Kentaro:* They aren't discussed openly, assertively very often. But in Japan a lot more is communicated nonverbally. If you guess that the other person is unhappy from the way they act, you might try to change to please them. But even then you wouldn't necessarily talk about the conflict directly.

*Question:* Would you say that the Japanese are better readers of nonverbal cues than Americans?

*Kentaro:* I do think they're more aware of nonverbal messages. But there are times when someone will misunderstand a nonverbal message. You might think a friend or a person at work is upset and try to change to make them happy, when they really weren't upset at all. But since nobody talks about their problems, these misunderstandings happen.

*Question:* Norie, does Kentaro hide his feelings very well?

*Norie:* No! He's more American than I am in this way. He will tell me how he's feeling sometimes. And even when he doesn't say anything, it's very easy to tell how he's feeling by his nonverbal communication.

*Question:* Do you appreciate his expressiveness?

*Norie:* Well, sometimes it makes me uncomfortable. I guess I appreciate it, but I'm still not used to communicating so directly. Kentaro's open communication is also hard for some of our Japanese friends to understand. We have a group of Japanese students at our church, and when Kentaro shows his feelings, they get very concerned since they're not used to seeing a Japanese man showing his emotions.

*Question:* Norie, it sounds like you're less comfortable facing conflicts than Kentaro?

*Norie:* That's right. I think it's partly my Japanese upbringing and partly just my personality but I don't like to confront people. For example, I was having a hard time studying and sleeping be-

*Continued*

**Info 7–1**    *Continued*

cause one of my housemates would wash her clothes late at night. I wanted her to stop, but I would never have talked to her directly. I asked my house mother to take care of the problem. Asking a third party is very common in Japan. She did, and now things are fine. Confronting my housemate directly might have caused a fight, and that would have been very unpleasant.

*Question:* Do you think Japanese culture is becoming more direct and assertive, following the American style of handling conflicts?

*Kentaro:* Maybe a little bit. But the traditions of not showing emotion and of being indirect are so strong that I don't think Japan will be very much like the U.S.A., at least not for a very long time.

*Source:* Except from LOOKING OUT-LOOKING IN, Seventh Edition by Ronald B. Adler and Neil Towne, Copyright © 1993 by Holt, Rinehart and Winston, Inc., reprinted by permission of the publisher.

face, interrelation, favor, seniority, status, power, credibility, interest, severity of the conflict, and gender.

## Face

*Face* refers to the projected image of a person's self in a relationship network (Ting-Toomey, 1988). It represents an individual's social position and the prestige that comes from the successful performance of one or more specific social roles that are well recognized by other members in the society (Hu, 1944). Positive-face comments praise the performance of roles, but negative-face comments tend to lower a person's social standing, or serve to deflect praise. Orientation to the use of face work is reflected in the conflict style a person selects. According to Ting-Toomey (1988), low-context cultures emphasize "I" identity, self-face concern, negative-face need, and direct verbal and nonverbal expression. In contrast, high-context cultures emphasize "we" identity, other-face concern, positive-face need, and indirect verbal and nonverbal expression.

Hwang (1987) indicated that in Chinese society face management is a power game often played by Chinese people. It is not only an important way to show off one's power, but also a method to manipulate "the allocator's choices of allocating resources to one's benefit" (p. 962). Losing one's face is one of the worst ways to injure one's self-esteem, which in turn results in emotional uneasiness or serious conflict. Thus, in Chinese society one has to utilize every kind of method to "earn face" (Chu, 1983), and to enhance another's face (Chiao, 1981). Lastly, Silin (1976) pointed out that the Chinese frequently use these methods to manage a modern social organization, and Pye (1982) indicated that giving face is the key to successful negotiation with the Chinese in business.

## Interrelation

*Interrelation* refers to the relationship between two parties. The relationship may be, for example, as friends, family members, supervisor and subordinate, or coworkers. Waggenspack and Hensley (1989) indicated that college students prefer to establish relationships with those who show less argumentativeness and aggressiveness in conflict situations. Leung (1988) confirmed that a conflict is more likely to be pursued with a stranger than with a friend. According to Chiao (1982), Jacobs (1979), Hwang (1987), and Yang (1982), maintaining a proper relationship is a way for the Chinese to avoid serious conflict and embarrassing encounters. Further study by Chang and Holt (1991) indicated that interrelation is not only a tool used to avoid conflicts, but it is also used as a social resource for solving conflicts among people. In other words, interrelations are "potential power in persuasion, influence, and control" (Chung, 1991, p. 9).

---

### Research Highlight 7–2

Who: Chang, H., & Holt. G. R.

What: "More Than Relationship: Chinese Interaction and the Principle of Kuan-hsi."

Where: *Communication Quarterly, 39,* 1991, 251–271.

Through an interpretive analysis of interviews with Chinese people in Taiwan, this article analyzes the principle of "kuan-hsi," which undergirds the functional aspects of Chinese interpersonal relationships.

Originally based on the Confucian principle that family relations are a microcosm of the larger society, the Chinese emphasis on relationship (kuan-hsi) has evolved into a social resource that may be at odds with Confucian ideals. The cultural concept "kuan-hsi," with its associated linguistic expressions, explains the Chinese atti-

tude toward the ingroup and the outgroup. Kuan-hsi can be established and maintained through a variety of acts of communication; once firmly established, it can be used to negotiate one's treatment by claiming oneself as an ingroup member. Within the context of kuan-hsi, communication is seen as a skill that can be used to facilitate one's instrumental relationships. Applied differentially to ingroup and outgroup members, and often involving intermediaries, strategic communication from the perspective of kuan-hsi suggests that social positioning can coexist with message elaboration.

Findings from this study challenge commonly held perceptions that the Chinese are collectivistic, concerned with social harmony as opposed to the individual, and indirect in their communication.

## Favor

*Favor* is conceptualized as a physical or psychological resource we can present to others as a gift in the process of social exchange (Hwang, 1987). Social exchange theorists believe that we initiate, maintain, and terminate relationships on the basis of real or perceived rewards and costs related to the relationship. Doing a favor to others is treated as a rewarding system that helps to maintain our relationships. In Chinese society, however, the rule of favor is based on the norm of reciprocity, that is, a favor for a favor (Wen, 1988). Relationship ties are usually broken when the rule is not followed. In order to maintain a harmonious relationship we must know how to do a favor for and return a favor to another.

---

**Research Highlight 7–3**

Who:    Hwang, K. K.

What:    "Face and Favor: The Chinese Power Game."

Where:    *The American Journal of Sociology, 92,* 1987, 944–974.

This article develops a conceptual framework to explain the Chinese relationship in the process of social interaction. The framework investigates the dynamic relationships among four of the most important concepts that affect the Chinese social interaction: *renqing* (favor), *mianzi* (face), *guanxi* (relation), and *bao* (repay).

*Renqing* has three meanings. First, it refers to our emotional responses when facing various daily situations. Second, it refers to a resource we can use in social exchanges. Finally, it refers to a set of social norms we have to follow to get along well with others. *Mianzi* refers to the social position or prestige that we gain through the successful performance of our specific role in the social network and that is recognized by others. Having *mianzi* is a

way to reach a good life within a Chinese social network. Thus, saving one's *mianzi* rather than losing one's *mianzi* becomes a golden rule in Chinese society.

*Guanxi* represents relationship between us and others. Three types of *quanxi* exist in Chinese society: (1) the expressive tie—mainly found in primary groups, it tends to produce feelings of affection, warmth, safety, and attachment and tends to be permanent and stable; (2) the instrumental tie—basically serves an instrument for us to attain a goal in the social network, (describes the tie between a customer and a salesperson, for example); and (3) the mixed tie—refers to a relationship in which we seek to influence other people by means of *renqing* and *mianzi.*

Finally, *bao* is the principle of reciprocity. In Chinese society one is supposed to repay things received from others. For example, in expressive-tie relationships, parents always expect the children to repay parental care.

The dynamic interaction of these

four concepts illustrates three principles of Chinese social interaction that distinguish it from Western social interaction:

**1.** The norms of *bao* are strongly emphasized and deeply ingrained in Chinese society.

**2.** The obligations of *bao* are formed by *renqing* according to the hierarchically structured network of *guanxi*.

**3.** The obligations of *bao* are negotiated through *mianzi,* and to lose or to save one's *mianzi* will in turn weaken or enhance social relations.

---

## Research Highlight 7–4

Who:    Chung, J.

What:    "Seniority and Particularistic Ties in a Chinese Conflict Resolution Process."

Where:    Paper presented at the annual meeting of the Eastern Communication Association, Pittsburg, Pennsylvania, April, 1991.

This paper analyzes the political crisis that happened in January and February 1990 in Taiwan and its resolution from three perspectives. The first perspective is that of the journalist/historian who collects and studies relevant documents and, whenever possible, interviews participants in the event. The second perspective is that of the intercultural theorist dealing with Taiwanese politics and history in English from the point of view of American scholarship, which has preconceptions about "foreign" cultures, in this case about how "Asians" respect their elders. This paper explicates notions about age and politics and also draws attention to similarities between U.S.

and Taiwanese uses of third-party mediation. Finally, the third perspective is that of communication theorists. The author draws on work in communication theory that pertains to conflict resolution, specifically to investigate third-party mediation in Taiwanese disputes.

The author analyzes and interprets some aspects of decision-making in the conflict resolution process and generates a model to explain the process. The model specifies two factors that regulate the decision of selecting eight elders as the mediators for resolving a crisis: particularistic ties and seniority. The author finds that the Chinese attach great significance to particularistic ties, or *Kuan-hsi,* in the social interaction process. To the Chinese, particularistic ties serve as potent sources of power in persuasion, influence, and control. The Chinese also show great respect to the elderly. In turn, seniority (age and length of service with the organization) becomes one of the most critical factors in determining one's status and authority within the organization.

## Seniority

*Seniority* is a concept that plays an important role in the social interactions of East Asian society. Although the aged receive respect in most human societies, compared to Western society, people in the Orient show a much higher degree of respect for the elders. For example, the aged enjoy a high status in Japan (Carmichael, 1991), and seniority is a major determining factor for status and authority in Japanese organization (Nishyama, 1971). Bond and Hwang (1986) specified that Confucian tradition accords the senior member of a relationship a wide range of prerogatives and power. In a case analysis of the conflict between two factions of a ruling party in the 1990 Taiwanese presidential election campaign, Chung (1991) reported that seniority and interrelation are the most determinants in the recruitment of mediators. The eight statesmen who served as conflict mediators in the case were between 78 and 92 years old.

## Status

Status and power are related concepts. Individuals with high status are usually more powerful (Emerson, 1964). *Status* refers to relative positions with respect to income, prestige, and power (Knupfer, 1969). Social status is found to be negatively related to alienation (Templeton, 1966). In other words, individuals with high social status are more likely to establish interrelations with others. Many studies have demonstrated the influence of status in the social interaction. For example, Sommer (1969) found that high-status persons are given greater prerogatives in social situations, especially in the way they use space. Lippitt, Polansky, Redl, and Rosen (1952) found that status strongly affects type and amount of communication. A person with high status is likely to have much more information about what is happening in a group. Furthermore, high-status persons are more likely to serve as mediators in conflict situations. Torrance (1955) indicated that what a high-status person says is valued much more than what a low-status person says. In Asian societies, especially in China, such status not only produces much power in the bureaucracy structure but also closely relates to face-saving and interrelations (Hwang, 1987; Sterba, 1978).

## Power

*Power* refers to the control by one party of resources valued by another party. According to Folger and Poole (1984), the power one exerts sustains moves and countermoves of the participants in conflict situations. Although the emphasis of power resources may be different in cultures, what is similar in most cultures is that power is the determinant of the kind of conflict styles individuals will select. Americans consider the control of material resources such as money and information to be a source of power (Nadler, Nadler, & Broome, 1985); the Japanese associate power with seniority (Prosser, 1978); and the Chinese use power as a dominant way to require foreigners to negotiate (Pye, 1982). Obviously, power is a highly influential factor in a conflict situation.

## Credibility

*Credibility* refers to the degree of trust one person has for another. Scholars have indicated that interpersonal trust has a significant impact on the communication process. For example, Deutsch (1968) found that perceived trust increases the amount of interpersonal communication. Griffin (1967) reported that an increase of trust produces changes in interpersonal relationships, including control over the interaction process and the increasing acceptance of others' influence. In particular, the degree of trust among people may determine whether persons adopt a cooperative or competitive stance in negotiations or conflict situations (Nadler, Nadler, & Broome, 1985).

## Interest

*Interest* is the degree of profit involved (or perceived to be involved) in the interaction of the conflicting parties. In a conflict situation, we tend to search for an outcome that constitutes a proper balance of conflicting interests (Nadler, Nadler, & Broome, 1985). Bacharach and Lawler (1981) called this phenomenon "equity appeals." The reciprocity and fairness deriving from the concept of interest affects both the conflict style and the results of the conflict.

## Severity of the Conflict

*Severity of the conflict* refers to the size of the potential gain or loss in a conflict. Starosta (1973) and Leung (1988) proposed that people are more likely to pursue a dispute when high stakes are involved. In other words, the size of loss in a dispute significantly affects an individual's likelihood of pursuing the conflict. A similar argument was made by Gladwin and Walter (1980) regarding the effect of the severity involved in conflict resolution strategies in multinational corporations.

## Gender

Various studies have been done in regard to gender and conflict. For example, research from Koberg and Chusmir (1989) and Nicotera (1995) indicated that men and women handle conflicts differently. Because the status of men and women differs from one society to another (Chen, 1988; Kohls, 1984), gender is a major factor that influences our decisions in a conflict situation.

**TABLE 7-3**    **Rank Order of the Ten Factors**

| Americans | Chinese |
|---|---|
| 1. Severity of conflict | 1. Severity of Conflict |
| 2. Interest | 2. Interrelation |
| 3. Credibility | 3. Credibility |
| 4. Interrelation | 4. Interest |
| 5. Power | 5. Seniority |
| 6. Seniority | 6. Power |
| 7. Face | 7. Face |
| 8. Favor | 8. Favor |
| 9. Gender | 9. Gender |
| 10. Status | 10. Status |

As previously mentioned, although the above dimensions exist in all societies, cultural contexts affect how persons approach or manage conflicts. Chen, Ryan, and Chen (1992) empirically studied differences between the Chinese and Americans in terms of these ten factors. They found that face, favor, seniority, and gender have more impact on the Chinese, while Americans consider interest and the severity of the conflict when they are in a conflict situation. However, when being asked to rank the ten factors in order of importance, the Chinese and the Americans show very similar results. Table 7–3 demonstrates this concurrence.

## EFFECTIVE MANAGEMENT OF INTERCULTURAL CONFLICTS

Effective conflict management of intercultural conflicts requires intercultural awareness and intercultural sensitivity. Chapters 10 to 12 present a detailed discussion of the two concepts. In a nutshell, intercultural awareness includes the knowledge of values, beliefs, and worldviews of our own and other's cultures, and intercultural sensitivity dictates that we must understand not only the differences between our culture and another's but must also show the sincerity to acknowledge, respect, and accept discovered differences. Based on this ability, Harris and Moran (1987) proposed a five-step method of managing conflicts across cultures: (1) describe the conflict in a way understood in both cultures; (2) analyze the conflict from both cultural perspectives; (3) identify the basis for the conflict from two cultural viewpoints; (4) solve the conflict through synergistic strategies; and (5) determine if the solution is working interculturally

(p. 257). Harris and Moran illustrated these steps using a case study of business dealing between the Americans and the British .

First, it is necessary to describe the conflict in a way understood in both cultures. Conflict occurs when American businesspersons do business with the British. Americans complain that it is very difficult to get a job done in Great Britain with efficiency. Their ambition and enthusiasm for job performance is usually forestalled by the self-restraint and indifference displayed by their British associates. To spend more time carrying out a job than one would in the United States always frustrates American businesspersons.

Second, it is necessary to analyze the conflict from both cultural perspectives. From the U.S. perspective, the British appear too soft and not aggressive enough in business, and they seem reluctant to make any changes or innovations. Thus, Americans may conclude that the British do not have the ability to engage in competition because they lack self-motivation and are ineffective in the business world. From the British perspective, Americans may appear impatient and too aggressive, and are always trying to prove themselves to their superiors. Given their long European cultural tradition, the British don't feel that it is necessary to tackle a problem in the way Americans do. To sacrifice the quality of their life or their casual nature simply to be more efficient is not worthwhile to the British.

Third, it is necessary to identify the basis for the conflict from two cultural viewpoints. The identification of basis refers to the analysis of the values or worldviews of both sides. Americans are very much oriented toward doing over being. They value hard work, competition, personal achievement, and determination, to make life better. Children are taught to believe that through individual effort they can move up on the social ladder, have more materialistic rewards, and gain more power and status. Based on this value system, Americans tend to believe that persons must be responsible for their own fate and rely on their own resourcefulness. This explains why Americans consider their British associates as less aggressive. In contrast, the British tend to value social class and a restricted educational system. Thus, work does not inspire the same social mobility and status in Great Britain as it does in the United States. There is a tendency in Great Britain for upper-class people to live a life of leisure and look down on the lower class and laborers. Also, the British do not put emphasis on the spirit of individual competitiveness. Instead, they value competition on behalf of one's group and nation. All these factors form the basis for conflict between the British and the Americans.

Fourth, it is necessary to solve conflict through synergistic strategies. Synergy refers to a dynamic process in which the opposing parties combine their actions and work by adapting and learning different viewpoints through empathy and sensitivity. Thus, before arriving in England the American employees should be aware of British customs, traditions, values, and belief system. The knowledge of cultural differences will make them more patient and tolerant in dealing with their British host. In addition to the knowledge of cultural differences, it is also useful to attend intercultural training programs to enhance the ability to be more empathic and sensitive to those of a different cultural background. The commonality of cultural traditions between the British and Americans may make cultural differences all the more difficult to understand or to accept. Chapter 12 presents detailed information about intercultural training.

Fifth, it is necessary to determine if the solution works interculturally. To assess the implementation of conflict management strategies it is necessary to conduct a survey after several months of the parties' working together. The survey should focus on the analysis of employees' attitudes and feelings from the standpoint of both cultures, especially to examine the degree of satisfaction in their intercultural dealings with each other.

In addition to Harris and Moran's model, Ting-Toomey (1994) provided some specific suggestions for effective conflict management based on individualistic and collectivistic cultures. Seven suggestions for people from individualistic cultures to enable them to deal with conflict effectively in a collectivistic culture are as follows:

1. Understand the opponent's face-maintenance assumptions in order to keep a balance between humility and pride and between shame and honor in interactions.
2. Save the opponent's face by carefully using go-between or informal consultation to deal with low-grade conflicts before they fall irrevocably into face-losing situations.
3. Give face to opponents by not pushing them into a corner with no leeway for recovering face.
4. Avoid using too much verbal expression, and learn how to manage conflicts by effectively reading implicit and nonverbal messages.
5. Be empathic by listening attentively and respecting the opponent's needs.
6. Put aside the effective communication skills practiced in the West and learn to use the indirect communication style.
7. Tolerate the opponent's tendency to avoid facing the conflict by being patient, thereby maintaining a harmonious atmosphere and mutual dignity.

Ting-Toomey also provided seven suggestions for people of collectivistic cultures to enable them to effectively manage conflicts with people from individualistic cultures:

1. Understand the conflict assumptions of low-context culture by learning to distinguish the task dimension of conflicts from the socioemotional dimension.
2. Learn to accept the individualistic style of managing conflict in which opin-

ions are openly and directly expressed and substantive issues of the conflict are focused.

3. Practice an assertive style of conflict behavior by defending one's own and the partner's right of speaking up on the issue and by learning how to reason systematically and logically.
4. Develop the sense of individual responsibility and use "I" statements to express one's feelings in the process of conflict management.
5. Develop the ability of verbal feedback and listening skills in order to clarify both parties' points of view.
6. Avoid the occurrence of too many silent moments in interactions by clearly and directly expressing one's concern about the issues.
7. Show a commitment to mutually and collaboratively work out conflict through responsible and constructive dialogues.

## RECAP

Conflicts are inevitable in the process of intercultural communication. To have unpleasant feelings during conflict is universal. This chapter first describes the nature and types of conflict, then discusses the impact of culture on conflict and conflict management from three perspectives: (1) thinking patterns, (2) language barriers, and (3) cultural context.

Ten factors that affect our reactions and decisions in a conflict situation are delineated: face, interrelation, favor, seniority, status, power, credibility, interest, severity of the conflict, and gender. Finally, two methods for the effective management of intercultural conflicts are suggested. The first method is based on Harris and Moran's model of conflict management, which includes five steps: (1) describe the conflict in a way understood in both cultures, (2) analyze the conflict from both cultural perspectives, (3) identify the basis for the conflict from two cultural viewpoints, (4) solve the conflict through synergistic strategies, and (5) determine if the solution is working interculturally. The second method is based on Ting-Toomey's suggestions for handling conflicts in individualistic and collectivistic cultures.

## RETHINK

While research concerning intercultural conflicts has gained in popularity over the last decade, three limitations continue to demand communication scholars' careful attention. First, the study of the relationship between cultural variability and conflicts still lacks a sound theoretical foundation. In recent years Ting-Toomey's studies on face-negotiation theory have provided a valuable contribution in this area. However, since Ting-Toomey's theory mainly focuses on the explanation of conflict resolution style from the perspectives of individualism and collectivism, the scope and heuristic power of the theory is still limited. Future research must provide an extension of Ting-Toomey's theory.

Second, although a cultural-variability perspective helps us understand how differences in cultural values guide our perceptions and behaviors in conflict situations, future research must examine how differences in cultural values lead to conflicts and "how members of a culture prioritize those dimensions or characteristics of their culture values" (Yu, 1995, p. 229). Yu pointed out that this kind of research—on the basis of daily interactions among people of different cultural backgrounds—would be helpful in identifying the loci of conflict when it occurs.

Finally, the universal nature of perceptions and feelings about conflict are topics that deserve more attention from communication scholars. Greater understanding of the universal commonalities of human reactions in conflict situations may enable us to explain how people from diverse cultures adapt universal paradigms and resources to the unique expectations of intercultural conflicts (Brown, 1991; Fiske, 1992; Strack & Lorr, 1990).

## QUESTIONS FOR DISCUSSION

1. Explain the types of conflict.
2. From the perspectives of thinking patterns, language barriers, and cultural context, discuss the impact of culture on conflict management.
3. Discuss how the following factors affect conflict management: face, expressions, interrelations, favor, seniority, status, power, credibility, interest, severity of the conflict, and gender.
4. Describe Harris and Moran's five-step method of managing conflicts across cultures.
5. Describe Ting-Toomey's suggestions for effective conflict management based on individualistic and collectivistic cultures.
6. What are the three theoretical limitations still hindering the study of intercultural conflict?

# ▶ Chapter 8

# Intercultural Adaptation

## *Objectives*

Upon completion of this chapter, you will

- Understand the nature of culture shock and intercultural adaptation.
- Be able to describe the aspects, forms, symptoms, and effects of culture shock.
- Understand the approaches to the study of intercultural adaptation.
- Understand the dimensions of intercultural adaptation.
- Be able to distinguish between **U**-curve and **W**-curve patterns of intercultural adaptation.
- Understand the models for the study of intercultural adaptation.

*Across the Fai river the orange becomes the tangerine—*
*Things will turn out differently in different localities or*
*surroundings.—CHINESE SAYING.*

Some persons who sojourn in a foreign country adapt well to the new environment within a short period of time, while others find the new environment to be a nightmare. One of the main reasons we may find an extended stay in an unfamiliar environment problematic is that the symbols most familiar to us in our daily lives have changed suddenly in the strange culture. We then start to consciously or unconsciously reject the new ways of life that cause us discomfort, promote our withdrawal from the culture, and make us fear contact with others. As we extend our stay in the new culture, however, we learn to function within its unfamiliar symbolic milieu. Until then, however, our difficulty in intercultural adaptation may incline us toward paranoia, depression, schizophrenia, and lack of confidence (Yeh, Chu, Klein, Alexander, & Miller, 1981).

Increased frequencies of interactions among people from different national cultures expose sojourners such as diplomats, international students, tourists, military personnel on foreign duty, missionaries working overseas, Peace Corps volunteers, business persons on assignment abroad, or new immigrants to new and unfamiliar cultural cues and contexts to which they must adapt. This chapter, then, deals with the following dimensions of intercultural adaptation: (1) culture shock and intercultural adaptation, (2) approaches to the study of intercultural adaptation, (3) dimensions of intercultural adaptation, (4) stages of intercultural adaptation, and (5) models for the study of intercultural adjustment.

## CULTURE SHOCK AND INTERCULTURAL ADAPTATION

*Intercultural adaptation* refers broadly to the process of increasing our level of fitness to meet the demands of a new cultural environment (Kim, 1988). It deals with how sojourners or new immigrants experience the distress caused by mismatches or incompatibility between the host culture and the culture of birth. In other words, intercultural adaptation is a process of dealing with maladjustment within a host culture.

Entrance into a new culture is generally accompanied by *culture shock.* We are unlikely to experience it suddenly, from a single event. More likely we will feel it gradually, from our day-in, day-out experience of navigating a different symbolic environment. Differences accumulate bit by bit (Kohls, 1984) and may most disorient us when we anticipate no difference to be present. According to Furnham and Bochner (1982), culture shock occurs "in the social encounters, social situations, social episodes, or social transactions between sojourners and host nationals," and it is "the reaction of sojourners to problems encountered in the dealings with the host members" (p. 172). In other words, we experience culture shock when many familiar cultural cues and patterns are severed, when living or working in an ambiguous environment for an extended period of time, when our values and beliefs are questioned in a new environment, and when we are continually expected to perform with appropriate skills and speed before we are able to understand clearly the rules of performance (Kohls, 1984).

Culture shock results from the processing of stressful situations, especially attempts to establish and maintain a relationship with those of the host culture. In order to reduce our problem of culture shock, we must learn to fit within the new symbolic environment. We must develop the ability to cope with the social and work demands of the host culture. Such adaptive difficulties involve six dimensions (Furnham and Bochner, 1982). First, the *formal relations* dimension deals with our understanding of the rules and customs of the host culture, especially when we are the focus of attention in the social interaction. Second, the *relationship management* dimension involves our ability to manage or initiate friendships and to understand host nationals. Third, the *public rituals* dimension refers to our ability to adapt to the public facilities of the host culture. Fourth, the *initiating contact* dimension concerns our initiating and maintaining of contacts and involves self-disclosure and self-presentation during our interaction with host nationals. Fifth, the *public decision-making* dimension involves our making choices regarding various public-issues. Finally, the *assertiveness* dimension deals with our ability to deal with what seems to us cases of hostility or rudeness.

Among these dimensions Furnham and Bochner further extracted the ten most difficult things we face in the process of intercultural adjustment: (1) making host friends of our own age; (2) dealing with somebody who is cross and aggressive; (3) approaching others or starting up a friendship; (4) appearing in front of an audience for the purpose of acting or speaking; (5) getting to know host nationals in depth; (6) understanding jokes, humor, and sarcasm; (7) dealing with host nationals who stare at us; (8) taking the initiative in keeping the conversation going; (9) spending time with host nationals we don't know very well; and (10) complaining in public or dealing with unsatisfactory service in the host culture.

Hammer, Gudykunst, and Wiseman (1978) also noted that to deal with culture shock or psychological stress in a host culture, we must effectively deal with eight potential problems we may encounter therein: (1) frustration, (2) stress, (3) anxiety, (4) different political systems, (5) pressure to conform, (6) social alienation, (7) financial difficulties, and (8) interpersonal conflict.

## Aspects of Culture Shock

When we experience the frustration of culture shock we may either reject the environment that causes us discomfort or may mentally regress to our own culture by feeling that everything from our own culture is more beautiful or important than local alternatives (Oberg, 1960). We may experience one or more of six common aspects of culture shock: (1) a feeling of strain that comes from our attempts at psychological adjustment; (2) a feeling of loss regarding friends and family, social status, and possessions; (3) a feeling of being rejected by or rejecting the host nationals; (4) a feeling of confusion in beliefs, values, and

**Research Highlight 8–1**

Who:    Furnham, A., & Bochner, S.

What:    "Social Difficulty in a Foreign Culture: An Empirical Analysis of Culture Shock."

Where:    In S. Bochner (Ed.) (1982), *Culture in Contact: Studies in Cross-Cultural Interaction* (pp. 161–198). New York: Pergamon.

One of the main purposes of this article is to explore out the nature and extent of the social difficulties sojourners encounter in the process of intercultural adjustment. The authors assert that social difficulties accounting for the phenomenon of culture shock are relative to three factors: (1) cultural differences—the greater the cultural differences, the greater the social difficulties; (2) individual differences—demographic and personality variables influence our ability to cope with a new environment; and (3) sojourn experience—the beginning of the visit to a new environment is especially important; sojourners tend to encounter fewer problems if they are carefully introduced into a new environment at the first visit.

One hundred fifty international students studying in England are the experimental subjects and fifty British students served as the control group in this study. The results from a forty-item Social Situations Questionnaire show that sojourners encounter social difficulty are encountered in six areas: (1) formal relations/focus of attention, (2) managing intimate relationships, (3) public rituals, (4) initiating contact/introduction, (5) public decision making, and (6) assertiveness.

The results further indicate the ten most difficult social situations identified by sojourners: (1) making friends of your own age with people of the host culture; (2) dealing with somebody who is cross or aggressive; (3) approaching others and starting up a friendship; (4) appearing in front of an audience; (5) getting to know people in depth, intimately; (6) understanding jokes, humor, and sarcasm; (7) dealing with people staring at you; (8) taking the initiative in keeping the conversation going; (9) being with people that you don't know very well; (10) complaining in public or dealing with unsatisfactory service.

This well-written article provides an extensive theoretical analysis of intercultural adjustment research. The experiment is effective and hypotheses are supported. The results lay a theoretical foundation for the study of culture shock.

role expectations; (5) a generalized feeling of anxiety, disgust, or surprise in the face of cultural differences; and (6) a feeling of impotence for being unable to cope with aspects of, or tasks in, the new environment.

Persons with an adaptive personality may experience these aspects of culture shock as only a brief, hardly noticeable phenomenon. Others, though, wrestle with all these aspects of culture shock for a period lasting from several months to one or two years.

## Forms of Culture Shock

Culture shock takes various forms. Six concepts have been used to describe culture shock: language shock, role shock, transition shock, culture fatigue, education shock, adjustment stress, and culture distance.

Smalley (1963) proposed that language shock occurs when we are unfamiliar with the host language. He argued that many sociorelational cues lie in the domain of human language. If we do not understand the language, we lose the ability to adjust ourselves to the new symbolic environment. *Role shock* refers to feeling of loss of personal status in an ambiguous new environment in which we make efforts to switch our role in order to fit and function well in the host culture (Higbee, 1969). *Transition shock* was used by Bennett (1977) to describe the distress we experience when trying to cope with the multitude of changes required by the host culture. It is similar to the state of losing a close family member, divorce, or geographic relocation. *Culture fatigue* was coined by Guthrie (1975) to describe the physical and psychological discomforts experienced by sojourners trying to adapt to a new culture.

*Education shock* is frequently used to describe what happens to international students who try to adapt themselves to academic life, especially when the learning situation is new and distressing (Hoff, 1979). *Adjustment stress* is a term used to indicate bodily physical tension that signals a person's readiness to face the challenges of the new cultural environment (Smith, 1955; Barna, 1983). Sojourners often experience a great deal of psychological pressure in the process of intercultural adjustment. Finally, *culture distance* refers to the distance between a sojourner's culture and the host culture and signals the degree of alienation, estrangement, and psychological distress the sojourner feels as a result (Babiker, Cox, & Miller, 1980).

## Symptoms of Culture Shock

The reaction to culture shock may differ greatly from person to person. For some, it may take only a few weeks to work through the psychological distress due to the cultural difference they experience; for others, it may take a long period of time to overcome the frustration of culture shock. In very serious cases, the only way to eliminate the problem caused by culture shock may be to return to familiar surroundings. If we are forced to stay in the host culture, our difficulty of intercultural adaptation may produce in us paranoia, depression, schizophrenia, and lack of confidence.

Thomas (1985) stated that symptoms of culture shock include depression, helplessness, hostility to the host country, feelings of anxiety, overidentification with our home country, feelings of withdrawal, homesickness, loneliness, paranoid feelings, preoccupation with cleanliness, irritability, confusion, disorientation, isolation, tension, need to establish continuity, defensiveness, intolerance of ambiguity, and impatience. Oberg (1960) vividly described the symptoms of culture shock as follows:

> *excessive washing of the hands; excessive concern over drinking water, food, dishes, and bedding; fear of physical contact with attendants or servants; an absentminded, faraway stare; a feeling of helplessness and a desire for dependence on long-term residents of one's own nationality; fits of anger over delays and other minor frustrations; delay and outright refusal to learn the language of the host country; excessive fear of being cheated, robbed, or injured; great concern over minor pains and eruptions of the skin; and finally, a longing to be back home, to be able to have a good cup of coffee and a piece of apple pie, to walk into a fast-food restaurant, to visit one's relatives, and, in general, to talk to people who really make sense. (p. 178)*

Earlier writings on culture shock picture it primarily as a psychological concern. Over time, however, it came to be seen also as a deficit in knowledge about the new culture and, as such, a concern of intercultural communication. Although the literature on culture shock primarily deals with the experience of persons who travel abroad for an extended period, clearly cultural variability may be sufficiently great to trigger symptoms of culture shock on a short-term

---

**Mini Case 8–1**

Huang was the firstborn son of a well-to-do family in Hong Kong. He had done well in his undergraduate studies at the University of Hong Kong and had been accepted for graduate studies at a prestigious American university. He made his initial adjustment fairly well, finding housing and joining a support group made up of other students from Hong Kong who lived near his university. After a time, however, he began to be disappointed in his work and was unhappy with life in America. He had become attracted to an American woman, but the relationship broke up because of personality differences. While not failing any of his classes, he was by no means among the best students in his department, as shown by both test scores and participation in class seminars. Not wanting his friends from Hong Kong to learn about his problems, Huang went to the student health center with complaints about upset stomach, severe headaches, and lower back pain. The doctor at the health center prescribed acetaminophen with codeine. Huang began to take the pills, but the problems did not go away.

Could you help to explain what's happening to Huang?

---

basis, e.g., within the United States and Canada themselves certain populations know little if any French or English. Similarly, being African American or Native American entails such contrast with the attitudes, roles, and values of the predominant white American culture that entry into the mainstream school system may resemble a sojourn to another country. Read Mini Case 8–1 and see whether you can answer the question from the perspective of culture shock.

## Effects of Culture Shock

As a transient experience, culture shock can be viewed as a transitional process of movement in which sojourners gradually become aware of and begin to adjust to cultural differences in a new environment. This process may lead in either of two directions, depending on individual personality.

In a positive sense, culture shock may contribute to individual growth. Adler (1987) pointed out that culture shock may promote several beneficial outcomes for sojourners. First, culture shock provides a learning opportunity that demands new responses from sojourners in coping with a constantly changing environment. Indeed, Hall (1976) and Stewart (1972) proposed that growth as an intercultural communicator would hardly be possible if we were to avoid a sojourn for fear of culture shock. Second, because most people have a tendency to pursue unique and special goals, culture shock can create an environment and serve as a motivational force for us to move to new levels of self-actualization.

Third, culture shock can give sojourners a welcome sense of challenge and achievement as a result of dealing with people from very different backgrounds. Fourth, the amount of learning increases when the level of personal anxiety is aroused to a certain degree. To most of us, culture shock offers us a high but not extreme level of anxiety that causes us to learn about a new culture and about ourselves.

Fifth, the experience from culture shock produces new ideas that, in turn, offer us a new set of behavioral responses for future unfamiliar situations. Our sojourn strengthens us in the future by teaching us how to learn from negative cultural feedback. Finally, the new ideas we acquire during our sojourn mostly result from drawing comparisons and contrasts. This practice helps us to deal with cultures that we have not yet experienced.

Culture shock may also lead to negative consequences. Draguns (1977) discussed problems that may be caused or aggravated by culture shock. First, affectively, culture shock constitutes an imbalancing experience. On one day,, we may experience the mood of mania and excitement, while, on another, we may feel hysteria, confusion, anxiety, and depression. This uncertainty may be detrimental to the psychological growth of some sojourners. Second, cognitively and perceptually, a set of desirable or proper behaviors in one culture might be considered bizarre or idiosyncratic in another. Sorting through feelings about cultural differences may take a long time or may prove impossible for some sojourners. We may become prone to judge the unfamiliar more harshly than we did before our sojourn.

## PERSPECTIVES ON THE STUDY OF INTERCULTURAL ADAPTATION

Furnham (1987) and Furnham and Bochner (1986) have identified eight theoretical foundations for the study of intercultural adaptation: movement as loss, fatalism, selective migration, appropriate expectation, negative life events, social support, a clash of values, and social skills deficit.

The viewing of *movement as loss* indicates that any kind of geographic movement entails the loss of familiar symbols and personal relationships. This feeling of loss is a cause of culture shock that is typically reflected in a range of psychological symptoms such as grief and mourning. The approach of *fatalism* suggests that many cultures are oriented to fatalistic beliefs in which people lack final control over the results of their behaviors. Sojourners from this kind of culture tend to act more passively in the process of intercultural adaptation. Thus, they may experience more problems in dealing with the host culture and may experience a high degree of culture shock.

The *selective migration* perspective, based on the notion of "natural selection" or "the survival of the fittest," suggests that sojourners who can adjust most easily to the effects of culture shock will become the prevailing types in the host culture. Therefore, the coping strategies used by the fittest group of sojourners can be used to help new sojourners or those who are less successful in the process of adaptation. The *appropriate expectations* approach argues that the degree of intercultural adaptation we may achieve can be evaluated by our expectations about living and possibilities for success in the host culture. It predicts that positive expectations about our successful performance will lead us to better adapt to the host culture.

The *negative life events* perspective underlines that any change in our daily life will cause a certain degree of physical and psychological discomfort. Sojourning in a new environment inevitably involves significant changes in our life. Thus, the speed of intercultural adaptation is influenced by the way sojourners cope with the stress and strain caused by drastic changes. The *social support* approach draws from attachment theory, social network theory, and psychotherapy. It explains that when we move to a new culture we suddenly lose many sources of social support. To provide necessary social supports is an effective way to reduce psychological problems and possible mental and physical stresses in the process of intercultural adaptation.

Differences in cultural values about the self, family, society, nature, and the supernatural have been used to explain the difficulties and distress sojourners experience in a new environment. The *clash of values* approach suggests that certain value orientations such as self-help and stoicism will help sojourners better adapt to the host culture. Finally, the *social skills deficit* approach emphasizes that persons who cannot adjust to the social conventions in their society will not adjust well to a new environment either. They may have trouble negotiating everyday social encounters whatever the culture. Chapter 12 discusses this approach in detail.

## DIMENSIONS OF INTERCULTURAL ADAPTATION

Change and difference are inevitable for sojourners in their encounter of the host culture. The process of adapting to a new culture can produce a feeling of loss of cultural identity in some and stimulate personal growth for others. Mansell (1981) pointed out that sojourners experience to one degree or another four emotional and affective states in the process of intercultural adaptation: alienation, marginality, acculturation, and duality.

*Alienation* causes a strong desire in sojourners to retain identification with their own culture. The rejection of the host culture leads us to limit our social circle to acquaintances or work contacts and to seek out our own nationals for social enjoyment. Unable to employ the necessary skills for adjustment, we feel out of sync with the host culture and want desperately to return home.

*Marginality* exists when sojourners get caught between two different cultures and do not clearly understand to which one they belong. The situation becomes ambiguous, and we are troubled by divided loyalties and uncertain self-identity. Social relationships for marginal sojourners tend to be functional and superficial with host nationals, rather than personal or intimate. As we remain reluctant to relinquish the major habits and customs of our own culture, our feeling of marginality often prevents us from appreciating or enjoying our own culture or that of the host.

*Acculturation* occurs when sojourners establish a strong need to adopt the way of living of the host culture. Our identification with the host culture means that the primary culture loses its importance. In this situation we are able to make intimate friends with the host nationals and are able gradually to replace some elements of our original culture with elements of the host culture. Yet, moving too quickly to adopt the new culture may pose frustrations and obstacles to our intercultural adaptation.

Finally, *duality* represents our ability to accommodate to both the original and the host culture while living in a new environment and our achievement of a sense of autonomy and bicultural independence. Such flexibility provides us with new skills to value cultural contrasts to integrate new and existing beliefs and rules. The attitudes of open-mindedness and flexibility are required in this situation to maintain an appropriate balance between continuity and growth.

# STAGES OF INTERCULTURAL ADAPTATION

Over the last decades scholars have tried to identify stages in the intercultural adaptation process. For example, Adler (1975) described intercultural adaptation as a transitional experience that moves from a low level to a high level of self-awareness and cultural awareness in a new environment. He found that the transitional experience of intercultural adaptation moves through the phases of contact, disintegration, reintegration, autonomy, and independence. Among the

---

**Research Highlight 8–2**

Who:    Adler, P. S.

What:    "The Transitional Experience: An Alternative View of Culture Shock."

Where:    *Journal of Humanistic Psychology, 15,* 1975, 13–23.

The purpose of this article is to investigate the transitions between intergroup and intercultural situations. More specifically, the article examines how our self-awareness is affected by culture shock.

The model of the transitional experience developed in this article is based on four assumptions: (1) modern life tends to be discontinuous and fragmentary; (2) culture is the foundation of experience; (3) people tend to be unaware of their own values, beliefs, and attitudes; (4) personality disintegration tends to occur when people enter a new environment. A successful cross-cultural experience involves moving from one set of values, beliefs, and attitudes to another.

According to the author, the transitional experience marks a movement from a lower state to a higher state of self- and cultural awareness. The process of transition occurs in five stages: contact, disintegration, reintegration, autonomy, and independence.

**1.** Contact—In this stage we are still saturated by our own culture. We continue to use cultural similarities and differences to rationalize our experiences and confirm our identity.

**2.** Disintegration—In this stage we gradually perceive the intrusion of cultural differences. Being aware of the differences decreases our self-esteem. We begin to feel the loss of cultural support ties and misread new cultural cues.

**3.** Reintegration—In this stage we begin to reject cultural differences by showing liking or disliking. Negative behaviors occur as a form of regaining self-esteem.

**4.** Autonomy—In this stage we are gradually able to negotiate cultural differences and gain the ability to survive in the new environment.

**5.** Independence—In this stage we can enjoy cultural differences and are able to create new meanings for situations.

In conclusion, the transitional experience is a dynamic process entailing both frustration and growth. The process is also a journey into the self. The more we are able to experience cultural diversity, the more we learn about ourselves. To successfully experience the cultural transition helps us survive in the "global village."

research on this area, **U**-curve and **W**-curve patterns are two popular models used to explain the developmental stages of intercultural adaptation.

## U-Curve Pattern

Lysgaard's (1955) study on 200 Norwegian Fulbright scholars in the United States first concluded that the process of intercultural adaptation moves through three phases: initial adjustment, crisis, and regained adjustment. The process can be described by a **U**-curve pattern, with high affect initially, followed by a drop in satisfaction, and ending with a period of recovery. Studies from Chang (1973), Deutsch and Won (1963), Morris (1960), Oberg (1960), and Smalley (1963) also confirmed the **U**-curve movement of intercultural adaptation. Generally, the **U**-curve pattern comprises four stages: honeymoon period, crisis period, adjustment period, and biculturalism period.

### Honeymoon Period

The *honeymoon* or *initial euphoria* stage is the initial period of intercultural adaptation. This stage is characterized by fascination with the new culture and by the excitement about all the new things we encounter in the host culture. In this stage we are still viewing the new environment from our own cultural perspective. Our curiosity in this stage often provides us a feeling of excitement and euphoria when we detect similarities and differences between the original and the new cultures. However, Adler (1975) pointed out that in this stage sojourners tend to perceptually neglect differences and to validate their cultural status and identity through the reinforcement of the similarities between the host culture and their own culture.

### Crisis Period

The *crisis period* is also called the hostility or frustration stage. Sojourners in this period must directly face the challenges of the new culture on a day-to-day basis. This stage is characterized by frequent confusion and disintegration as we confront differences in values, beliefs, behaviors, and lifestyles. Activities that we take for granted suddenly become insurmountable problems. Such problems often lead to a feeling of rejecting or being rejected by the host culture. Smalley (1963) indicated that the increasing sense of being different, isolated, and inadequate to the demands of the host culture also lead sojourners to assert the superiority of their own culture. The symptom of being too ethnocentric tends to challenge the sojourners' personality and to confuse their identity. If the sojourners are unable to overcome these problems, severe depression and withdrawal will ruin the sojourners' life in the new environment.

### Adjustment Period

Efforts to cope with the problems in the crisis period gradually provide sojourners with new ways to live in the new culture. Sojourners begin to learn how to respond and adapt appropriately to the new environment by following the social and cultural norms of the host nation. Thomas and Althen (1989) referred to this period in which sojourners also begin to appreciate and respect the new culture and to develop sensitivity toward cultural differences as the *recovery stage*. Sojourners now regain a certain degree of effectiveness, relaxation, and comfort, and have less difficulty accommodating both the positive and negative aspects of the host culture. A sense of autonomy and self-efficacy arise from this gradual *adjustment period* that not only improves our ability to survive in the new culture without the assistance of cultural cues from the home culture, but also marks a growth in our personal flexibility (Adler, 1975).

### Biculturalism Period

*Biculturalism,* or the mastery period, is the last stage of the **U**-curve pattern. In this stage, we may still experience occasional anxiety and frustration, but we have cultivated an understanding of the host culture and can begin to work and play in the new environment with a feeling of enjoyment. We have recovered or nearly recovered from the symptoms of culture shock. According to Adler (1975), this stage is marked by attitudes and behaviors that are independent from the influence of our birth. It is this fully developed autonomy that provides us with the freedom and capacity for dual cultural identity, awareness of being in control of creative enjoyment, aesthetic appreciation for the contrasts of cultures, development of satisfactory interpersonal relationships, and a high level of commitment toward both cultural contexts (Mansell, 1981).

## W-Curve Pattern and Reentry Shock

If sojourners decide to remain in the host nation, the adaptation process usually ends at the **U**-curve pattern. But, if sojourners plan to return to their home countries, they may face a similar process of adaptation to their own cultures. Gullahorn and Gullahorn (1963, 1966) extended the **U**-curve pattern to describe the process of *reentry* or *reverse culture shock*. They used the "**W**-curve" to represent the pattern of sojourners' readjustment to their own cultures.

The **W**-curve pattern suggests that when we return home, we must proceed through the four stages of the **U**-curve pattern once again. Although we may experience less trauma and adopt faster when we readjust to our own culture, culture shock is again inevitable. Kohls (1984) recommended five steps to help sojourners feel mentally and behaviorally at home again soon:

**1.** Share the feelings about the experience abroad with sympathetic friends or relatives without bragging about it.

**2.** Temporarily act like a foreigner by asking questions about the home culture, just as you did when you arrived in the new culture.

**3.** Ask a friend to help you figure out what went on while you were abroad by listing items such as new slang, new technological products, new music, and new social events.

**4.** Join different social groups such as temples, churches, clubs, and professional organizations to gain more information about your original culture.

**5.** Find people from your original culture with international experiences, or locate foreign nationals to share common experiences you have experienced since your return.

## MODELS FOR THE STUDY OF INTERCULTURAL ADAPTATION

Two recent approaches provide a new perspective to the study of intercultural adaptation: Dialectic and transformative learning models.

### *A Dialectical Model*

Based on psychological drive theory, Anderson (1994) proposed a dialectical model for the study of intercultural adaptation. The model argues that intercultural adaptation is a cyclical and recursive process in which sojourners try to solve problems and overcome obstacles embedded in the interactions with the host culture. How we choose to respond will create our own adjustment patterns. Our effort to penetrate into a new culture can lead to a fundamental change that delivers us a sense of "rebirth." Thus, drive or motivation is the force that moves us to reach the goal of intercultural adaptation. Without this motivation, our experience of instability or imbalance in the process of intercultural adaptation will impede our ability to act in an appropriate way.

Anderson's model is composed of six principles: First, intercultural adaptation is a motivated, goal-oriented process in which sojourners learn to accommodate to the new culture. The accommodation process requires them to cope with three categories of obstacles:

**1.** The clashes of cultural differences especially regarding values, attitudes, and beliefs between the home and host cultures.

**2.** The loss of the familiar symbols used in home culture that define our identity.

**3.** The social incompetency caused by the lack of appropriate perceptual sensitivity and behavioral flexibility in the host culture.

Second, the intercultural adaptation and learning processes are reciprocal and interdependent. The obstacles or cultural barriers we must encounter in the new environment require us to learn the parameters of the situation and to develop strategies to solve our problems. Those cultural barriers are what Barna

## Research Highlight 8–3

Who:    Barna, L. M.

What:   "Stumbling Blocks in Inter-
        cultural Communication."

Where:  In L. A. Samovar & R. E.
        Porter (Eds.) (1994), *Inter-
        cultural Communication: A
        Reader.* Belmont, CA: Wads-
        worth.

The ultimate goal of intercultural adaptation is to reach a state of intercultural
communication competence that enables sojourners to meet the challenges
posed by intercultural interaction. In
this article the author delineates six
stumbling blocks sojourners must overcome in order to be competent in
intercultural communication: assumptions of similarities, language differences, nonverbal misinterpretations,
preconceptions and stereotypes, the
tendency to evaluate, and high anxiety.

First, assuming people are similar
to ourselves is natural and may reduce
our discomfort in dealing with people
of different backgrounds, the tendency
often leads to misunderstanding or rejection in intercultural communication.
Because there is no universal principle
enabling people to understand each
other, we need to treat each interaction
as an individual case.

Second, language differences in
vocabulary, syntax, idioms, and dialects cause difficulties in intercultural
communication. The most serious problem is the assignment of a single mean-

ing to a word or phrase of the host language. It is important that sojourners
learn the various connotative meanings
of the words in the host language.

Third, nonverbal misinterpretations are more difficult to overcome
than language differences, because our
culture teaches us to live in a specific
sensory reality. Unlike verbal language,
learning the meanings of nonverbal expressions is more effective in an informal way.

Fourth, preconceptions or stereotypes may help us make sense about
the surrounding environment and feel
more secure in the process of intercultural communication. They reduce our
sensitivity toward the stimuli of new
environment.

Fifth, the tendency to evaluate
causes us to jump to conclusions about
people's behaviors in intercultural interactions. It prevents us from trying to
comprehend others' thoughts and feelings and from being open-minded. To
look and listen empathically is essential
in intercultural interaction.

Finally, anxiety—the tension or
stress caused by ambiguous situations—It underlies and compounds the
previous five stumbling blocks. For example, stereotyping and the tendency
to evaluate often serve as defense
mechanisms to alleviate the stressful
feeling of being in a new environment.
Thus, overcoming anxiety is fundamental to reducing the incidence of the
other five stumbling blocks.

(1994) called "stumbling blocks," including assumption of cultural similarities, language differences, nonverbal misinterpretations, preconceptions and stereotypes, tendency to evaluate, and high anxiety.

Anderson indicated that sojourners may react in any of four ways to obstacles presented by the new environment: changing the environment, changing oneself, doing nothing, or walking away. Unless the sojourners choose to do nothing or physically withdraw from the environment, both changing the environment and changing oneself in order to reach the goal of intercultural adjustment demand learning. For instance, we may choose to change ourselves by learning the host culture's language if we find language is a barrier.

Third, intercultural adaptation implies a stranger-host relationship. We are strangers in a foreign land (Gudykunst & Hammer, 1987; Gudykunst & Kim, 1992). The status of newcomers and marginal persons make the intercultural adaptation process take place in the context of a stranger-host relationship. In order to move from outsider status into the inside world, we must modify our thinking and behavioral patterns to fit the frame of reference of the host culture. In some collectivistic cultures, the clear distinction between outsiders and insiders may pose cognitive confusion and emotional discomfort for the sojourners.

Fourth, intercultural adaptation is a cyclical, continuous, and interactive process. As a dynamic and complex process, intercultural adaptation involves interaction among three dimensions: affective, cognitive, and behavioral. Based on our reactions to these three dimensions of the new culture, we begin to influence and change the environment and to be influenced and changed by it. This interaction also represents a continuous and cyclical process in which we constantly face and try to overcome the obstacles caused by the new environment. The process is cyclical because it reflects the ups and downs and repetitive sequences of affective, cognitive, and behavioral reactions to facing and generating responses to the obstacles. The responses generated when we face the obstacles may lead us to be successful participants in the host culture in which we become free of the iterative and recursive loop of facing and generating responses to cultural obstacles. In other words, we become bicultural. If, however, we fail to generate effective and appropriate responses to the obstacles, we either become returnees by going back to our home culture or escapers by avoiding problem solving in the host culture.

Fifth, intercultural adaptation is ongoing. Studies in intercultural adjustment tend to overemphasize the failure or success of coping with the problems or obstacles. Actually, to most sojourners, the adjustment process falls between the two extremes. In other words, our adaptation is an incomplete one in which we can never be affectively, cognitively, or behaviorally identical to host nationals. Thus, focusing on the relative degree or level of the coping process is far more important than dicotomizing the process into either failure or success.

Finally, intercultural adaptation implies personal development. Adjusting to a new environment is a developmental event that requires sojourners to develop appropriate strategies to overcome the obstacles caused by the new culture. Thus, intercultural adaptation challenges us and pushes us to change affectively, cognitively, and behaviorally in order to fit ourselves to the lifestyles of the new environment.

Although this dialectical model is not new, it integrates a wide range of literature in the area of intercultural adaptation and reconnects it to sociopsycholgocial adjustment theory. It becomes a heuristic model that can be used to analyze different types of sojourners regardless of the length of time they stay in the host culture and the depth of their interaction with the host nationals.

## A Transformative Learning Model

Living in a new culture for a period of time, we will inevitably experience transformation. Intercultural adaptation, then, is a tranformative process in which we gradually learn to convert ourselves, through communication activities, from a newcomer to a competent communicator in the host culture. Based on Mezirow's (1978, 1981, 1991) transformative learning theory and Kim and Ruben's (1988) intercultural transformation theory, Taylor (1994) developed a learning model for becoming interculturally competent to explain the process of intercultural adaptation.

Transformative learning explicates the change sojourners undergo by examining how they interpret their experiences in the host culture in order to reach understanding, appreciation, and respect. The change of meaning structure for our experiences results from instrumental learning and communicative learning (Mezirow, 1990). Instrumental learning is based on empirical-analytic discovery in which sojourners learn new ways of interpretation through solving task-oriented problems and learning the manner in which hosts assign cause-and-effect relationships. Communicative learning is a process of cognitively understanding the cultural presuppositions concerning concepts such as values, feelings, freedom, and love. The transformative learning model of intercultural adaptation consists of three dimensions: the precondition to change, the process, and the outcome.

The *precondition to change* refers to culture shock that serves as a catalyst for transformation in the process of intercultural adaptation. As Kim and Ruben (1988) indicated, it is in this situation that we attempt to regain the internal balance by coping with the cultural difficulties caused by the host culture. The efforts to make this kind of psychological adjustment become the precondition for individual transformation and growth.

Taylor related Mezirow's (1991) ten-phase transformation process:

1. A disorienting dilemma.
2. Self-examination with feelings of guilt or shame.

**3.** A critical assessment of epistemic, sociocultural, or psychic assumptions.

**4.** Recognition that one's discontent and process of transformation are shared and that others have negotiated a similar change.

**5.** Exploration of options for new roles, relationships, and actions.

**6.** Planning of a course of action.

**7.** Acquisition of knowledge and skills for implementing our plans.

**8.** Provisional adoption of new roles.

**9.** Building of competence and self-confidence in new roles and relationships.

**10.** A reintegration into one's life on the basis of conditions dictated by one's new perspective. (p. 168)

Among these phases, the disorienting dilemma represents the precondition for sojourners for transformation as a result of culture shock. Phases 9 and 10 represent the *outcome* dimension. The *process* dimension can be treated as an extension of the intercultural adaptation models introduced by Adler (1975), Kim (1988), Kim and Ruben (1988), Mansell (1981), Torbiorn (1982), and Yoshikawa (1987).

The old bottle is filled with new wine in the outcome dimension. Through a persistent learning process, we are transformed from awkward newcomers into competent communicators in the new culture. Our growth as sojourners is seen in our affective, cognitive, and behavioral performance. Affectively, we are more in touch with our own emotions and moods and become more empathetic to host nationals' conduct. Cognitively, we become more capable and flexible in dealing with ambiguous situations. Behaviorally, we show the ability to confidently play the different social roles required by the host culture.

Although this model may suffer from the limitation of treating the learning process as a universal model that reflects the Western autonomous and self-directed worldview, it adequately explains how the sojourners develop a new perspective in the process of intercultural adaptation and heuristically links the theories of intercultural adaptation and intercultural competence.

## RECAP

Increasing contact among people from different cultures around the globe demands understanding of the process of intercultural adaptation. This chapter examines intercultural adaptation from the perspective of culture shock and further explores the dimensions and developmental stages of intercultural adaptation and approaches to its study. Two new models of intercultural adaptation study are also described that will serve to guide future research.

Five topics of culture shock are discussed: (1) the nature of culture shock, (2) aspects of culture shock, (3) forms of culture shock, (4) symptoms of culture shock, and (5) effects of culture shock.

## Research Highlight 8–4

Who:     Kim, Y. Y.

What:    "Cross-Cultural Adaptation: An Integrative Theory."

Where:   In R. L. Wiseman (Ed.) (1995), *Intercultural Communication Theory* (pp. 170–193). Thousand Oaks, CA: Sage.

This article aims to develop an integrative theory of intercultural adaptation. Three "open-systems" assumptions form the basis of the theory: (1) humans have an inherent drive to adapt and grow; (2) adaptation to one's social environment occurs through communication; and (3) adaptation is a complex and dynamic process.

Three concepts form the foundation of this integrative theory: deculturation and acculturation, the stress-adaptation-growth dynamic, and intercultural transformation. Acculturation is the process of learning the elements of the host culture to be a member of it. The acculturation process inevitably involves discarding old cultural habits (deculturation). This acculturation-deculturation process normally causes stress and requires sojourners to adapt to the stress. The stress-adaptation process leads to personal change and growth. Therefore, the entire process of cross-cultural adaptation represents a process of intercultural transformation by which sojourners become functionally and psychologically suited to the new environment and finally achieve intercultural identity.

Based on the above conceptual foundation, the author develops a structural model of intercultural adaptation. The model is comprised of six dimensions. The first dimension, *host communication competence,* includes cognitive, affective, and operational competence in the host culture. The second dimension, *host social communication,* includes interpersonal and mass communication in the host culture. The third dimension, *ethnic social communication,* includes ethnic interpersonal and mass communication. The fourth dimension, *environment,* includes host receptivity, host conformity, and ethnic group strength. The fifth dimension, *predisposition,* includes preparedness, ethnicity, and personality. Finally, the dimension of *intercultural transformation* includes functional fitness, psychological health, and intercultural identity.

Eight approaches to the study of intercultural adaptation are delineated: (1) movement as loss, (2) fatalism, (3) selective migration, (4) appropriate expectation, (5) negative life events, (6) social support, (7) clash of values, and (8) social skills deficit.

Four dimensions of intercultural adaptation are explained: (1) alienation, (2) marginality, (3) acculturation, and (4) duality.

A **U**-curve pattern of intercultural adaptation is comprised of four stages: (1) honeymoon period, (2) crisis period, (3) adjustment period, and (4) biculturalism period. A **W**-curve pattern is also used to explicate the reentry adaptation process.

Finally, a dialectical model of intercultural adaptation developed by Anderson and a tranformative learning model for intercultural adaptation are discussed.

## RETHINK

As a critical concept of intercultural communication, intercultural adaptation needs much further study. Several suggestions from Kim (1986, 1989) and Searle and Ward (1990) for future research deserve mention here.

First, the terms used to describe sojourners' experience in a new culture are vague. Those terms commonly used, including *acculturation, adaptation, adjustment, assimilation, integration, resocialization, transculturation,* and *transformation,* need to be conceptually defined. Second, the differences and similarities of the intercultural adaptation process as experienced by sojourners and immigrants should be clarified. Third, the influences of institutional factors on the intercultural adaptation process, including the sojourner's original society, the host society, and the ethnic community to which he or she belongs, need to be considered. Finally, theory-based research needs to be encouraged. Most studies lack conceptual correspondence and methodological appropriateness. The two theory-based models delineated in this chapter can serve to direct research on the intercultural adaptation process.

## QUESTIONS FOR DISCUSSION

1. What are the six common aspects of culture shock?
2. Describe the six forms of culture shock.
3. Describe the symptoms of culture shock specified by Oberg.
4. Compare the positive and negative effects of culture shock.
5. Describe the eight theoretical foundations for the study of intercultural adaptation.
6. Explain the four patterns of emotional and affective states in the process of intercultural adaptation.
7. Describe the stages of **U**-curve pattern of intercultural adaptation.
8. Compare and contrast the dialectical model and transformative learning model of intercultural adaptation.
9. What needs to be considered in the future study of intercultural adaptation?

# ▶ **Chapter 9**

## **Listening between Co-Cultures**

### *Objectives*

By the completion of this chapter, you will

- Understand that language and experience are only partially shared by persons within a culture.
- Observe how denying someone's co-cultural differences can privilege one person over another.
- Investigate how persons from domestic co-cultures can develop a common ground of listening.
- Possess some tools for use in listening between co-cultures.
- Consider intercultural listening as the constructing of narratives between people of diverging cultures.

> *Freedom to speak, freedom to listen. . . . However ardently we disagree. . . . [i]t is from our diversity, our tolerance of diversity, our reasoning together from many different convictions we hold that the chief strength of our people derives.—LYNDON BAINES JOHNSON*

Within the African American rhetorical tradition, messages get co-created. One party begins a message, but is often joined by others, who add emphasis or words of appreciation or extensions of the thought. The interactants may seek to establish a pleasing rhythm of circular, communal interaction. In the black church or similar gathering, speaker and listener urge one another on with call and response, with messages and expressions of delight, amplifications, encouragement, and echoes of words just said. Conceptually, it becomes difficult to say for sure who is the "speaker" and who the "listener."

Across town, in a public school kindergarten class, an African American child similarly echoes the words of the teacher, only to be warned that he or she should "listen," and not "interrupt" the teacher. And, in a nearby junior high school, a white teacher begins a lesson, white students complete their sentence, and then attend to the teacher. After all, this is the mainstream rule for "listening" respectfully to a teacher. Some African American students, on the other hand, complete their thought and then turn their full attention to the teacher. In their case, a "thought" requires several sentences. Tragically, notes to parents or suspensions follow what, to the teacher of the dominant culture, appears to be clear-cut "interruptions," "disrespect," and "failure to listen" by the African American students (Patton, 1986). Mainstream schools likely enforce the expectations and rules of the dominant culture, and it should not be surprising that the reasons for minority student suspensions contain frequent reference to listening and communication "mismatches" between the rules of the mainstream culture and those of domestic co-cultures (Patton, 1986). Mini case 9–1 shows potential problems of co-cultural listening.

Can it be the case that co-cultural children resort to distinctive cultural patterns of listening in defiance of the teacher in a deliberate attempt to undermine his or her authority? Don't nine years of public schooling impress upon co-cultural children the "correct" way to listen and to "pay attention"? Alternatively framed, how many years of contact with co-cultural children does it take for a mainstream teacher to adjust to major variations in rules for "listening attentively and with respect"? Why does he or she feel obliged to use

---

**Mini Case 9–1**

Hamilton High School had a faculty meeting to decide on the calendar for the coming academic year. Midway through the meeting, Thelma proposed inviting the governor to come to a school assembly to discuss his thoughts on the need for greater civility in the schools. The idea got talked about, and then the meeting turned to other subjects. Later, Fred again asked whether the school would invite the governor to speak. At this point, the faculty agreed to invite him. The chair of the meeting thanked Fred for his great idea, while Thelma looked on in anger.

Discuss the process by which Fred got credit for an idea that was initiated by Thelma. Does this case have any implications for co-cultural listening?

institutional power to discipline co-cultural children who perform listening and speaking acts in accordance with the rules that have been passed on to them by their culture?

Along these lines, Kochman (1981) describes differences in talking and listening styles among African American and white communicators. The dominant white pattern is to express a thought, change the pitch of the voice, and await a response. A common pattern for the African American, Anglophone Caribbean, or Asian (North) Indian co-culturals is to join midway in the sentence of the previous speaker and to assume a place in the conversation without a pause or a shift in tone of voice. The result can be frustration for the white listener who would like to join the conversation but cannot find a culturally convenient method to shift from "listener" to "speaker." Differences in listening thus contribute to friction among white and black co-culturals.

A text by Kochman, *Black and White Styles in Conflict* (1981), invites us to reach two implicit conclusions. First, the book hints that it is the black style that differs from the white style rather than the reverse. The black style seems "at fault" for being distinctive, and the white style becomes the ground against which to view the black "difference." Second, listening differently invites "conflict." The veiled message is that the mainstream pattern is the norm, and that those who depart from the mainstream invite trouble. If only co-culturals (or women, or youths) would "listen" right, goes the thinking, things would be okay.

Those of Northern and Western European ancestry in the United States tend to define the norm and to challenge those who depart from it. The implicit message is that African Americans would do well to learn and adopt the white style of turn-taking (Harrigan, 1985), hence, of listening, for the sake of reduced interethnic conflict. The implicit thinking of the dominant group seems to be, "Why should the mainstream communicator be taught to accommodate differences in listening by nondominant co-culturals? Why not require women and nondominant co-culturals to make the necessary adjustments?"

To date almost no research has tackled the question of listening between co-cultures. Because listening is a vital skill both within and across cultures and because, in a microcosm, the study of listening raises nearly every other concern that we feature in our text, we build this chapter, in the absence of a large body of research literature, by combining research on listening within monocultural populations with the authors' experience with domestic co-cultures. We add the findings of the few studies that touch on cultural concerns in listening with reflections on listening from philosophers of meaning and with logical extensions of existing research that was not conducted specifically with listening in mind.

The literature on listening even within a single culture provides few definitive answers: Is listening an external or an internal matter? Is it an active or passive act? Is it something only one party does while the other talks, or does the listener somehow shape the message? Are interpersonal listening and listening to a lecture equivalent acts? Is reading a lot like listening? Does listening represent product or process? Does "comprehensive" listening (for overall meaning) differ from "critical" listening (to persuasive messages)? Are typologies of listening useful or unproductive? Is empathy a necessity for listeners, or is it a fiction? We touch on some of these questions in the development of our thoughts on listening between cultures. The discussion is separated into five sections: (1) levels of listening, (2) components of intercultural listening, (3) intercultural listening as qualitative research, (4) stepping outside to listen, and (5) narrative listening.

## LEVELS OF LISTENING

There are three levels of listening: (1) intrapersonal listening, (2) interpersonal intracultural listening, and (3) intercultural listening.

### *Intrapersonal Listening*

If we can be said to have a self, we form and develop this self through conversations within our inner mind, by talking with those of our own language group, and by interacting with significant members of society and family. Especially if we choose to be "rhetorically sensitive" and to "highly self-monitor," we rehearse in our minds how our ideas will sound to another interactant. The theory of symbolic interactionism states that we become who we are through this ongoing interaction of mind, self, and society (Mead, 1934). Our internal dialogue, our listening to ourselves, incorporates references to what we have heard others say around us and about us. Even in our quietest thoughts we echo image and concept, schemas (Edwards & McDonald, 1993; Thorndyke & Yekovich, 1981), and characterization that we have learned from others in our society during the course of social listening.

Within our own community, we learn to estimate what others are saying, and what they mean (Edwards & McDonald, 1993). We are aware of common possibilities and usage, and we do not always attend to each and every word that is spoken. We do not experience the increased "processing load" that we do when the discourse of the other is not typical of our community's speech. Edwards & McDonald maintain:

> *it is not usually necessary for a listener to pay attention to individual components of an utterance unless the context is unfamiliar or unexpected . . . or when a speech pattern differs markedly from one's own, as in listening . . . to a dialect. (p. 43)*

The willingness to continue to listen even as the processing load increases is one quality of listening competence from Allen and Brown (1976) that is endorsed by Ridge (1993, p. 8).

Philosophers propose that there is no way for persons to negotiate the world, if not through words (Ricoeur, 1976). Either, as some persons believe, the "things" of the world can be named and dealt with "objectively," without changing them. Or, as we argue for the purpose of this chapter, our link with realities outside is through linguistic realities inside, or "linguisticality" (Ricoeur, 1976). Our words name things, and the names we use for things convey beliefs about them and attitudes toward them. Our culture looks at a pencil and comments on its usefulness for writing. A Native American culture looks at the same object and describes it as being longer than it is wide. To Bantu Africans it is first sized up as "not alive," as an object. As mainstream Americans, we draw up a four-legged piece of furniture, sit upon it, and speak of it as a "chair." A Native American culture may say that a thing is "chairing" when it is used for sitting, but does not consider it to be a chair. These distinctions, while they may not prevent a person from one culture from talking with someone from another culture, indicate an active role in construing reality for our language.

The fact that words within my mind are not those words within the mind of the speaker of another language offers little difficulty for intracultural communication. For so long as I talk to myself, I do not expose my misperceptions and misrepresentations of another's realities. While I listen to myself, the questions of culture that I face are expressed in frames that are familiar to me. I may experience "self shock" (Zaharna, 1988) when I try to use my familiar frames to contain unfamiliar ideas and concepts and experiences, but my problems are not yet felt at the level of "listening."

Our meanings for things may be hierarchic: We start with broad categorizations for a thing; for example: It is Middle Eastern. We add further differentiation: It is a building. We qualify our differentiations: It is a place of worship for Muslims, a mosque. If our experience with such things is plentiful, we add several further layers to this description, about its designer or its history or about whether it was damaged in a particular war. Contrarily, if we have had little experience with the thing, all examples of the thing fall into the same broad category for us. All Asians "look alike" and "get A's in math." We fail to differentiate "Chinese" from "Japanese," and falsely consider Iranians as "Arabs."

A contrasting theory from Rosch (1973) poses the possibility that we first learn a "prototype" level for thing, for example, "dog," before branching to "Labrador retriever" and "dachshund," or moving upward in abstraction to "animal." We start with a familiar case and then move to finer differentiations or toward greater abstractions. Our intrapersonal assignment of meaning begins with the most familiar category, then branches upward or downward. This view of processing could also explain the use of stereotypical listening, whereby we start with the description we learned first, before qualifying that description.

There are two contrasting perspectives at the intrapersonal level. One is that we have a "self." That self more or less represents the product of our conscious mind. Therefore, when we frame a message for another person we construct a message to be sent, we hope unchanged, to the other party. Information theorists look for ways to see that "noise" of one kind or another does not somehow erode our original message. That message should arrive at its destination intact. By this view, we are fully and self-consciously aware of our original message and listening is something that takes place "out there," in the mind of another. We are fully aware what message was sent and know precisely what message should be replicated by a capable listener.

A contrasting view is that we are not completely visible to ourselves (Berry, 1993). Further, our words for things never have a single meaning but rather, spoken at different times, could scold on one occasion and give a compliment on another. The link between our words and things "out there" is somewhat established for our own language community, but also it is unique to us. Indeed, when we hear our own words played back to us we may have second thoughts about what we actually "meant." Our words take meaning only as they provide links to a specific context. By this view, listening takes on an internal focus; it asks us to explain how our ideas were framed, and how we are using our words to "point" to external realities. We extend this position for our analysis in this chapter.

## Interpersonal Intracultural Listening

The persons who speak our language and who constitute our immediate family and community share a common base of symbolization. Therefore, when any one member of the community who is minimally competent speaks words to another member of that community, the listener can likely grasp a significant part of the speaker's meaning. Though words are not permanently connected to things, they seem to be so for other members of our linguistic community. We share the same frames and are united in *homophily,* the assumption of likeness, with those around us.

Over the course of time, the common pool of meanings we draw from in our conversations comes to reflect the usage of the most publicly prominent members of our community. When males play a dominant role in the public sphere, the words we share tend to be men's words. Foss and Foss (1991) propose that women may have their own places where they use language in ways that are familiar and comfortable for them, but women who enter mainstream organizations may feel a need to learn a man's language, to move toward "androgyny," and to adopt the linguistic frames and conventions of the male members of the organization (Coakley & Wolvin, 1990). Few sources ask male members of organizations to seek androgyny, that is, to speak and to listen more like women. The burden falls onto the co-cultural person to stop being "different." Women who are socialized in North America tend to hint at their inner thoughts through kinesics, to ask more questions, to mirror more of what the other speaker has said (Emmert, Emmert & Brandt, 1993). Men from within the same linguistic community may frame this as an indication of a lack of toughness or resolve. Listening frames, then, differ by gender even within a single linguistic community (Borisoff & Hahn, 1992).

If frames differ within a single community of speakers what, then, occurs between co-cultural groups within a single nation? We present an example drawn from an ethnographic study in Canada (see for details Starosta & Hannon, 1997). A 1990 dispute started between Canadian Mohawks and the provincial authorities in Quebec. The police were French Canadians, and they demanded to speak with a representative from the matriarchal Mohawk community:

> *We sent out a woman to negotiate, but the French chauvinists [Quebec police] do not treat their women as equals. They told us to send out a man. It is our tradition to take the guidance of women before we make decisions. A second time they told us, send out a man to talk. We sent out our spiritual advisor to explain to them that they should talk to our women and the French police said, "At last, a man! Now we can talk!" We then called back the advisor and again sent out a woman to speak for us. For several months they had to negotiate with a woman.*

As a precondition for "listening," the police demanded to speak with someone that they framed as "worth listening to," someone "with authority." Their linguistic and cultural frames (allegedly) defined women as largely irrelevant to the task of serious negotiation.

As negotiations proceeded, the Canadian and Quebecois authorities rapidly grew impatient with the pace of the proceedings. They claimed that the Mohawks would not negotiate. Their frames demanded a rapid settlement of issues. The Mohawk community, though, was geared toward protracted talking and protracted listening aimed at generating consensus:

> *We Mohawks will talk forever. All First Nation Aboriginal people will talk and talk. The Canadian police said we would not negotiate when we wanted to add "Ancestral" to their description of the disputed [Ancestral] Pines. They broke off talks, and gave us one phone line to be used only when we were ready to surrender to authorities. We work slowly because we operate by consensus. Even children join our discussions. We listen to what everyone has to say, and only then we know what we must do.*

The listening of the three co-cultural groups (the Anglophone Canadians, the Francophone Quebecois, and the Anglophone Mohawks) differed with regard to time frame. To many Montrealers the dispute began in 1990. To many Mohawks the dispute dated with the arrival of the first French settlers hundreds of years earlier.

The European, linear time frame is often posed within technological societies as the "standard" and cyclical variations, mythic views of time, event time, or other variations are disparaged as deviant. The empowered definition becomes that of the numerically dominant co-culture (Vinson, Johnson & Hackman, 1993). Mahatma Gandhi therefore chided a European reporter with the words that the European culture needs immediate results. He, a Hindu whose culture believes in rebirth, could "wait 40 or 400 years" for India's independence (Starosta, 1993).

Finally, three elements are emphasized at the interpersonal intracultural listening level: empathy, openness, and history.

### Empathy

"Listen empathically" is a dictum that is advanced for listeners both within and across cultures: See from another's perspective, walk in another's shoes, put yourself in the place of the other. Empathic listening, as discussed by Arnett and Nakagawa (1993) and by Stewart (1993), is viewed as a fiction. It is based on a view of the world that says the task of listening is to passively reproduce the thoughts of the speaker in the mind of the listener. This view, says Stewart (1993), leads us to the "reification of self" by which means we falsely move "from a conceptual question to make it an empirical one" (p. 371) and sets us to looking for reproducible meanings and states of mind. Stewart proposes that we move beyond the search for the internal feelings of the communicator in our analysis to portray "the meanings given birth between partners in relationship" (pp. 374–375). The emphasis on "meanings between" in place of "meanings within" leads us to consider the communication that draws persons together toward a "third culture."

### Openness

Here we return to the thinking of meaning-centered philosophers Heidegger, Ricoeur, and Gadamar (see Littlejohn, 1995), who all call for us to explore the act of communication as a communing in a world of partially shared meanings (Stewart, 1993, pp. 381–382). They ask us to choose among the myriad things that words can mean within our linguistic community and to tie the words to possible contexts. If we can restore the original context, or nearly restore the context, listening will have resulted. This trying-on of contexts does not and cannot proceed unilaterally. Instead, we bounce ideas off one another in order to achieve a more perfect understanding. Stewart (1993) quotes Ricoeur:

---

**Research Highlight 9–1**

Who:    Stewart, J.

What:    "Interpretive Listening: An Alternative to Empathy."

Where:    *Communication Education, 32*, 1983, 379–391.

Stewart's article is an outgrowth of the 1981 conference of the International Listening Association. Stewart builds on the work of Arnett and Nakagawa that calls for the development of alternatives to models of empathetic listening.

Stewart begins with an observation that the listening literature views listening as a primary skill, but that little writing "identifies the nature of the listening process or specifies its qualities or components. Stewart believes that writers in hermeneutic phenomenology can advance the understanding of listening.

Philosophers work toward more toward the reproduction, not the production, of meaning. Heidegger, Gadamer, and Ricoeur, however, move the study of meaning from a place *within* communicators to a place *between* them. "Being-in-the-world" requires going beyond text.

Language is viewed as "polysemic, or prone to having different meanings with varying contexts. The listener must show an "openness" to possible meanings and interpretations that go beyond the familiar. *Prejudice,* or the starting point of the interactant, must be suspended as a point of reference in order to listen with openness.

*Linguisticality (Sprachlichkeit)* implies that language does not represent things, it does not portray set realities. Rather, Stewart endorses the idea that the world is linguistic and that a given set of words can only evoke the most familiar set of conventions to approximate a common or a cultural usage. Says Plato, "the true being of things becomes accessible precisely in their linguistic appearances."

*Play* indicates a to-and-fro, give-and-take negotiation of meaning. Genuine listening creates surprises for both interactants and introduces the unforeseen. The result of the "play" of listening can be a decentering of the interactants, leading to the "fusion of horizons."

Listening, according to Stewart, can move beyond inferences about internals states to study the interactants' communicative action.

---

*interpretation is a process by which, in the interplay of question and answer, the interlocutors collectively determine the contextual values which structure their conversation. (p. 389)*

Openness, then, is the give-and-take between communicators that is required to recreate a common contextual frame for understanding. That frame is the original frame of neither party. Instead, it is something common to the two interactants. Understanding is "co-constituted."

### History

Our meanings result from experience. In part, this experience is linguistic, since our words predispose us to a particular view of the world. But history takes many forms, and is similar to our usage of "culture." "Understanding is developed in a neutral process between historically-contexted subjects . . . , an 'I' and a 'Thou'" (Stewart, 1993, p. 383). Within this view, our particular history gives to us a "prejudice," a particular view of the world. Since all persons bring a prejudice, a presumptive view of the meaning of things to the interaction, the prejudices of each party must be subjected to the demands of openness. "Anyone who listens is fundamentally open" (p. 383).

## INTERCULTURAL LISTENING

Thus far we have dealt with interactants who share some semantic space, that is, they share socialization in a particular geographic location and history and share to some degree *linguisticality* (the understanding of things outside by reference to usage within a given linguistic community.) Persons of the same culture or co-culture recognize some common frames of history and concept and use some of the same categories to process a message.

The notion of linguisticality, a shared semantic space provided for members of a language community, does not hold as easily for those who have different native languages. Sociolinguists have long maintained that a difference in language or dialect corresponds rather directly to a difference in some other feature of social life.

In practice, we consider less believable those within our own nation who speak with different regional accents or dialects (Johnson & Buttny, 1982). Elsewhere in the world, a difference in vocal rhythm or pronunciation points to a difference of caste, tribe, ethnic origin, class, or religion. Recall from an earlier chapter, for instance, how the Amish English vocabulary and the lexicon of other U.S. Americans diverge.

Three issues can be raised at the level of intercultural listening: listening across emotions, fusing horizons, and selective listening.

### Listening across Emotions

White males commonly attribute to women and to African Americans in the United States, among others, that they are emotional (Kochman, 1981). While listening across emotions can raise the energy needed to process messages (Thomas, 1994), the conclusion that the co-cultural speaker is "emotional" can block openness of exchange because such name-calling tends to terminate the exchange. Context building, history sharing, and the search for common meaning are soon disregarded. Speicher (1994) develops the idea that the co-cultural person who speaks with emotion usually speaks rationally. Persons can be both passionate and logical about a given idea, especially when they speak from a position of relative powerlessness.

### Fusing Horizons

The blocking of interaction because we are locked in our own parochial view of the world prevents "the fusion of horizons" that accompanies all successful listening (Stewart, 1993). A person with no horizon can see only himself or herself. Great importance is given to the person's own point of view, because the world centers on that person. (At the cultural level, we speak of *ethnocentrism* or *xenophobia*). When we push back the edges of our horizon, defending our personal interpretations becomes of little importance. Instead, we begin to see listening between cultures to be the best avenue to take perspectives and to "see ourselves as others see us."

When we see ourselves in perspective, we recognize ourselves to be en-culturated and socialized entities. The person who "sees farther" places himself or herself into perspective. That person seeks out conversations across cultures and listens across difference to further broaden his or her horizon. The goal is to attain a higher universality than we could know alone. We confront our prejudice, our culture, our gender, our historicity, while our counterpart does the same. We must be mindful, not mindless, of differences in meanings and their processing. We must reduce our taken-for-granteds and seek to grow from every exchange across gender, language, or culture. Of course, we expect no less of the other interactant who builds, with us, a common ground, a third culture. John Stewart refers to this joint creation of experience as our "spiritual child" (1990, p. 26).

Putting aside our use of our own historical and cultural reference points to listen to the message of another is no easy task. Cooper (in press) considers words drawn from a speech by Khallid Abdul Muhammed, a spokesman for Unity Nation, who was criticized in a one-page newspaper advertisement by members of the Jewish community. Muhammed's words were quoted, for example, about the desirability of killing white South Africans. Cooper then placed these words before two groups of students, one white and the other African American. The white students largely thought the words to represent "hate speech," and some responded with counterthreats. Black students, in many cases, said Muhammed was not engaging in hate speech. He was expressing anger, or he was taking rhetorical license to engender pride in being black. Differences in the presumptive worlds of black and white students are powerfully dramatized by Cooper's analysis.

### Selective Listening

We do, indeed, hear what we expect to hear in a message. Witkin (1993) recounts the example of:

*a friend whose professional career was focused on the prevention and reduction of racial and religious discrimination [who] caught a glimpse of a billboard advertising a product. He thought he saw the words* racial issues, *when in fact the message was about* facial tissues. *(p. 38)*

Pursuing why we hear such differences takes us too far toward the "out there" analysis of human psychology and removes us from the "in between" analysis of intercultural listening that concerns us here. When prejudices, history, and a sense of the powerlessness of many co-culturals cause us to limit authentic listening; when the usage of the dominant group as the standard for correctness and the presence of unnegotiable schemas in our minds cause us to distort what we hear from the other party, we are far from effective listening. We develop few shared symbols, we promote no openness, we seek to broaden no horizons, and we cease to move toward the fostering of a place between, a third culture. A part of us that is most distinctively human dies.

## COMPONENTS OF INTERCULTURAL LISTENING

Based on the previous discussions, we can consider listening between co-cultures to be the "reciprocal attending to verbal and nonverbal messages of someone of differing history, linguisticality, and socialization in an attempt to create a ground of mutual understanding." This definition is comprised of four components of intercultural listening: reciprocal attending; verbal and nonverbal messages; differing history, linguisticality, and socialization; and mutual understanding.

### *Reciprocal Attending*

The monocultural literature on listening often stresses the role of speaker versus the role of listener. When speaker and hearer are viewed as the same in principle, then listening research goes no further to understand or to compensate for differences in socialization. The belief that within a single culture differences of gender, power, and linguisticality "do not matter" or "make no difference" soon leads to the glossing of difference on the part of the speaker and to an affirming of power on the part of the dominant group: Understanding is assumed by the dominant communicator, even in its absence.

By stressing listening between cultures to be a reciprocal (i.e., mutual) process, we emphasize that neither party may legitimately lay claim to the position of "standard" against which to measure the "other." If either party enters into intercultural interaction with the expectation that only the other must adapt to the messages that are offered, we propose that only pseudo-listening can occur. It is false intercultural listening if one party expects adjustments in the other interactant but remains unwilling or unable to change his or her own orientation toward the other.

## Verbal and Nonverbal Messages

The literature on monocultural listening tends to adopt an "external" approach in which it becomes the responsibility of the listener to replicate the message of the speaker in his or her own mind. This approach draws us toward psychology to see why it may be that the listener attends to only parts of the message, distorts other parts of the message, and recalls only a portion of the message that has been incompletely attended to. The *information theory* frame also presents an external view: The "message" must be conveyed through some "channel" in the face of "noise" in a way that the message "received" is the same as the message sent. The best listener, then, is a channel who can pass any possible message of the source free of distortion of any kind. Likewise, the often-cited belief in empathic listening tries to see that the message received and the message sent are one and the same message. Earlier we mentioned that the meaning of the sender and receiver can never be one and the same, try as we might to make it so. We move beyond this view in our thinking.

The "external" approach to listening is limiting in the process of intercultural listening. Placing listening "out there" promotes a one-way flow of information. If feedback is allowed, it functions only to emphasize the importance of the original message, not to invite the co-initiation of distinctive messages on the part of the other interactant.

Also, though, we mentioned that the "internal" analysis of listening (within the initiator) is mainly useful within a single cultural setting. When the sender and receiver grow up with a common language and a shared history, we may become interested in how the sender tries to "point to" things of the external words through the use of his or her messages, but differences in language repertoire and the absence of common frames seldom arise as listening concerns.

If neither the external nor the internal approach to listening proves very useful to study listening between co-cultures, we then must focus on the "mutual and reciprocal" creation of meaning. Many meanings, of course, stem from the use of words. Writers on nonverbal communication, however, propose that vocalics, the use of time, the significant use of space, the physical orientation of the speaker and listener, gesture, temporal, and other nonlinguistic features of a message can serve to gain attention or to qualify message meaning. Indeed, nonverbal aspects of communication may be an especially poignant means of conveying feelings toward a subject. The focus on reciprocal interaction requires very close attention to nonverbal features of the communication.

Stewart (1983) and Arnett and Nakagawa (1983) write of "interpretive lis-

---

**Research Highlight 9–2**

Who:    Arnett, R. C., and Naka-
        gawa, G.

What:   "The Assumptive Roots of Em-
        pathetic Listening: A Critique."

Where:  *Communication Education,
        32,* 1983, 368–378.

The article departs from the pioneering
work of Ralph Nichols on listening.
Nichols and those who wrote from
1948 to 1978 identified listening and
empathy as two of the ten most
frequent communication concerns in
the communication literature. Interpersonal communication researchers
tended to study "empathetic," "non-
directive," therapeutic," "relational,"
"critical," "responsive," or "analytic" listening.

The authors question the philosophical assumptions behind the interpersonal approach to listening. They
subject the idea of empathy to scrutiny,
they ask where meaning falls during
listening, and they seek to identify so-

cial consequences and limits for effective listening.

Empathy (or the German *Ein-
fuhlung*) was studied by communication specialists since 1909. The authors
posit that the idea of empathy falsely
dichotomizes speaker and receiver.
They propose that listening and the
assignment of meaning take place
between, not within, sender or receiver.

The authors accept the hermeneutic notion that all information processing introduces personal bias or
prejudice. To this extent meaning can
never be "transferred," and empathy
can never be complete. Also, cultural
bias renders listening an in-between,
as-if, inferential process.

The authors call for the development of alternatives to the internal,
empathetic, duplication-of-feelings approach to listening. Perhaps the search
for "meaning between" would offer a
viable alternative to the model of "empathetic listening."

---

tening" by which means all interactants "constitute meanings" and through
which we seek the "co-constituing of understanding." This level of listening involves both verbal and nonverbal attentiveness.

## Differing History, Linguisticality, and Socialization

Within a given cultural setting writers commonly assume the presence of a
common pool of language and concepts. The notable exception has been the
separate treatment of women's communication and the subsequent development of a literature on androgynous (gender-neutral) communication. At times,
this literature touches on aspects of listening. If culture were a river, most listening researchers would look at the a river and see it as conceptually the same
river. This view tends to empower those persons who hold positions of privilege within the society.

A variation on this metaphorical view of rivers is that, by sifting through the silt that has been carried to the river's mouth, we can detect where the river has been. We find traces of soil and objects that washed into the flowing river along every point of its history. This seems, to us, an ethnographer's view of rivers: The mainstream is the culture, but it can be analytically viewed according to its many component traditions. We do not see this view of domestic culture as likely promoting research on intercultural listening.

Therefore we subscribe to a third view of rivers and of cultures. By this view, the river does not exist except as a collection of the waters provided by various tributaries. No tributary is the river but each, in collection with the others, generates the river. The history of many different units somehow fuses to become the history of the whole. This metaphor accords most closely with our view of domestic communication, that is, that no tributary is the river and that no co-culture is the culture. The river receives its final identity when the bulk of the tributaries have joined their waters, but the streams of Spanish and Arabic and Hindi that enter the river, the eddies of men and women, the rapids of Jews and Buddhists and Christians, remain distinguishable elements of the whole. In such a national setting we see hope for a flood of theories of listening across culture.

Within this third view of culture we find room to recognize differences in region, in power, in class, in gender socialization, in ethnicity, in religion, in language, and in conceptualization. Persons who listen within such a culture must be on the alert for possible co-cultural variation that goes beyond their expectations. It is a fallacy to assume a unitary *history*. A reporter once told an American that the Vietnamese conflict was the first war that Americans did not win. The response was that the reporter was not from the southern states since the South had, in fact, lost a war before. We dare not assume a unitary language: The courts in Oakland, California, opted in 1996 to consider ebonics (black English) as a distinct language. And we cannot assume the same socialization for all U.S. citizens except for the commonality that accrues slowly over the years through exposure to the same prime-time television programming. The load of processing communication as a listener within a single nation may not be as great as it will likely be across national lines, but it can still be very formidable.

While interaction with those of different national cultures holds the greatest potential to inspire theory building in intercultural listening, the astute communicator will see a need to recognize differences of linguisticality, history, and conceptualization even before looking abroad. It may be the study of differences in gender socialization that leads to a heightened awareness of the co-cultural interactant as culturally "distinct." A study by Cumber and Braithwaite (1996) indicates that when persons in the U.S. Southwest think of "cultural difference" they naturally think of co-cultural variation, but when inhabitants of the Great Plains states consider cultural variation they think of cultures of other nations. If this is the case, states with large populations of Native Americans, Asian Americans, and Hispanic Americans may possibly lead the search for a theory of co-cultural listening. Although the literature on African American communication could also provide deep insights on listening between cultures, much of such research to date reports on the monocultural context of the black church.

## Mutual Understanding

In Chapter 6, on relationship building, we advanced some thoughts on the building of third cultures. We return to these thoughts, and to others that we discussed earlier in this chapter, to deal with mutual understanding: expanding horizons, openness, and to a focus between interactants, not within them.

As suggested earlier, to think of listening as an attempt at direct transfer of meaning from one person to another cannot move us beyond information theory or theories of perceptual distortion. We also stated that moving to within the communicator tempted us to overlook co-cultural differences and differences of national cultures as factors affecting ease of listening. We offered the view that listening between co-cultures is the attempt on the part of all parties to develop a common pool of symbols, concepts, and meanings that would promote the smooth exchange of information.

Our sources introduced the idea that we must *decenter* our communication, that is, to move to a wider horizon in order to view our own cultural grounding as relatively accidental. Through a process of openness, of give-and-take, we must detach ourselves from some of our common cultural usages in order to seek a place in-between, a place that is built and sustained by communicated messages. To move to this place in-between may take new skills in language, new attitudes, and a deeper sense of our prejudice and history. All of these factors are subject to reconsideration when we truly listen between cultures.

We have asked in our presentation of the third-culture model of intercultural relationships what would motivate persons to expose themselves deeply to the culture of another. Also we have heard the question repeatedly whether a person would really want to move to a place where a new way of communicating becomes primary. Our thinking on intercultural listening relies on the willingness to place some of ourselves on to the bargaining table in the interest of expanding our personal (or business) horizons. We achieve this by conceptualizing listening as an active process that is engaged in by two or more persons simultaneously. To this extent, we do not see the "lecture" mode of listening whereby one person talks and the other attends as being a useful foundation for intercultural listening. Rather, we add the defining feature of an *added processing load* requiring us to frame messages at the same time as we are decoding them.

For the present authors, listening is an active process that takes into account all available verbal and nonverbal cues to achieve a common basis of interpretation and understanding. Our search for a theory of intercultural listening leads us to examine comprehensive listening (for overall meaning) rather than critical listening (for persuasive messages). (Intercultural listening may be the pre-condition that makes some critical listening possible for messages from other cultures.) While the monocultural study of listening has produced certain typologies of listeners, listening modes, and the like, we do not see that the sorting of listeners into types and listening into modes provides great insight for the study of intercultural listening. Finally, we have rejected empathy (Bruneau, 1989, 1993) as a model for intercultural listening: (1) it probably is no more than an "as if" construct; (2) it privileges the thoughts of one interactant over the other; (3) it suggests a one-way flow of interaction; (4) it promotes an external view of listening; and (5) we prefer a model of intercultural listening that is the product of the communicative interaction of both parties, not just one.

If the external view of listening is a product of a *positivist* outlook in which the receipt of messages is a quantifiable thing, the internal view of listening is mostly *interpretive*. This means that the way a given person uses language to "point to" things "out there" becomes of interest in and of itself. Our advocacy of an in-between focus is most closely wed to a *critical* research stance. In a critical study we advance an idealized view of the world, explain its advantages, and demonstrate that the adoption of this view offers the advantage of rendering us more complete, fuller human beings. This process does not require strict measurement, and it moves us outside the thinking of any particular person. What is obvious to the researcher is the creation of "a place between." What we experience is an awareness of ourselves as historically situated, enculturated, prejudiced persons. Through intercultural listening we aspire to rise above our cultural limitations.

## INTERCULTURAL LISTENING AS QUALITATIVE RESEARCH

When we move beyond positivism, that is, the idea that the world is "out there" and does not change when we think or talk about it, we must offer ways to talk about a world that changes with our descriptions. To this end, qualitative researchers have developed procedures to investigate the thinking of particular persons and to search for regularities in the thinking of groups of persons. We move from viewing persons as "objects" who "contain" bits of culture to a view of choice-making persons who, with their talk, "constitute" the meanings of things.

Some approaches that qualitative researchers have used to find out how persons constitute their world are very much the same processes we as intercultural listeners can use to learn how our counterparts understand the world:

**1.** Grounded theory: We listen closely and attentively to the actual discourse of the other party.

**2.** Bracketing assumptions: We are clear to ourselves about our prejudices and assumptions, so that we may discount our own thinking to more accurately hear the thinking of the other.

**3.** Experience rich: We acquire enough examples of the other's discourse that we can see beyond superficial levels and hasty generalizations.

**4.** Member checks: We take problematic interpretations back to the other party to see if we have heard and interpreted somewhat accurately what the other party has said.

**5.** Constant comparison: We listen to the other in a variety of contexts so that we can see which parts of the other person continue throughout all contexts and which are situational.

**6.** Ongoing researcher audit: We use our excess thinking space (research on listening indicates that we have extra capacity to think about messages while they are being presented) to ask, "Is the other party starting from a different positioning? Am I shutting the other party out by thinking from my own culture?"

**7.** External audit: We turn to specialists on a culture or co-culture, as needed, to double-check our emerging insights.

**8.** Recognize patterns: We offer our conclusions as provisional, not as final products. Eventually we identify themes, form categories, and develop a common language with the other party. At least until then, we open ourselves to new possibilities.

**9.** Expect the unexpected: Interpretive research that contains no surprises leads us to ask why we tried to learn of the other's thinking or if we succeeded in accessing the other person's distinctive views. And intercultural listening that provides no surprises leads us to ask if we have blocked off important insights with the closedness of our listening approach.

**10.** Await epiphanies: We move toward a position of equality with the other. A history of inequality, land theft, patriarchy, colonialism, homophobia, and World War II internment camps, as a few examples, may mean that parties to intercultural listening must work out feelings of privilege and work through feelings of disempowerment before a "place between" can be generated through intercultural listening.

## STEPPING OUTSIDE TO LISTEN

Two demands of intercultural listening may seem self-contradictory. On the one hand, we must step outside ourselves, we must expand our horizons, so that we may attach proper importance to the things of our culture and so that we may give appropriate value to the positions of the other. On the other hand, we must achieve greater clarity and resolution. What we believe to be on the other's "map" should indeed be there. What we hear should be meant as received. We should become aware if our perceptions are attuned to the perceptions of the other. We seek at one and the same time a panoramic view of interaction and sharp resolution. Can we achieve both breadth and depth at the same time?

Stepping outside of ourselves has been advocated by cognitive psychologists such as Edward C. Stewart and by cultural anthropologists including Edward T. Hall for over two decades. Their proposal is that we seek exposure to those of other cultures for extended periods of time so that we may then return to our culture with the ability to see ourselves as cultural beings who simply occupy one culture out of many, many possibilities. Hall urged us to go "beyond culture," while Stewart pioneered the contrast-American role-play training technique to move us outside of our cultural moorings.

To achieve resolution we should learn a foreign language, take area studies courses, and read the literature of the persons of other cultures. We should use academic training to acquaint us with the history, power relationships, and culture of our counterparts. Failing this, we should turn to informants of the interactants' culture to help us to interpret things that are not clear to us that we think may be cultural or co-cultural in origin. When we obtain a certain comfort level with our counterparts we will then seek greater clarity and resolution by asking questions and by being questioned in turn.

Intercultural trainers and educators have long debated the merits of pursuing culture-general (horizon-widening) and culture-specific (achieving clear cultural resolution) approaches to instruction. We feel that parallel concerns await the listener between co-cultures but that resolution will probably not be motivated without first expanding horizons. The difference in learning to listen between co-cultures and nations is that for international listening our instructor will have to "stand in" for his or her culture, and the process of creating a common semantic space may therefore be more formal than would be common in the case of our co-culturals.

## NARRATIVE LISTENING

In this chapter we entered uncharted territory together. To our knowledge, the topic of listening between co-cultures has not explicitly been breached as such, though some research literature certainly seems to apply. Now we extend our thinking to propose a model of intercultural listening as *narrative*. Let us consider a set of premises about ourselves as communicators:

**1.** We are active interpreters of what we hear.
**2.** We take new knowledge and somewhat consciously mix it with what we already know and believe.

**3.** We relate the things we recount of our private life and of our cultural life as narratives, that is, as connected stories about things.

**4.** We try to make our narratives internally consistent and consistent with known and believed "facts."

**5.** When we talk about new things we fit them in with our previous understandings of events while adding statements about motivations, heroes, villains, morals, and the like.

**6.** Persons of other cultural and co-cultural backgrounds engage in these same narrative processes but reach variant explanations and conclusions about things "out there."

If we look at ourselves and at other persons who characteristically tell stories—about ourselves, our community, our world(s)—we soon consider the role of the narrative listener, the person who listens "across cultural stories" and who blends elements from one story with elements of another. We may find that we, as listeners to intercultural narratives, function as "naive qualitative researchers" who use some of the same data-gathering strategies that are used by ethnographers and others in the field.

## Sense-Making

We "make sense" of things by posing logical connections among external events and also by connecting external events with constructs and values we hold dear. By defining relationships among concepts and events, we come to an interpretation of the reality around us. Our interpretations are shaped by our perceptions, by our sense of logic, and by our notions of right and wrong.

We give significance to external events by relating them to our internal structures and needs and then frame the results of this process as explanatory narrative accounts. Our narrative accounts, our stories about things "out there," are more or less consistent internally, more or less shared within our community or culture, more or less consistent with external facts, and more or less dramatically compelling (Fisher 1984, 1985a, 1985b, 1987; Metzger, Weber, Springston & Larsen 1991; Starosta & Hannon, in press). Notes Friedman (1993):

> *Stories give coherence to people's experiences in particular contexts, involve intentions and feelings, and operate as integrated, holistic units. Narratives reflect a discrete mode of thought, evidenced by how we impose a narrative structure upon human experiences and how stories capture our attention. . . . Most extant literature on listening, however, does not address narratives independently from other forms of discourse. (p. 201)*

Truthfulness and accuracy are not our sole determining factors in producing narratives. The "truth" may not be popular, and we may not believe it

---

**Research Highlight 9–3**

Who:     Fisher, W. R.

What:    "The Narrative Paradigm: An Elaboration."

Where:   *Communication Monographs, 52,* 1985, 347–367.

Fisher extends his work on narrative that he introduced in the March of 1984 in Communication Monographs. Here he addresses how narrative theory relates to some other approaches.

Social science tries to answer how people come by the stories that guide their behavior through the study of attribution theory and the like. Narrative theory, too, "seeks to account for how people come to adopt stories. . . ." A person's narrative recounting should serve to predict actions that are related to the person's understanding.

Social science, though, tends to overlook values and oughtness; that is, whether someone should adhere to a story. It ignores consideration of good and bad, virtue and evil, that are assessed in the study of narrative.

Narrative approaches assess "prob-

ability" and "fidelity," not "effectiveness" and "success." They call for critical self-awareness and conscious choice. One person's narrative might be another's rationalization.

Narratives must cohere without obvious contradictions. Also, they must meet the standard of representing "good reasons." They involve questions of fact, relevance, consequence, consistency, and transcendence.

Structuralist, semiotic, or deconstructionist study is formal and aims to locate higher-order meanings. Narrative, by contrast, is a paradigm of viewing discourse. Each paradigm has its own standards of inquiry. Narrative is a way of interpreting discourse that invites critique of reliability, trustworthiness, or desirability as a guide for human action.

Persons are viewed as storytellers who use warrants of value to rationalize their choices. Narrative theory aims at "practical wisdom and humane action." Ordinary discourse is "symbolic action that creates social reality."

---

(Perelman, 1963). Or that which is "true" may serve to paint us as villains, such that many true stories cannot or will not be told. Instead, we ask a "good" narrative account to be "plausible" after factoring in our personal knowledge, our prejudices, and the prejudices of those with whom we regularly interact. Also, we recount stories that "tell well." Good narratives promote retelling, they make or suggest clear-cut moral judgments, and they provide a framework that gives order to a selected set of circumstances in a way that is in keeping with what we and our community or culture want to believe. We aim at offering coherence and "good reasons."

For a given historical and linguistic community, only certain stories potentially prove plausible; when we substitute an audience that includes persons with other experiences, cultures, and predilections, the same narrative no longer proves compelling (Settle, 1996). The credibility and plausibility of narrative accounts rest as much upon personal and community belief as upon demonstrable truths.

Narrative accounts come to be construed by members of an interpretive community as truth. That is, members of our community tend to agree as to whom is good or bad, justified or unjustified, selfish or altruistic, and as to which act may or may not count as proper (Starosta, 1971). The wounding of youths in a New York City subway is viewed either as abhorrent, or as a morally courageous act, within the latitude of acceptance of specific receiving communities. Explains Farrell (1993), "There is always a strain between the world in which discourses appear, and the interiorized subjectivity that gives meaning to the discourse itself" (p. 149).

Narratives' rationales may be used in a predictive manner, that is, to specify what actions can be justified. Likewise narratives serve to rationalize acts already completed. Proactive justifications comprise "recounted narratives," whereas narratives used to justify completed actions comprise "enacted narratives" (Fisher, 1984, 1985a, 1985b, 1987; Metzger et al., 1991).

## The Media and Co-Cultural Narratives

Because narrative accounts prove compelling only for those who share a common history and linguisticality, multiple explanations and judgments arise for the same historical events. In other words, different persons who "listen to" or "read" our historical "texts" commonly arrive at variant readings of that text. The character who is "good" in one reading becomes the "villain" of another reading of ostensibly the same historical text. It may be that the text itself is inherently ambiguous or the multiple meanings reside within the minds of the respective listeners.

Those of a dominant group must decide what listening ("reading") they will extend to narrative accounts of nondominant communities, choosing amongst responses that range from (1) actively welcoming the competing account as an example of diversity; (2) merely tolerating the different account; (3) rendering the discrepant narrative invisible; (4) asserting "the truth" about the "mistaken" accounts recounted in the discrepant narrative; (5) converting those to "truth" who discover ironic (i.e., subversive) readings of mainstream texts; (6) castigating those who believe in a way that the dominant group does not sanction; or (7) taking decisive, violent action against those whose readings of texts differ from their own. In other words, the treatment of co-cultural persons who tell variant narrative accounts of events from those sanctioned by the dominant community ranges from the enjoyment of a good alternative story, on the one hand, to the elimination of the "false" storyteller, on the other (Starosta & Hannon, in press). To this list we add the possibility of perceptually distorting the alternative text so that the "difference" does not have to be recognized.

# HOW TO LISTEN ACROSS CULTURES

If we accept that new information is placed into a framework of what we already know and believe it is up to us to decide whether this will be a largely conscious or an unconscious process, we can use our excess thinking space by (1) trying to reduce the need to consider new ideas; (2) accepting the added demands of seeing and hearing novel messages; (3) waiting as long as possible before merging the story of another into our own narrative; or (4) using reciprocal questioning to build a common narrative with the other cultural interactant. These choices take increasing amounts of effort and should yield increasing degrees of reward. Mini case 9–2 serves to familiarize us with these skills.

## *Reducing the Need to Consider New Ideas*

One option is for us to cling to our prejudice and to make other persons adapt their knowledge to us, not the reverse. We can avoid learning other languages, avoid topics that could cause us cultural discomfort, and use our processes of active perception to distort the ideas of the other party. In this way we will see no difference, speak no difference, hear no difference. This is probably a popular option for listeners, since it places only a modest demand upon us as listeners. Unfortunately, this failure to process novel stimuli produces, at best, pseudo-intercultural listening. We hear only the echo of our own voice.

## *Accepting the Added Demands of Seeing and Hearing Novel Messages*

Once we accept that we are part of a limited community of history and linguisticality, our first important step toward achieving full-fledged intercultural listening is to expose ourselves to novel messages. Our first steps in this direction may be modest, since we need to develop the opportunity and the linguistic tools to enable us to meet with those of other cultures and co-cultures.

Each step we take in the direction of deliberate listening to those of other perspectives makes subsequent steps easier. We start to develop intercultural competencies and to hone our new skills with each new contact. Eventually, some of our message-processing strain is relieved, and we start to listen more easily across difference. Our steps at intercultural listening may start with the one-way exchanges of films and public speeches or lectures; more and more, though, we shift toward face-to-face, mutual interaction with physically present persons. Our simultaneous need to process messages at the same time as we initiate them temporarily introduces new challenges to our success. We pause

---

**Mini Case 9–2**

Prem is a graduate student from India you have come to know. The two of you talk a lot, and you finally ask about something that strikes you as peculiar. Each month, Prem takes $250 from his university assistantship and sends it to India to his family. You are on an assistantship yourself and you know that, if the roles were reversed, you could not afford to send money back home. You ask Prem, "Is your family poor?" Prem says they are middle-class. You say, "Did they ask you to send them money?" Prem says, "No. They would not do that! I do it on myself." He goes on, "They think everyone in States is rich." You are puzzled with his answer.

Devise a listening strategy that will explore both your American perceptions and Prem's Indian perceptions. Role-play the conversation that ensues. Have "external auditors" critique the conversation for mutual listening sensitivity.

---

to recognize that our counterpart must be undergoing this same processing strain as well.

## Waiting as Long as Possible before Merging the Story of Another into Our Own Narrative

We are the definitive expert on our own linguisticality and history, at least for a given intercultural listening exchange. We have learned long ago how things fit together, what matters and what does not, who is virtuous and who is villainous, and what things are worth pursuing or discarding. In our intercultural listening exchange we meet a person with his or her own stories, and these narratives also speak from a position of assumed, definitive expertise. Yet, elements of the two accounts conflict.

Since we come with the wish to listen authentically, we hesitate to prefer one account of things "out there" over another. Yet some elements of the other account start to sound attractive, and some of our own story lines start to strike us as implausible. The longer we listen without shutting the other interactant out, the more we realize that a new story could be framed that coherently tells about the things that we had been taking for granted over the years but that tells the story differently from what we earlier supposed to be correct. We discover that some new ways of telling our stories can be as consistent, compelling, and logical as those we always accepted. Our counterpart goes through this same process of realization.

The longer we wait before choosing one narrative line or set of explanations over another, the more likely we are to emerge with a hybrid story, one that takes the most appealing elements of each distinctive telling of events. To-gether, we form a new basis for interaction that is not one view, not the other, yet is both views.

## Using Reciprocal Questioning to Build a Common Narrative with the Other Cultural Interactant

Now we reach a stage of consolidating our narrative accounts. Instead of as-suming that we see the world in a joint way, we make inquiries. First we ask about facts, and ask for translations of difficult concepts into different language. The process of simple clarification reduces our processing load and helps to clarify where ideas may have gone through an errant process of translation.

After some time we develop a common linguistic usage. Soon we extend our questioning to ideas and their implications. When we do so, we reveal our cultural moorings and expose our nativist prejudices. We rely on the knowl-edge that both interactants are putting themselves at risk by moving to in-creasingly sensitive areas of inquiry. This process may abruptly halt if either of us starts to listen judgmentally. Reciprocal questioning, at least in its initial stages, relies on a suspension of disbelief and on the possibility that the other person's story line may make a better narrative than that of our own experi-ence. Indeed, the novel narrative of the other gets intermixed with our pool of experience and we emerge as changed persons. We "can't go home again."

Stage by stage we have created a third culture, a co-cultural narrative com-munity of two. We listen between cultures and co-cultures because we feel the urge to tell a better story than our cultural insularity will let us tell alone.

## RECAP

We began by looking at the research literature on listening. Probably because most listening researchers have come from a community that shares a common history and gender, little thought has been given to listening across or between cultures. (Some mention has been made of women's communication and of dialect.) Most of the existing research looks for ways to decode a message in exactly the same way it was intended. Since this monocultural approach priv-ileges some persons over others and is not easily adaptable to joint hearing and listening, we questioned these assumptions.

The literature on listening favors the dominant cultural group. It renders listening a passive process. It takes a message orientation, not a processing ori-entation. It assumes commonality. We found ourselves offering a theory of listening to widen our perspectives, to step outside ourselves, to develop a semantic space between two interactants that differed from the initial space of either one. We adopted some methods that were developed by qualitative researchers to help us with this task.

Finally, we framed a view of listening between co-cultures as a sharing of stories. That exchange had to move in both directions in an authentic attempt to actively understand how the other party framed his or her reality. Our movement toward the creation of a third culture was motivated in equal part by the necessity to know and by the wish to tell a better narrative.

## RETHINK

Some elements that were combined for this chapter are novel to the study of listening. In particular, the thoughts on qualitative methods and on narrative listening are yet to be tested.

We are on more familiar ground with our call for active listening that occurs simultaneously on the part of both parties. Also, we were able to draw on some work on linguisticality to deal with distinctive worlds of meaning of persons from different cultures or co-cultures.

Our focus on domestic co-cultures, including women and those of differing religious traditions, was the product of a few leads from other researchers, but it gained a prominence that we did not find elsewhere in the listening literature.

In short, this chapter represents an attempt to co-create with the first generation of text readers and with future researchers a new path to be traveled by listening research. We are not yet certain where this path will lead. We do know that much listening research has been conducted from a positivistic tradition wherein message received and message sent are compared for accuracy. We did not take this path. Less work had been done to say that listening research could help us to re-create the world of the processor of messages. It could help us to see how that person's symbols related to things "out there." This (interpretive) approach proved more useful for our work.

But we still felt the urge to move listening between cultures to a level of co-interpretation by persons who had experienced historical inequalities and misperceptions. This took us in a critical direction, where we were obliged to set out a course of action that would improve interunderstanding among the persons who talked and listened with one another across co-cultural difference. We know of no other critical approach to listening.

Because of the newness of our approach, it seems wise to await feedback from students and from the research community about the possible strengths or weaknesses of our approach. For the moment, we think of our work as provisional.

## QUESTIONS FOR DISCUSSION

1. Differentiate between positivist, interpretive, and critical approaches to research.
2. Trace listening research through each of the above stages.
3. Is listening between co-cultures identical to listening between national cultures? Why or why not?
4. Is there a way to study people who are merging their separate cultural narratives through the process of listening? Would we do such research as a neutral observer? Would we ask the interactants to debrief their process?
5. Think of the best and the worst co-cultural listeners you know. Give four qualities that distinguish the best from the worst listeners.

# ▶ Part IV

## Application

# ▶ Chapter 10

## Cultural Diversity and Multiculturalism

### *Objectives*

Upon completion of this chapter, you will

- Gain insight into the challenge of cultural diversity.
- Understand cultural diversity in organizations.
- Know how to manage a culturally diverse workforce.
- Understand the nature of multicultural education.
- Understand the stages of the multiculturalism process.
- Know the meaning and components of intercultural sensitivity.
- See the relationship between intercultural sensitivity and training programs.

> *All human beings live in what for them is a multicultural world, in which they are aware of different sets of others to whom different cultural attributions must be made, and of different contexts in which the different cultures of which they are aware are expected to operate.*
> —*W. H. GOODENOUGH*

"Who a person is" results both from socialization into "the ways of a nation" and from ethnic, cultural, and gender socialization. Those of the majority population sometimes insist that a single individual or group of individuals typifies our "nation" or "culture" most perfectly and that others should "become like them" or "leave" (—a doctrine known as *nativism*) (Short, 1988). Persons who identify strongly with domestic co-cultures, as well as those who have arrived recently from other nations, experience a tension between national and ethnic identity that may or may not decrease over time. The choice to identify completely with the national majority is not entirely their own, since enculturation stems both from individual intent and from majority permission (Rich, 1973).

In the United States, demographic shifts serve to question a belief in the "melting pot and assimilation philosophy" that has held sway for decades

---

### Research Highlight 10–1

Who:    Adler, P.

What:    "Beyond Cultural Identity: Reflections on Cultural and Multicultural Man."

Where:    In L. A. Samovar & R. E. Porter (Eds.) (1985), *Intercultural Communication: A Reader* (pp. 410–425). Belmont, CA: Wadsworth.

To become a successful citizen of global society, or a multicultural man, has long been a dream of human beings. What is a "multicultural man?" This essay attempts to answer that question.

The author defines multicultural man as "the person who is intellectually and emotionally committed to the fundamental unity of all human beings while at the same time he recognizes, legitimizes, accepts, and appreciates the fundamental differences that lie between people of different cultures" (p. 411–412). Multicultural persons are able to embody personal attributes and characteristics to facilitate and catalyze contact between people of different cultural backgrounds. Thus, multicul-tural man is a "new kind of man," who is capable of adjusting to different cultures and incorporating them into his life without losing sight of his true identity.

Three characteristics reflect the personality of multicultural persons: (1) they are psychologically adaptive to a new culture; (2) they are constantly undergoing personal transitions through the process of enculturation and deculturation; and (3) they maintain indefinite boundaries of the self for openness to change.

Finally, the ability of multicultural persons to live in different environments indicates that they constantly face tensions and stresses. The risks to their well-being are fivefold: (1) they become vulnerable in the effort to maintain indefinite boundaries of the self; (2) they can easily become persons of multiphrenic or diffused identity; (3) they can easily lose the sense of their own authenticity; (4) they risk becoming unimpaired, uncommitted, and unaffected persons; and (5) they may develop a detached and aloof attitude to mock persons different from them.

(Lewis-Chung, 1992). On the one hand, each of us grows up under the influence of a national culture. On the other, co-cultural identities (nonmajority ethnic, nationalistic, regional, or linguistic groupings) compete for our allegiance with other identities that go beyond the boundaries of any single nation (e.g., international organizations and trade alliances). We hear calls for us to become the "multicultural man [*sic*]" whose loyalties and identifications transcend nation, culture, language, and ethnicity (Adler, 1982). This chapter explores the topic of multiculturalism from seven perspectives: (1) the challenge of cultural diversity, (2) cultural diversity in organizations, (3) managing the culturally diverse workforce, (4) techniques for diversity management in organizations, (5) multicultural education, (6) stages of the multiculturalism process, and (7) the need for intercultural sensitivity.

## THE CHALLENGE OF CULTURAL DIVERSITY

In 1940, 70 percent of immigrants to the United States originated from Europe. Half a century later, 15 percent come from Europe, 37 percent from Asia, and 44 percent from Latin America and the Caribbean. The current ethnic breakdown for the United States includes 80 percent white, 12 percent black, 6.4 percent Hispanic, and 1.6 percent Asian. Given no new exclusionary legislation, by the year 2050 the population of U.S. white ethnics will decrease to 60 percent, while Asians increase tenfold, Hispanics triple their numbers, and African Americans increase their proportion but slightly (Nieto, 1992).

Shifts in the U.S. population structure gradually influence the country's educational system and organizational life. Educationally, although about 27 percent of U.S. public school students are persons of color, African American and Latino student populations presently dominate 22 of the 25 largest central-city school districts. (The actual proportion of substantially segregated high schools has changed little in over forty years since the *Brown versus Board of Education* school integration decision.) Co-culture majority school systems may increase in number by the year 2000.

Meanwhile, the number of U.S. children who speak a non-English language will increase from 2 million in 1986, to 5 million by 2020 (Natriello, McDill, & Pallas, 1990; Vadivieso & David, 1988). The influx of nonnative speakers of English requires the educational system to develop a curriculum that meets the needs of recent immigrants and their children, promotes learning, and accommodates differing communication styles of recent immigrants that may not match those of teachers and counselors (Sue, 1994).

Persons of co-cultures within the United States consume more goods and services than do any of the country's trading partners, and will constitute 25 percent of the U.S. economic market by the year 2000 (Foster, Jackson, Cross, Jackson, & Hardiman, 1988). If companies are to attract and retain new

## Research Highlight 10–2

Who:    Sue, D. W.

What:   "A Model of Cultural Diversity Training."

Where:  *Journal of Counseling and Development, 70,* 1991, 99–104.

Demographic changes have made our society a multicultural, multiracial, and multilingual place. How to increase our cultural sensitivity and knowledge of various racial-ethnic groups becomes important for us to survive in this culturally diverse world. This article addresses this issue by developing a model for assessment and training of cultural diversity in organizations. The model is built on three concepts : functions, barriers, and competencies.

Three organizational functions affect diversity training and intervention: (1) *recruitment* (labor pool) dictates that modern organizations attract more culturally diverse members; (2) *retention* (corporate culture) refers to the efforts organizations make to accommodate the needs of co-cultural members and to make them feel comfortable in their working environment; and (3) *promotion* (career path) refers to the openness of equal access and opportunity in organizations.

Three organizational barriers interfere with diversity training and intervention: (1) different communication styles and personal attributes, (2) interpersonal discrimination and prejudice toward the co-cultural members regarding their ability in serving certain positions, and (3) systemic barriers that institutionalize inequality between racial or ethnic groups.

The three dimensions of organizational competencies include: (1) appropriate beliefs and attitudes toward co-cultures; (2) knowledge of our own and other cultures' values, worldviews, and norms; and (3) verbal and non-verbal skills for multicultural communication.

After integrating the three organizational functions a 3 × 3 × 3 matrix (i.e., functions—recruitment, retention, promotion; barriers—differences, discrimination, systemic factors; competencies—beliefs/attitudes, knowledge, skills) becomes the basis of the model of cultural diversity training. In other words, a total of twenty-seven cells can be identified for multicultural training intervention. Moreover, appropriate training programs and techniques can be developed for each cell to fulfill the needs of multicultural organizations.

The model for cultural diversity training developed by the author in this article is heuristic. It is not only applicable to business and industry but to other forms of organization, such as institutions of higher education.

workers, they must recruit persons of varying heritages and ethnicity. Companies that fail to promote minorities and women to higher levels of management in the organization will lose their competitive edge (Morrison & Von Glinow, 1990). Therefore, companies must begin now the creative planning and the introduction of new workplace configurations in order to make best use of the talents of nontraditional employees (Goldstein & Gilliam, 1990).

The changing origins of workers and students in the American society require new flexibility on the part of existing workers and managers. Similarly, the changing cultural character of neighborhoods, schools, and the workplace calls for us all to adapt to the unfamiliar. The readiness of individual and organizational decisions to mutually accommodate in encounters across "difference" will be an important measure of the nation to come.

## CULTURAL DIVERSITY IN ORGANIZATIONS

Our best projections document a trend toward a culturally more diverse workplace. For United States business to succeed in the competitive world, diverse workers and companies, women and men, must find ways to effectively combine their efforts. As persons of ethnic co-cultures, immigrants and women enter the workforce in increasing numbers, corporations must learn to understand their workers both as group members and as individuals.

The head of ASTD's Institute for Workplace Learning, Anthony Carnevale, noted that inclusiveness is crucial to organizations. New competitive conditions change the way we work, and these changes eventually outstrip the importance of demographics. Success increasingly relies on the ability of persons to communicate with those of different backgrounds (Galagan, 1991). Unfortunately, while diversity may be on the minds of many personnel directors, it is seldom in their action plans. For instance, a survey conducted in 1989 by the American Society for Training and Development for 121 executives from Fortune 500 companies on issue of workforce diversity shows that only 27 percent of the companies provide training programs on diversity and that their programs are mainly for executives. In 1990, the same magazine surveyed fifty subscribers of *Training & Development Journal* and found that "diversity" was ranked twelfth in a list of fourteen priorities (Galagan, 1991).

Diversity looms as one of the biggest learning challenges of the near future. By failing to recognize the importance of demographic trends and of the trends toward multinational commerce, and by failing to adjust our beliefs about the contributions that those of diverse backgrounds can make, we will lose their valuable and creative inputs. We can further examine cultural diversity issues in organizations from four perspectives: (1) the report of the U.S. Department of Labor, (2) gender impact, (3) ethnic impact, and (4) business impact.

### Report by the U.S. Department of Labor

The "Workforce 2000: Work and Workers for the 21st Century" report, by the U.S. Department of Labor (1987), indicated five demographic facts that will influence the American workforce by the year 2000:

**1.** The population and the workforce will grow more slowly than at any time since the 1930s: This means a slow expansion of the U.S. economy, with a shift in the economy more toward luxury goods and convenience services.

**2.** The average age of the population and the workforce will rise, and the pool of young workers entering the labor market will shrink: The decline of young people in the labor force will, on the one hand, bring in more experienced and reliable older workers and, on the other hand, render the workforce less flexible and adaptable.

**3.** More women will enter the workforce: Women will rapidly enter various high-paying professional and technical fields. The demand for day care, more time for pregnancy leave, child-rearing assistance, and part-time, flexible, and stay-at-home jobs will increase.

**4.** Co-cultural groups will constitute a larger share of new entrants into the labor force: It is estimated that nonwhites will double their current share of the new entrants and reach 29 percent of the workforce by the year 2000.

**5.** Immigrants will represent the largest share of the increase in the population and the workforce since the World War I: It is estimated that approximately 600,000 documented and undocumented immigrants will enter the United States annually until the year 2000. Their participation in the workforce will dramatically reshape the U.S. economy.

The combination of these demographic changes means that, by the year 2000, the structure of the American workforce will be very much different from what we see today. In particular, immigrants, women, and nonwhite workers will make up more than five-sixths of the new workers. Fine (1991) drew a picture of the future American workforce by explicating two facts: First, the workforce will be much more diverse than it is now. Although white males will continue to outnumber other groups in the next decade, they will constitute a shrinking proportion of new entrants into the workforce. The new workforce will show a greater diversity of gender, race, age, culture, and language. Second, the demands for workers in the next decade will exceed the supply of those previously deemed as "qualified," therefore creating intense competition among organizations for workers.

The implications of Workforce 2000 are profound, and organizations will have to understand different mind-sets and cultural perspectives to adjust to diversity. They must initiate a mutual learning process in which they change, while simultaneously inducing changes in ("resocializing") their new employees.

## Gender Impact

Participation by women in the workforce has changed dramatically over the years. With the enactment of new laws and the changing needs of society, women have gone from working largely in the home, to being limited to cer-

**Research Highlight 10–3**

Who:   Fine, M. G.

What:   "New Voices in the Work-place: Research Directions in Multicultural Communication."

Where:   *Journal of Business Communication, 23,* 1991, 259–275.

The purpose of this article is to develop a framework, based on the assumption of cultural differences, that can be used to explore multicultural communication in modern organizations.

Borrowing ideas from postmodernism and feminism, the author describes two core processes of the framework. First, *resisting privileged discourse* refers to the recognition of the "assumption of difference" as the organizational norm. Multicultural communication is a process of multiple discourses and multiple interpretations of reality. Any voice that seeks to dominate should be resisted. In other words, organizations should not privilege only one form of discourse. Sec-

ond, *creating harmonic discourse* provides an environment for people to work together toward a common goal. Multicultural discourse requires not only all voices to retain their own identity but also to form an orderly and congruously holistic discourse.

The author then proposes four research directions for multicultural communication study in modern organizations from a feminist perspective: (1) to document organizational discourse across demographic differences in order to recognize that there exist other forms of discourse and further to respect the integrity of different forms, (2) to document and analyze organizational discourse in which privilege is asserted so that strategies for resistance can be developed, (3) to document discourses that resist privilege in order to how an individual can resist privileging of the dominant discourse, and (4) to document multicultural organizational discourse so that a harmonic discourse in the organization can be created.

tain positions such as teachers to (legally) being able to hold any position for which they can show preparation.

Fernandez (1991) pointed out that the influx of women into the workforce continues to increase. In 1960 women represented about 33 percent of the workforce, but in 1980 they constituted 43 percent and will represent at least 47 percent by the year 2000. Although women in the United States enjoy more freedom in the business world than in many other countries, they still participate on an inequitable basis in the workforce. According to Jackson (1992) and Fernandez (1991), although about 35 percent of the population of the executive, management, and administrative workforces were women in 1987, almost doubling from 1972, only 19 of 4,012 of the highest-paid officers and directors were women. These figures document that males are still dominant in the superior positions. Salary disparities similarly persist by gender.

We may question whether differences in educational levels are primarily the cause of the inequitable distribution of women in the workforce. Fernandez (1991) indicated that this seems unlikely, because in 1989 women received 52 percent of undergraduate degrees. They constituted approximately 31 percent of those receiving MBA degrees, 39 percent of law degrees, and 13 percent of engineering degrees (Jackson, 1992).

As the proportion of women continues to increase in the workplace, gender diversity has become a major issue for organizational life. Basically, contemporary organizations face two gender diversity challenges. First, they must ensure that women's abilities and talents are appropriately utilized on the job. With women representing such a large portion of the workforce, maximizing their full potential becomes necessary to raise productivity and keep the organizations competitive and successful. Second, employers must balance women's job duties and their responsibility for family care (women continue to serve disproportionately as primary family caretakers.) Employers must develop maternity leave and flexible time plans that allow women to meet their family responsibilities so that women who opt to enter the business world may do so. Although various improvements regarding women in the workplace have been implemented, many goals remain to be achieved. Companies must decide how far they will change to accommodate the needs of their female employees, and how much androgyny (a gender-neutral style of communication) they will seek from their female workers.

## Ethnic Impact

The management of cultural diversity in organizations requires a closer examination of various ethnic issues. Persons who live within a single national culture differ from each other because of variations in socialization, region, religious training, and political climate. The United States offers a good example. The U.S. culture comprises many ethnic groups, including African Americans, Native Indians, Asian American, and Hispanic Americans. Further, within the given domain of these ethnic classifications variations exist. For example, "Asian Americans" lumps together Chinese, Filipinos, Japanese, Koreans, and Pakistanis. "Hispanic Americans" combines Mexican Americans and Puerto Ricans, Cubans and Spaniards (Jackson, 1992). Similarly, North American Indians now seek to restore their legal status as members of separate, sovereign nations.

Aburdene (1990) and Williams (1990) pointed out that Asians, Hispanics, and African Americans together make up 20 percent of the American population and will increase at a rate seven times faster than the population as a whole. Increases in the numbers of co-culturals will crucially influence the structure of organizations.

Companies must recognize within their particular organization the legacy of the past political isolation of these populations. They must promote skills in

## Research Highlight 10–4

Who: Aburdene, P.

What: "How to Think Like a CEO for the 90's."

Where: *Working Woman*, September, 1990, 134–137.

A successful CEO in the nineties won't merely think big, he or she must think "meg." Aburdene is co-author of the book *Megatrends 2000*. In this article he summarizes the nine major trends specified in *Megatrends 2000* that future leaders must master:

**1.** Evolve a global orientation. *Globalization* is the word that best characterizes the 1990s and beyond. The CEO of the 1990s must gaze far beyond America's shores to realize how an organization fits into the big picture.
**2.** Invest in a foreign language. Although English is a common language for international business, using our partner's native language in business interaction is a way to show great respect. This linguistic investment will pay immediate dividends.
**3.** Create corporate vision. The corporate vision is the organizing force behind corporate decisions. Leadership must create the vision that informs people about the direction the company is going in and how it will get there. The CEO will be buried in the global 1990s without a clear picture of the company.
**4.** Be a good public speaker. In order to sell the idea of corporate vision the CEO must possess effective communication skills, such as precise writing and speaking. Similarly, in order to carry out the corporate vision the CEO must know how to effectively communicate with the company's human resources.
**5.** Realize what the arts can do for your company. Because of the increase women in the workforce, the arts have replaced spectator sports as society's top leisure activity in the 1990s. Corporate support of the arts has flourished. Associating one's company with the arts becomes an expensive way to reach affluent consumers.
**6.** Practice the "bring out the best in people" leadership style. Because half of the workforce today attended or graduated from college, authoritarian management does not work anymore. The CEO of the 1990s must also know how to help employees achieve their own goals.
**7.** Be attuned to environmental concerns. The global environment has become the main concern after the end of the cold war. Any CEO with an effort to keep the company on the right track cannot afford to ignore environmental issues in the 1990s.
**8.** Plug into the new electronic heartland. Electronic and telecommunication technology will continue to disperse people from cities to any place it can be carried. Through the use of modems and fax machines, we can communicate with people anywhere. The CEO of the 1990s must know how to plug into an international grid of information technology from every corner of the world.
**9.** Learn to manage cultural diversity. As mentioned in this chapter, immigration trends have made the world a multicultural society. The CEO of 1990s must possess effective cross-cultural skills to lead a diversified workforce and to deal with multinational business.

cultural understanding and sensitivity by implementing training programs at all levels of the organization and must foster greater trust and acceptance among their diverse workers. Organizations must accept as legitimate the existence of differing values, attitudes, behavioral styles, and ways of thinking within and among various co-cultural groups. Only a familiarity with the different ways that various co-cultural groups prefer to participate in organizational life can provide a cohesive workforce for continuing business operations. Enlightening all employees as to co-cultural variation not only provides new insight into others but also holds the capacity for greater creativity, idea generation, and increased understanding and acceptance of others (Thomas, 1991).

## Business Impact

So far, most organizations view the demands of cultural diversity as coping with demographics, meeting legal requirements, and being "good corporate citizens." However necessary, these actions are not sufficient to sustain the full impact of cultural diversity on business. According to Thomas (1991), unless the challenge of cultural diversity is treated as a business issue, a company will be unable to deal with it, because recognizing cultural diversity means changing aspects of the business operation of the entire company.

An increasingly diverse workforce compels organizations to recognize the unique needs and cultural backgrounds of its workers and to assume greater responsibility for employees' education, health, and well-being (Wozniak, 1991). These measures would, in turn, attract a wider range of applicants. By responding to identified differences among their personnel, companies stand to gain enormous competitive advantages.

Cox and Blake (1991) indicated that an organization's ability to attract, retain, and motivate culturally diverse employees may yield great advantages for the organization, especially in light of business globalization, because compared to a homogeneous workforce, a heterogeneous workforce can better anticipate and avoid market problems and can be more creative in their solutions (Buhler, 1993).

As mentioned above, managing cultural diversity in organizations involves not only an understanding of the concept but also the implementation of techniques necessary to utilize workers to their full capacities. Workers of various cultural identities must be mentored and promoted. Also, corporations must meet the various needs of such diverse groups by implementing counseling and training. Many organizations today realize the need for intercultural training and have thus enlisted either in-house or outside consulting firms to implement such programs. (According to recent evidence, combining in-house and external trainers apparently helps to avoid training that exacerbates differences or that does not address the needs of the particular company). The American Management Association reports that the presence of a formal diversity program usually leads to higher co-cultural representation within management

**Mini Case 10–1**

M. Legrand is a French engineer who works for a Japanese company in France. One day the general manager, Mr. Tanaka, calls him into his office to discuss a new project in the Middle East. He tells M. Legrand that the company is very pleased by his dedicated work and would like him to act as chief engineer for the project. It would mean two to three years away from home, but his family would be able to accompany him and there would be considerable personal financial benefits to the position—and, of course, he would be performing a valuable service to the company. M. Legrand thanks Mr. Tanaka for the confidence he has in him but says he will have to discuss it with his wife before deciding. Two days later he returns and tells Mr. Tanaka that both he and his wife do not like the thought of leaving France and so he does not want to accept the position. Mr. Tanaka says nothing but is dumbfounded by his decision.

Why is Mr. Tanaka so bewildered by M. Legrand's decision?

*Source:* From R. Brislin, K. Cushner, C. Cherrier, & M. Yong, *Intercultural Interaction: A Practical Guide,* copyright © 1986 by Sage Publications. Reprinted by permission of Sage Publications.

in the organization. Mini Case 10–1 illustrates an example of cultural diversity in modern organizations.

## MANAGING A CULTURALLY DIVERSE WORKFORCE

Managing a culturally diverse workforce requires an overall examination of the organization. An analysis of the company's specific needs must precede the implementation of the most effective training regimen. Organizations must also be aware of the advantages of a culturally diverse workforce and use this knowledge to achieve success. Management must take into account the mission, vision, values, policies, procedures, systems, and practices of the company, while observing three operational principles: planning, organization, and leadership (Rhinesmith, 1991).

### Planning

The dramatic changes that have taken place in the workplace and those that will occur in the near future demand that organizations plan ahead. Organizations must incorporate systems into the working environment through which a further understanding of cultural diversity can be reached. Digital Equipment and Ford serve to illustrate the impact of cultural diversity on organizations, as well their ability to function as global entities (Galagan, 1991). Digital Equipment has been prepared for the arrival of a new workforce since its founding in 1972. The company planned a new and different way of dealing effectively with the inclusion and use of people of ethnic and gender differences at all positions and levels. Likewise, Ford created and refined internal personnel structures and systems to help ensure fair and equal treatment of all employees. The company has educated employees to understand and appreciate diversity.

Rhinesmith (1991) suggested that ideal planning for a company with a multicultural and global perspective should include: (1) a cultural and global inspiring mission, (2) a cultural and global corporate vision, (3) cultural and global information sources and systems, and (4) decision-making criteria that reflect global and local culture values. Naturally, a company must confront diverse cultural issues before making the transformation from a corporate entity to a global entity (Gordon, 1992).

## Organization

To meet the needs of the changing workforce and to function competitively in the multinational environment, organizations need to reorganize their policies and programs. In doing so, they should ensure that they promote increased awareness and appreciation of cultural diversity and that no single set of cultural rules prevails (Edwards, 1991). The effort to accommodate cultural diversity should aim to bring a new and richer business outlook (Winikow, 1991).

SCIENCETECH is a good example. The company has attempted to diversify its managerial ranks in response to demographic changes, its goals being not only to manage but to value cultural diversity. Some questions guiding SCIENCETECH's reorganization included: What constitutes diversity? How and why does an organization decide that diversity is a value? Who actually decides? How are the definitions and goals communicated within the organization? What are the organization's public statements regarding the diversity effort? What are the formal and informal communication practices within the organization regarding the value of diversity (Fish, 1991)? All these questions helped to establish criteria for reorganization, including: (1) clearly defined levels of authority and delegation based on diverse cultures; (2) culturally coherent decision making policies; (3) formal and informal networking and integration mechanisms reflecting diverse culture needs; and (4) cross-functional and cross-unit coordination councils representing the diverse cultures (Rhinesmith, 1991). To this should be added formal and informal mentoring programs for diverse employees.

## Leadership

As organizations seek to enter the global market and to welcome a culturally diverse workforce, leadership plays a key role. Adding persons to the workforce who come from diverse backgrounds means little if managers do not adopt a global mind-set and understand how to manage such a workforce. Providing successful leadership requires the ability to frame problems in the ways that diverse employees frame them. Otherwise, the company's "solutions" are those only of one party, leaving the other party or parties to feel misunderstood and, over the course of time, alienated from the company's operations. Correspondingly, employees need to make an effort to understand the company's needs and perspectives.

Cultural, religious, gender, and ethnic diversity issues are the fundamental management issues leadership has to face (Winikow, 1991). Companies must realize that training to gain improved understanding and awareness of diverse issues is an ongoing need; it is not just a one- or two-day program, but it represents a process of continuous reinforcement.

Successful leadership possesses the following abilities: (1) to scan the global and multicultural environment for trends and ruptures, (2) to develop global and multicultural visions and mind-sets, (3) to build global and cross-cultural bridges and alliances, (4) to reframe global and multicultural problems to create new solutions, (5) to communicate cross-culturally in an effective way, (6) to practice global and multicultural team leadership in an environment of equals, and (7) to develop a global and diverse corporate culture (Rhinesmith, 1991). Info 10–1 illustrates a case of management in a culturally diverse organization.

### Info 10–1

*Managing Cultural Diversity*

James Dillard, president of Systems Computers, Inc., knows both the workplace and the customer base are changing. He has read *Workforce 2000*. In fact, he does not know anyone who has not read it. He also knows that many of his senior managers could care less about affirmative action, and many openly resent attempts at hiring with concerns for work force diversity.

James Dillard feels differently. He believes the future rests on having a work force that represents the diverse composition of Systems Computers' customers, a group that is increasingly minority and female. He believes that

to design low cost computer products for the future requires a knowledge of customers that cannot come from an all-white male group or any single group for that matter. Among his senior managers, only Charlie Nighthorse agrees with him. Charlie, a Native American, has long advocated pluralism as a corporate objective of Systems Computers, Inc.

Dillard was pleased to see the article on U.S. West in the *Washington Post* (Lynne Duke, "Employer Puts Pluralism First," *Washington Post,* National Weekly Edition, August 12–16, 1991). According to the *Post,* U.S. West was assembling "pluralistic slates" of job

*Continued*

**Info 10–1**   *Continued*

candidates to ensure minorities and women are considered for new jobs and internal promotions. U.S. West, like Systems Computers, is heavily white male at the top. The article cited progress in attracting and promoting a diverse work force but also described concerns expressed about quotas by some U.S. West personnel, including minorities and females.

At his next staff meeting Dillard gave copies of the U.S. West article to all present. He asked the vice-president of personnel to think about a new approach for recruitment and promotions based on a "pluralistic slate" of candidates. He pointed out that A. Gary Ames, CEO of U.S. West Communications, had been quoted as saying that he would personally nix any high-level promotion that was not recommended from a pluralistic slate of candidates. Several staff members objected to Dillard's request suggesting it went too far and was not based on solid business judgment. Dillard countered he was concerned that Systems Computers did not have a sufficient pipeline of fe-

males and minorities employed to effectively penetrate top management ranks over the next several years. He persisted with his assignment to the vice-president although it was clear serious objectives existed.

Six weeks later, the vice-president for personnel made his first report to Dillard's staff meeting. He suggested a new management performance appraisal system, which would give significant credit to managers who recruited or promoted from among pluralistic slates of candidates. The credit would be received even if the final selection for a job was a white male. Although no quotas were to be established, all managers would be required to attend in-house diversity training workshops. Charlie Nighthorse expressed concern that the approach was not strong enough. Several staff members seemed relieved. Dillard did not know; his concern rested with the attitudes of his senior staff. He wondered what he might do to help them understand that managing a culturally diverse workforce was good business.

*Source:* From FUNDAMENTALS OF ORGANIZATIONAL COMMUNICATION by Pamela Shockley-Zalabak. Copyright © 1991 by Longman Publishers. Reprinted with permission.

# TECHNIQUES FOR DIVERSITY MANAGEMENT IN ORGANIZATIONS

Based on the three principles for managing a culturally diverse workforce (planning, organization, leadership), a wide variety of specific techniques for implementing managerial policy can be generated. Conrad (1994) grouped these techniques into four categories:

**1.** Managing and rewarding performance based on the foundation of diversity: Management should cultivate an environment in which all employees can demonstrate their ability and values to the organization, regardless of their race, culture, or gender, and in which employees can dare to be creative and innovative. For appraisal systems to be developed and implemented that focus on performance and outcomes, top management in the organization must be committed to promoting diversity and to providing training and educational programs designed to increase employees' positive attitudes toward diversity by promoting awareness of and sensitivity toward cultural differences within the organization. Work appraisals might combine core standards common to all the workforce with other standards elected by the workers that would highlight their special qualities. Management would thereby shift from "seeing no difference" to "rewarding beneficial difference" among its employees.

**2.** Matching people and jobs: The programs for diversity management assume each employee possesses a variety of abilities that change over time. Thus, the company benefits most that provides employees with opportunities to pursue career goals that maximize their changing abilities. In other words, a successful organization with diversity management is able to create an environment in which employees can fully utilize their skills, interests, and abilities and can equally get a chance to be promoted and receive increasingly complex assignments.

**3.** Keeping employees informed and involved: Companies should establish a free and open communication climate in the organization for implementation of diversity management. In a culturally diverse organization the special focus should be on individual differences in the process of participative decision making or power sharing.

**4.** Supporting diverse work styles and life needs: The organization should ask employees' needs and then develop flexible programs that can individualize the organizational policy and benefits within the constraints imposed by budgets and concerns for fairness.

## MULTICULTURAL EDUCATION

As we move toward multiculturalism and globalization it is not only the business world that must adapt to changes, the academic sector must deal with the trend as well. In the classroom, the necessity to accommodate cultural diversity is becoming more apparent. Education not only helps new immigrants to make sense of the local culture, it offers individuals insights and skills they need to survive in the changing world. Only through multicultural and global education can people learn about those problems and issues that cut across ethnic, national, and gender boundaries and learn to understand how other groups process experience in ways that may differ from our own perceptions.

---

**Mini Case 10–2**

Mrs. Jane Simpson enjoyed her job as departmental secretary in a large, well-respected university in the United States. She enjoyed trying to be helpful to students as they worked their way through departmental and university regulations on their way toward their bachelor's, master's, and doctoral degrees. One day, a student from India entered the departmental office and began demanding attention to his various problems with his visa, low course grades, and his thesis adviser.

He never used words such as "please" and "thank you," talked in a tone of voice reminiscent of a superior talking to subordinates, and gave orders to Mrs. Simpson. Mrs. Simpson counted slowly to 10, but her anger did not subside. She went to see the department chairperson to see if someone else could work with this student in the future.

How would you help Mrs. Simpson sort out her feelings about this incident?

---

*Source:* R. Brislin K. Cushner, C. Cherrie, & M. Yong, *Intercultural Interactions: A Practical Guide,* copyright © 1986 by Sage Publications. Reprinted by permission of Sage Publications.

Mini Case 10–2 demonstrates a potential problem caused by cultural differences in an educational environment.

Multicultural education raises four significant issues: (1) exposure to multicultural perspectives, (2) maintaining cultural identity, (3) developing intercultural communication skills, and (4) diversification of curriculum.

## Exposure to Multicultural Perspectives

New cultural influences enter not only the workforce but also the classroom. Bennett (1990) pointed out that approximately 25 percent of U.S. school-age children are ethnic minorities. As these numbers increase, cultural differences become an everyday reality that cannot be overlooked. The educational system that restricts the understanding of cultural diversity will suffer from losing the richness of values, lifestyles, and perspectives of ethnic groups (Corner, 1984).

Academic exposure to the multicultural environment will provide students with the skills to excel in the real world. As the business world adjusts its views to fit a changing society, the academic environment must do the same. Because students ultimately return to the world outside the school, the more fully they learn to recognize and to respect differences in the beliefs, values, and worldviews of people of varying cultural extraction, the more effectively will they promote a multicultural society beyond the classroom.

## Maintaining Cultural Identity

Multicultural education concerns not only the individual identity but also the collective cultural identity. Multicultural education functions to help students rediscover their culture of origin and to strengthen, maintain, and create feelings of belonging to a community and of respect for culturally diverse values. Even if the courts had not ordered that school systems adapt to culturally different persons (as in the *Lau* and *Martin Luther King* decisions), schools should understand that problems occur at both the individual and societal level when individuals are forced to reject their racial or ethnic cultures (Corner, 1984). They need a cultural comfort zone within which to operate, before venturing into the cultural unknown.

Exposing students to differences in thinking and practice of foreign and domestic cultures promotes intergroup contact that, in turn, offers students the chance to see themselves through the eyes of those of other cultures. Multicultural education therefore assists students, regardless of their ethnic background, to function successfully within their own and within another's ethnic culture.

## Developing Intercultural Communication Skills

Modes of communication differ among various ethnic groups. As students learn about various cultures, they become aware of the typical communication patterns of students of other cultures. Soon, students generalize their knowledge beyond the classroom and try out their understanding in the larger world outside the school. By providing both abstract and personal knowledge of typical communication preferences within culturally defined groups, multicultural education prepares students to learn other cultural features besides the verbal.

Following is a list of some sample ethnic traits that might be common to students and parents of students who are encountered in a multicultural education environment. (The observations should not be treated as absolutes, since culture provides a range of possibilities for communicators. Individual communicators may or may not display the predicted communication features.)

**1.** *Vietnamese.* They shake hands; they also bow; they smile most of the time; but they do not show their true feelings. They tend to speak in a monotonous tone, to increase the focus on message content, not on emotion. They have a strong sense of hospitality. They do not like to be touched on the head and do not touch each other on the head. They hold a reverence for elders.

**2.** *Cambodians.* They bow but do not shake hands, especially the women. They distrust outsiders. They do not understand pointing. They do not like to have their heads touched, and they do not like to "towered over" by someone else. They do not like loud voices.

**3.** *Puerto Ricans.* They have a close sense of personal space. They maintain a relaxed demeanor. They do not segregate themselves according to age categories. They tend to compliment possessions very much. They do not mind being interrupted. They seldom talk about formal issues over meals.

**4.** *Colombians.* They will shake hands but not with a strong grip. Titles are very important to them. They usually have their father's last name as their middle name and their mother's last name for their last name.

**5.** *Asian Indians.* Only urbanized Indians shake hands. They have a relaxed sense of time. They tend not to date prior to marriage. They may interrupt the speaking of others. They maintain a strong respect for secular and religious teachers. Many practice dietary restrictions. They tend not to participate in classroom discussions. They like clearly defined tasks and exercise close supervision over their subordinates.

**6.** *African Americans.* They may be more consensus-oriented than European Americans and generally function well in group modalities. They tend to value oral expression. They like to develop an individual, distinctive verbal and nonverbal style. Most can switch codes between black English vernacular (Ebonics) and standard English. They like to know where a person individually stands on an issue. Their proxemic distances tend to be closer than those of European Americans.

These examples reveal that an awareness of cultural traits includes both verbal and nonverbal communication, is situation-specific, and occurs at many levels of intricacy. Providing students with an understanding of the communication and interaction that is most prevalent within cultures (and teaching the existence of exceptions to the most common patterns) enables students to communicate more effectively and appropriately with "others" both within their society and elsewhere within the world.

## Diversification of Curriculum

To respond to changing demographics and to increasing globalization, academic institutions must use their curricula to foster multicultural thinking and thereby improve student attitudes toward ethnic, gender, and cultural diversity. To this end, educators must not only explore new areas of study but also acquire new teaching methods and new class organization styles (Nixon, 1985).

The study of cultural diversity must be an integral part of the entire curriculum and not be limited to social studies, humanities, or language classes in order for students to learn how different ethnic groups have influenced and contributed socially in all areas. For the successful implementation of a multicultural curriculum to be achieved, diverse experiences such as seminars, visitations, committee work, guest speakers, community involvement, and workshops combined with factual lectures are also effective (Corner, 1984).

# STAGES OF THE PROCESS OF MULTICULTURALISM

Multiculturalism is a dynamic process that moves us towards cultural expansion, awareness, sensitivity, and competence. This process can be viewed as a sequence of conceptual stages, seven of which have been identified by Wurzel (1988):

**1.** *Monoculturalism.* Ethnocentrism is dominant at this stage, in which individuals nourish their own pride and vanity and perceive other cultures as strange and inferior. The tendency to measure others against our own culture serves the purpose of helping our own group to survive and offers us a social identity. At the monocultural stage we are not aware of the inevitable and universal characteristics of ethnocentrism, until we have intercultural communication experience.

**2.** *Cross-cultural contact.* At this stage multiculturalism begins to emerge when we directly or indirectly contact persons from different cultural backgrounds. The contrasting of cultural traits leads us to recognize some differences between ourselves and others, which we then process with curiosity or with frustration. We first process those differences that contrast most directly with our own cultural practice.

**3.** *Cultural conflict.* Cultural conflict (incongruity) appears because of the presence of differing cultural patterns and the clash of ethnic stereotypes. Such conflict may cause miscommunication and reinforce our prejudice toward people of other groups. Symptoms of cultural shock (feelings of depression, alienation, and marginality) may appear at this stage. Students who first encounter different cultural populations in the classroom may experience stress or may be removed by their parents to private schools or to largely segregated suburban schools. Alternatively, the "different" students may be channeled into separate "tracks" from those of the mainstream students.

**4.** *Educational interventions.* An effective educational intervention can help to reduce cultural conflicts and to develop a multicultural perspective. Curricular programs containing multicultural components can improve communication problems posed by cultural differences. A successful educational program serves two purposes: (1) educating students to examine, understand, and respect their own cultural values, and (2) educating students to acknowledge and understand their common humanity as well their cultural differences. Educational interventions aim to alleviate dogmatism by developing in students a provisional attitude toward knowledge: that is, their cultural practices are arbitrary, and their knowledge is incomplete. Preference for the familiar does not authorize judgment of the unfamiliar.

**5.** *Disequilibrium.* As a result of educational interventions that introduce new cultural information, students begin to experience a feeling of disequilibrium. According to Ackerman (1958), disequilibrium refers to the process of balanc-

ing one's need to protect sameness and continuity and the need to accommodate changes. In a multicultural setting, students will find that their previously
held knowledge is challenged, and they begin to reconsider their own beliefs.
Disequilibrium leads to awareness.

**6.** *Awareness.* At this stage students start to understand the concept of culture
and to emerge from the confinement of ethnocentrism. They move toward a
new equilibrium in which they show a better accommodation of new cultural
knowledge.

**7.** *Multiculturalism.* The achievement of a multicultural perspective reflects a
new mental and emotional consciousness that lets students face and accept the
diversity of cultural reality. Students at this stage become "multicultural" (Adler,
1982). Multicultural persons possess three characteristics: (1) they are psycho-
culturally adaptive and situational in their relationships to others and their connections to culture; (2) they are ever undergoing personal transitions through
a process of cultural learning; and (3) receptive to change, they maintain neither a fixed nor predictable boundary of the self.


# THE NEED FOR INTERCULTURAL SENSITIVITY

Survival in this multicultural world requires the ability to see through the eyes
and minds of people from different ethnic, sexual, and cultural backgrounds.
Intercultural sensitivity is a quality that enables people to achieve a multicultural mind-set.

## What is Intercultural Sensitivity?

Bronfenbrener, Harding, and Gallwey's study (1958) is one of the earliest dealing with the concept of sensitivity. They propose two kinds of sensitivity: sensitivity to the generalized other and sensitivity to individual differences (i.e.,
interpersonal sensitivity). McClelland (1958) considered sensitivity to the generalized other as the ability to be sensitive to the social norms of one's own
group, while Bronfenbrener et al. treated interpersonal sensitivity as the ability to distinguish how others differ in their behavior, perceptions, or feelings.
Intercultural sensitivity is similar to Bronfenbrener et al.'s notion of interpersonal sensitivity.

Hart and Burks (1972) and Hart, Carlson, and Eadie (1980) further treated
sensitivity as a mind-set applied in one's everyday life whereby one accepts
personal complexity, avoids communication inflexibility, interacts consciously,
appreciates the ideas exchanged, and tolerates intentional searching.

Based on Gudykunst and Hammer's (1983) three-stage intercultural training model and Hoopes's (1981) intercultural learning model, Bennett (1984)

explained intercultural sensitivity as a developmental process in which we transform ourselves effectively, cognitively, and behaviorally from an ethnocentric state to an ethnorelative state. This transformation process includes six stages: (1) denial—in which we deny the existence of cultural differences among people; (2) defense—in which we attempt to protect our own worldview to counter the perceived threat of cultural difference; (3) minimization—in which we attempt to protect the core of our own worldview by concealing differences in the shadow of cultural similarities; (4) acceptance—in which we begin to accept the existence of behavioral differences and underlying cultural differences; (5) adaptation—in which we become empathic toward cultural differences and become bicultural or multicultural; and (6) integration—in which we apply ethnorelativism to our own identity and can experience "difference as an essential and joyful aspect of all life" (p. 186). This model of intercultural sensitivity views intercultural sensitivity not only as an affective and cognitive ability but also as a precondition for being interculturally competent.

Finally, Bhawuk and Brislin (1992) developed an instrument for measuring intercultural sensitivity from an individualism/collectivism perspective. The authors argued that intercultural sensitivity should include three elements: (1) an understanding of the different ways we can behave, (2) open-mindedness concerning the differences we encounter, and (3) the behavioral flexibility we demonstrate in a new culture.

Based on the literature cited in this section, we conceptualize intercultural sensitivity to be a "positive drive to accommodate, understand, and appreciate cultural differences in promoting an appropriate and effective behavior in intercultural communication." According to this definition, intercultural sensitivity is a dynamic and a multidimensional concept describing individual's active desire to motivate themselves to understand, appreciate, and accept differences among cultures. Such motivation springs from the expectation of positive outcomes from intercultural interactions.

## Intercultural Sensitivity and Training Programs

Interculturally sensitive persons better adjust to a new environment within any cultural setting than do persons with less sensitivity. The recognized importance of intercultural sensitivity in a multicultural world leads us to examine the concept from different perspectives. Along these lines, more and more intercultural training programs have been initiated to foster intercultural sensitivity. Those training programs include "T-groups," critical incidents, case studies, role playing, and cultural orientation programs (Seidel, 1981; Yum, 1989).

A common goal of intercultural training is to increase our awareness of cultural differences to develop our communication potential while lessening our likelihood of misunderstandings. In other words, intercultural training programs aim to "develop an appreciation and understanding of cross-cultural differences and to [instill] some of the necessary abilities, such as an increased awareness and sensitivity to cultural stimuli and better human relations skills" (Seidel, 1981, p. 184). Morgan and Weigel (1988) also indicated that the major purpose of these training programs is to develop intercultural sensitivity. Intercultural sensitivity has been viewed as a first step toward intercultural communication competence (Bennett, 1984, 1986; Hammer, 1989; Harris & Moran, 1989; Parker, Valley, & Geary, 1986).

Because intercultural sensitivity is key to a positive outcome in intercultural encounters, its meaning should become evident from an examination of intercultural training programs. Intercultural training programs commonly fall into one of six types: affective training, cognitive training, behavioral training, area simulation training, cultural awareness training, and self-awareness training (Brislin, Landis, & Brandt, 1983; Gudykunst & Hammer, 1983; Gudykunst, Hammer, & Wiseman, 1977; Seidel, 1981). Chapter 11 describes in detail intercultural training programs.

## Components of Intercultural Sensitivity

Intercultural communication scholars have advanced many components of intercultural sensitivity. This section discusses six of them: ethnorelativism, respect for cultural differences, adaptability, perspective-taking, open-mindedness, and acknowledgment of others' needs. All these components are essential for us to interact productively in a multicultural society.

### Ethnorelativism

Bennett (1984) proposed that the development of intercultural sensitivity demands new awareness and attitudes for us to manage intercultural differences. Gains in intercultural sensitivity lead us to more interculturally appropriate and sensitive meanings. According to Bennett (1986), the development of intercultural sensitivity moves from an ethnocentric stage to the final ethnorelative phase. He sees people as progressing from a narrow, inward-looking view to a broad-mindedness.

Bennett (1984) defined ethnocentrism as "assuming that the world-view of one's own culture is central to all reality" (p. 33). Samovar and Porter (1988) likewise defined ethnocentrism as the negative evaluation of different cultures. These definitions imply three negative tendencies we all share: first, the tendency to formulate a narrow and defensive social sense of identity about our own culture (Stewart & Bennett, 1991); second, the tendency to develop stereotypes that generalize about people from other cultures without recognizing their individual differences; and, third, the tendency to assume our culture is normal and natural and to form negative judgments of other cultures based on this assumption (Stewart & Buoyant, 1991). Blubaugh and Pennington (1976) identified ethnocentrism (the posing of "differences that make a difference") as the basis of racism. Ethnocentrism, egocentrism, and racism share common dynamics (Buoyant, 1984).

By contrast, *ethnorelativism* denies that cultural differences "make a difference." Ethnorelativism maintains that "cultures can only be understood relative to one another; there is no absolute standard of rightness or goodness that can be applied to cultural behavior; cultural difference is neither good or bad; it is just different" (Buoyant, 1984, p. 46). One who is ethnorelative understands that it is a fallacy to practice "negative difference." Each culture has its unique way of judging and comparing cultural dissonance (McPhail, 1991). Ethnorelative individuals do not measure cultural dissonance against the scale of their own cultural values. Instead, they accept it, and allow difference to be difference.

### Respect for Cultural Differences

The initial step in practicing enthorelativism is to accept that cultural differences are inevitable and welcome (Buoyant, 1984). Cultural differences fall into two categories: behavioral (manifest) and cultural value (tacit) differences. While behavioral differences make their appearance verbally and nonverbally, cultural values refer implicitly to "the goodness or desirability of certain actions or attitudes among members of a culture" (Stewart & Buoyant, 1991, p. 14). We infer value indirectly, from disparity in the organization of reality (Kluckhohn & Strodtbeck, 1961; Stewart, 1972).

In cognitive terms, intercultural sensitivity is our awareness that we must cope with a unique and challenging task. This occurs when culturally unfamiliar persons are engaged in an encounter. According to Hart and Burks (1972), sensitive awareness reflects a sincere desire to deal with sometimes overwhelming uncertainties and doubts in a situation. Intercultural sensitivity charges us with the task of ascribing coherent meanings to seemingly disjointed and nonsensical differences.

To aid in our effort, Turner (1968) stressed the importance of discovering "central cultural themes" in a particular culture. Central cultural themes are shared worldviews or patterns of a culture (Benedict, 1946). Turner (1968) suggested that, to understand central cultural themes, we must understand the dynamics that produce the various cultural features. From learning the patterns of other cultures, we develop skills in empathy and appreciation that help us coexist (Stewart, 1978). Understanding results in an internalized, broadened concept of the world (Buoyant, 1986). Because cultures differ fundamentally in the way they create and maintain worldviews, they also interpret events differently. This makes the comprehension of *worldview* important for intercultural sensitivity. Cultural myopia and its annoying and irritating outgrowth of provinciality and rigid evaluation of alien cultures, must be seen as unwise (Barnlund, 1988). A culturally sensitive outlook permits the recognition, acceptance, and appreciation of unfamiliar views and ideas. The interculturally sensitive person, like the rhetorically sensitive person, understands that an idea can be rendered in various forms (Hart & Burks, 1972). Therefore, interculturally sensitive individuals tend to recognize, accept, and appreciate cultural differences in culturally diverse environments.

### Adaptability

According to Hart and Burks (1972), an interculturally sensitive person is willing to undergo the strain of adaptation. Spitzberg and Cupach (1984) considered adaptability the ability to alter roles and strategies in concurrence with situational demands. They also argue that adaptability resembles behavioral flexibility, as they both "represent a stable individual's ability to produce consistent and effective responses in others by adjusting to varied situations" (p. 36). Bochner and Kelly (1974) conceptualized behavioral flexibility as the ability to choose an appropriate response to different situations. Adaptability or behavioral flexibility is also an important component that leads individuals to be interculturally competent (Chen, 1989, 1990; Martin, 1987; Wiemann, 1977).

Interculturally sensitive persons are adaptable beings with a complex network of selves (Hart, Carlson, & Eadie, 1980). They desire to practice the unwelcoming and grueling procedure of adjustment because they recognize the complex dynamics of interpersonal communication. Their willingness derives from their culturally diversified habits of thinking. Interculturally sensitive persons select the persona from their repertoire of selves that matches the dynamics of the culturally diverse situation. Thus, interculturally sensitive individuals play roles that are recognizable to those of other cultures.

### Perspective-Taking

Intercultural sensitivity also requires assuming the chameleon role of perspective-taking. Piaget (1932) and Mead (1934) recognized our capacity for perspective-taking by practicing nonegocentric behavior. Stewart and Buoyant (1991) suggested that perspective-taking is the ability to put aside our personal perception. Buoyant (1979) described perspective-taking as "acknowledging the other person's different experience, having a willingness to participate in that experience and behaving in ways appropriate to it" (p. 419). Coke, Bateson, and McDavis (1978) contended that perspective-taking allows us to possess a higher degree of feeling of sympathy and concern toward others—hence the display of identification, understanding, and consideration toward others that follows from perspective-taking. Davis (1983) has validated that perspective-taking ability allows us to "anticipate the behavior and reactions of others, therefore facilitating smoother and more rewarding interpersonal relationships" (p. 115).

Barnlund (1988) pointed out that, in perspective-taking, an interculturally sensitive person searches for "symbols that will enable him or her to share the other's experiences" (p. 9). Interculturally sensitive persons thus refuse to play the same role for every situation or context (Hart et al., 1980). Moreover, high perspective-takers are also relatively selfless, showing concern for the other interactant's feelings and reactions (Davis, 1983). As a result, the identification of similar perspectives creates a mutual understanding that leads to the establishment of a rapport. Thus, interculturally sensitive persons are likely to be high perspective-takers in multicultural encounters.

### Open-Mindedness

Culturally sensitive persons are slow to make judgments of others. They avoid "splintering," the practice of jumping to conclusions without sufficient data (Hart & Burks, 1972). By being open-minded or nonjudgmental in intercultural associations, those of other cultures are able to fully explain themselves and be sincerely listened to (Ruben, 1988). Intercultural sensitivity is the avoidance of issuing rash judgments about the inputs of others. Only when sufficient information has been gathered through non-judgmental listening will evaluation and appraisal take place. In this way, the other parties are psychologically satisfied that they have been actively listened to. This, in turn, promotes cordiality and positiveness. An open mind elevates the intercultural relationship to a higher level and promotes trust in spite of difference.

### Acknowledgment of Other's Needs

Yum (1989) highlighted the emotional quality of sensitivity, the understanding of other people's needs. Smith (1966) stated that, because sensitivity motivates us to understand other people, it makes us more receptive to new events and people. It also prepares us to participate in a learning process. Sensitivity moves us to a higher level of ethnorelativism: integration. According to Buoyant (1986), the person who has integrated differences is "one who can construe differences as processes, who can adapt to those differences, and who can additionally construe himself or herself in various cultural ways" (p. 186).

In integration, we find a most crucial skill of intercultural sensitivity. Evaluating phenomena during the process of integration necessitates adopting another cultural frame of reference to interpret events and people. Perry's (1970) "contextual relativism" and Buoyant's (1986) "contextual evaluation" are important concepts in the evaluation of phenomena relative to cultural context. Our quickness to distinguish and decipher communication patterns and to avoid negative displays of ethnocentrism facilitates intercultural experiences and enhances relationship development. Therefore, being sensitive is having consideration for others, being receptive to their needs and differences, and being able to transfer such emotions to actions (Smith, 1966). In short, interculturally sensitive individuals are more likely to understand and consider others' needs in multicultural encounters. Even when disagreeing, an interculturally sensitive person will leave the other feeling confirmed and validated.

# RECAP

The cry for intercultural understanding is echoed repeatedly today. Intercultural understanding is absolutely vital for people to lead harmonious and meaningful lives together in a culturally pluralistic world. Buoyant (1979) went to the heart of the problem in asserting that the noble goal of attaining a greater degree of intercultural understanding must be accompanied by a shift from ethnocentrism to ethnorelativism. Only through this process of transformation can the cultural differences be turned from a problem into an opportunity.

This chapter examines multiculturalism and its impact on organizational life and the educational system. The chapter also discusses the important role intercultural sensitivity plays in a multicultural society, first explaining that increasing cultural diversity, especially in American society, has offered and will continue to offer new challenges. To see beyond difference, to make changes in the workplace and the schools to make the most of the opportunities presented to us by diversity, is our primary challenge.

The chapter considers the impact of cultural diversity for business. Managing a culturally diverse workforce is examined from three operational perspectives: planning, organization, and leadership. The chapter proposes four strategies of diversity management for organizations: (1) managing and rewarding performance based on the foundation of diversity, (2) matching people and jobs, (3) keeping employees informed and involved, and (4) supporting diverse work styles and life needs.

In the educational setting four significant issues regarding multicultural education are considered: (1) exposure to multicultural perspectives, (2) maintaining cultural identity, (3) developing intercultural communication skills, and (4) diversifying the curriculum. Seven stages of the process of multiculturalism are identified: (1) monoculturalism, (2) cross-cultural contact, (3) cultural conflict, (4) educational interventions, (5) disequilibrium, (6) awareness, and (7) multiculturalism.

The last section of the chapter stresses the need for intercultural sensitivity in multicultural societies. The concept is defined, the relationship between intercultural sensitivity and intercultural training programs is explained, and six components of intercultural sensitivity are explicated: (1) ethnorelativism, (2) respect of cultural differences, (3) adaptability, (4) perspective-taking, (5) open-minded, and (6) acknowledgment of other's needs.

# RETHINK

The notion of a "global village" pairs two contradictory elements: "global" (inclusive) and "village" (exclusive). On the one hand, it dissolves boundaries; on the other, it maintains them. Drawing from the Indian and Chinese tradition of finding wisdom in paradoxes, we propose starting with a zone of culturally familiar space from which to operate. Then, from within this space, the practice of inclusiveness can widen our horizons and can invite learning.

It is inclusiveness that prevents differing identities and ideologies from developing mutual intolerance. In this vein, Mahatma Gandhi refused to recognize anyone as an enemy. He regarded his opponents as being good persons, who were differently persuaded (Starosta, 1992). Similarly, writers such as Oliver (1965) and Condon and Yousef (1975) have considered cultural conditioning as a form of societal persuasion whose rules had come to be perceived as natural. Inclusiveness takes account of the full range of human possibilities. Its driving force is commitment to tolerance. In pursuit of tolerance and inclusiveness, the Southern Poverty Law Center in Alabama distributes free learning materials on *Teaching Tolerance* to thousands of U.S. educators twice each year.

Regrettably, each step toward tolerance awakens voices of resistance. A policy of affirmative action generates resistance that decries "reverse privilege." The practice of de facto privilege that has, over the years, benefited the majority, must be expanded to include national minorities. Steps must be taken to see that all persons are "privileged" to participate in the process of selection (Mann, 1996). Only when such "privilege" is extended to historically excluded groups do those who have benefited from exclusiveness begin to recognize that privilege has been conferred.

The exercise of power by majorities in the interest of exclusiveness is sometimes subtle. When an ardent proponent of Unity Nation gave a speech at a white university, the Black Student Association at that university was told to repudiate his views. When he spoke at a historically black university (where CBS's *Eye to Eye* falsely identified him as a "black Muslim"), the university administration was asked to disassociate themselves publicly from his message. By contrast, when a white extremist spoke at an Ivy League school, representatives of minority student groups were told not to complain that the university promoted a policy of "free speech." The de facto privilege of speaking one's individual mind was extended only to the white extremist speaker (Berry, 1994). When individuals of an identifiable minority sought to share in the de facto privilege of speaking biased messages, their group was singled out for attention (Cooper, 1997).

The tug-of-war between inclusiveness and exclusiveness often takes the form of debates on differences in the community, the workplace, and the classroom. The introduction of women's studies or African American studies curricula is viewed by some as inclusive, but by others as divisive. Teaching from an Afrocentric perspective is seen as providing safe space for self-discovery by some, and as working against national integration by others.

The role communication is to play in multicultural societies must be closely monitored by intercultural scholars. Will intercultural education serve as the foundation for cooperation among mutually tolerant groups? Definitive answers to questions of inclusiveness and commitment await further research. Until these answers are found, those who teach intercultural communication must seek ways to value diversity while, at the same time, moving beyond the traditional walls of privilege and exclusiveness. Literature dealing with the issue of multiculturalism is still scarce. Intercultural communication scholars must pay more attention to multicultural issues in the future.

## QUESTIONS FOR DISCUSSION

1. Why must we face cultural diversity issues?
2. Describe five demographic factors that will influence the U.S. workforce by the year 2000.
3. What is the impact of the interplay of gender, ethnicity,, and business on modern organizations?
4. Describe the three operational principles that must be considered in the process of managing a culturally diverse workforce.
5. Explain techniques that can be used to manage diversity in organizations.
6. Describe four significant issues for multicultural education must face.
7. Describe Wurzel's seven stages of the multiculturalism process.
8. Explain the components of intercultural sensitivity.
9. What are the potential problems of multiculturalism?

# ▶ Chapter 11

## Intercultural Communication Competence

### *Objectives*

Upon completion of this chapter, you will

- Be able to define competence and intercultural communication competence.
- Understand the approaches to the study of intercultural communication competence.
- Understand the dimensions and components of intercultural communication competence.

> *Compose oneself before trying to move others; rest and ease one's mind before speaking; make one's relations firm before asking for something from others.—I CHING*

It is a legacy of Hinduism, Buddhism, and Taoism to strive to make the self "right" before entering into dealings with others. Yet, only through interaction with others can a sense of the community emerge. Interaction across individuals and among communities calls for "competent" communication. The idea of communication competence necessarily takes us beyond the self to regard the other. Although the study of communication competence dates indirectly back to Aristotle's *Rhetoric,* only a handful of scholars currently deal with communication competence by considering cultural factors. In what we have portrayed as a world that is driven by intercultural imperatives, we find surprisingly few studies of intercultural communication competence. This chapter explores intercultural communication competence by separating the discussion into four parts: (1) the nature of communication competence, (2) culture and communication competence, (3) approaches to the study of intercultural communication competence, and (4) a model of intercultural communication competence.

## THE NATURE OF COMMUNICATION COMPETENCE

Although the study of intercultural communication can be dated back to the works of political scientists and anthropologists in the 1940s and 1950s, the topic of intercultural communication competence remains a fresh area. Intercultural communication competence is the only means whereby we can move beyond cultural differences in order to succeed in intercultural interactions. But, "What is intercultural communication competence?" Before we answer this question we first need to understand what is "competence."

### *Definition of Competence*

One early study considered competence "an organism's capacity to interact effectively with its environment" (White, 1959, p. 297). White viewed competence as a basic human need and proposed the measure of competence to be the degree to which a person produces the intended effect from interaction with the environment. In other works, our competence increases as our awareness of relevant factors increases (Argyris, 1965a, 1965b).

Competence was also defined as the acquired ability to interact effectively (Foote & Cottrell, 1955; Holland & Baird, 1968). This definition sees communication competence as an inherent ability that relates neither to personal intellect nor to education. However, Weinstein (1969) proposed that communication competence increases through socialization and that we learn it incidentally, rather than through deliberate effort. Weinstein viewed competence as the acquired ability to manipulate the interaction in response to personal goals.

Bochner and Kelly (1974) expanded the concept of competence to include both interactants by defining competence as "the ability to relate effectively to self and others" (p. 280). That is, to be competent, we must not only feel we are competent, but our ability should be observed and confirmed by our counterparts. Under this definition, communication competence can be judged by "(1) abilities to formulate and achieve objectives, (2) ability to collaborate effectively with others, and (3) ability to adapt appropriately to situational or environmental variation" (p. 288).

Finally, Wiemann (1977) synthesized the concept of competence from the human relations, social skills, and self-presentation perspectives. He conceptualized communicative competence as "the ability of an interactant to choose among available communicative behaviors in order that he [*sic*] may successfully accomplish his own interpersonal goals during an encounter while maintaining the face and line of his fellow interactants within the constraints of the situation" (p. 198). This definition simultaneously argues that competent communication is other-oriented and that communicators have to successfully accomplish their own goals. All these conceptualizations focus on perceived effectiveness in an interaction.

Whereas some scholars conceive of communication competence as a function of perceived effectiveness, others look at communication competence from the viewpoint of appropriateness. For example, Backlund (1978) reviewed the various definitions of communication competence and defined communication competence as "the ability to demonstrate a knowledge of the socially appropriate communicative behavior in a given situation" (p. 26).

Allen and Wood (1978) offered one set of rules for appropriateness:

1. Say just enough—not too little or too much.
2. Don't say something that's false—or speak about something for which you lack evidence.
3. Relate your contribution to the topic and situation.
4. Be clear about what you are saying, and say it "with dispatch."

They stressed the four elements of appropriateness: quantity, quality, relevancy, and manner of message sending in interaction. Thus, communication competence is comprised of two elements: effectiveness and appropriateness.

## Definition of Intercultural Communication Competence

Intercultural communication competence is defined as much the same way as the above-mentioned intracultural definitions (Lustig & Koester, 1996). The only difference is, in addition to looking at communication competence as effective and appropriate interaction, intercultural communication scholars place more emphasis on contextual factors. They conceived of communication competence not only as effective and appropriate interaction between people, but as effective and appropriate interaction between people who belong to particular environments. This orientation resembles that of communication scholars who emphasize competence as a context-specific behavior (Spitzberg & Cupach, 1984). Thus, we conceive of intercultural communication competence as "the ability to effectively and appropriately execute communication behaviors to elicit a desired response in a specific environment." This definition shows that competent persons must not only know how to interact effectively and appropriately with people and environment, but also know how to fulfill their own communication goals using this ability.

## CULTURE AND COMMUNICATION COMPETENCE

The addition of cultural factors complicates the study of intercultural communication competence. Culture, in its broadest sense, represents the way of human life of a group (Tylor, 1958). Thus, we see that different cultures generate distinctive value systems and perceptions of meaning. Because the specific cultural milieu serves as the measure of our communication competence, we need to investigate "the breadth and depth of the impact of culture on communication behavior, and the salience of particular communication behavior to members of different cultures" (Cooley & Roach, 1984, p. 14). Based on this point of view, we examine some approaches developed to study intercutural communication competence.

## APPROACHES TO THE STUDY OF INTERCULTURAL COMMUNICATION COMPETENCE

Dinges (1983) and Collier (1989) have classified the study of intercultural communication competence into different approaches. Dinges (1983) proposed six approaches to investigate intercultural communication competence: overseasmanship, subjective culture, multicultural person, social behaviorism, topology and intercultural communicators approaches.

### Overseasmanship Approach

The *overseasmanship* approach, first presented by Cleveland, Mangone and Adams (1960), identifies common factors in effective performance when we sojourn in another culture. (A sojourn is an extended, nonpermanent stay abroad.) To be competent, we must show the ability to convert lessons from a variety of foreign experiences into effective job-related skills.

### Subjective Culture Approach

The *subjective culture or isomorphic attribution* approach requires us to have the ability to understand the causes of interactants' behaviors and reward them appropriately, and to modify suitably our behaviors according to the demands of the setting (Triandis, 1976, 1977). This ability to understand the reasons other cultures give for their behavior must be based on accurate understanding of the differences in cognitive structure between cultures.

## Multicultural Person Approach

The *multicultural person* approach emphasizes that a competent person must be able to adapt to exceedingly difficult circumstances by transcending usual adaptative limits (Adler, 1975, 1977). We must learn to move in and out of contexts, to maintain coherence in different situations, and to be dynamic.

## Social Behaviorism Approach

The *social behaviorism or culture learning* approach emphasizes that successful intercultural coping strategies depend more on predeparture experiences, such as training and sojourning in another country, than on our inherent characteristics or personality (Guthrie, 1975). That is, to be competent we must learn discriminative stimuli to obtain social rewards and to avoid punishments that would create hardship in intercultural interaction (David, 1972). By learning social taboos in an unfamiliar setting, for example, we can avoid accidentally alienating ourselves from others.

## Typology Approach

The *typology* approach develops different models of intercultural communication competence. Most of the models place sojourners' behavioral styles on to a continuum from most to least effective. For example, Brislin (1981) proposed that a successful intercultural interaction must be based on the sojourner's attitudes, traits, and social skills. Brislin claims nonethnocentrism and nonprejudicial judgments to be the major attitudes for effective intercultural interaction. Ethnocentrism is the judgment of an unfamiliar practice by the standards and norms familiar to us from our own culture. The major adaptive variables include personality strength, intelligence, tolerant personality, social relations, potential for benefit, and task-orientation. Lastly, the social skills consist of knowledge of subject and language, positive orientation to opportunities, effective communication skills, and the ability to use personal traits to complete tasks.

## Intercultural Communicators Approach

The *intercultural communicators* approach emphasizes that successful intercultural interaction centers on communication processes among people from different cultures. In other words, to be competent we must show the ability to establish interpersonal relationship by understanding our counterparts through the effective exchange of verbal and nonverbal behaviors (Hall, 1959, 1966, 1976).

These approaches represent key directions for the study of intercultural communication competence. The next section presents a model of intercultural communication competence based on the six approaches.

## DIMENSIONS AND COMPONENTS OF INTERCULTURAL COMMUNICATION COMPETENCE

According to Chen (1989), intercultural communication competence has four dimensions: personality strength, communication skills, psychological adaptation, and cultural awareness. Figure 11–1 illustrates the dimensions and components of intercultural communication competence, and the following section discusses them.

### *Personality Attributes*

*Personality attributes* refers to the traits that constitute an individual's personality. These traits stem from our unique experiences within a culture and reflect, in part, our heredity. The main personal traits that affect intercultural communication competence include self-concept, self-disclosure, self-awareness, and social relaxation.

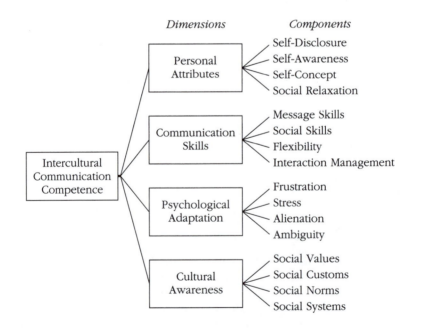

**FIGURE 11-1**   **Dimensions and Components of Intercultural Communication Competence**

## Self-Concept

*Self-concept* refers to the way in which we view ourselves. It not only is fundamental to how we communicate but mediates how we relate to the world. One of the most important elements of self- concept is self-esteem. It has been found that the communication behaviors of high-self-esteem individuals and low-self-esteem individuals differ significantly. Adler and Towne (1987) itemized some of these predicted differences: persons with high self-esteem, as opposed to persons with low self-esteem, more likely think well of others, are accepted by others, perform well when being watched, feel more comfortable when working with superiors, and can defend themselves against the negative comments of others.

Ehrlich (1973) also showed that people with high self-esteem generally feel more positively toward outgroup persons than do those with low self-esteem. In intercultural encounters, self-esteem helps us to meet psychological stresses. Other aspects of self-concept that affect intercultural communication competence include self-reliance, an optimistic outlook, and a stable extroverted personality.

## Self-Disclosure

*Self-disclosure* refers to the willingness of individuals to openly and appropriately reveal information about themselves to their counterparts. "Appropriate" self-disclosure varies among cultures, as do the allowable topics of conversation, for persons at one or another level of intimacy, at a given level of the social hierarchy. Adler and Towne (1987) proposed that self-disclosure must be intentional and that information revealed to others must be significant and previously unknown to others. Self-disclosure is one of the main elements of individual competence in communication, and it can lead to achievement of personal communication goals (Bochner & Kelly, 1974; Parks, 1976).

The contextual ambiguity common to interactions with people from different cultures produces predictably high levels of uncertainty. Reduction of the uncertainty level can often be achieved through mutual self-disclosure. Chen's (1989, 1990, 1993) studies demonstrate self-disclosure to be one of the components of intercultural communication competence, especially regarding depth and breadth of self-disclosure. This finding helps to illustrate the social penetration model, developed by Altman and Taylor (1973), wherein relationships develop from superficial to more personal levels through the depth and breadth of information individuals disclose to their counterparts.

## Self-Awareness

The implementation of conversationally competent behaviors in interaction requires *self-awareness*, the ability to monitor or to be aware of ourselves (Spitzberg & Cupach, 1984). Self-awareness helps individuals adjust more smoothly to other cultures (Brislin, 1979; Triandis, 1977). Self-monitoring, a concept closely related to self-awareness, facilitates competent intercultural communication. According to Snyder (1974), when we are high in self-monitoring we stay particularly sensitive to our counterparts' expressions and self-presentation, and know how to use these behavioral cues to guide our own self-presentation. Snyder included in high self-monitoring factors such as the following:

1. Concern with social appropriateness of one's self-presentation.
2. Attention to social comparison information as cues to situationally appropriate expressive self-presentation.
3. The ability to control and modify our self-presentation.
4. Our use of this ability in particular situations.
5. The modification of our expressive behavior and to meet the requirements of particular situations.

### Social Relaxation

*Social relaxation* is the ability to reveal little anxiety in communication. Anxiety, according to Herman and Schield (1961), usually originates from our lack of security in entering a new situation. The new situation presents us with a series of crises when we first enter the host culture (Gudykunst & Hammer, 1987) .

The symptoms of social anxiety include undue perspiration, shakiness, postural rigidity, vocal unevenness, and lowered response tendencies (Spitzberg & Cupach, 1984). In other words, to be effective in intercultural communication we must surmount what Barna (1979) called stumbling blocks. One of these is a feeling of anxiety that accompanies communication with those from different cultures. Obviously, social relaxation is important to intercultural interaction.

To summarize, we become more competent in intercultural communication as we acquire the following personal attributes: (1) a positive self-concept, (2) appropriate self-disclosure, (3) self-awareness, and (4) less anxiety and more social relaxation.

## Communication Skills

Communication skills are the verbal and nonverbal behaviors that enable us to be effective in interactions with others. Such behaviors in intercultural communication include message skills, behavioral flexibility, interaction management, and social skills.

### Message Skills

*Message skills* require that we acquire not only a knowledge of the host language but also show the ability to use it. Competent intercultural communication begins with message skills. Chomsky (1965), for example, emphasized linguistic competence that pertains to the knowledge of rules underlying the use of language. Competent persons must be able to code skillfully and to create recognizable messages in the process of communication. Barna (1979) affirmed that a good understanding of the interactant's language and the ability to recognize the meaning of nonverbal behavior comprise two major elements of intercultural communication competence.

Besides language itself, message skills include the ability to use descriptive and supportive messages in the process of interaction. *Descriptiveness* refers to our use of concrete and specific feedback as opposed to our judgment of another's behaviors. *Nonjudgmentalism* helps us to avoid defensive reactions from our counterparts. *Supportiveness* is the sine qua non of effective communication. It requires us to know how to support others effectively and to reward them in communication by cues such as head nods, eye contact, facial expressions, and physical proximity (Hammer, 1989).

### Behavioral Flexibility

*Behavioral flexibility* indicates the ability to select an appropriate behavior in different contexts and situations (Bochner & Kelly, 1974). A behaviorally flexible person must demonstrate the abilities of accuracy and adaptability when attending to information and must be able to perform different behavioral strategies in order to achieve communication goals (Parks, 1976).

As one dimension of intercultural communication competence, we express behavioral flexibility through verbal immediacy cues, in which we know how to use different kinds of intimate verbal behaviors to establish interpersonal relationships. Thus, behaviorally flexible persons must be good at "the alternation and co-occurrence of specific speech choices which mark the status and affiliative relationships of interactants" (Wiemann, 1977, p. 199). According to Wheeless and Duran (1982), behavioral flexibility also includes feeling comfortable while interacting with people from different cultures.

### Interaction management

By *interaction management* we mean the ability to speak in turn in conversation and to initiate and terminate the conversation appropriately. In other words, we deal with the ability of individuals to "handle the procedural aspects of structuring and maintaining a conversation" (Spitzberg & Cupach, 1984, p. 46). This implies knowing how to develop a topic smoothly in interaction and allow equal opportunity for all participants to share the time of discussions. Interaction management was treated as one of the major dimensions in Ruben's (1976) *Intercultural Behavioral Assessment Indices* to measure intercultural communication competence.

To be effective in communicative interaction we must realize that: (1) interruptions are not permitted, (2) only one person may talk at a time, (3) speaker's turns should alternate appropriately, and (4) speakers should pay full

---

### Research Highlight 11–1

Who:   Ruben, B. D.

What:  "Assessing Communication Competence for Intercultural Adaptation."

Where: *Group and Organization Studies, 1,* 1976, 334–354.

In this article the author argues that outcome assessment of intercultural training is a recurrent problem faced by scholars in different disciplines. The purpose of this article is to develop an instrument that can be used to behaviorally assess communication competence in intercultural training programs.

After a thorough review of previous literature, the author identifies seven dimensions of behavioral competence in intercultural communication and then creates an index using the seven dimensions as an instrument to testing intercultural communication competence. The seven dimensions include:

**1.** Display of respect—the ability to show positive regard for another person, including behavioral cues such as eye contact, body posture, voice tone, and general displays of interest in intercultural interaction.

**2.** Interaction posture—the ability to use nonjudgmental and descriptive ways to respond to others' statements. The more competent we are, the more descriptive and less evaluative or judgmental we tend to be.

**3.** Orientation to knowledge—the ability to distinguish that different persons have different ways of interpreting themselves and the world around them: first and most important, intrapersonal orientation; then interpersonal orientation and cultural orientation; and, last, physical orientation.

**4.** Empathy—the ability to see others from their points of view. In intercultural communication empathic persons sense their interactants' feelings and thoughts through their expressions.

**5.** Self-oriented role behavior—the ability to be functionally flexible in different kinds of role behaviors. There are three kinds of role behaviors: task roles, relational roles, and individualistic roles.

**6.** Interactional management—the ability to initiate, take turns in, and terminate a conversation in the process of intercultural interaction. A person with high interaction management skills knows how to provide equal opportunity for conversation to all interactants.

**7.** Tolerance of ambiguity—the ability to face an ambiguous situation or a new environment with little discomfort. In other words, persons with high tolerance of ambiguity tend to be less nervous or frustrated and adapt to a new culture rapidly.

---

attention to their counterparts (Wiemann, 1977). Wiemann's standards appear to be based on European conventions, since African and African American interaction regulation allows two speakers to talk at one time, at least briefly. Moreover, "call-and-response" behavior may be falsely interpreted by Euro-Americans as an "interruption," whereas it actually signifies the co-creation of messages.

*Interaction involvement,* which closely resembles interaction management, is a measure of how we perceive a topic and situation to involve our concept of self and self-reward (Spitzberg & Cupach, 1984). It indicates a person's empathic and other-oriented ability in interaction. A fundamental element of the interpersonal communication process, interaction involvement depends on three competencies: responsiveness, perceptiveness, and attentiveness (Cegala, 1981, 1984).

### Social Skills

Communication skills also include *social skills,* such as empathy and identity maintenance. Empathy has been long recognized as essential to efficacy in interpersonal communication. We practice empathy when we project ourselves "into another person's point of view so as momentarily to think the same thoughts and feel the same emotions as the other person" (Adler & Towne, 1987, p. 95). Empathy allows us to sense what is inside another's mind or to step into another's shoes. It is also called *affective sensitivity, telepathic or intuition sensitivity,* or *perspective-taking.*

A highly empathic individual not only possesses abilities such as reciprocity of affect displays, verbal response showing understanding, and active listening but also can respond accurately to another person's feelings and thoughts. Empathy has been confirmed to be as one of the traits that produce intercultural communication competence (Bennett, 1979, 1986; Yum, 1988).

Identity maintenance allows us to affirm our counterpart's identity. Because the need to learn who we are prompts us to communicate with others, competent persons not only need to understand themselves in interaction but also need to inform their counterparts about who they are (Collier, 1994; Collier & Thomas, 1988; Hecht & Ribeau, 1991). Likewise, in order to achieve smooth interaction, competent persons must know how to respect their counterparts' identity. Parks (1976) mentioned that we usually learn the ability of identity maintenance through experience, and the use of identity maintenance skills must vary with different situations and different personal goals.

To summarize, we become more competent in intercultural communication when we exhibit the following communication skills: (1) message skills, including knowing the host language and the abilities of descriptiveness and supportiveness in the process of interaction; (2) behavioral flexibility; (3) interaction management, including the ability of initiating, maintaining, and terminating a conversation; and (4) interaction involvement, including the ability to be responsive, perceptive, and attentive in interaction.

## Psychological Adjustment

Psychological adjustment refers to our ability to acclimate to a new culture. It entails a complex process through which we acquire the ability to fit in the new cultural environment (Kim & Gudykunst, 1988). That is, psychological

## Research Highlight 11–2

Who:      Collier, M. J.

What:     "Cultural and Intercultural Communication Competence: Current Approaches and Directions for Future Research."

Where:    *International Journal of Intercultural Relations, 13,* 1989, 287–302.

The article gives an overview of the approaches to the study of intercultural communication competence based on three issues raised by the author: (1) unclear or inappropriate conceptualization of culture or intercultural communication, (2) the validity and consistency of ontological and epistemological assumptions about intercultural communication competence made by scholars, and (3) the theoretical perspectives adopted by scholars in the study of intercultural communication competence relative to the goals of the research.

Four approaches to the study of communication competence across cultures are discussed: (1) ethnography of speaking approaches, (2) cross-cultural attitude approaches, (3) behavioral skills approaches, and (4) the cultural identity approach.

First, the ethnography of speaking approaches argue that (1) culture, as a system of symbols and meanings transmitted through history, is an emergent product of discursive text and conduct of interactions; thus, competence must be a contextual phenomenon; (2) ontologically, an interdependent relationship exists between conduct, meanings, and members of the cultural group; epistemologically, interpretive approaches are ways of knowing the participants' conduct in a naturalistic environment, and (3) the goal of ethnography is to describe the membership in a particular culture or community.

Second, cross-cultural approaches argue that (1) culture is a set of shared ideas about patterned behaviors of group members; thus, dimensions of cultural variability can be identified; (2) through the understanding of specific and general cultural features we can reach intercultural communication competence; and (3) the goal of these approaches is to increase our understanding of others' cultures in order to be more tolerant and respectful of cultural differences.

Third, behavioral skills approaches argue that (1) culture is affiliated with a nation; thus, intercultural communication occurs when two persons from different nations encounter; (2) ontologically, human beings' actions are goal-directed and they exercise a free in for making choices; epistemologically, through the self-report process, we are able to identify the behavioral skills of members of various cultures; and (3) the goal of these approaches is to increase international and global interdependence.

Finally, the cultural identity approach argues that (1) like ethnography, culture is an emergent system of symbols, meanings, and norms that is transmitted throughout history; cultural identity, then, is shaped in the interaction of cultural systems—thus, intercultural communication competence is the ability to appropriately and effectively manage our own and respect others' cultural identity in the process of inter-cultural interaction; (2) from an onto-logical standpoint, members of cultural groups are expected to understand the meanings of cultural symbols and norms and to know how to negotiate cultural identity appropriately; episte-mologically, cultural identity and cul-tural competence can be described based on textual analysis or on im-pressions of the respondents immedi-ately after the interaction; and (3) the goal of this approach is to "understand why particular conduct is viewed as appropriate and effective and what can be learned to help individuals improve the quality of their own experience " (p. 295).

adaptation represents our general psychological well-being, self-satisfaction, and contentment within a new environment. As indicated in Chapter 8, Lysgaard (1955) proposed the **U**-curve hypothesis to explain the three steps of psychological adaptation: initial adjustment, crisis, and regained adjust-ment. The hypothesis indicates that adjustment does not increase at a constant level. Rather, it may start out easy, then stall before eventually recovering its momentum.

The crisis stage is generally termed *cultural shock.* The symptoms of cul-tural shock were delineated in Chapter 8. For competent people, these symp-toms represent temporary phenomena that will be overcome after a short period of time. However, with less competent persons, these symptoms could persist for the duration of the sojourn. If a person cannot return home, the difficulty in cross-cultural adaptation may cause serious psychological or psy-chiatric problems such as schizophrenia, paranoia, depression, and lack of con-fidence (Yeh, Chu, Klein, Alexander, & Miller, 1981). This underlines the importance of competency in adapting to a new culture. By contrast, other writ-ers consider culture shock to be a cognitive deficit more than a psychological disorder.

In general, psychological adjustment is typically associated with a person's ability to cope with situations such as frustration, stress, alienation, and ambi-guity caused by the host culture. That is, according to Furnham and Bochner (1982), psychological adjustment indicates how a person handles "social diffi-culties." Social difficulties tend to increase when the differences between the host culture and the sojourner's culture become greater.

Persons with high ambiguity tolerance tend to show little visible discom-fort, little confusion, and little nervousness in a new environment. They can quickly adapt to situational demands with no noticeable personal, interper-sonal, or group consequences and can cope with the changing environment rapidly and comfortably. These abilities, in turn, tend to lessen feelings of frus-tration, alienation, and stress experienced by sojourners in a new culture (Ruben & Kealey, 1979).

In addition, the ability to deal with psychological stress in a new environment is one of the main elements for intercultural communication competence. The ability includes the skills needed to cope effectively with frustration, interpersonal conflict, pressure to conform, financial difficulties, social alienation, different political systems, and general anxiety. These collective traits show that a psychologically well-adjusted person can effectively cope with the feelings of stress, frustration, alienation, and ambiguous situations in a new culture. This makes effective psychological adaptation a key variable for competency in intercultural interaction (Searle & Ward, 1990; Ward & Searl, 1991; Wiseman & Abe, 1986).

To summarize, we become more competent in intercultural communication when we display psychological adaptation, which includes four elements: (1) our ability to deal with stress, (2) our ability to deal with feelings of frustration, (3) our ability to deal with feelings of alienation, and (4) our ability to deal with ambiguous situations caused by the new environment. Mini Case 11–1 illustrates the psychological stress we may experience in an ambiguous intercultural situation.

## Cultural Awareness

*Cultural awareness* refers to understanding the conventions of the host culture that affect how people think and behave. Each culture shows different thinking patterns. We encounter frequent problems in intercultural communication when we misunderstand thinking patterns. To be effective in intercultural interaction we must first learn the preferences of the host culture for supporting arguments and determining knowledge. Understanding a host culture enables us to modify our communication patterns to be congruent with the cues of unfamiliar interactants. Changing behavior to be congruent with host nationals or

---

**Mini Case 11–1**

An American family traveling in Florence, Italy, wanted to experience a true Italian meal while on their vacation. The family had eaten many typical Americanized Italian meals but was looking forward to tasting the authentic variety. The restaurant they chose did not take reservations and was extremely crowded with locals from the nearby communities. The Americans waited silently while more and more Italians entered and were seated and served. It did not seem to bother the family that they were being overlooked or just put off.

How do you explain the restaurant's behavior toward the Americans and the Americans' toleration of it?

*Source:* Lauren Maselli, University of Rhode Island.

---

**Mini Case 11–2**

John is an American visiting Egypt who has been invited to attend a dinner party at the home of an Egyptian friend. The dinner is superb, the host obviously having gone out of his way to entertain John. At the close of the evening, John thanks his friend for the incredible dinner. After shaking his friend's hand and walking to his car, John senses that he has said or done something to offend his friend.

Why was John's Egyptian friend offended?

---

*Source:* Jeanette Santos, University of Rhode Island.

with co-culturals helps us reach a mutual understanding (Hall & Whyte, 1963; Hecht, Sedano, & Ribeau, 1993)

Cultural awareness resembles the concepts proposed by Kluckhohn and Turner. Both sources emphasize the importance of cultural knowledge for effective intercultural communication. Kluckhohn (1948) asserted that cultural awareness requires understanding the "cultural map"; "if a map is accurate, and you can read it, you won't get lost; if you know a culture, you'll know your way around in the life of a society" (p. 28). Turner (1968) indicated that to be aware of a culture means to catch the "culture theme"—the thread that goes through a culture and organizes a culture as a recognizable system. It acts as a guideline to people's thinking and behavior, and appears repeatedly in daily life. Mini Case 11–2 demonstrates the importance of cultural awareness in the process of intercultural communication.

The key components of a cultural map or a cultural theme that affect intercultural communication competence include social values, social customs, social norms, and social systems. Intercultural communication competence requires an understanding of these components.

To summarize, we become more competent in intercultural communication as we acquire a high degree of cultural awareness, including understanding of the host culture's (1) social values, (2) social customs, (3) social norms, and (4) social systems.

## RECAP

As we encounter ever greater cultural and co-cultural diversity, careful study of intercultural communication competence becomes increasingly important. Only with mastery of intercultural communication competence can persons from different cultures communicate effectively and appropriately. This is why

Sitaram and Cogdell (1976) proclaimed that "all people of the world should study intercultural communication." This dictum, while broad, emphasizes the necessity of learning more about members of other cultures.

While communication competence has been studied for many years, its application to intercultural interaction continues to evolve. This chapter extracts some perspectives on intercultural communication competence from the existing literature. The chapter considers how the variable of *competence* influences the intercultural setting. The six types of competence discussed in the chapter include fundamental, social, interpersonal, linguistic, communicative, and relational competence. These types of competence can be treated as the key dimensions of communication competence. The chapter also argues the inseparability of the culture and communication competence.

We offer six approaches to the study of intercultural communication competence: overseasmanship, subjective culture, multicultural person, social behaviorism, typology, and social skills approaches. These lead to a model of intercultural communication competence that comprises four dimensions: (1) personal attributes, including self-concept, self-disclosure, self-awareness, and social relaxation; (2) communication skills, including message skills, social skills, behavioral flexibility, and interaction management; (3) psychological adjustment, including the ability to handle feelings of frustration, stress, alienation, and ambiguity caused by the host culture; and (4) cultural awareness, including the understanding of social values, customs, norms, and systems.

## RETHINK

Several research challenges remain for the study of intercultural communication competence. First, as the concept of intercultural communication competence grows more sophisticated, it has become confused with the definition of the term *competence* and embroiled in the argument as to whether competence is an inherent ability or a learned ability. This chapter proposes that competence should refer to the strength of personal attributes and to communication skills. In other words, both inherent and learned abilities (*traits* and *states*) should be considered and included. Neither trait nor state, taken alone, can account for competence.

Another problem centers on whether competence refers to the interactant's knowledge or performance. Chomsky (1965) considered competence to be simply the knowledge of the speaker-hearer's language. Phillips (1983) added the concepts of competence, skill, and effectiveness as follows: competence is "understanding situations and their requirements," skill is "demonstrated ability to meet requirements," and effectiveness is "the ability to accomplish specific goals" (p. 33). By this classification, Chomsky's competence is merely the first step in achieving communication competence. Both definitions of competence focus more on an individual's knowledge than upon the ability to perform based on that knowledge. This chapter indicates that both knowledge and performance must be considered elements of intercultural communication competence.

Finally, the confusion between effectiveness and competence must be resolved to arrive at a definition of communication competence. Many scholars (e.g., Hammer, Gudykunst, & Wiseman, 1978) used *effectiveness* to mean "competence." Others (e.g., Ruben, 1976, 1977; and Ruben and Kealey, 1979) used *effectiveness* and *competence* interchangeably. The terms' usage must be made crystal-clear in future studies. Obviously, the term *competence* is preferable, especially in an intercultural communication setting; as indicated previously, effectiveness is only one of two variables for conceptualizing competence. The second variable, *appropriateness,* plays a role of equal significance. In other words, to be competent in an intercultural interaction, individuals must communicate effectively and appropriately.

Within a multicultural workforce, researchers need to document the conflicts arising from the need mold workers of other cultures so that they are competent in the culture of that company and the need to widen the company's definition of competence to allow the genius of ethnically and culturally different workers to emerge. That competence is a reciprocal function—one that calls for considerable expertise on the part of both interactants—is an interesting premise for future investigation.

The second research challenge is to operationalize intercultural communication competence. To do so, we must first determine: what measurement criteria to use. This chapter proposes four traits—personal attributes, communication skills, psychological adjustment, and cultural awareness—that can be used to measure intercultural communication competence. Future study will likely offer further criteria. Next, we must decide what reporting methods to use in assessing intercultural communication competence. Use of a self-report scale, other-report scale, or the two together is possible. Because intercultural communication competence involves personal attributes and behavioral skills, some researchers argue in favor of a combination of self- and other-report methods. Though the use of both methods in tandem increases the external validity of the data, it becomes difficult to bridge any discrepancy between the self- and other-report measures unless a more acceptable scale is created. This problem becomes critical in an intercultural communication setting (Lustig & Spitzberg, 1993). For example, people from different cultures may have different perceptions or attitudes toward the process of the study, including items of the scale and the way to operate it (Martin, 1993).

Finally, another research challenge is to determine the traits individuals must possess to be considered "competent." For example, is it enough for individuals to possess communicative ability, or must they possess other abilities such as personal attributes, psychological adaptation, and cultural awareness?

## Research Highlight 11–3

Who: Lustig, M. W., & Spitzberg, B. H.

What: "Methodological Issues in the Study of Intercultural Communication."

Where: In R. L. Wiseman & J. Koester (Eds.) (1993), *Intercultural Communication Competence* (pp. 153-167). Newbury Park, CA: Sage.

The authors of this article argue that all attempts to study intercultural communication competence must address six issues: *what, who, when, where, why,* and *with what effect.*

First, *what* refers to the content of research. Five issues are involved in the study of intercultural communication competence: (1) level of abstraction—concerns whether to assess intercultural communication competence at a micro- or macro-level; (2) assessment equivalence—concerns whether to use a specific or a general approach to study intercultural communication competence; (3) level of analysis—concerns what unit should be used for the purpose of studying intercultural communication competence; (4) types of comparison—concerns selecting one of the four general ways (typicality, variability, association, and pattern) to compare the communication behaviors; and (5) content level—concerns the content of communication behaviors for the purpose of the research.

Second, *who* refers to the locus of evaluation. Should intercultural communication competence be measured by the interactant, by the interactant's counterpart, or by an observer? The authors suggests that strictly psychological information should be collected by using the self-report method; more public and discrete information can be collected by using other-report methods.

Third, *when* refers to chronological assessment of intercultural communication competence. Three categories are involved in this issue: (1) whether to conceptualize intercultural communication competence as an "episodic" or "dispositional" phenomenon; (2) whether to use a cross-sectional or longitudinal research design; and (3) whether to take a short-term or a long-term perspective toward intercultural communication competence.

Fourth, *where* refers to the role of context in the study of intercultural communication competence. Is intercultural communication competence a contextual phenomenon? If it is, how do researchers tackle the complexity of the intersecting of contexts such as physical setting, actor purposes, cultural milieu, and relational definition?

Fifth, *why* refers to the relevance of research in intercultural communication competence. Is competence treated equally as an important concept in different cultures? What are the meanings and values each culture attributes to on the concept of competence?

Finally, *with what effect* refers to ethical issues in the study of intercultural communication competence, including what position to take in the continuum of moral absolutism and moral relativism, the relationship between researchers and research participants, and the relationship between researchers and their host-culture colleagues.

Communication scholars must investigate whether the measurement of intercultural communication competence varies with the number of competence components assessed, or because of other factors. An equally provocative question concerns the interrelationships among the supposed components of intercultural communication competence.

One final problem concerning the dimensions and components of intercultural communication competence must be mentioned. Because the study of intercultural communication competence remains an interdisciplinary effort, scholars from different fields might generate different dimensions, terms, and components for intercultural communication competence. The dimensions and components of intercultural communication competence discussed in this chapter represent one perspective among many. It must be stressed that these dimensions and components are not definitive or exhaustive. Future research may serve to standardize the dimensions and components for the study of intercultural communication competence.

## QUESTIONS FOR DISCUSSION

1. Describe what is the difference between the meanings of *communication competence* and *intercultural communication competence.*
2. Explain Dinge's six approaches to the study of intercultural communication competence.
3. Discuss the dimensions and components of the model of intercultural communication competence.
4. What are the challenges for future research on intercultural communication competence?

# ▶ Chapter 12

## Intercultural Training

### *Objectives*

Upon completion of this chapter, you will

- Understand the importance of intercultural training.
- Understand the effects and goals of intercultural training.
- Know the models and techniques of intercultural training.
- Know how to evaluate intercultural training.

> *Intercultural communication involves my indicating to you the rules which govern my understanding and behavior of my culture, and you indicating to me the rules which govern them in your culture, and our showing a mutual respect of their similarities and differences*
> —*S. S. KING*

The above statement indicates that all cultures are interwoven by preferences and expectations that we may call rules. Our ability to interact effectively with individuals from cultures that are different from our own is based on our understanding of these cultural rules and their force. Through this knowledge we predict whether our counterparts will communicate in a particular way, and we learn to adjust our communication to respect the expected differences in cultural rules. Intercultural communication training programs move us toward such a state of functional cultural understanding. This chapter focuses on the topic of intercultural training. The discussion is divided into five parts: (1) the reasons for intercultural training, (2) the effects of intercultural training, (3) the goals of intercultural training, (4) the models of intercultural training, and (5) the evaluation of intercultural training.

## WHY INTERCULTURAL TRAINING?

Our ability to communicate with people from other cultures is the primary skill that allows us to function in an expanding global economy and among an increasingly diverse population here in the United States. According to Fontaine (1986), over 1.7 million Americans live and travel abroad for business, military service, religious activities, and diplomatic affairs each year. While Americans travel the world as tourists and students, those from other cultures also travel and work in the United States.

Intercultural interaction among persons with differing cultural rules has increased rapidly in the past few decades and will likely continue to accelerate in the United States and abroad. We must decide what communication practices will work in intercultural settings. Intercultural training programs are developed to improve interactional effectiveness by increasing our familiarity with customs of the host culture, with differences in perceptions, with the pool of meanings within the society, and with the use of varying nonverbal cues.

Domestically, cultural diversity poses problems of national reidentification. The rapid increase in non-European citizens and residents speaks to the need for a multicultural focus for career education and development (Locke & Parker, 1991). This multicultural perspective helps us understand ourselves and others in a changing historical and cultural context. It demands of an awareness of both human differences and commonalities. Professionals in business and education are called upon to infuse their practices with an awareness of their own personal and cultural background and experiences as well as those of their clients. They are called upon to promote positive self-concepts and to advocate career choices regardless of cultural background, to encourage understanding of the contributions of all cultural groups, and to develop effective intercultural communication skills (Rifenbary, 1991). Intercultural training programs can help to fulfill these quests.

## EFFECTS OF INTERCULTURAL TRAINING

Effective intercultural training should expand our worldview, that is, those attitudes, values, opinions, and beliefs by which we perceive the world. Our worldview is influenced by our cultural heritage and life experiences in a specific cultural group. One liability of a multicultural society is the tendency on the part of its various members to assume that everyone shares or must share identical characteristics, as would the members of any self-identified group. Intercultural training begins with the understanding of cultural differences and teaches us to recognize that people are a complex product of gender, ethnicity, and individuality (Gainor & Forrest, 1991). Through effective intercultural training we acquire a wider repertoire of knowledge and skills to interpret the worldviews and communication patterns of people of different cultures.

Good intercultural training affects our cognition, affect, and behavior beneficially in a variety of ways (Brislin, Landis, & Brandt, 1983). Cognitively, trainees come to (1) understand more about each other's points of views; (2) use fewer negative stereotypes in thinking about people of different cultures; (3) recognize greater complexity in their own and others' cultures; and (4) develop a "world-minded" attitude just as they gain a greater knowledge of their own culture.

Affectively, effective intercultural training enhances (1) enjoyment in interacting with people of different cultures; (2) expectations that we can establish good relationships with people of different cultures; and (3) the pleasure of living in an unfamiliar cultural environment.

Behaviorally, effective intercultural training helps us (1) develop better interpersonal relationships in a work groups whose members represent different cultural backgrounds; (2) better adjust to the different kinds of stress caused by cultural differences; (3) achieve better job performance; (4) feel more at ease while interacting with people of different cultures; and (5) achieve the goals we set for ourselves in intercultural communication.

Kohls (1984) narrowed the proposed impact of intercultural training on participants to the following elements:

- Preparation for participants' physical move to a new culture
- Comprehension of survival and logistical skills in a new culture
- The ability to verbally and nonverbally communicate with the host nationals
- The reduction of social blunders in the new culture
- Enhanced sense-making in the face of cultural variability
- The application of the worldviews of the host nationals
- The ability to cope with cultural shock
- Facilitation of positive feelings in the process of intercultural adjustment
- Transformation of the trainee into a bicultural person
- The expansion of the self and of cultural understanding

# GOALS OF INTERCULTURAL TRAINING

Because the ability to interact effectively with persons from different cultures has become a means of survival in an increasingly interdependent society, intercultural training programs must teach trainees to increase their awareness and understanding of cultural differences and to further increase their communication potential while lessening the likelihood of misunderstanding. In a larger sense, the objective of intercultural training is to help people successfully live and work in a new cultural environment. To achieve this objective, intercultural training programs may need to disregard the conceptual distinction between education and training.

Historically, the distinction of education and training has been discussed by scholars from different disciplines (Albert & Triandis, 1985; Bennett, 1986; Kohls, 1980). To these scholars, training basically deals with the issue of "how" and education deals with the issue of "why." Training programs frequently apply a skills approach that involves behavioral objectives. They tend to minimize conceptual groundwork and require participants to demonstrate behavioral ability outside the program (Bennett, 1986). Education, on the other hand, helps participants understand the theoretical background of learning. It requires learners to demonstrate and apply what they learn in creative ways to a new environment.

While emphasizing the skills approach, an effective intercultural training program necessarily involves exposing participants to the educational "why" element. The distinction between education and training therefore blurs in intercultural training programs. Recently, many scholars have used the words "trainer" and "educator" interchangeably to denote that both training and education should be presented in every intercultural training program. In addition, participants of intercultural training programs are referred to as "trainees," "students," or "learners."

The conceptual convergence of education and training requires intercultural training programs to achieve a variety of specific goals. For example, Warren and Adler (1977) identified eight goals of intercultural training: (1) to provide information on other cultures; (2) to provide professional skills for individuals to work in a specific culture; (3) to develop the ability to tolerate differences of cultural attitudes, beliefs, and values; (4) to help trainees acquire language skills; (5) to develop the ability to appropriately respond behaviorally in a new cultural environment; (6) to help trainees deal with culture shock; (7) to develop the capacity for cultural self-awareness; and (8) to enable trainees to experience a new culture in a positive way.

This list of intercultural training goals is similar to Seidel's (1981) model in which intercultural training programs are used to enable the trainees to

- Attain a practical working knowledge of a particular foreign language.
- Acquire management and interpersonal skills in an intercultural setting.
- Achieve a better understanding of their own culture as a basis for increased sensitivity to an understanding of the culture of assignment.
- Accept and be tolerant of values, beliefs, attitudes, and behavior patterns that might be quite different from their own.
- Communicate more effectively with persons from other cultures as well as from their own.
- Develop a more creative and effective approach to problem solving and goal setting by the application of modern management techniques.
- Acquire new learning skills that will to increase their interest in continued learning during the cross-cultural experience.
- Experience fewer problems of adjustment by achieving heightened self-understanding and self-awareness so that they are better able to perform within the requirements of a new cultural environment.
- Acquire new learning skills that will enable them to become sensitive and to respond appropriately to the subtleties of the new culture. (pp. 189–190)

## MODELS OF INTERCULTURAL TRAINING

With goals such as the above in mind, scholar-trainers have offered a series of models for intercultural training. A few of the many possibilities follow:

Gudykunst, Hammer, and Wiseman (1977):

- Intellectual approach
- Behavioral approach
- Area simulation approach
- Cultural awareness approach
- Self-awareness approach
- Interaction approach

Triandis (1977):

- Affective training
- Cognitive training
- Behavioral training
- Specific training
- General training
- Self-insight training

Brislin (1979):

- Attribution training
- Cognitive training
- Behavioral modification training
- Experiential training
- Self-awareness training

Bennett (1986):

- Intellectual model
- Area training model
- Self-awareness model
- Cultural awareness model

These models, which show great similarities, and can be grouped into six categories: the classroom model, the simulation model, the self-awareness model, the cultural awareness model, the behavioral model, and the interactional model.

## The Classroom Model

The classroom model may be the most popular approach used in intercultural training programs. It is also called the "intellectual" or the "university" model and usually applies the curricular offerings of educational system (Harrison & Hopkins, 1967). The model proposes that, through cognitive understanding of customs, values, people, geography, and habits of a specific culture, we can effectively adapt to the culture without experiencing discomfort caused by cultural differences.

Because the staffing process required by this model tends to be easy and the participants are able to relate their learning experience to the materials used in this type of training, satisfactory outcomes of the training are usually achieved (Bennett, 1986). Moreover, lectures, films, readings, and different kinds of presentations are normally applied to this model to help participants know more about a culture (Downs, 1969).

Although the model has the strength of conveying content knowledge to assist participants to understand a specific culture, the lack of congruence between classroom environment and lived experience in another culture becomes its insurmountable limitation. In other words, this model only teaches participants "what to learn," not "how to learn." Teaching participants to gain knowledge of a culture without knowing how to perform or adapt behaviorally to it will not guarantee success at living or working in a new culture (Hoehn, 1968).

## The Simulation Model

The simulation model was formed in response to criticism of the classroom model. According to Bennett (1986), this model focuses on the affective and experiential processes of training participants by involving them in an environment that closely resembles a specific culture. It is designed to help motivate participants in their interactions with people from different cultures and to increase their sensitivity to other cultural groups. The basic assumption of this approach is that after trainees have really experienced living in a place resembling the host culture, they will develop a set of new behaviors and methods of problem solving that will enable them to better adjust to the culture

---

**Research Highlight 12–1**

Who:  Gudykunst, W. B., & Ting-Toomey, S., & Wiseman, R. L.

What:  "Taming the Beast: Designing a Course in Intercultural Communication."

Where:  *Communication Education, 40,* 1991, 272–285.

This article addresses the major issues instructors face in teaching intercultural communication. The discussion focuses on philosophical issues, pedagogical issues, course content, and resources and teaching techniques.

Four philosophical issues in teaching intercultural communication addressed include:

**1.** conceptualizing intercultural communication—should the instructor conceive of intercultural communication as a unique area of study?
**2.** applying culture-general versus culture-specific approaches—should the instructor teach specific information about a given culture and how to interact with its members or teach generalities concerning people from different cultural or ethnic backgrounds?
**3.** explaining cultural variability in communication—should the instructor teach cultural similarities and differences by focusing on the dimensions of cultural variability?
**4.** explaining intercultural communication—to what degree should the instructor rely on theories of intercultural communication while teaching the course?

Two pedagogical issues that are addressed include: (1) balance of the cognitive, affective, and behavioral components of intercultural communication, and (2) the instructor's style of teaching, including language usage and treatment of stereotypes appearing in lectures and texts.

In terms of course content, the authors specify several course objectives and possible assignments and outline a syllabus. They also list some primary resources and discuss effective techniques.

(Gudykunst, Hammer, & Wiseman, 1977; Gudykunst, Ting-Toomey, & Wiseman, 1991).

When this model is used in intercultural training programs, participants are encouraged to interact with host families and other members of the culture and to experience the environmental variability of the field setting in order to directly experience the consequences of their communication styles and strategies. Through this trial-and-error process the participants gradually overcome their feeling of frustration and begin to become accustomed to the ways of behavior in that specific culture.

According to Wright (1970), this model of intercultural training demonstrates four advantages: (1) program participants rather than program trainers are the focus of the training; (2) program participants are required to be responsible for their behaviors in the training process; (3) the model emphasizes the acquisition of problem-solving skills rather then the transmission of cultural knowledge; and (4) the model teaches participants how to learn through a real interaction experience. However, the model also shows two disadvantages. First, it is difficult to duplicate an overseas environment. An inappropriate simulation procedure often leads to failure in living or working in the host culture. Second, the model does not truly teach the culture of the host nation: The training intervention lasts from a day to a few weeks and cannot possibly provide extensive cultural knowledge in such a limited time. The integration of the classroom model and the simulation model could promote a more effective intercultural adaptation process for programs participant (Gudykunst, Hammer, & Wiseman, 1977).

## The Self-Awareness Model

The self-awareness model assumes that understanding ourselves as cultural beings is the basis of better adjustment to a new culture (Chen, 1989). T-Group (i.e., Training Group), a basic form of sensitivity training, is the most popular training technique used in this model. The purpose of the model is to teach participants how psychological forces operate in groups and how their own behaviors influence others. It trains people to be sensitive to others' expressions and use behavioral cues to guide their own self-presentation.

Although self-awareness is important for being effective in intercultural communication, its focus on the internalized processes of an individual cannot adequately teach participants about factors involved in cultural interaction. The ethnocentric orientation of the model may put participants in a disadvantaged situation. Furthermore, the model does not provide participants with a framework of conceptual knowledge with which to analyze future situations. It does not teach them how to go beyond the self-awareness level to demonstrate their behavioral ability (Bennett, 1986; Downs, 1969).

## The Cultural Awareness Model

This model contrasts with the self-awareness model in its focus on the understanding of cultural knowledge rather than on self-knowledge. It assumes that in order to successfully interact with people from other cultures we have to understand our own and the other's cultural values, norms, customs, and social systems (Chen, 1990). The model postulates understanding our own culture (i.e., cultural self-awareness) as well as the other's culture (i.e., cultural awareness). It argues that the knowledge of ourselves as a cultural being is the foundation of knowing others in terms of their own culture (Kraemer, 1975). It aims to teach participants to recognize their own cultural values and contrast them with those of other cultures so that, by applying their insights, they can improve the quality of their intercultural interactions (Bennett, 1986). The model further maintains that, unless we understand our own cultural identity to be only one possibility among numerous others, we may ethnocentrically condemn the unfamiliar ways of other persons to be inferior to our own.

Based on the cognitive process, this model usually adopts a general perspective of cultural understanding instead of stressing the understanding of a specific culture. Trainees are expected to process the specific content of the new culture in light of general principles they have learned prior to contact with the other culture.

Cultural awareness training is built on a strong theoretical base, which adds to the popularity of the model. Through the training programs participants can reach not only intellectual understanding but also an affective tolerance of cultural differences in the process of intercultural communication (Bennett, 1986). Nevertheless, applying general cultural knowledge in dealing with a specific cultural task may prove difficult, especially when training programs are designed following the Western cultural mode, oriented toward verbal skill and individualism. Moreover, it may be hazardous for participants to compare and contrast their own culture to others. Similarities may be neglected, differences exaggerated, and slight differences may become major sources of conflict. In one author's conversations with Edward C. Stewart, he learned that Peace Corps experience as shown that adaptation to cultures where great difference is anticipated may go more smoothly than adaptation to other locales where differences are expected to be minimal. To master the complex process of preparing for other cultures by becoming more aware of our own may take more time than a regular training program can offer (Bennett, 1986).

## The Behavioral Model

The behavioral model of intercultural training teaches participants specific behavioral skills of a specific culture. It assumes that by learning a set of the host culture's behavioral skills, we can function effectively in the culture (David,

1972). According to Brislin and Pedersen (1976), to reach the goal of behavioral training the trainers have to model the appropriate behaviors used by a specific culture, and the training usually takes place in a simulated environment. The training process is expected to reduce the uncertainty and anxiety participants might feel in their encounters with people in the simulated culture. In the baFá baFá (Shirt, 1977) and Barnga (Thiagarajan & Steinwachs, 1990) simulation programs participants can observe the influences of a simulated culture in interaction with those of other simulated cultures.

Although the behavioral model of intercultural training focuses on solutions to concrete problems and the training programs are generally explicit and clearly designed, they contain several limitations (Brislin, Landis, & Brandt, 1983; Gudykunst & Hammer, 1983). First, great demands are placed on trainers, who must have thorough knowledge of a specific culture and be able to concretize a set of appropriate behavioral skills. These demands make it difficult to find competent trainers. Second, little data can be offered to confirm that the understanding of a culture's behavioral skills really helps participants better adjust to the culture. Finally, focusing on a set of behavioral skills ignores the dynamics of a culture. Cultural reality, in its complexity, cannot easily be reduced to a teachable (trainable) set of behavioral skills.

## The Interaction Model

In the interaction model created by Gudykunst et al. (1977) participants are required to directly interact with members of the host culture. It assumes that after experiencing face-to-face interaction with the host nationals in an intercultural training program, participants will feel more comfortable living and working in the host culture. Through the experiential learning process participants figure out the value systems and appropriate behavioral patterns of the host culture. The model is commonly applied to the intercultural workshop programs held on college campuses. International students or other people from the specific culture are usually invited to attend the workshop to provide trainees with an opportunity for face-to-face interaction.

The advantage of this model is that people of the host culture can provide more comprehensive resources than a trainer can. The disadvantage of the model is that people of the host culture may idealize or distort their own culture and may not able to present a real picture of it. This problem leads to difficulty in developing guidelines for program participants (Brislin, Landis, & Brandt, 1983).

Overall, each model of intercultural training shows strengths and weaknesses. Applying a single model may not sufficiently prepare participants to function appropriately and effectively in a new cultural environment. Depending on the nature and purpose of the training, a combination of methods is recommended. According to Foster and Danielian (1966), an integrated approach incorporating two or more models into the training program can maximize and maintain the desired results.

## INTERCULTURAL TRAINING TECHNIQUES

The intercultural training programs based on the models previously mentioned must devise specific training techniques. The coordination of training content and techniques leads to a more effective outcome. The following section discusses five fundamental and typical techniques often used in current intercultural training programs, including role playing, case studies, critical incidents, cultural assimilators, and simulations.

### Role Playing

In role-play exercises participants are assigned a role and asked to simulate real-life behavior. Different problem-solving situations based on life in the host culture can be designed somewhat spontaneously. The participants play the roles of the people involved and develop potential solutions. The technique is a good way to transform trainees from observers of another culture into participants within it, by having them role-play themselves in a situation simulating the host culture environment (Seidel, 1981).

Several specific objectives can be effectively accomplished by using the technique of role playing in intercultural training programs (Barnak, 1980):

- Practicing and learning intercultural communication skills.
- Practicing the executing of certain actions or solutions in a specific situation.
- Exploring reactions and feelings in a simulated situation.
- Encouraging involvement.
- Enabling greater understanding of the thinking and behavioral patterns of people from different cultures.

Example 12–1 is an example of role playing.

One form of role playing is psychodrama, in which the trainer tries to arouse strong emotions that are appropriate to the task of dealing with situations in the other culture or with co-cultural groups within the same culture. However, it takes advanced training to channel strong emotional responses in a productive direction (Starosta, 1990).

### Case Studies

Case studies are realistic descriptions of complex cultural events. Although the exact event the case study specifies will never take place, situations that it

## Example 12–1: Role Playing

A girl of 17 is able to visit a foreign country for the first time this summer, using her own savings and with some help from her parents. Fortunately, one of her former school chums, a boy named Sim, lives in the capital and has invited her to stay with him and his family. After being a guest of Sim's family for a week, the girl must get an extension of her visa so she can stay longer. She appears at the Immigration Office with her passport, expecting to meet with one of the immigration officers.

Assume one of the following roles:

### The Visitor: Role A

Today is the last day for obtaining an extension to your visa. You regret having to spend half the day in a government office, especially since Sim's family was hoping to take you to a local festival. You have heard about red tape and inefficiency in countries like these. You hope the visa won't take too long so you can enjoy the rest of the day.

### The Official: Role B

You have held this immigration job for several years now. Much of the work is routine. Lately, your government has been concerned about the large numbers of young people from Western countries who have come here to visit. Many of them, because of their sloppy dress and long hair, are considered a bad influence on the local customs. Some officials think that they introduce drugs and other bad habits to the young people.

You enjoy talking to young people, especially from European countries. It helps you practice your English. As you talk to this young woman, you discover she is here on her own and visiting a local young man here in the capital. This is not the usual thing for a young girl. If she is not a proper girl, her application would present a problem. Besides, visa applications sometimes take time.

In playing either role, you are to act exactly as though this were a real situation, and you may say or do anything you feel will be appropriate.

*Source:* S. Thiagarajan and B. Steinwachs. *Intercultural Sourcebook: Cross-Cultural Training Methodologies,* David S. Hoopes and P. Ventura, eds., reprinted with permission of Intercultural Press, Inc., Yarmouth, ME. Copyright 1979.

closely resembles reality enables us to effectively analyze and resolve the problems it poses. A good case study has unlimited potential for getting participants to think about, analyze, discuss, diagnose, and generate solutions. Thus, a good case study should help participants identify (1) the points of view of the characters are involved in the case, (2) the possible outcomes of the case and the effects on the characters in the case, and (3) their reaction to the case and to the characters in the case (Hoopes & Pusch, 1970). In other words, case studies are designed "to develop a method of approaching situations that will

## Research Highlight 12–2

Who:     Starosta, W. J.

What:    "Thinking Through Intercul-
         tural Training Assumptions
         in the Aftermath."

Where:   *International Journal of
         Intercultural Relations, 14,*
         1990, 1–6.

This article provides a critical analysis
of the intercultural training profession
by questioning training effectiveness
and trainer ethics. More specifically,
the article focuses on the ethical responsibilities of trainers who conduct
training sessions where the modification of trainees' prejudicial attitudes
and behaviors serves as the main objective. The author uses *psychodrama,*
a training technique used to facilitate
prejudice reduction among trainees in
a national conference of a professional
society, as an example for his analysis.
The psychodrama technique aims to
create an "emotionally intense" experience for both parties that requires the
trainer to adopt and act out a verbally
confrontational racist, ageist, sexist,
and ethnocentric persona while the
trainees endure the trainer's verbal and
prejudicial abuse.

The author raises several questions and ethical dilemmas about the
technique and provides possible solutions for those within the intercultural training profession. He scrutinizes
trainers' use of "abbreviated" forms of
methods such as the psychodrama to
facilitate prejudice reduction when
their ultimate responsibility is the
maintenance of participants' mental
well-being. Furthermore, the author

questions the long-range good of such
simulations in that they never produce
any final answers. He calls upon those
trainers who do conduct such sessions
to produce more convincing evidence
of their utility than testimonials and/
or personal accounts. Also, the author
distinguishes between prejudice due
to lack of information and the deep-
seated, internalized beliefs of a hard-
ened bigot.

In addition, the author argues that
the psyches of both the trainers and
trainees are at risk with such methods
and encourages debriefing not only for
the participants but for the trainers as
well. He labels "pseudo-trainers" those
trainers who conduct such psychodrama sessions despite their belief that
they will not change prejudicial behavior in the real world, and he questions
their professional ethics. He asserts that
just as licensed psychiatrists and psy-
chotherapists must work on their own
mental health, so must trainers struggle
with their own "isms"; those who claim
they only deal with prejudice in the
world "out there," as opposed to their
own, are not qualified to lead a simulated prejudice reduction training
session.

The author ends by offering several alternative strategies and techniques to trainers who wish to conduct
a prejudice reduction session, including training that prevents the enactment of any prejudiced behavior;
training that separates knowledge def-
icits from deep-seated prejudice; and
training that offers testimonials from
formerly prejudiced persons. Additionally, the author clarifies and justifies the

need for a mandatory debriefing session at the end of any intensely emotional simulated intercultural training exercise. Finally, the author challenges those within the field of intercultural communication to maintain a critical perspective on the training and development of their profession.

---

facilitate maximum understanding of those situations, of the people in them, and of the several outcomes that might result when one or another of the people emphasizes certain values rather than others" (Ross, 1980, p. 142).

Hoopes and Pusch (1979) and Ross (1980) further pointed out that good case studies are expected to do the following:

- Describe a specific situation that is closely analogous to the reality.
- Focus on the experience, thus centering discussions on the actual situation, giving participants a feeling of involvement in the situation.
- Emphasize the particular rather than general situation.
- Involve participants as decision-makers in the process of analyzing the situation.
- Have an appropriate time frame for the discussion.
- Generate participants' appreciation of important intercultural problems.

Example 12–2 is an example of case study.

---

**Example 12-2: Case Study**

The frail, old almost totally blind lady appeared at every clinic session and sat on the dirt floor enjoying the activity. She was dirty and dishevelled, and obviously had very little, even by Malaysian *kampong* (local village) standards.

One day the visiting nurse happened upon this woman in her *kampong*. She lived by herself in a rundown shack about ten feet by ten feet. When the nurses asked the woman how she obtained her food, the woman said she was often hungry, as she only received food when she worked for others—pounding rice, looking after the children, and the like.

The nurse sought to obtain help for the woman. It was finally resolved that she would receive a small pension from the Department of Welfare, which would be ample for her needs.

At each weekly clinic, the woman continued to appear. She had become the center of attention, laughed and joked freely, and obviously enjoyed her increased prestige. No change was noted in her physical status, however.

*Continued*

---

**Example 12-2: Case Study**   *Continued*

She continued to wear the same dirty black dress and looked no better fed.

The nurse asked one of the rural health nurses to find out if the woman needed help in getting to a shop to buy the goods she seemed so sorely in need of.

In squatting near the woman, the rural health nurse noted a wad of bills in the woman's basket. "Wah," she said: "It is all here. You have spent nothing. Why is that?"

The woman laughed and then explained: "I am saving it all for my funeral."

*Discussion Guide*

In Malaysia

1. How do people approach activity?
2. What are the important goals in life?
3. What is the nature of social reciprocity?
4. What is the attitude toward problem solving?
5. What is the nature of property?
6. What are the relationships between man and nature?
7. What personal qualities are valued?
8. What are the attitudes toward change?

---

*Source:* S. Thiagarajan and B. Steinwachs. *Intercultural Sourcebook: Cross-Cultural Training Methodologies,* David S. Hoopes and P. Ventura, eds., reprinted with permission of Intercultural Press, Inc., Yarmouth, ME. Copyright 1979.

## Critical Incidents

Case studies enable participants to maximize their understanding of simulated problem-solving situations and thereby acquire knowledge of a host culture's value systems. Because their use as a training tool is relatively time-consuming, trainers turn to *critical incidents* in order to stimulate discussion (Hoopes & Pusch, 1979). Critical incidents are often incorporated into the cultural-awareness model of intercultural training.

A critical-incident case study should be based on real-life experiences with people of other cultures. Moreover, it should depict a controversy or source of conflict that reflects cultural values or other aspects of a culture. Barnak (1980) indicated that critical incidents are used to accomplish the following objectives:

- Introduce participants to new aspects of another culture.
- Help participants understand the problems they may face.
- Provide participants with various methods they can use in a particular situation.

- Require participants to work with group members who have different points of view.
- Train participants to make appropriate decisions while encountering people with different cultural values.

Example 12–3 is an example of critical incident.

## Cultural Assimilators

A *cultural assimilator* is a variant of the critical-incident case study that is used to help participants better understand their own and other cultures. A typical cultural assimilator is composed of a critical incident, a question regarding the cultural problem it raises, and four or five potential answers to the question, along with the rationale for each. Although all the answers are applicable to the problem, only one of them adequately addresses it from the perspective of the specific culture. For the purpose of cultural self-awareness, participants answer the question from their own cultural perspective (Brislin, 1986).

---

**Example 12–3: Critical Incident**

A Japanese and an American corporation are meeting to discuss a business proposal. The meeting is taking place in a fancy restaurant, and the Japanese men all arrive dressed in identical blue suits. The Americans, each dressed in his own individual style, greet the other men with vigorous handshakes and a few slaps on the back. The Japanese men extend their business cards, which are quickly pocketed by the Americans, and they all sit down.

The Americans proceed to give an elaborate description of their plans, specifically explaining what they wish to accomplish and stating the many mutual benefits their deal would bring about. The Americans are very confident about their presentation and con-

sider it to be simple and easy to follow. Also the Americans want their Japanese counterparts to be at ease and enjoy themselves; therefore the entire meeting is conducted in a friendly and casual manner.

The Japanese men sit quietly listening to the proposal without making any indication as to what they think of it. After dinner they thank the Americans and kindly refuse the deal without asking a single question or making a single comment, even though the Americans suggest they take some time to think it over.

Why did the Japanese so rapidly refuse an offer that could have been beneficial to them?

---

*Source:* Andres Fekete, University of Rhode Island.

A well-designed cultural assimilator can help participants (Brislin, Cushner, Cherrie, & Yong, 1986):

- Develop skills in empathy.
- Learn to consider others' feelings or thinking before making decisions.
- Realize that there are alternative ways to solve a problem.
- Recognize the stereotypes or prejudices they have that prevent them from understanding people of other cultures.
- See differences and commonalities between people of different cultures.

Example 11–4 is an example of cultural assimilator.

---

**Example 12–4: Cultural Assimilator**

An American family living in Japan for one year wanted their son (age 10) to attend a Japanese elementary school. When they indicated this to their landlord, he appointed his English-speaking daughter to act as a go-between (*chukaisha*). The boy was duly enrolled and began school. He had to take a lunch (*bento*) every day, so he took a regular American meal of sandwich, chips, cookies, and drink. The teacher subsequently contacted the go-between to notify with the parents about the inappropriateness of the lunch and to request that they provide a more Japanese-style *bento*.

Why was the school teacher perturbed by the child's American-style lunch?

**1.** The teacher feared that the Japanese children would become dissatisfied with their own lunches.
**2.** It was felt the lunch was not sufficiently nutritious.
**3.** The typical Japanese *bento* has symbolic significance, and it was felt that the child was breaking with tradition.

**4.** Conformity in Japanese society is valued more than individuality.

*Rationales for the Alternative Explanations*

**1.** You selected 1. This is possible, but this thought was probably not uppermost in the teacher's mind. Please choose again.
**2.** You selected 2. The lunch is probably less nutritious, but there is a more likely explanation. Please choose again.
**3.** You selected 3. The *bento* is usually made in a traditional manner; however, it is not the breaking of tradition or the desecration of any symbol that upset the teacher but a more fundamental conflict rising from the difference between American and *bento* lunches. Please choose again.
**4.** You selected 4. This is the best choice. Conformity is a dominant characteristic of Japanese society and the teacher possibly feared that such individuality could set a bad example or lead to teasing or ostracism of the boy.

---

*Source:* From R. Brislin, K. Cushner, C. Cherrie, & M. Yong, *Intercultural Interactions: A Practical Guide,* copyright 1986 by Sage Publications. Reprinted by permission of Sage Publications.

## Simulations

Although implementation of the *simulations* technique is a time- and energy-consuming process, it remains one of the most powerful tools of experiential learning used in intercultural training programs. The group format and game structure provide a highly stimulating learning environment. The forming of group cohesion at the beginning of the simulation and gradual involvement in the simulated situation lead to case in association and to interpersonal sharing among the participants and enables them to practice intercultural communication skills (Schnapper, 1980).

The simulation is designed to teach participants about the basic facts and characteristics of culture. It gives the participants experience and opportunities to observe and interact with those who represent another culture in the simulation. In addition, the simulation can create a feeling similar to that the participants are likely to experience in the real cultural situation (Seidel, 1981).

The simulation technique used in intercultural training programs can fulfill the following objectives (Schnapper, 1980):

- Increase participants' awareness of their own and others' cultural identities.
- Understand the potential problems we may encounter in the process of adapting to a new culture.
- Stimulate meaningful discussions about cultural differences.
- Allow participants to practice new roles and express themselves in a non-threatening situation.
- Draw participants into the simulation game emotionally so that they learn principles of intercultural communication through direct involvement.

baFá baFá, developed by Gary Shirts (1973), is one of the most commonly used simulation games in intercultural training programs. The game divides participants into two hypothetical cultural groups: Alphas and Betas. The two cultures represent two distinct sets of values and communication patterns. The alpha culture represents a patriarchal system in which established rituals are required to develop social relationships, while the beta culture represents an egalitarian one in which effective bargaining skills are emphasized (Gudykunst & Hammer, 1983).

Through a process of cultural exchange members in each cultural group are sent to the other group to learn and gather information about the culture. Following the cultural exchange process a discussion session is held. Participants are encouraged to share their feelings about the exploration in the other culture. Although the whole game of baFá baFá takes one to four hours to complete, it is very effective in helping participants develop cultural self-awareness and cultural awareness. In addition, the game provides participants with a chance to play new roles in a different culture, which enables participants to acquire effective intercultural communication skills.

Another simplified simulation game is Barnga (Sivasaliam & Thiagarajan, 1990). Its authors describe the playing procedure as follows:

*BARNGA is so easy to use that its procedure is a joy for both the experienced and the inexperienced game facilitator. The game almost immediately involves all its players and supplies are easily procurable. Careful planning of the follow-up debriefing period helps assure that all participants will become aware of and reflect on the learnings of the exercise. The game works like this. Players form small groups of, say, 4 to 6 players each. Each group sits separated from the others. They receive a modified deck of cards (each deck containing only the same few cards) and a sheet of rules for playing a new card game called "Five Tricks." They have a few minutes to study the rules and practice playing the game. Once everyone has the hang of it, the facilitator collects the rule sheets and at the same time imposes a strict command of "no verbal communication." This means that players may gesture or draw pictures if they wish, but may neither speak (orally or by signing) nor write words. Clearly, communication, should it be needed, is going to be more difficult henceforth. Since the game is so simple and so short, this artificial barrier to communication forces the players, within the simulated setting, to be as creative and alert as possible.*

*Frequently at this point there is a little nervous laughter, some stifled last words, and finally a settling into playing "Five Tricks" without the written rules and in silence. The facilitator then announces a tournament. As in any tournament, some players leave their home table and move to another, some from that other table have moved to yet another, and so on. They sit down at their new table, look around, and begin at once playing "Five Tricks." Shortly thereafter an almost imperceptible change is felt in the room, then expressions of uncertainty. . . . murmurs of frustration . . . chuckles . . . fists banging on tables. The tournament, with more movement to other tables, continues for another ten minutes or so amidst growing uncertainty, frustration, laughter, banging on tables. Sometimes someone is all ready to claim a "trick" when someone else reaches out and takes it. Sometimes someone makes an effort to draw a picture clarifying an uncertainty. Sometimes whoever was at the table first prevails, sometimes the more aggressive. When, during the debriefing, the facilitator probes for what might have been going on, someone takes another player to task for not learning the rules correctly. Someone else confesses that she never was very good at cards. Someone else speaks about others trying to cheat.*

*And several suggest that each table originally had applied a dif-*

Source: S. Thiagarajan and B. Steinwachs. "Barnga", in *Intercultural Sourcebook: Cross-Cultural Training Methodologies*, David S. Hoopes and P. Ventura, eds., reprinted with permission of Intercultural Press, Inc. Yarmouth, ME. Copyright 1990.

*ferent set of rules. Some are sure of this, others think it might be true; others hadn't considered it. Here is the beauty of Barnga—everything appears to be the same, and in fact almost everything is the same, yet great confusion, uncertainty, misunderstanding, and misjudgments fill the room because of just a few differences in rules. Even those who understand that the rules are different (and many do) are not necessarily clear about how they are different. And even those who understand how they are different have difficulty bridging the communication barriers to work out a solution. These concepts spark the energy generated by the game and provide the starting point for a group follow-up discussion rich in observations of how what happened can be seen as metaphors for what happens in real life.*

## EVALUATION OF INTERCULTURAL TRAINING

Evaluation is the key to the success of intercultural training programs. An effective evaluation not only helps trainers maximize limited training resources but also shows the critical link between the contributions of training programs to participants' performance and the programs' capacity to promote intercultural awareness. The challenges to and opportunities for evaluation of intercultural trainings are tremendous. But the risks are great as well. A poor evaluation may put the whole program in jeopardy (Brinkerhoff, 1989).

The process of intercultural training evaluation involves three factors: the trainer, the participant, and the organization that sponsors the training program. Ideally, all these factors are needed to measure whether successful learning has been achieved. According to Seidel (1981), an effective evaluation procedure should include three components: (1) a pretraining test to measure the participants' performance level, attitudes, and amount of information about the host culture; (2) the means to record behavioral changes in the participants during the training program; and (3) a method to determine long-term effects on participants' ability to cope with a new culture. In other words, the evaluation should demonstrate whether the participants have developed cultural awareness, cultural sensitivity, and cultural competence in intercultural communication settings after taking the training program. These abilities can be categorized as follows (Renwick, 1980):

- Participants' knowledge of the fundamental characteristics of their own and other cultures and their accurate perceptions of people from another culture
- Open attitudes toward people of another background
- Effective skills to analyze cultural differences that may cause conflicts in the process of intercultural encounters
- Development of appropriate communication patterns in intercultural communication

**Research Highlight 12–3**

Who:   Renwick, G. W.

What:  "Evaluation: Some Practical Guidelines"

Where: In M. D. Pusch (Ed.) (1979). *Multicultural Education: A Cross Cultural Training Approach* (pp. 205–255). La Grange Park, IL: Intercultural Network.

In this article the author searches for the answer to the question "How do you know whether students or participants are more competent after attending a multicultural education or training program?" Two steps are suggested: (1) recognize the importance of evaluation and commit yourself to doing it, and (2) ask a number of question regarding the evaluation process.

Further examination of the evaluation of multicultural education and training programs poses eight questions: (1) Who is to do the evaluation—someone from outside or the teacher or trainer? (2) For whom is evaluation being done—the students and program participants, the teacher and the trainer, administrators, colleagues, or outsiders? (3) When should the evaluation be done—during the program to find out how things "are going" and/or before the program to find out how

things "should go"? (4) What is to be measured among five major categories—knowledge, perceptions, attitudes, skills, and patterns of behavior? (5) How are the measurements is to be done, depending on objectives and timing—paper and pencil (self-report, including checklists, rank ordering, scales, written training exercises, critical incidents, case studies, films, and photographs, sentence completion, questions, and journal), discussion (self-report), enactment (teacher-report, perhaps peer-report), production (teacher-report, perhaps peer-report), observation (teacher-report, perhaps peer-report), and unobtrusive measures (teacher-report)? (6) How are the results to be tabulated—by checklists, scales, multiple choice questions, or essay questions? (7) What is the appropriate format for the findings—checklists, scales, or essay responses and observation? and (8) How are the findings to be interpreted and used? The best time for interpretation of the findings is immediately after the tabulation. Interpretation includes three steps: begin with a general introduction of the program; then sort out the most important findings after examining all the results; and finally, interpret the results by asking "So what?"

Four kinds of evaluation of intercultural training programs are possible (Seidel, 1981): self-evaluation by the participants, external evaluation of the participants, self-evaluation of the instructional system, and external evaluation of the training programs. *Self-evaluation by the participants* can be used to measure their progress and examine their qualifications. This effort will, in turn, further their understanding of the objectives and goals of the intercultural training program. *External evaluation of the participants* can be made by the trainers or by outside observers who do not involve themselves in the training process. *Self-evaluation of the instructional system* is often used when the trainers and participants feel the need for an evaluation phase in the process of intercultural training. This method can use formal discussion or a survey questionnaire as the evaluation format. Finally, the purpose of the *external evaluation of the training programs* is to critique and compare the training programs by applying an objective standard and thereby gauge their impact. All these evaluation methods can be supplemented by using techniques such as check lists, rank ordering, scales, written training exercises, critical incidents, sentence completion, journal writings, observation, and discussion.

## RECAP

With the advent of more contact among diplomats, students, military personnel, religious groups, business and professional people, and international tourists, intercultural training has become increasingly important. As members of the global society, we must develop the ability to expand our worldview by increasing our understanding of culture and its impact on communication behaviors; enhance our ability to recognize and appreciate cultural similarities and differences; and further improve our skills of intercultural communication. Only through the process of intercultural training can we effectively achieve these goals.

This chapter delineates the effects and goals of intercultural training and examines six training models, including the classroom model, the simulation model, the self-awareness model, the cultural awareness model, the behavioral model, and the interactional model. Furthermore, it discusses five of the most common techniques used in the training models—role playing, case studies, critical incidents, cultural assimilators, and simulations—and examines the procedures used to evaluate intercultural training programs.

## RETHINK

Although intercultural training programs are frequently used, two major problems in their structuring need to be addressed. As mentioned previously, a common goal of intercultural training is to increase awareness of cultural differences in order to develop our communication potential while lessening the likelihood of misunderstandings. Participants seek to "develop an appreciation and understanding of cross-cultural differences and to acquire some of the necessary abilities, such as an increased awareness and sensitivity to cultural stimuli and better human relations skills" (Seidel, 1981, p. 184). In other words, the advocates of intercultural training programs often assert that an effective intercultural training can increase our capacity for intercultural awareness, intercultural sensitivity, and intercultural competence. Unfortunately, these concepts are used interchangeably by intercultural communication practitioners without clearly conceptualizing them.

As we have discussed, *intercultural awareness* refers to cognitive understanding of cultural knowledge; *intercultural sensitivity* refers to the affective capacity to recognize, acknowledge, and respect cultural differences; and *intercultural competence* is the behavioral ability to adapt to a new culture (Chen & Starosta, 1996). Obviously, confusion in the use of these concepts will affect the quality of intercultural training programs and their evaluation as well.

The second problem is that intercultural training programs as they are currently practiced are mostly atheoretical. Seldom do intercultural training programs fully explore the theoretical foundation of the interventions. This problem may cause fragmentation and inconsistency in terms of program arrangement, training process, and training results.

Future research or application of intercultural training programs must make an effort to correct their conceptual and theoretical deficiencies.

## QUESTIONS FOR DISCUSSION

1. Discuss the beneficial effects of intercultural training on our cognition, affect, and behavior.
2. Explain the goals of intercultural training.
3. Compare and critique the six models of intercultural training.
4. Compare and contrast the five techniques of intercultural training.
5. Describe the methods used for the evaluation of intercultural training.

# ▶ Part V

## Ethical Issues and the Future

# ▶ Chapter 13

## Ethics and the Future of Intercultural Communication

### *Objectives*

Upon completion this chapter, you will

- Be able to define the term *ethics*.
- Understand why we need to study intercultural communication ethics.
- Gain insight into theories of ethical study.
- Understand the principles and rules of intercultural communication ethics.
- Understand the future development of intercultural communication study.

*Ethical principles represent, in a sense,*
*a territorial imperative.*
*—DEAN C. BARLUND*

*We have a genuine opportunity to make the world of*
*the future a little better than it would otherwise be, but*
*there is no guarantee that we will actually do so.*
*—EDWARD CORNISH*

Might it be easier to research what a thing is, rather than what it might be? Could this be why descriptive research has so little to say about ethics, or about the way the future of intercultural communication should unfold? With this chapter we explore two topics that intercultural communication scholars sometimes neglect: ethical issues and the future of intercultural communication. Our examination of ethical questions in intercultural communication centers on (1) the nature of intercultural communication ethics, (2) ethical principles of intercultural communication, (3) ethical rules for intercultural communication, and (4) propositions for ethical intercultural communication. Our discussion then moves to the future of intercultural communication, focusing on three concerns: (1) increasing or decreasing intercultural communication, (2) unity versus division, and (3) the study of intercultural communication.

## THE NATURE OF INTERCULTURAL COMMUNICATION ETHICS

When we practice intercultural communication, we judge and evaluate one another's behaviors. Our judgments or evaluations are often based on our cultural learning, and we may not even be conscious of our reference to cultural learning to make such judgments. When we judge, when we attribute right and wrong to communication choices, when we favor one way of symbolizing experience over another, we enter the realm of ethics.

### Ethics Defined

Communication ethics pertains to our means or methods of enacting behaviors and to the goals, to intentions, and consequences of our behaviors (Fletcher, 1966). In other words, ethics considers how we should communicate. It asks what is right or wrong, good or bad, and what standards and rules should guide our conduct. Thus, for example, when we choose a communication strategy and ask if it is right or wrong in the way that it affects another person, we are said to deal with the ethical issues of human communication (Johannesen, 1978). Ethics, then, can be defined as "the science of judging human ends and the relationship of means to those ends," and "the art of controlling means so that they will serve specifically human ends" (Garrett, 1966, p. 4).

### Why Study Intercultural Communication Ethics?

Our definition of ethics suggests that ethical issues are relevant to the elements of human communication, including sender, receiver, encoding, decoding, feedback, and context. It is important that communication scholars specify appropriate moral standards in order to promote healthy and appropriate communication behaviors. In the intercultural communication setting, when differing cultural contexts influence our interaction, ethical issues become more complex and more nearly unique. Hamnett (1978) specified four reasons that questions of intercultural communication ethics differ from cases where only a single national or domestic culture is involved. First, the variety of behavioral norms among different cultures means that ethical standards vary too. Second, the knowledge that is extracted by intercultural communication research may be conducted by outside scholars whose research may be detrimental to the host culture. Third, using models, techniques, or theories from other cultures to analyze the phenomena of a separate culture may promote the drawing of false conclusions. Finally, the collaboration of scholars from foreign and host countries may be an ethical precondition for collecting valid data about intercultural communication. These reasons and others require the study of intercultural communication ethics.

## Theories of Ethical Study

Like other concepts in this text, ethics can be examined from multiple perspectives. Lowenstein and Merrill (1990) offered dichotomies to explore ethical issues: universalism vs. relativism, objectivism vs. subjectivism, attitudinalism vs. consequentialism, and deontologicalism vs. teleologicalism.

### Universalism vs. Relativism
Proponents of ethical universalism take the position that there is a constant and universal ethical principle that applies to all societies at any time. Thus, what is wrong in one place will be wrong elsewhere, without regard to place, time, and circumstance. Based on this view, ethical universalists believe that no ethical problem is unique to intercultural communication.

Proponents of ethical relativism hold the view that ethics is closely related to motive, intuition, and emotion. They believe that while people from different cultures may share common needs, interests, or feelings, their ways of acting upon these internal states varies because of cultural differences. Thus, ethical relativists would not judge another's behaviors by using their native ethical standards. Adhering to their own contextualized truths in intercultural interactions could only lead to conflict.

### Objectivism vs. Subjectivism
As an advocate of ethical universalism, the ethical objectivist maintains that all ethical principles are based on truths that can be rationally demonstrated and that are independent of personal speculation. Thus, ethical standards must be found outside of us, not within the individual. The ethical subjectivist, as an advocate of ethical relativism, considers all ethical principles to be based on the

mental state of the individual. Ethics therefore reflects the preference of a person. What I think good is good, and what I think ugly is ugly.

## Attitudinalism vs. Consequentialism

Attitudinalism is a kind of ethical subjectivism. Anything that is congruent with one's attitude is judged as right. By way of contrast, ethical consequentialism uses the consequences of the conduct as a standard to define ethics. The means is not so important as the end. For example, when the Chinese leader Deng Xiao Pin proclaimed that "no matter if it's a good cat or bad cat, as long as the cat knows how to catch mice, it's a good one," he took the view of ethical consequentialism. Similarly, Indira Gandhi, when asked if she would resort the use of force to bring down the birth rate in India, told a Western reporter India might mix "a little compulsion with our persuasion" (Starosta, 1987).

## Deontologism vs. Teleologism

Instead of using the consequences of our conduct as the basis for an ethical standard, ethical deontologism focuses on the action itself for the judgment of rightness and wrongness of our conduct. As Lowenstein and Merrill indicated, the intuitionist journalist is a good example of ethical deontologist who often uses his or her natural and spontaneous conscience as a reliable guide for what is wrong or right.

Ethical teleologism is similar to ethical consequentialism. It advocates that the pleasure or displeasure of the action gives us the standard to perceive ethics. For example, it doesn't matter if a journalist did a right or wrong thing to produce a news article, provided that the reader felt pleasure from reading it (Lowenstein & Merrill, 1990).

While all the above theories approach the ethical issues from different perspectives, they can be treated as the extension of ethical universalism and relativism. From the perspective of ethical relativism Condon (1981) argued that intercultural communication ethics is especially related to cultural values. For example, Condon specified several U.S. cultural values that differ from those of other cultures. Characteristically many Americans (1) are individualistic rather than relational, (2) practice symmetrical rather than complementary relationships, (3) tend to be low context rather than high context, (4) welcome moderate change rather than resist it, and (5) seek more choices rather than accept those they are given. Ethical problems emerge when we fail to take account of such differences in cultural tendency when we examine intercultural interaction.

From the perspective of ethical universalism, however, Schwartz (1990) argued that many universal values such as achievement, security, and hedonism exist in different cultures. Such parallels indicate that people of different cultures share similar values. The argument is supported by studies from several other scholars, including Brown (1991), Fiske (1992), and Schwartz and Sagiv

**Research Highlight 13–1**

Who:    Condon, J. C.

What:   "Values and Ethics in Communication Across Culture: Some Notes on the North American Case."

Where:  *Communication, 6,* 1981, 255–265.

This article delineates the relationship between ethics, cultural values, and communication. The author argues that differences in culture can be attributed to varying value and ethical standards in intracultural and intercultural communication. Though people may be unaware of the influence of their culture, their values and ethics serve as strong guidelines for communication.

The author further argues that ethical principles may transcend a culture, but the meanings of those ethical principles are confined by the values of that specific culture. For example, ethical standards in North America are affected by five main cultural values: (1) individualism, (2) symmetrical relationships, (3) low context, (4) emphasis on change, and (5) selecting among choices (rather than accepting givens).

Based on these North American values, the author describes the ethical standard of communication. He states, "Communication is ethical when it permits free access, without personal or social pressure, to accurate information, and which allows for the expression of the same so that reasoned choices may be made and individually desired goals may be achieved" (p. 263). In other words, unethical communication refers to "limited access to and the limiting of information; pressure to express what one does not believe or to remain silent when one wishes to speak out; deliberate falsification of information" (p. 263).

Thus, because of the differences of values among cultures, problems will arise when we apply this ethical principle of communication to other cultures. Moreover, the author concludes, because the process of adjusting to another culture is very slow or perhaps never complete, adjustment to others' cultural values that leads to the appreciation of a different ethical standard is virtually an impossible goal to set for ourselves.

(1995). The phenomenon of universal values in different cultures is used by such researchers as the foundation for a universal ethics of intercultural communication.

We make the case that a more appropriate way to examine intercultural communication ethics is to integrate both universal and relative perspectives. In other words, although we realize that different ethical codes are required by different cultures because of the dissimilarities of cultural value orientations, we also recognize that a set of universal principles of intercultural communication ethics can be generated. The following sections focus on the general ethical principles and rules that should be applied to the process of intercultural communication, but they do not advocate that contextual differences be neglected.

# PRINCIPLES OF ETHICAL INTERCULTURAL COMMUNICATION

A prominent "universal" principle of ethical intercultural communication is that of *reciprocity,* "Communicate unto others as you wish others to communicate unto you" (Tyler, 1978). This general rule is balanced against four behavioral standards: mutuality, nonjudgmentalism, honesty, and respect.

## Mutuality

*Mutuality* indicates that we must try our best to locate a common space for interaction with an interactant from another culture. We should expect that the shared symbolic space may be neither that of our own cultural upbringing, nor that of the culture of the other interactant. Both parties must actively search for a mutual symbolic ground that allows the fullest and clearest possible exchange of ideas. If either party demands that the interaction be conducted solely in his or her own cultural terms, without flexibility, that interactant has created barriers to successful intercultural communication.

## Nonjudgmentalism

Based on open-mindedness, *nonjudgmentalism* demands a willingness to express ourselves openly when the situation is appropriate and to accept other's expressions. It allows information to flow freely and entails a willingness to recognize, appreciate, and accept different views and ideas in intercultural interactions. Nonjudgmentalism aims to allow both sources of information and opportunities to distribute information uncontrolled and unfettered. To reach this goal it is important to recognize the different scale of values in different cultures and to trust one another.

## Honesty

The principle of *honesty* involves the self and communication partners. It implies that the information is true as the sender understands it. In other words, we should see things as they are rather than as we would like them to be. The most important step toward honesty is to be fully aware of our personal and cultural biases in the process of intercultural communication. In addition to self-honesty, we are obliged to be honest to our communication partners.

## Respect

The principle of *respect* demands that interactants protect the basic human rights of their partners in the process of human communication. Respect is based on our sensitivity to understand and acknowledge other people's needs. In this sense it relates to our observations on nonjudgmentalism. In other words, we have to know that an idea can be rendered in multiform ways. To show our respect for cultural differences is to fulfill our responsibility toward preserving the dignity of our partner as a human being and to interact without deception.

With mutuality, nonjudgmentalism, honesty, and respect, we are able to establish an environment in which an authentic dialogue between people from different cultures can be fostered. These principles also dictate several ethical rules for intercultural communication.

## ETHICAL RULES FOR INTERCULTURAL COMMUNICATION

Five specific ethical guidelines for intercultural communication can be derived from the five ethical principles: promote voluntary participation in the interaction; seek individual focus prior to a cultural one; maintain the right to freedom from harm; accept the right to privacy of thought and action; and avoid imposing personal biases.

### Promote Voluntary Participation in the Interaction

It is fundamental in all intercultural interactions that participation be voluntary. Voluntary participation means that interactants fully and accurately understand the nature of the interaction that may cause potential social and psychological discomforts. Coerced participation in intercultural communication especially violates the ethical principles of mutuality and respect.

### Seek Individual Focus Prior to Cultural Focus

An authentic dialogue is needed to allow the uniqueness of each individual to emerge. Although each culture programs its members to think and behave in certain ways, variations among individuals do exist. Seeking an individual focus prior to a cultural one prevents us from falling into the trap of cultural stereotyping, a practice that leads us to apply group perception that denies an individual's uniqueness.

Thayer (1987) pointed out that ethical communication must allow interactants to express themselves and understand their partners on their own terms rather than confining itself to social convention. In other words, to be ethical in intercultural communication, the focus must be on the expressions that are emitted from the individual who has consciously examined the beliefs and ideologies imposed by the culture. Intercultural trainers could be taught to adopt this ethical framework.

## Maintain the Right to Freedom from Harm

Based on the principle of honesty, intercultural interactants must not impose physical, social, or psychological harm to their counterparts. This requires us to avoid manipulating others by acting or behaving in a socially questionable way that would cause anxiety and to avoid uncovering socially or psychologically sensitive topics such as raising the question about sexual practices or using obscene gestures that are taboo in the other culture. These kinds of messages may not only put our counterparts in an embarrassing situation but also have the potential to produce negative consequences.

## Accept the Right to Privacy of Thought and Action

The ethical principle of mutuality does not mean that the intercultural interactants are allowed to intrude on each other's privacy. An authentic intercultural dialogue must be based on the principle of respecting others' privacy. We should gain the acknowledgment and consent of our counterparts when we try to initiate a conversation for any specific purpose. The rule also dictates that we should avoid, either inadvertently or by choice, disclosing private information about our intercultural partners that may cause embarrassment.

## Avoid Imposing Personal Biases

Because reality is socially constructed by our own culture, what is perceived to be the truth can vary among different cultures. Thus, the culturally imposed perceptions are often subjective and tend to foster personal bias in the process of intercultural communication. It is important that ethical intercultural interactants should understand this kind of personal biases and avoid using these personal biases to deliberately deceive or mislead their counterparts (Kale, 1994). Deception originating from personal biases often causes damage to the ability of interactants to trust each other.

The obligation to take ethical responsibility is the most basic requirement for the success of intercultural communication. We have to learn how to integrate these rules of conduct or moral codes into a general pattern of our daily life so that intercultural communication is a rewarding experience. Following

**Research Highlight 13–2**

Who:    Kale, D. W.

What:    "Peace as an Ethic for Intercultural Communication."

Where:    In L. A. Samovar & R. E. Porter (Eds.) (1994), *Intercultural Communication: A Reader* (pp. 435–444). Belmont, CA: Wadsworth.

In explaining how peace is the foundation of intercultural communication ethics, the author first gives a definition of *communication ethics* (which is similar to the definition in this chapter) and then distinguishes between cultural relativism and universal ethics. Although cultural relativism posits that each culture develops its own system of cultural values based on principles peculiar to that culture, the author argues that we can use the "human spirit"

(which is a value universal in all cultures) as the basis of developing a universal code of communication ethics.

Through this universal "human spirit" we can create a world in which people of different cultural backgrounds can live together peacefully. Thus, a universal code of intercultural communication ethics could be developed based on the following four principles: (1) "ethical communicators address people of other cultures with the same respect that they would like to receive themselves," (2) "ethical communicators seek to describe the world they perceive as accurately as possible," (3) "ethical communicators encourage people of other cultures to express themselves in their uniqueness," and (4) "ethical communicators strive for identification with people of other cultures" (pp. 438–439).

are twelve propositions regarding ethical intercultural communication for further reflection.

### *Propositions for Ethical Intercultural Communication*

Proposition 1:    The Ethical Intercultural Communicator (EIC) perceives people to be equal, even when their beliefs differ.

Proposition 2:    The EIC actively seeks out and interacts with persons of diverse ethnicity and national origin.

Proposition 3:    The EIC listens carefully and nonjudgmentally.

Proposition 4:    The EIC questions patiently to ascertain intended meanings.

Proposition 5:    The EIC is slow to reach closure. He or she allows that misunderstanding often arises from out-of-awareness cultural differences.

Proposition 6:    The EIC solicits and provides feedback to ascertain that messages were received as intended.

Proposition 7:    The EIC seeks to learn the culture and language of the Other in considerable detail.

Proposition 8:    The EIC works from the belief that the Other is rational when understood in cultural context.

Proposition 9:    The EIC places a positive value on cooperation and conflict reduction.

Proposition 10:   The EIC seeks synergy in dealings with the Other. (For example, a nation includes those of different languages, religions, and gender orientations. None should be given the chance to speak as a surrogate for the whole.)

Proposition 11:   The EIC seeks to include all voices in the interaction.

Proposition 12:   The EIC sets only those conditions for the Other that will be honored equally by the Self.

We now turn our discussions to the future of the field of intercultural communication. We consider, in turn, (1) the impetus for future intercultural communication research, (2) two prominent issues facing the future development of the field, and conclude with (3) thoughts on how directions for the future may finally be determined.

## THE FUTURE OF INTERCULTURAL COMMUNICATION

Is the future of human society predictable? Futurists may tell us that it is not possible to predict what the future will look like or what will happen in the future, because the future is a constantly evolving process rather than a predetermined event. However, as human beings, by making one choice over some other, we affect what is likely to happen. As Cornish (1990) indicated, there is no guarantee that we will actually try to influence the direction of future changes, but if we do, we certainly can make the future better than what it would have been. Thus, by identifying some of the possibilities for the future, we can visualize more clearly the sorts of choices that could make a larger difference. Based on this perception, this section focuses on discussion of some future possibilities in the transformative process of intercultural communication. The discussion is separated into three parts: (1) increasing or decreasing intercultural contact, (2) unity versus division, and (3) the study of intercultural communication.

# INCREASING OR DECREASING INTERCULTURAL CONTACT

As mentioned in Chapter 1, given the four trends of technology development, globalization of the economy, widespread population migration, and the development of multiculturalism, a more interdependent world is emerging. These forces will definitely increase contacts among people with different cultural and ethnic backgrounds. They also increase diversify domestic cultures. Let's examine the impact of these forces for change from international and domestic perspectives.

## International Perspective

The continuous development of technology and the globalization of the economy will shorten the distances between peoples and soon revolutionize our lives. According to Conway (1993), in addition to new ventures in energy, space, and scientific research, "super projects" will forge new global links through communication and transportation technology and will soon have a strong impact internationally. Super projects such as land linking, the airport challenge, high-speed-railroads, and telecommunications links will bring the people and nations of the world closer together (Conway, 1993).

### Land Linking

The "Eurotunnel" that connects England and European continent is probably the most publicized land-link project in the twentieth century. Upon its completion last year, worldwide significance for geoeconomic developments was immediately evident. The "Great Belt Road" in northern Europe is also a multi-billion-dollar project that will eventually connect Denmark's Zealand Island and the Jutland peninsula, running between Sweden's Malmoe and Copenhagen, and between Lolland in south Denmark and Germany. Other super projects are also under way or being planned on in different continents: the new Panama Canal project; the Southern Seaboard Development Program plans for connecting Thailand and the Malay peninsula; the proposal for connecting Africa and Europe that is continuously discussed in the United Nations; the plan to link Italy and Sicily; the proposed bridge to link Egypt and Saudi Arabia; a potential bridge to connect Colombia, Uruguay, and Buenos Aires in South America; a possible link between Asia and North America through the Bering Strait; and a proposed sea tunnel to link England and Ireland.

### The Airport Challenge

The airport challenge is clearly mirrored in the construction of new international airports. For example, the new Kansai international airport in Osaka,

Japan can be used to relieve the problem of overcrowding in Tokyo's Narita airport. The Japanese are also building a modern airport at Nagoya that can help improve the overall airport situation in Japan. Airport officials in Hong Kong also ambitiously plan to build a new international airport or a small island, along with a system of transportation links such as bridges and tunnels to provide access to the new airport. Major airport projects are also under way in Munich, Germany, and Lyon, France. In the United States, the Denver airport has been completed.

Because it is so expensive to acquire land and build or renovate new airports, the concept of The Airport City has gained wide currency. "The Airport City" will be built over water or on available land, and will be planned as would a new town, with its own unique features.

### High-Speed Railroads

The success of the "bullet train" in Japan and the high-speed trains in France has encouraged many countries to launch such projects. For example, the Community of European Railroads plans to link all major cities in Europe. The Madrid-Seville line in Spain began to operate in 1992. Italy plans to build Turin-Venice and Milan-Naples links. Russia plans to link St. Petersburg and Moscow. Australia proposes to connect Sydney and Melbourne via Canberra. Other countries, such as Belgium, South Korea, Canada, and United States, are all proposing new high-speed railroads to link major cities in their countries. The new systems linking major cities in various countries will make international transit more efficient in the years to come.

### Telecommunications Links

New communication systems will continue to link peoples and nations tightly together. For example, the global Fiber Optics Cable Network will soon connect Japan, the United Kingdom, and the United States. Motorola is developing a small low-earth-orbit satellite that can provide services for global personal communication. General Motors is also negotiating to install an advanced cellular and satellite telecommunications system in Russia. Finally, the British Telecom has built a global telecommunication network that combines voice, data, and video transmissions to serve London, New York, Sydney, and Frankfurt through computerized exchanges.

These super international projects draw a picture of a future world in which national boundaries have become obsolete, at least for the more technological nations. In the case of less technologically developed nations, telecommunication trends may amplify differences among nations and promote friction among peoples.

Intercommunication among diverse people will become part of our daily life. As mentioned in Chapter 1, a mind-set by which we can see things through the eyes of others will become a survival tool for living in the future global society.

## Domestic Perspective

Immigration has made the United States a truly multicultural country. The trend will not be reversed even if the U.S. Congress passes stricter laws to limit the number of new immigrants to the United States. In addition to the impact of changing demographics mentioned in Chapter 1, including multicultural classrooms, multiethnic neighborhoods, and the multiethnic workplace, we can expect that future domestic developments will require further integration in the economic, environmental, social, cultural, and spiritual domains.

According to Wishhard (1990), the need for integration is reflected especially in the development of the economy. The key economic trends and events the United States must face in the future include (1) increased demand for new knowledge from the world's research laboratories; (2) a shift from a self-sufficient national economy to an integrated system of global production; (3) continuous challenges from Japan, China, and India, and from potential joint ventures between Russian and European and Japanese companies; (4) rising national debt that brings with it a deterioration in the strength of credit; (5) restructuring of major corporations as they adapt to a fast-changing environment; (6) demand for better employee education; and (7) the need to develop a new corporate leadership style to cope with the economic shift from heavy industry toward services and high technology.

Moreover, social, economic, and cultural changes will inevitably transform the values Americans live by. Mitchell (1990) grouped future American values into four categories comprising nine American lifestyles:

**1.** The first category of *need-driven values* is comprised of "survivors," who are intensely poor, despairing, unskilled, and far removed from the cultural mainstream, and "sustainers," who are angry, rebellious, resentful, living on the edge of poverty, and participating in an underground economy.

**2.** The second category of *outer-directed values* is comprised of "belongers," who are middle-class Americans who are rather conventional, contented, sentimental, and deeply stable; "emulators," who are ambitious and competitive, and who strive intensely for success; and "achievers," who are self-assured, materialistic, and prosperous, and who tend to be able leaders.

**3.** The third category of *inner-directed values* is comprised of "I-Am-Me" persons, who are dramatic, impulsive, inventive, and narcissistic; "experientials," who are self-centered, artistic, seeking direct experience, and intensely oriented to inner growth; and "societally conscious" persons, who are successful, mature, influential, mission-oriented, and very concerned with societal issues.

**4.** The last category combines *outer- and inner-directed values* and is comprised of "integrated" persons who are psychologically mature, tolerant, and understanding and who are able to adopt a coherent outlook on life.

There is no doubt that domestic development make the United States a more diverse nation in which skilled intercultural communication will be required so that people with different backgrounds can work together peacefully to make the nation a better place in which to live. Indeed, reconciling the types of persons described above will, itself, call for powerful skills in intercultural and interethnic communication. The alternative is increasing social alienation and disaffection.

# UNITY VERSUS DIVISION

Internationally, because of the progress in technology and globalization of the economy, we are moving toward a global society in which we will be obliged to learn how to live interdependently and productively with people of different national backgrounds. Domestically, because of the influx of immigrants and because one-third of U.S. society will soon be nonwhite, we are becoming a multicultural society in which ethnic diversity will be a norm of daily life. Can we guarantee that this transformational process will reach an ideal state of synergy in the long run? In other words, will the future bring, domestically and internationally, a more united world or multiple antagonistic worlds? Two challenges related to this question deserve further examination: those of ethnocentrism and gender impact.

## *Ethnocentrism*

Culture is of its nature ethnocentric. It teaches its people to see the external environment through a local lens. Ethnocentrism forms the boundary of different groups. To develop one's cultural identity it is necessary to be enthnocentric. However, ethnocentrism often causes problems in the process of intercultural communication, because it provides only a limited choice of human thinking and behavioral patterns, and these limited possibilities cannot explain human experience in its entirety. Will the increasing amount of intercultural communication within and between cultures in the future reinforce attitudes of ethnocentrism and xenophobia? Or will the interactions of different cultures bring forth a state of ethnorelativism? These remain important issues in the study of intercultural communication. Bennett's (1986) developmental model explaining the transition from ethnocentrism to ethnorelativism serves as the point of departure for our discussion.

According to Bennett, the basic concept of the model is "difference." We must first recognize that cultural differences exist among people of different cultures. In other words, the ability to comprehend and experience cultural differences is the foundation upon which we must address the problems of ethnocentrism. Bennett pointed out that the continuum stretching from ethnocentrism to ethnorelativism is comprised of six stages: denial, defense, minimization, acceptance, adaptation, and integration. Chapter 10 mentioned the six stages. Here we extend the discussion in more detail.

First, a *denial of cultural differences* is the core of ethnocentrism, which may occur because of the lack of physical or social contact with persons from other cultures. The denial of cultural differences often leads to the symptom of "projected cognitive similarities," or the tendency to think of others as similar to us. What we practice is perforce the way they practice. For example, because individualism and privacy are part of life in the United States and in Northern Europe, an ethnocentric bias would cause us to think that the Japanese also emphasize individualism and privacy. This is not the case. Cultural awareness training, discussed in Chapter 12, is one of the best techniques to help us improve the denial problem.

In the second stage we may defend against cultural differences to protect the centrality of our worldview. The feeling of threat to our worldview follows the recognition of cultural differences. We turn to three common defense mechanisms in this stage: denigration of difference, cultural superiority, and reversal of position. *Denigration of difference* refers to the attribution of undesirable characteristics to all members of culturally different groups. *Cultural superiority* is based on the assumption that our culture is better than any other. *Reversal of position,* the belief that the host culture is superior to our own culture, is a common result of the colonial experience. To move successfully toward ethnorelativism it is important to emphasize the commonality of cultures, especially their positive aspects.

The *minimization* stage focuses on projected similarities of cultures. Although cultural differences are recognized and tolerated to some degree, they are trivialized. Physical universalism and transcendent universalism are two common forms of minimization. *Physical universalism* indicates that human behaviors are basically innate. The awareness of universal patterns of behavior is sufficient for being successful in intercultural communication. By contrast, *transcendent universalism* implies that human beings are products of transcendent laws that are invariably valid in intercultural communication. The stage is critical because it involves the initial steps toward ethnorelativism. Using training methods such as simulations, sharing reports of personal rewarding intercultural experiences, and using persons from other cultures as resources can help us to negotiate this stage.

In the *acceptance stage* cultural differences are accepted and respected. This fourth stage represents a gradual movement away from the influence of ethnocentrism. Cultural differences are considered as inevitable and of interest in intercultural communication. From the acceptance of behavioral differences we move to a recognition of the underlying cultural value differences. To achieve a higher level of ethnorelativism, we need to associate the appreciation of cultural value differences with respect for unfamiliar behaviors.

The *adaptation stage* represents a process of integrating respect for cultural value differences into observable behavior. Bennett pointed out that empathy and cultural pluralism are the two most common forms of this stage. Empathic communicators are able to adapt to cultural differences by temporarily adopting their counterparts' worldviews. *Empathy* greatly increases the possibility of understanding others. *Cultural pluralism* moves us to become the "multicultural person" indicated by Adler (1982) through which we begin to move freely among different worldviews and practices. Providing real-life opportunities for interactions with people in other cultures is the best way to promote skills in adaptation and to move us to the ultimate stage of ethnorelativism.

The final stage is the *integration of cultural differences*. Ability in integration enables a person not only to genuinely adapt to cultural difference but also to enjoy experiencing such differences in intercultural interactions. The integration stage is the culmination of intercultural sensitivity. Bennett indicates that in this stage the only problem we may still face is that of ethics. After integrating the cultural differences, we may find it is still difficult for us to construe the ethical system that guides our conduct. Given differences in psychological makeup and historical circumstance, not all persons will be equally able to enjoy the experience of cultural difference.

## Gender Impact

Can men and women get along? This perennial question continues to echo in the study of human communication. Research has consistently found that males and females differ significantly in terms of assumptions about communication and the use of communication rules (Coates & Cameron, 1989; Tannen, 1990). Wood (1994) summarized differences between male and female communication that have been supported by research, primarily research in the United States (p. 160):

**1.** Women use talk to build and sustain rapport with others; men use talk to assert themselves and their ideas.
**2.** Women share and learn about others through self-disclosing; personal disclosure can make men feel vulnerable.
**3.** Women use talk to create symmetry or equality; men use talk to establish status and power.
**4.** Women treat matching experiences with others as understanding and empathy; men treat it as a competitive strategy to command attention.

**5.** Women express understanding of feelings to support others; men do so to seek advice or solve a problem.

**6.** Women tend to take turns and include others in conversation by encouraging them to express opinions; men tend to interrupt more and talk in their own way.

**7.** Women use responses to indicate that they care about what others are saying; men tend to use responses to make a point.

**8.** Women are more tentative and allow others to contribute their ideas; men are more assertive, to be perceived as confident and in command.

These differences, however much culture-bound, demonstrate that those of differing gender socialization hold different perspectives on how, when, and why to communicate with each other. In attempting to integrate feminine and masculine cultural perspectives, four principles recommended by Wood (1994) deserve our attention: (1) show respect for gender differences by suspending judgment in cross-gender communication; (2) recognize the validity of different communication styles by realizing the different goals, patterns, and standards of the feminine and masculine cultures; (3) seek translation cues by asking what the partner wants; and (4) enlarge our own communication repertoire to include patterns of the other gender by means of continuous learning.

## THE STUDY OF INTERCULTURAL COMMUNICATION

Living in a world that is moving toward a global society demands of us a more systematic and comprehensive study of intercultural communication. Because the study of intercultural communication will identify the knowledge and skills that enable people to develop a global mind-set and succeed in the future world, it is important to examine the future direction and application of intercultural communication study from three perspectives: education, research, and business.

### Education

The trend toward globalization will directly challenge higher education. Colleges and universities, as the institutes of higher educational, must endeavor to provide an environment in which students can understand the nature of global society and learn the skills for effectively communicating with people of diverse cultures. The key to success in facing the challenge academically is to internationalize the curriculum—in other words: (1) programs to internationalize the curriculum should be instituted; (2) multidimensional and interdisciplinary programs should be well integrated throughout the university or college; and (3) these programs should be of sufficient depth and intensity to enable substantial numbers of students and faculty to function well in different cultures and move toward ethnorelativism (Johnston & Edelstein, 1993). To summarize, internationalizing the college curriculum should help students and faculty

**1.** understand the goal of globalization in making future choices,

**2.** understand sensitizing cultural concepts that will assist them in their interaction with people from other cultures,

**3.** change aspects of their performance such as cultural self-perception and emotional and cognitive acquisitions in order to reach a higher level of empathy,

**4.** govern their performance and emotions in working and in living with people from other cultures by increasing their adaptability, and

**5.** adopt a changed way of perceiving and behaving so that they can improve their social performance in other cultures (Stewart, 1979). To this we would add that such a curriculum should encourage students and faculty to work against all measures that forcibly segregate and isolate cultural and ethnic populations on the campus.

Effectively internationalizing the college curriculum includes four common dimensions: language study, study abroad, interdisciplinary collaboration, and scholarly ethnorelativism (Johnston & Edelstein, 1993).

### Language Study

Language is one of the main elements that clearly distinguishes one culture from another. It is the most important vehicle we use to encode messages. In the process of communication if we cannot speak the language, immediately we experience difficulty. All the components of language, including vocabulary, syntax, dialects, slang, and idioms, cause difficulties in understanding. In addition, language and culture are interdependent. Language is a product of our culture, and our culture is a product of language use. Language affects the way we think, our attitude, and behavior. The inability to understand each other verbally, and the misinterpreting of each other's messages are sources of conflict among people. Thus, learning a new language plays an important role in the process of internationalizing the college curriculum. In order to help students to be competent and proficient in acquiring a new language, traditional methods of instruction should be supplemented by new methods that include instructional technology—computer software, satellite links, and interactive video discs.

### Study Abroad

Study abroad not only helps students improve their language proficiency and competency but also provides them with a great opportunity to understand another culture through direct interaction with the host nationals. Programs of study abroad should not be limited to white, middle-class females who are from highly educated professional families and who have studied humanities in Western Europe (Johnston & Edelstein, 1993). Students from diverse social classes, races, and ethnicities should be encouraged to study abroad through the support of college programs. Students should also be encouraged to study in different countries. Moreover, the quality and impact of the experience abroad should be reflected in the students' work after they return home. In other words, study abroad should be integrated into the academic life of the student and the college.

## Interdisciplinary Collaboration

Interdisciplinary collaboration can bridge the gaps among disciplines by transcending the limit of departmental and geographic frames of reference. The International Engineering Program (IEP) at several colleges provides a good example. Students in the program can simultaneously earn a B.A. degree with a major in German and a B.S. degree with an engineering major. Other institutes of international business can also collaborate with the languages departments to offer joint programs modeled on the IEP. These programs provide breadth, depth, and maturity to the international curriculum of the university. Although some disciplines such as computer science, mathematics, and physics, are not necessary components of such a curriculum, the trend of globalization will inevitably lead practioners in these fields to make contact with their counterparts in other countries. Interdisciplinary collaboration within the college or among colleges from different countries can broaden students' perspectives to better adapt to the global society.

## Scholarly Ethnorelativism

Scholarly ethnorelativism aims to produce internationally minded students and scholars through a process of "asking new questions and reformulating old ones, collecting data from new and possibly far-flung sources, and generalizing from sufficiently diverse observations" (Johnston & Edelstein, 1993, p. 15). Institutional efforts to motivate students and faculty to investigate different cultures are the best means to combat the problem of scholarly ethnocentrism, which promotes a self-centered, narrow-minded worldview.

All these educational initiatives for the world of the future must be integrated with the components of intercultural communication. It is the responsibility of the field of intercultural communication to contribute its resources to promote and fulfill this educational demand. For whatever reason, programs in intercultural communication have appeared first where the local community has experienced cultural difference firsthand. These sites include historically black colleges and universities (HBCUs), schools with a large international student population, schools with a religious affiliation that promotes missionary preparation, and schools where immigrant populations have strongly shaped the character of the institution. In the central United States, where rural residents seldom directly interact with urban residents and where questions of culture seem somehow less salient, few strong intercultural curricular programs have emerged. Indeed, what counts as "diversity" differs according to different regions of the country and their historical conditioning (Cumber & Braithwaite, 1996).

## Business

As indicated in Chapter 1, the progress of communication and transportation technology has made markets more accessible and defined business interests more globally. This trend will continue to demand a greater understanding between nations and between ethnic groups. The knowledge and skills of intercultural communication will then play an increasingly important role in the future business world. Certainly, cultural problems that cannot be resolved within a nation will prove no easier to resolve among nations. The question is; What can the study of intercultural communication contribute to create a mindset that leads us to be successful in the global business world? According to Harris and Moran (1987), five attitudinal imperatives based on intercultural knowledge and skills will be needed in an age of economic interdependence:

**1.** Possessing a cosmopolitan mind with a sensitive, innovative, and participative ability to operate comfortably in a global or pluralistic environment.

**2.** Acknowledging the importance of intercultural communication by recognizing cultural influences on personal needs, values, expectations, sense of self, and roles.

**3.** Becoming culturally sensitive, by integrating the understanding of culture in general with insights gained from service in multicultural organizations or from activities that bring us into contact with ethnically and culturally different persons.

**4.** Adjusting to the norms of a new culture, whether that be a domestic co-culture or another national culture.

**5.** Building upon similarities and common concerns, while integrating and understanding differences, to promote our personal growth and to aid us in our dealings with other cultures that are, as yet, unfamiliar to us.

Clearly, the attitudes requisite for a global economy force us to reexamine our isolation and to prepare to deal with a wide variety of persons from a broad range of cultural backgrounds. The search for mutually acceptable guidelines for conducting economic exchange as trade barriers are lowered entails frequent intercultural communication.

## Research

From the perspective of research the future of intercultural communication study will continue to be informed by methodological pluralism, cultural diversity, and ethical complexity. As indicated in Chapter 1, the history of intercultural communication study demonstrates the incompleteness of any single methodological or theoretical orientation. To date, mainstream theories in the field of intercultural communication are Western-oriented. We predict that more universal, non-western theories will be developed in the near future. Methodologically, quantitative methods have dominated the field since its inception. Qualitative-interpretive studies have emerged in the 1990s, joined by critical studies and a resurgence in rhetorical analyses. This development will lead to both competition and cooperation among intercultural communication scholars. An optimistic outlook for intercultural communication study depends on triangulation among the various methods of intercultural inquiry, in which multiple methods are used to compensate for the others' deficiencies.

Two issues related methodologically and theoretically that may persist include the demarcation between academicians and practioners and agreement on the parameters of the field. The first issue concerns defining the borderline between theory and practice. Historically, the field of intercultural communication study is based on attempts to solve practical problems encountered in different cultures. In other words, the first priority of intercultural communication study is practice. Its basic concern is the improvement of intercultural adjustment rather than purely intellectual or academic interest (Smith, 1977). This can explain why training programs are emphasized so much in this field. The practical orientation emphasis of intercultural communication may mislead us to believe that the theoretical foundation of intercultural communication is of little importance. For a sound future development of intercultural communication study, it is critical for us to understand that robust theory is the key to success of any practice of intercultural communication. The practical orientation of any field cannot negate the need for rigorous theory and research. They are the two sides of a coin, and their complementarity is essential.

The lack of agreement on the exact parameters of the field will continue to haunt intercultural communication scholars. Conceptual inconsistency is found in scholars' definition of intercultural communication and their delineation of subject matter. As indicated in Chapter 1, Rich classified intercultural communication into five forms, including intercultural, international, interracial, interethnic, and contracultural communication. Integrating the conceptual definitions and the study of these five forms of intercultural communication is a critical challenge to scholars. Moreover, whether intercultural communication should be considered as an independent field of study or of human communication study also deserves close attention in the future. In other words,

## Research Highlight 13–3

Who:   Starosta, W. J.

What:   "Re-centering Culture in Intercultural Communication."

Where:   *Arizona Communication Journal, 19,* 1993, 19–26.

This article argues that culture serves as the starting point of any communication study. The author deconstructs current intercultural communication literature and reveals popular orthodoxies within the individual disciplines.

Researchers within each subfield assert that intercultural communication is solely a special case in their field. For example, intrapersonal communication researchers determine that the exact position of contact between communicators of different cultures is the individual mind, cognitions, attitudes, and perceptions. With such a perspective, intercultural adjustment is a function of "self shock." Intrapersonal communicologists, therefore, do not assume it necessary to consider issues of a cultural group's identity, cultural history, gender or power relationships as influences on a communication episode.

Interpersonal communication scholars rival intrapersonal assumptions by stating that intercultural communication is a special case within their discipline. They argue that culture introduces no new challenges to two- or three-person communication that are not already present in intracultural exchanges. They claim that importance of societal sense-making overrides the need to know individual processes.

Mass communication scholars argue that the term *intercultural communication* describes the projection of mass-mediated messages and symbols across culture. Thus, the images of cross-cultural exchanges exemplify and teach principles of intercultural communication that negate the need for similar learning in face-to-face exchanges. Finally, rhetorical communication scholars stress that intercultural communication relies mainly on the function of rhetoric.

Based on the above analyses, any communication study is a study of cultural phenomena. In other words, culture is the center of all communication studies. Ultimately, the author contests the effort of each discipline to stand without culture. Furthermore, the author challenges communication scholars to specify which cultural perspective (for example, the United states, Euro-American) they use in conducting their research and making their methodological choices.

Finally, the author states that the competition regarding intercultural communication between sub-disciplines denies us a comprehensive understanding of intercultural communication. This exclusionary rivalry prevents scholars outside of, for example, the Western perspective from contributing intercultural research within the scholarly community and earns it the label of "unscientific." Voices and perspectives are marginalized that ultimately could enhance understanding of the ubiquitous nature of culture in communication.

should intercultural communication become an extension of interpersonal or mass communications study, or does it represent a research area that penetrates into interpersonal, group, organizational, and public communication concerns (Starosta, 1993)?

This is an identity issue intercultural communication scholars must address in the future. The conceptual definition of intercultural communication naturally affects the subject matter to be studied. Examining the extant intercultural communication textbooks, we find that they commonly cover basic ideas about communication and culture, cultural perception, verbal and nonverbal communication, and intercultural communication competence. Other topics such as intercultural training, conflict management, and multiculturalism are still not emphasized by scholars. Scholars must reach a consensus about the subject matter of intercultural communication study.

Finally, the ethical complexity of intercultural communication demands more attention from scholars. In terms of the research process itself, intercultural communication scholars must address the following questions (Hamnett & Porter, 1979; Streeton, 1975; Tapp, et al., 1974):

**1.** To what degree should the conduct of intercultural communication researchers be answerable to the expectations of their own culture versus the target culture? Do those of the target culture, in fact, "own" the research?
**2.** To what degree should benefits of the research accrue to the target culture?
**3.** To what extent should intercultural communication scholars utilize the theoretical frameworks and methodologies of the target culture to analyze and explain the phenomena from that culture?
**4.** To what extent should intercultural communication researchers collaborate with scholars in the target culture to account for communication phenomena in their respective societies?

## RECAP

This chapter focuses on ethical issues and the future of intercultural communication study. In the discussion of the nature, principles, rules, and propositions of ethical intercultural communication, the concept of *ethics* is introduced, a rationale for the study of intercultural communication ethics is provided, and four theoretical propositions—universalism vs. relativism, objectivism vs. subjectivism, attitudinalism vs. consequentialism, and deontologicalism vs. teleologicalism—are examined in relation to the behavioral norms of mutuality, disclosure, honesty, and respect. In addition, five ethical rules to promote successful intercultural communication are suggested: (1) participating voluntarily in the interaction, (2) seeking an individual focus prior to a cultural one, (3) enjoying the right to freedom from harm, (4) enjoying the right to privacy of thought and action, and (5) seeking to eliminate personal biases. Finally, twelve propositions for ethical intercultural communication are listed for further speculation.

The discussion of the future of intercultural communication is divided into three parts. First, increasing or decreasing intercultural communication is discussed from domestic and international perspectives. Second, unity versus division is discussed from two angles: ethnocentrism and gender impact. Finally, the future study of intercultural communication is explained from three perspectives: education, business, and research.

## QUESTIONS FOR DISCUSSION

1. Why is it important to study intercultural communication ethics?
2. Compare and contrast the theories of ethical study discussed in this chapter.
3. Describe the principles of ethical intercultural communication.
4. Explain the guidelines for ethical intercultural communication.
5. Will intercultural contact be increasing or decreasing in the future?
6. Will the world move toward unity or separateness?
7. Discuss the future direction and application of intercultural communication study from the perspectives of education, research, and business.

# References

Aburdene, P. (1990). How to think like a CEO for the 90's. *Working Woman*, September, 134–137.

Ackerman, N. W. (1958). *The psycho-dynamics of family life*. New York: Basic Books.

Adler, M. K. (1977). *Pidgins, creoles, and lingua franca*. Hamburg: Helmut Buske Verlag.

Adler, N. J. (1980). Cultural synergy: The management of cross-cultural organizations. In W. Burke & C. D. Goodstein (Eds.), *Trends and issues in O.D.: Current theory and practice*. San Diego, CA: University Associates.

Adler, N. J. (1991). *International dimensions of organizational behavior*. Belmont, CA: Wadsworth.

Adler, P. S. (1975). The transitional experience: An alternative view of culture shock. *Journal of Humanistic Psychology, 15*, 13–23.

Adler, P. S. (1977). Beyond cultural identity: Reflections upon cultural and multicultural man. In R. Brislin (Ed.), *Culture learning: Concepts, applications, and research*. Honolulu: University Press of Hawaii.

Adler, P. S. (1982). Beyond cultural identity: Reflections on cultural and multicultural man. In L. A. Samovar and R. E. Porter (Eds.), *Intercultural communication: A reader* (pp. 389–405). Belmont, CA: Wadworth.

Adler, P. S. (1987). Culture shock and the cross-cultural learning experience. In L. F. Luce & E. C. Smith (Eds.), *Toward internationalism* (pp. 14–35). Cambridge, MA: Newbury.

Adler, R. B., & Towne, N. (1987). *Looking out/looking in*. New York: Holt, Rinehart and Winston.

Adler, R. B., & Towne, N. (1990). *Looking out/looking in*. Chicago: Holt, Rinehart and Winston.

Albert, E. S., & Triandis, H. C. (1985). Intercultural education for multicultural societies: Critical issues. *International Journal of Intercultural Relations, 9*, 319–338.

Allen, R. R., & Brown, K. L. (Eds.) (1976). *Developing communication competence in children: A report to the Speech Communication Association's national project on speech communication competencies*. Skokie, IL: National Textbook Company.

Allen, R. R., & Wood, B. S. (1978). Beyond reading and writing to communication competence. *Communication Education, 27*, 286–292.

Allport, G. W. (1958). *The nature of prejudice.* New York: Doubleday Anchor.

Altman, I., & Taylor, D. (1973). *Social penetration: The development of interpersonal relationship.* New York: Holt, Rinehart and Winston.

Anderson, L. E. (1994). A new look at an old construct: Cross-cultural adaptation. *International Journal of Intercultural Relations, 18,* 293–328.

Andersen, P. A. (1986). Consciousness, cognition, and communication. *Western Journal of Speech Communication, 50,* 87–101.

Andersen, P. A. (1994). Explaining intercultural differences in nonverbal communication. In L. A. Samovar & R. E. Porter (Eds.), *Intercultural communication: A reader* (pp. 229–239). Belmont, CA: Wadsworth.

Andrews, P. H., & Baird, J. E. (1989). *Communication for business and the professions.* Dubuque, IO: Wm. C. Brown.

Argyle, M. (1975). *Bodily communication.* New York: International Universities Press.

Argyris, C. (1965a). Explorations in interpersonal competence—I. *Journal of Applied Behavioral Science, 1,* 58–83.

Argyris, C. (1965b). Explorations in interpersonal competence—II. *Journal of Applied Behavioral Science, 1,* 255–269.

Arnett, R. C., & Nakagawa, G. (1983). The assumptive roots of empathic listening: A critique. *Communication Education, 32,* 4, 368–378.

Asante, M. K. (1980). Intercultural communication: An inquiry into research directions. In D. Nimmo (Ed.), *Communication Yearbook, 4* (pp. 401–411). New Brunswick, NJ: Transaction.

Asante, M. K., Blake, C., & Newmark, E. (Eds.) (1979), *Handbook of intercultural communication.* Beverly Hills, CA: Sage.

Asante, M. K., & Gudykunst, W. B. (Eds.) (1989). *Handbook of international and intercultural communication.* Newbury Park, CA: Sage.

Babiker, I., Cox. J., & Miller, P. (1980). The measurement of culture distance and its relationship to medical consultations, symptomatology and examination performance of overseas students at Edinburgh University. *Social Psychiatry, 15,* 109–116.

Bacharach, S. B., & Lawler, E. J. (1981). *Bargaining: Power, tactics, and outcomes.* San Francisco, CA: Jossey-Bass.

Backlund, P. (1978). Defining communication competence. In C. Larson, P. Backlund, M. Redmond, & A. Barbour (Eds.), *Assessing functional communication.* Annandale, VA: SCA/ERIC.

Bagby, J. W. (1957). A cross-cultural study of perceptual pre-dominance in binocular rivalry. *Journal of Abnormal and Social Psychology, 54,* 331–334.

Baker, H. D. R. (1979). *Chinese family and kinship.* London: Macmillan.

Barna, L. M. (1979). Intercultural communication stumbling blocks. In R. E. Porter & L. A. Samovar (Eds.), *Intercultural communication: A reader* (pp. 291–298). Belmont, CA: Wadsworth.

Barna, L. M. (1983). The stress factor in intercultural relations. In D. Landis & R. W. Brislin (Eds.), *Handbook of intercultural training,* Vol. 2. New York: Pergamon.

Barna, L. M. (1994). Stumbling blocks in intercultural communication. In L. A. Samovar & R. E. Porter (Eds.), *Intercultural communication: A reader* (pp. 337–346). Belmont, CA: Wadsworth.

Barnak, P. (1980). Role-playing. In D. S. Hoopes & P. Ventura (Eds.), *Intercultural Sourcebook: Cross-cultural training methodologies* (pp. 7–10). Washington D.C.: SIETAR.

Barnlund, D. C. (1975). *Public and private self in Japan and United States.* Tokyo: Simul.

Barnlund, D. C. (1988). Communication in a global village. In L. A. Samovar, & R.E. Porter (Eds.), *Intercultural communication: A reader* (pp. 5–14). Belmont, CA: Wadsworth.

Barnlund, D. S. (1974). The public and private self in Japan and the United States. In J. C. Condon & M. Saito (Eds.), *Intercultural encounters with Japan: communication-contact and conflict.* Tokyo: Simul Press.

Barnlund, D. S. (1989). *Communication style of Japanese and Americans: Images and reality.* Belmont, CA: Wadsworth.

Baxter, L. (1984). An investigation of compliance-gaining as politeness. *Human Communication Research, 10,* 427–456.

Berry, M. (1993). The development of self-reflexive listening. *Journal of the International Listening Association,* Special Issue, 83–93.

Berry, M. (1994). Colloquium participant on "Hate Speech," Howard University.

Becker, C. B. (1986). Reasons for the lack of argumentation and debate in the Far East. *International Journal of Intercultural Relations, 10,* 75–92.

Beebe, S. (1974). Eye contact: A nonverbal determinant of speaker credibility. *Speech Teacher, 23,* 21–25.

Beier, E. G., & Zautra, A. (1972). Identification of vocal communication of emotions across cultures. *Journal of Consulting and Clinical Psychology, 34,* 166.

Belay, G. (1993). Toward a paradigm shift for international and intercultural communication: New research directions. *Communication Yearbook 16* (pp. 295–306). Newbury Park, CA: Sage.

Benedict, R. (1946). *Patterns of culture.* New York: Penguin Books.

Bennett, C. I. (1990). *Comprehensive multicultural education.* Boston, MA: Allyn and Bacon.

Bennett, M. J. (1977). Transition shock: Putting cultural shock in perspective. In N. C. J. Jain (Ed.), *International and intercultural communication, 4.* Falls Church, VA: Speech Communication Association.

Bennett, M. J. (1979). Overcoming the golden rule: Sympathy and empathy. In D. Nimmo (Ed.), *Communication Yearbook* (pp. 407–433). New Brunswick, NJ: Transaction.

Bennett, M. J. (1984). *Towards ethnorelativism: A developmental model of intercultural sensitivity.* Paper presented at the annual conference of the Council on International Exchange, Minneapolis, Minnesota.

Bennett, M. J. (1986). A developmental approach to training for intercultural sensitivity. *International Journal of Intercultural Relations, 10,* 179–196.

Berger, C. R. (1979). Beyond initial interactions: Uncertainty, understanding, and the development of interpersonal relationships. In H. Giles, & R. St. Clair (Eds.), *Language and social psychology.* Oxford: Basil Blackwell.

Berger, C. R., & Calabrese, R. (1975). Some explorations in initial interactions and beyond: Toward a developmental theory of interpersonal communication. *Human Communication Research, 1,* 99–112.

Bhawuk, D. P. S., & Brislin, R. (1992). The measurement of intercultural sensitivity using the concepts of individualism and collectivism. *International Journal of Intercultural Relations, 16,* 413–436.

Birdwhistell, R. L. (1970). *Introduction to kinesics.* Philadelphia: University of Pennsylvania Press.

Blubaugh, J. A., & Pennington, D. L. (1976). *Exercising differences in interracial communication.* Columbus, OH: Merill.

Bochner, A. P., & Kelly, C. W. (1974). Interpersonal competence: Rationale, philosophy, and implementation of a conceptual framework. *Speech Teacher, 23,* 279–301.

Bond, M. B., & Hwang, K. (1986). The social psychology of Chinese people. In M. H. Bond (Ed.), *The psychology of the Chinese people* (pp. 213–266). Hong Kong: Oxford University Press.

Bond, M. H. (1991). *Beyond the Chinese face: Insight from psychology.* New York: Oxford University Press.

Borden. G. A. (1991). *Cultural orientation: an approach to understanding intercultural communication.* Englewood Cliffs, NJ: Prentice Hall.

Borisoff, D., & Hahn, D. F. (1992). Dimensions of intimacy: The interrelationships between gender and listening. Journal of the *International Listening Association, 5,* 23–41.

Bourhis, R. Y. (1979). Language in ethnic interaction: A social psychological approach. In H. Giles & R. St. Jacques (Eds.), *Language and ethnic relations* (pp. 117–141). Oxford: Pergamon.

Brinkerhoff, R. O. (1989) (Ed.). *Evaluating training programs in business and industry.* San Francisco, CA: Jossey-Bass.

Brislin, R. W. (1979). Orientation programs for cross-cultural preparation. In A. J. Marsella, R. G. Tharp, & T. J. Ciborowski (Eds.), *Perspectives on cross-cultural psychology* (pp. 287–303). New York: Academic Press.

Brislin, R. W. (1981). *Cross-cultural encounters: Face-to-face interaction.* New York: Pergamon.

Brislin, R. W. (1986). A cultural general assimilator: Preparation for various types of sojourns. *International Journal of Intercultural Relations, 10,* 215–234.

Brislin, R. W., Cushner, K., Cherrie, C., & Yong, M. (1986). *Intercultural interactions: A practical guide.* Beverly Hills, CA: Sage.

Brislin, R. W., Landis, D., & Brandt, M. E. (1983). Conceptualizations of intercultural behavior and training. In D. Landis & R. W. Brislin (Eds.), *Handbook of intercultural training: Issues in theory and design,* Vol. 1 (pp. 1–35). New York: Pergamon.

Brislin, R. W., & Pedersen, P. (1976). *Cross-cultural orientation programs.* New York: Gardner Press.

Bronfenbrener, U., Harding, J, & Gallwey, M. (1958). The measurement of skill in social perception. In McClelland, D. C. (Ed.). *Talent and society.* New York: Van Nostrand.

Broome, B. J., & Christakis, A. N. (1988). A culturally sensitive approach to tribal governance issue management. *International Journal of Intercultural Relations, 12,* 107–124.

Brown, E. E. (1991). *Human universals.* Philadelphia: Temple University.

Bruneau, T. (1989). Empathy and listening: A conceptual review and theoretical directions. *Journal of the International Listening Association, 3,* 1–20.

Bruneau, T. (1993). Empathy and listening. In A.D. Wolvin & C.G. Coakley (Eds.), *Perspectives on Listening.* (pp. 185–200). Norwood, NJ: Ablex.

Buber, M. (1958). *I and thou.* New York: Scribner's.

Buhler, P. (1993). Understanding cultural diversity and its benefits. *Supervision,* July, 17–19.

Buoyant, C. I. (1991). *Comprehensive multicultural education.* Boston: Allyn and Bacon.

Buoyant, M. J. (1979). Overcoming the golden rule: Sympathy and empathy. In D. Nimmo (Ed.), *Communication Yearbook, 3* (pp. 407–433). Newbury Park, CA: Sage.

Buoyant, M. J. (1984). *Towards ethnorelativism: A developmental model of intercultural sensitivity.* Paper presented at the Annual Conference of the Council on International Exchange, Minneapolis, Minnesota.

Buoyant, M. J. (1986). A developmental approach to training for intercultural sensitivity. *International Journal of Intercultural Relations, 10,* 179–196.

Burgoon, J. K., Buller, D. B., & Woodall, W. G. (1989). *Nonverbal communication: The unspoken dialogue.* New York: Harper and Row.

Carmichael, C. W. (1991). Intercultural perspectives of aging. In L. A. Samovar & R. E. Porter (Eds.), *Intercultural communication: A reader* (pp. 128–135). Belmont, CA: Wadsworth.

Cegala, D. J. (1981). Interaction involvement: A cognitive dimension of communicative competence. *Communication Education, 30,* 109–121.

Cegala, D. J. (1984). Affective and cognitive manifestations of interaction involvement during unstructured and competitive interactions. *Communication Monographs, 51,* 320–338.

Chang, H., & Holt, G. R. (1991). More than relationship: Chinese interaction and the principle of Kuan-hsi. *Communication Quarterly, 39,* 251–271.

Chang, H. B. (1973). Attitudes of Chinese students in the United States. *Sociology and Social Research, 58,* 66–77.

Chen, G. M. (1988, November). *A comparative study of value orientations of Chinese and American families.* Paper presented at the annual convention of the Speech Communication Association, New Orleans, Louisiana.

Chen, G. M. (1989). Relationships of the dimensions of intercultural communication competence. *Communication Quarterly, 37,* 118–133.

Chen, G. M. (1990). Intercultural communication competence: Some perspectives of research. *The Howard Journal of Communication, 2,* 243–261.

Chen, G. M. (1990). Cultural value orientations and language acquisition: An application to overseas Chinese education. World Chinese Language (Ed.), *Essays on Chinese language teaching and application* (pp. 39–51). Taipei: Shuei Shen.

Chen, G. M. (1992). A test of intercultural communication competence. *Intercultural Communication Studies, 2,* 63–82.

Chen, G. M. (1992). The change of Chinese family value orientations in the United States. *Journal of Overseas Chinese Studies, 2,* 111–121.

Chen, G. M. (1993). Self-disclosure and Asian students' abilities to cope with social difficulties in the United States. *Journal of Psychology, 127,* 603–610.

Chen, G. M. (1994). Self-disclosure and Asian students' abilities to cope with social difficulties in the United States, *Journal of Psychology, 127,* 603–610.

Chen, G. M. (1995). Differences in self-disclosure patterns among Americans versus Chinese: A comparative study. *Journal of Cross-Cultural Psychology, 26,* 84–91.

Chen, G. M. (1996, November). *Feng Shui: The Chinese art of space arrangement.* Paper presented at the 1996 annual convention of he Speech Communication Association. San Diego, California.

Chen, G. M., & Chung, J. (1994). The impact of Confucianism on organizational communication. *Communication Quarterly, 42,* 93–105.

Chen, G. M., Ryan, K., & Chen, C. C. (1992, October). *Some determinants of conflict dominance: A comparative study.* Paper presented at the annual convention of the Speech Communication Association, Chicago, Illinois.

Chen, G. M., & Starosta, W. J. (1996). Intercultural communication competence: A synthesis. *Communication Yearbook, 19,* 353–384.

Cheng, C. Y. (1987). Chinese philosophy and contemporary human communication theory. In. D. L. Kincaid (Ed.), *Communication theory: Eastern and western perspectives* (pp. 23–44). New York: Academic Press.

Chiao, C. (1981). *Chinese strategic behavior: Some central principles.* Paper presented at the Conference on Content of Culture, Claremont, California.

Chiao, C. (1982). Guanxi: A preliminary conceptualization. In K. S. Yang and C. I. Wen (Eds.), *The Sinicization of social and behavioral science research in China* (pp. 345–360). Taipei: Academia Sinica.

Chomsky, N. (1965). *Aspects of the theory of syntax.* Cambridge: MIT Press.

Chu, R. L. (1983). *Empirical researches on the psychology of face.* Doctoral dissertation, Taipei, Taiwan: National Taiwan University.

Chua, E. & Gudykunst (1987). Conflict resolution style in low- and high-context cultures. *Communication Research Reports, 4,* 32–37.

Chung, J. (1991, April). *Seniority and particularistic ties in a Chinese conflict resolution process.* Paper presented at the annual conference of the Eastern Communication Association, Pittsburgh, Pennsylvania.

Chung, J. (1992, November). *Electronic mail usage in low-context and high-context cultures.* Paper presented at the annual meeting of Speech Communication Association, Chicago, Illinois.

Cleveland, H., Mangone, G. J., & Adams, J. C. (1960). *The overseas Americans.* New York: McGraw-Hill.

Coakley, C. G., & Wolvin, A. D. (1990). Listening pedagogy and androgyny: The state of the art. *Journal of the International Listening Association, 4,* 33–61.

Coats, J., & Cameron, D. (1989). *Women in their speech communities: New perspectives on language and sex.* London: Longman.

Coke, J., Bateson, C., & McDavis, K. (1978). Empathetic meditation of helping: A two-stage model. *Journal of Personality and Social Psychology, 36,* 752–766.

Cole, M. (1989, November). *A cross-cultural inquiry into the meaning of face in the Japanese and United States cultures.* Paper presented at the annual convention of the Speech Communication Association, San Francisco, California.

Collier, M. J. (1989). Cultural and intercultural communication competence: Current approaches and directions for future research. *International Journal of Intercultural Relations, 13,* 287–302.

Collier, M. J. (1994). Cultural identity and intercultural communication. In L. A. Samovar & R. E. Porter (Eds.), *Intercultural communication: A reader* (pp. 36–44). Belmont, CA: Wadsworth.

Collier, M. J., & Thomas, M. (1988). Cultural identity: An interpretive perspective. In Y. Y. Kim & W. B. Gudykunst (Eds.), *Theories in intercultural communication* (pp. 99–120). Newbury Park, CA: Sage.

Condon, J. C. (1977). *Interpersonal communication.* New York: Macmillan.

Condon, J. C. (1981). Values and ethics in communication across culture: Some notes on the North American case. *Communication, 6,* 255–265.

Condon, J. C., & Yousef, F. (1975). *An introduction to intercultural communication.* Indianapolis, IN: Bobbs-Merrill.

Conrad, C. (1994). *Strategic organizational communication.* New York: Harcourt Brace College Publishers.

Conway, M. (1993). Super projects: New wonders of the world. *The Futurist,* March-April, 25–28. Cooley, R. E., & Roach, D. A. (1984). A conceptual framework. In R. N. Bostrom (Ed.), *Competence in communication: A multidisciplinary approach* (pp. 11–32). Beverly Hills: Sage.

Cooper, B. (in press). 'It's going to be a rough ride, buddy!': An analysis of the collision between 'hate speech' and 'free expression' in the Khallid Abdul Muhammed controversy. *The Howard Journal of Communications, 8.*

Corner, T. (1984). *Education in multicultural societies.* New York: St. Martin's Press.

Cornish, E. (1990). Introduction: The possibilities of the future. In E. Cornish (Ed.), *The 1990s and Beyond* (pp. 5–7). Bethesda, MD: World Future Society.

Cox, H., & Blake, S. (1991). Managing cultural diversity: Implications for organizational competitiveness. *Academy of Management Executive,* August, 45–56.

Cronen, V. E., & Shuter, R. (1983). Forming intercultural bonds. In W. B. Gudykunst (Ed.), *Intercultural communication theory* (pp. 89–118). Beverly Hills, CA: Sage.

Cumber, C. J., & Braithwaite, D. O. (1996). A comparative study of the perceptions and understanding of multiculturalism. *The Howard Journal of Communications, 7,* 271–282.

David, K. (1972). Intercultural adjustment and applications of reinforcement theory to problems of culture shock. *Trends, 4,* 1–64.

Davis, M. H. (1983). Measuring individual differences in empathy: Evidence for a multidimensional approach. *Journal of Personality and Social Psychology, 44,* 113–126.

Davitz, J. R., & Davitz, L. J. (1961). Nonverbal vocal feeling. *Journal of Communication, 11,* 110–117.

Deutsch, M. (1968). The effects of cooperation and competition upon group process. In D. Cartwright & A. Zander (Eds.), *Group dynamics* . New York: Harper and Row.

Deutsch, S. E., & Won, G. Y. M. (1963). Some factors in the adjustment of foreign nationals in the United States. *Journal of Social Issues, 19,* 115–122.

Devito, J. A. (1992). *The interpersonal communication book.* New York: Harper Collins.

Dinges, N. (1983). Intercultural competence. In D. Landis & R. W. Brislin (Eds.), *Handbook of intercultural training* (Vol. 1): *Issues in theory and design* (pp. 176–202). New York: Pergamon.

Dodd, C. H. (1977). *Perspectives of cross-cultural communication science.* Dubuque, IA: Brown.

Dodd, C. H. (1982). *Dynamics of intercultural communication.* Dubuques, IA: Brown.

Dodd, C. H. (1991). *Dynamics of intercultural communication.* Dubuque, IA: Brown.

Downs, J. F. (1969). Fables, fancies and failures in cross-cultural training, *Trends, 7, 3.*

Draguns, J. G. (1977). Problems of defining and comparing abnormal behavior across cultures. In L. L. Adler (Ed.), *Issues in cross-cultural research* (pp. 664–675). New York: New York Academy of Science.

Eakins, B. W., & Eakins, R. G. (1991). Sex differences in nonverbal communication. In L. A. Samovar & R. E. Porter (Eds.), *Intercultural communication: A reader.* Belmont, CA: Wadsworth.

Edman, P., & Friesen, W. V. (1972). Hand movement. *Journal of Communication, 22,* 353–354.

Edwards, A. (1991). Cultural diversity in Today's corporation. *Working Women,* January, 45–51.

Edwards, R., & McDonald, J. L. (1993). Schema theory and listening. In A. D. Wolvin & C. G. Coakley (Eds.), *Perspectives on listening* (pp. 60–77). Norwood, NJ: Ablex.

Ekman, P., & Friesen, W. V. (1969). The repertoire of nonverbal behavior: Categories, origins, usage and coding. *Semiotica, 1,* 49–98.

Ekman, P., & Friensen, W. V. (1975). *Unmasking the face.* Englewood Cliffs, NJ: Prentice Hall.

Ekman, P., & Friensen,, W. V. (1983). Felt, false and miserable smiles. *Journal of Nonverbal Behavior, 6,* 238–252.

Emerson, R. M. (1964). Power-dependence relations. *Sociometry, 27,* 282–298.

Emmert, P., Emmert, V. & Brandt, J. (1993). An analysis of male-female differences on the listening practices feedback report. *Journal of the International Listening Association,* special issue, 43–55.

Enrlich, H. (1973). *The social psychology of prejudice.* New York: Wiley.

Erickson, B., Lind, E. A., Johnson, B. C., & O'Barr, W. M. (1978). Speech style and impression formation in a court setting: The effects of powerful and powerless speech. *Journal of Experimental Social Psychology, 14,* 266–279.

Farrell, T. B. (1993). On the disappearance of the rhetorical aura. *Western Journal of Communication, 57,* 147–158.

Fernandez, J. P. (1991). *Managing diverse work force.* Massachusetts: Lexington Books.

Fine, M. G. (1991). New voices in the workplace: Research direction in multicultural communication. *Journal of Business Communication, 23,* 259–275.

Fischer, H., & Merrill, J. C. (Eds.) (1976). *International intercultural communication.* New York: Hastings House.

Fish, S. L. (1991). Preparation for the year 2000: One corporation's attempt to address the issues of gender and race. *The Howard Journal of Communications, 3,* 61–72.

Fisher, W. R. (1984). Narratives as a human communication paradigm: The case of public moral agreement. *Communications Monographs, 51,* 1–22.

Fisher, W. R. (1985a). The narrative paradigm: An elaboration. *Communication Monographs, 52,* 347–367.

Fisher, W. R. (1985b). The narrative paradigm: In the beginning. *Journal of Communication, 35,* 74–89.

Fisher, W. R. (1987). *Human communication as narration: Toward a philosophy of reason, values, and action.* Columbia: University of South Carolina Press.

Fiske, A. P. (1992). The four elementary forms of sociality: Framework for a unified theory of social relations. P*sychological Review, 99,* 689–723.

Fletcher, J. (1966). *Situation ethics: The new morality.* Philadelphia: Westminster.

Folger, J. P., Poole, M. S., & Strutman, R. K. (1993). *Working through conflict.* New York: Harper Collins.

Fontaine, G. (1986). Roles of social support systems in overseas relocation: Implications for intercultural training. *International Journal of Intercultural Relations, 10,* 361–378.

Foote, N. N., & Cottrell, L. S. (1955). *Identity and interpersonal competence.* Chicago: University of Chicago Press.

Foss, S., & Foss, K. (1991). *Woman speak: The eloquence of women's lives.* Skokie, IL: Waveland Press.

Foster, B. G., Jackson, G., Cross, W. E., Jackson, B., & Hardiman, R. (1988). Workforce diversity and business. *Training and Development Journal,* April, 15–19.

Foster, R., & Danielian, J. (1966). *An analysis of human relations training and its implications for overseas performance.* Technical Report 66–15, HumPRO.

Friedman, P. G. (1993). Listening for narrative. In A.D. Wolvin & C.G. Coakley (Eds.), *Perspectives on listening.* (pp. 201–216). Norwood, NJ: Ablex.

Fromkin, V., & Rodman, R. (1978). *An introduction to language.* New York: Holt, Rinehart and Winston.

Furnham, A. (1987). The adjustment of sojourners. In Y. Y. Kim & W. B. Gudykunst (Eds.), *Cross-cultural adaptation: Current approaches* (pp. 42–61). Beverly Hills, CA: Sage.

Furnham, A., & Bochner, S. (1982). Social difficulty in a foreign culture: An empirical analysis of culture shock. In S. Bochner (Ed.), *Culture in contact: Studies in cross-cultural interaction* (pp. 161–198). New York: Pergamon.

Furnham, A., & Bochner, S. (1986) *Culture shock: Psychological reactions to unfamiliar environments.* London: Methuen.

Gainor, K. A., & Forrest, L. (1991). African American women's self-concept. *Career Development Quarterly, 39,* 261–273.

Galagan, P. (1991). Tapping the power of a diverse workforce. *Training and Development Journal,* March, 61–72.

Gallois, C., Franklyn-Stokes, A., Giles, H., & Coupland, N. (1988). Communication accommodation in intercultural encounters. In Y. Y. Kim & W. B. Gudykunst (Eds.), *Theories in intercultural communication* (pp. 157–185). Newbury Park, CA: Sage.

Garrett, T. M. (1966). *Business ethics.* New York: Appleton-Century-Crofts.

Giles, H. (1973). Accent mobility: A model and some data. *Anthropological Linguistics, 15,* 87–105.

Giles, H., & Johnson, P. (1981). The role of language in ethnic group relations. In J. C. Turner & H. Giles (Eds.), *Intergroup behaviour* (pp. 199–243). Oxford: Basil Blackwell.

Giles, H., & Powesland, P. F. (1975). *Speech style and social evaluation.* London: Academic Press.

Gladwin, T. N., & Walter, I. (1980). *Multinationals under fire: Lessons in the management of conflict.* New York: John Wiley.

Gleason. L. B. (1989). *The development of language.* Columbus, OH: Merrill.

Glenn, E. S., & Glenn, C. G. (1981). *Man and mankind: Conflict and communication between cultures.* New Jersey: Norwood.

Goldstein, I. L., & Gilliam, P. (1990). Training system issues in the year 2000. *American Psychologist, 45,* 143.

Gordon, G. (1992). This man knows what diversity is. *Communication World,* December, 8–12.

Griffin, K. (1967). Interpersonal trust in small-group communication. *Quarterly Journal of Speech, 53,* 224–234.

Guan, S. J. (1995). *Intercultural communication.* Beijing: Peking University Press.

Gudykunst, W. B. (1983). Uncertainty reduction and predictability of behavior in low- and high-context cultures: An exploratory study. *Communication Quarterly, 31,* 49–55.

Gudykunst, W. B. (1985). Intercultural communication: Current status and proposed directions. In B. Dervin & M. J. Voigt (Eds.), *Progress in communication sciences, 6,* (pp. 1–46). Norwood, NJ: Ablex.

Gudykunst, W. B. (1987). Cross-cultural comparison. In C. R. Berger & S. H. Chaffee (Eds.), *Handbook of communication science* (pp. 847–889). Beverly Hills, CA: Sage.

Gudykunst, W. B. (1994). *Bridging differences.* Newbury Park, CA: Sage.

Gudykunst, W. B., & Hammer, M. R. (1983). Basic training design: Approaches to intercultural training. In D. Landis and R. W. Brislin (Eds.), *Handbook of intercultural training,* Vol. 1 (pp. 118–154). New York: Pergamon.

Gudykunst, W. B., & Hammer, M. R. (1987). Strangers and hosts: An uncertainty reduction based theory of intercultural adaptation. In Y. Y. Kim & W. B. Gudykunst (Eds.), *Cross-cultural adaptation: Current approaches* (pp. 106–139). Newbury Park, CA: Sage.

Gudykunst, W. B., Hammer, M. R., & Wiseman, R. L. (1977). An analysis of an integrated approach to cross-cultural training. *International Journal of Intercultural Relations, 2,* 99–110.

Gudykunst, W. B., & Kim. Y. Y. (1984). *Methods for intercultural communication.* Beverly Hills, CA: Sage.

Gudykunst, W. B., & Kim, Y. Y. (1992). *Readings on communicating with strangers.* New York: McGraw-Hill.

Gudykunst, W. B., & Nishida, T. (1984). Social penetration in close relationships in Japan and the United States. In R. Bastrom (Ed.), *Communication Yearbook, 7.* Beverly Hills, CA: Sage.

Gudykunst, W. B., & Nishida, T. (1986). The influence of cultural variability on perceptions of communication behavior associated with relationship terms. *Human Communication Research, 13,* 147–166.

Gudykunst, W. B., & Ting-Toomey, S. (1988). *Culture and interpersonal communication.* Newbury Park, CA: Sage.

Gudykunst, W. B., & Ting-Toomey, S. (1988). Affective communication across cultures. *American Behavioral Scientist, 31,* 384–400.

Gudykunst, W. B., Ting-Toomey, S., Sudweeks, S., & Stewart, L. P. (1995). *Building bridges: Interpersonal skills for a changing World.* Boston: Houghton Mifflin.

Gudykunst, W. B., Ting-Toomey, S., & Wiseman, R. L. (1991). Taming the beast: Designing a course in intercultural communication. *Communication Education, 40,* 272–285.

Gullahorn, J. T., & Gullahorn, J. E. (1963). An extension of the U-curve Hypothesis. *Journal of Social Issues, 19,* 33–47.

Gullahorn, J. T., & Gullahorn, J. E. (1966). American students abroad: Professional versus personal development. *Annala, 368*, 43–59.

Guthrie, G. M. (1975). A behavioral analysis of culture learning. In R. W. Brislin, S. Bochner, & W. J. Lonner (Eds.), *Cross-cultural perspectives on learning.* New York: Wiley.

Folger, J. P., & Poole, M. S. (1984). *Working through conflict: A communication perspective.* Glenview, IL: Scott, Foresman.

Hall, E. T. (1959). *The silent language.* Garden City, NY: Doubleday.

Hall, E. T. (1966). *The hidden dimension.* Garden City, NY: Doubleday.

Hall, E. T. (1976). *Beyond culture.* Garden City, NY: Anchor.

Hall, E. T. (1984). *The dance of life: The other dimension of time.* Garden City, NY: Doubleday.

Hall, E. T. (1994). Monochronic and polychronic time. In L. A. Samovar & R. E. Porter (Eds.), *Intercultural communication: A reader* (pp. 264–271). Belmont, CA: Wadsworth.

Hall, E. T., & Hall, M. R. (1987). *Understanding cultural differences.* Yarmouth, ME: Intercultural Press.

Hall, E. T., & Hall, R. H. (1989). *Understanding cultural differences: Germans, French and Americans.* Yarmouth, ME: Intercultural Press.

Hall, E. T., & Whyte, W. F. (1963). Intercultural communication: A guide to men of action. *Practical Anthropology, 9*, 83–108.

Hammer, M. R. (1987). Behavioral dimensions of intercultural effectiveness: Application and extension. *International Journal of Intercultural Relations, 11*, 5–88.

Hammer, M. R. (1988, November). *Communication skills and intercultural communication competence: A review and research agenda.* Paper presented at the annual meeting of Speech Communication Association, New Orleans, Louisiana.

Hammer, M. R. (1989). Intercultural communication competence. In M. K. Asante and W. B. Gudykunst (Eds.), *Handbook of international and intercultural communication* (pp. 247–260). Newbury Park: Sage.

Hammer, M. R., Gudykunst, W. B., & Wiseman, R. L. (1978). Dimensions of intercultural effectiveness: An exploratory study. *International Journal of Intercultural Relations, 2*, 382–392.

Hamnett, M. P. (1978). Ethics and expectations in cross-cultural social science research. In N. C. Asuncion-Lande (Ed.), Ethical perspectives and critical issues in intercultural communication (pp. 44–61). Falls Church, VA: SCA.

Hamnett, M. P., & Porter, D. (1979, March). *Problems and prospects in Western approaches to cross-national social science research,* Paper presented at the annual meeting of SIETAR convention. Mexico City, Mexico.

Harrigan, J. A. (1985). Listeners' body movements and speaking turns. *Communication Research, 12*, 233–250.

Harris, P. R., & Moran, R. T. (1987). *Managing cultural differences.* Houston, TX: Gulf.

Harris, P. R., & Moran, R. T. (1989). *Managing cultural differences.* Houston, TX: Gulf.

Harrison, R., & Hopkins, R. (1967). The design of cross-cultural training: An alternative to the university model. *Journal of Applied Behavioral Science, 3*, 341–60.

Hart, R. P., & Burks, D. M. (1972). Rhetorical sensitivity and social interaction. *Speech Monographs, 39*, 75–91.

Hart, R. P., Carlson, R. E., & Eadie, W. F. (1980). Attitudes toward communication and the assessment of rhetorical sensitivity. *Communication Monographs, 47*, 1–2.

Hawes, F., & Kealey, D. J. (1981). An empirical study of Canadian technical assistance. *International Journal of Intercultural Relations, 5*, 239–258.

Hecht, M. L., & Ribeau. S. (1991). Sociocultural roots of ethnic identity: A look at black Americans. *Journal of Black Studies, 21*, 501–513.

Hecht, M. L., Sedano, M. V., & Ribeau, S. R. (1993). Understanding culture, communication, and research: Applications to Chicanos and Mexican Americans. *International Journal of Intercultural Relations, 17*, 157–166.

Herman, S., & Schield, E. (1961). The stranger group in cross-cultural situation. *Sociometry, 24*, 165–176.

Heslin, R., & Alper, T. (1983). Touch: A bonding gesture. In J. M. Wiemann & R. P. Harrison (Eds.), *Nonverbal interaction* (pp. 47–75). Beverly Hills, CA: Sage.

Higbee, H. (1969). Role shock—A new concept. *International Educational and Cultural Exchange, 4*, 71–84.

Hoehn, A. J. (1968). *The need for innovative approaches for training in intercultural interaction.* Report 9–68, HumPRO.

Hoff, B. L. R. (1979). *Classroom-generated barriers to learning: International students in American higher education.* Ph.D. diss., United States International University, San Diego.

Hofstede, G. (1980). Motivation, leadership, and organizations: Do American theories apply abroad? *Organizational Dynamics*, Summer, 42–63.

Hofstede, G. (1983). National cultures in four dimensions. *International Studies of Management and Organization, 13*, 46–74.

Hofstede, G. (1984). *Culture's consequences.* Beverly Hills, CA: Sage.

Hofstede, G., & Bond. M. H. (1988). The Confucius connection: From cultural roots to economic growth. *Organizational Dynamics, 16*, 5–21.

Hoijer, H. (1994). The Sapir-Whorf hypothesis. In L. A. Samovar and R. E. Porter (Eds.), *Intercultural communication: A reader* (pp. 194–200). Belmont, CA: Wadsworth.

Holland, J. L., Baird, L. L. (1968). An interpersonal competence scale. *Educational and Psychological Measurement, 28*, 503–510.

Homans, G. C. (1958). Social behavior as exchange. *American Journal of Sociology, 63*, 597–606.

Hoopes, D. S. (1981). Intercultural communication concepts and the psychology of intercultural experience. In M. D. Pusch (Ed.), *Multicultural education: A cross-cultural training approach.* Chicago: Intercultural Press.

Hoopes, D. S., Pusch, M. D. (1979). Teaching strategies: The methods and techniques of cross-cultural training. In M. D. Pusch (Ed.), *Multicultural education: A cross cultural training approach* (pp. 104–204). La Grange Park, IL: Intercultural Network.

Hoopes, D. S., & Ventura, P. (1980) (Eds.). *Intercultural Sourcebook: Cross-cultural training methodologies.* Chicago, IL: Intercultural Press.

Hu, H. C. (1944). The Chinese concept of "face." *American Anthropology, 46*, 45–64.

Hsu, F. L. K. (1953). *Americans and Chinese: Two ways of life.* New York: Abelard-Schuman.

Hsu, F. L. K. (1981). *Americans and Chinese: Passage to differences.* Honolulu: University of Hawaii Press.

Hwang, K. K. (1987). Face and favor: The Chinese power game. *American Journal of Sociology, 92*, 944–974.

Hwang, K. K. (1988). Renqin and face: The Chinese power game. In K. K. Hwang (Ed.), *The Chinese power game* (pp. 7–56). Taipei: Juliu.

Hymes, D. (1971). Competence and performance in linguistic theory. In R. Huxley & E. Ingram (Eds.), *Language acquisition: Models and methods* (pp. 3–26). New York: Academic Press.

Irwin, G. (1972). *American tramp and underworld slang.* Ann Arbor, MI: Gryphon.

Ishii, S. (1982). Thought patterns as modes of rhetoric: The United States and Japan. *Communication, 11.*

Ishii, S., & Bruneau, T. (1994). Silence and silences in cross-cultural perspective: Japan and the United States. In L. A. Samovar & R. E. Porter (Eds.), *Intercultural communication: A reader* (pp. 264–271). Belmont, CA: Wadsworth.

Jackson, S. E. (1992). *Diversity in the workplace.* New York: Guilford Press.

Javidi, A., & Javidi, M. (1991). Cross-cultural analysis of interpersonal bonding: A look at East and West. *The Howard Journal of Communications, 3*, 129–138.

Jocobs, B. J. (1979). A preliminary model of particularistic ties in Chinese political alliances: Kan-ching and Kuan-hsi in a rural Taiwanese township. *China Quarterly, 78*, 237–273.

Jocob, P. E., Teune, H., & Watts, T. (1968). Values, leadership and development: A fournation study. *Social Science Information, 7*, 49–92.

Johannesen, R. L. (1983). *Ethics in human communication.* Prospect Heights, IL: Waveland.

Johnson, F. L. & Buttny, R. (1982). White listeners' responses to "sounding black" and "sounding white": The effects of message content on judgments about language. *Communication Monographs, 49*, 33–49.

Johnston, J. S., & Edelstein, R. J. (1993). *Beyond borders: Profiles in international education.* Association of American Colleges and American Assembly of Collegiate Schools of Business.

Johnston, W. B., & Packer, A. H. (1987). *Workforce 2000: Work and workers for the 21st century.* Indianapolis, IN: Hudson Institute.

Kale, D. W. (1994). Peace as an ethic for intercultural communication. In L. A. Samovar & R. E. Porter (Eds.), *Intercultural communication: A reader* (pp. 435–444). Belmont, CA: Wadsworth.

Kaplan, R. B. (1966). Cultural thought pattern in inter-cultural education. *Language Learning, 16*, 1–20.

Keesing, R. M. (1975). Linguistic knowledge and cultural knowledge: Some doubts and speculations. *American Anthropologist, 81*, 14–35.

Kelly, H. H., & Thibaut, J. W. (1978). *Interpersonal relations: A theory of interdependence.* New York: Wiley.

Kim, Y. Y. (1986, November). *Cross-cultural adaptation: A critical assessment of the field.* Paper presented at the annual meeting of the Speech Communication Association, Chicago, Illinois.

Kim, Y. Y. (1988). *Communication and cross-cultural adaptation: An integrative theory.* Philadelphia: Multilingual Matter.

Kim, Y. Y. (1988). Intercultural adaptation. In M. K. Asante & W. B. Gudykunst (Eds.),

*Handbook of international and intercultural communication* (pp. 273–294). Newbury Park, CA: Sage.

Kim, Y. Y., & Gudykunst, W. B. (Eds.) (1988). *Theories in intercultural communication.* Newbury Park, CA: Sage.

Kim, Y. Y., & Gudykunst, W. B. (Eds.) (1988). *Cross-cultural adaptation: Current approaches.* Beverly Hills: Sage.

Kim, Y. Y., & Ruben, B. D. (1988). Intercultural transformation. In Y. Y. Kim & W. B. Gudykunst (Eds.), *Theories in intercultural communication* (pp. 299–321). London: Sage.

Kincaid, D. L. (1987). *Communication theory: Eastern and Western perspectives.* New York: Academic Press.

King, S. S. (1989) (Ed.). *Human communication as a field of study: Selected contemporary views.* Albany, NY: SUNY Press.

Klaw, S. (1971). Two weeks in a T-group. In R. W. Siroka, E. K. Siroka, & G. A. Schloss (Eds.), *Sensitivity training and group encounter: An introduction* (pp. 36–51). New York: Grosset and Dunlap.

Klopf, D. W. (1995). *Intercultural encounters: The fundamentals of intercultural communication.* Englewood, CO: Morton.

Kluckhohn, C. (1948). *Mirror of man.* New York: McGraw-Hill.

Kluckhohn, C. (1951). Values and value-orientation in the theory of action. In T. Parsons & E. Shils (Eds.), *Toward a general theory of action* (pp. 388–433). Cambridge, MA: Harvard University Press.

Kluckhohn, C., & Strodbeck, F. (1961). *Variations in value orientations.* Evanston, IL: Row, Peterson.

Knapp, M. L. (1980). *Essentials of nonverbal communication.* New York: Holt, Rinehart and Winston.

Knapp, M., & Vangelisti, A. (1992). *Interpersonal communication and human relationships.* Boston: Allyn and Bacon.

Knupfer, G. (1969). Portrait of the underdog. In R. W. O'Brien, C. C. Schrag, & W. T. Martin (Eds.), *Readings in general sociology* (pp. 298–304). New York: Houghton Mifflin.

Koberg, C. S, & Chusmir, L. H. (1989). Relationship between sex role conflict and work-related variables: Gender and hierarchical differences. *Journal of Social Psychology, 129,* 779–791.

Kochman, T. (1981). *Black and white styles in conflict.* Chicago: University of Chicago Press.

Kochman, T. (1982). *Black and white: Styles in conflict.* Chicago, IL: University of Chicago Press.

Kohls, L. R. (1979). *Survival kit for overseas living.* Yarmouth, ME: Intercultural Press.

Kohls, L. R. (1980). Issues in cross-cultural training. In N. Asuncion-Landé (Ed.), *Ethical perspectives and critical issues in intercultural communication* (pp. 86–94). Falls Church, VA: SCA.

Kohls, L. R. (1984). *Survival kit for overseas living.* Yarmouth, ME: Intercultural Press.

Kohls, L. R. (1984). *The values Americans live by: Introduction.* Washington, DC: Meridian House International.

Kraemer, A. (1975). Cultural self-awareness and communication. *International Education and Cultural Exchange, 10,* 13–16.

Krug, L. (1982). Alternative lifestyle dyads: An alternative relationship paradigm. *Alternative Communications*, *4*, 32–52.

Lederer, W. J., & Burdick, E. (1958). *The ugly American*. Greenwich, CT: Fawcett.

Leeds-Hurwitz, W. (1990). Notes in the history of intercultural communication: The foreign service institute and the mandate for intercultural training. *Quarterly Journal of Speech*, *76*, 268–281.

Leo, J. (1983, December 19). Reprogramming the patient. *Time*, p. 79.

Leung, K. (1988). Some determinants of conflict avoidance. *Journal of Cross-Cultural Psychology*, *19*, 125–136.

Levinger, G. (1983). The embrace of lives: Changing and unchanging. In G. Levinger & H. L. Raush (Eds.), *Close relationships: Perspectives on the meaning of intimacy* (pp. 1–16). Amherst: University of Massachusetts Press.

Lewis-Chung, W. V. (1992, June). *Attitudinal issues in multicultural education: The college student experience*. Paper presented at the Philip White Scholars' conference.

Lin, Y. (1984). *The introduction of philology*. Taipei: Cheng Chung.

Lindin, O. G. (1974). Harmony with nature in Chinese thought and opposition to nature in Western thought. *Journal of Intercultural Studies*, *1*, 5–9.

Lippitt. R., Plansky, N., Redl, F., & Rosen, S. (1952). The dynamics of power. *Human Relations*, *5*, 37–64.

Littlejohn, S. W. (1995). *Theories of human communication*. Belmont, CA: Wadsworth Press.

Locke, D. C., & Parker, L. D. (1991). *A multicultural focus on career education*. (ERIC Reproduction Service No. ED 348).

Lowenstein, R. L., & Merrill, J. C. (1990). *Macromedia: Mission, message, and morality*. New York: Longman.

Lu, X., & Chen, G. M. (1995, August). *Language change and value orientations in Chinese culture*. Paper presented at the 5th International Conference on Cross-Cultural Communication: East and West, Harbin, China.

Lustig, M. W., & Koester, J. (1996). *Intercultural competence: Interpersonal communication across cultures*. New York: Harper Collins.

Lysgaard, S. (1955). Adjustment in foreign society: Norwegian Fulbright grantees visiting the United States. *International Social Science Bulletin*, *7*, 45–51.

Ma, R. (1990). An exploratory study of discontented responses in American and Chinese relationships. *Southern Communication Journal*, *55*, 305–318.

Ma, R. (1991, April). *Contexts of discontented responses in Chinese and North American cultures*. Paper presented at the annual convention of the Eastern Communication Association, Pittsburgh, Pennsylvania.

Ma, R. (1992). The role of unofficial intermediaries in interpersonal conflicts in the Chinese culture. *Communication Quarterly*, *40*, 269–278.

Mader, T. F., & Mader, D. C. (1990). *Understanding one another*. Dubuque, IA: Brown.

Madonik, B. (1990). I hear what you say, but what are you telling me? *Canadian Manager*, *15*, 18–20.

Mann, M. N. (1996). Personal Communication. September 3. Mandelbaum, D. C. (Ed.) (1949). *Selected writings of Edward Sapir*. Berkeley, CA: University of California Press.

Mansell, M. (1981). Transcultural experience and expressive response. *Communication Education*, *30*, 93–108.

Martin, J. N. (1987). The relationships between student sojourner perceptions of inter-cultural competencies and previous sojourner experience. *International Journal of Intercultural Relations, 11,* 337–355.

Martin, J. N. (1993). Intercultural communication competence: A review. In R. L. Wise-man and J. Koester (Eds.), *Intercultural communication competence* (pp. 16–32). Newbury Park, CA: Sage.

Martin, J. N., & Hammer, M. R. (1989). Behavioral categories of intercultural communi-cation competence: Everyday communicators' perceptions. *International Journal of Intercultural Relations, 13,* 303–332.

Matawi, A. (1995). *Proxemics among male and female Saudi Arabian undergraduates in Saudi Arabia and the United States.* Diss., Howard University.

McClelland, D. C. (1958). Review and prospect. In McClelland, D.C. (Ed.), *Talent and society.* New York: Van Nostrand.

McPhail, M. L. (1991). Complicity: The theory of negative difference. *Howard Journal of Communications, 3,* 1–13.

Mead, G. H. (1934). *Mind, self, and society.* Chicago: University of Chicago Press.

Mead, R. (1990). *Cross-cultural management communication.* New York: Wiley.

Meade, R. D., & Whittaker, J. O. (1967). A cross-cultural study of authoritarianism. *Jour-nal of Psychology, 72,* 3–7.

Mehrabian, A. (1972). *Nonverbal communication.* Chicago, IL: Aldine.

Mehrabian, A., & Williams, M. (1969). Nonverbal concomitants of perceived and in-tended persuasiveness. *Journal of Personality and Social Psychology, 13,* 37–58.

Metzger, J. G., Weber, D. W., Springston, J. K., & Larsen, P. D. (1991). Recounted and enacted narratives: The genesis and endurance of community as found in the treaty rights debate. *Howard Journal of Communications, 3,* 36–60.

Mezirow, J. (1978). *Education for perspective transformation.* New York: Center for Adult Education, Columbia University.

Mezirow, J. (1981). A critical theory of adult learning and education. *Adult Education Quarterly, 32,* 3–24.

Mezirow, J. (1990). *Fostering critical reflection in adulthood.* San Francisco, CA: Jossey-Bass.

Mezirow, J. (1991). *Tranformative dimensions of adult learning.* San Francisco, CA: Jossey-Bass.

Miller, G., & Steinberg, M. (1975). *Between people.* Chicago: Science Research Associ-ates.

Mitchell, A. (1990). Nine American Lifestyles: Values and societal change. In E. Cornish (Ed.), *The 1990s and beyond* (pp. 12–22). Bethesda, MD: World Future Society.

Morain, G. G. (1987). Kinesics and cross-cultural understanding. In L. F. Luce and E. C. Smith (Eds.), *Toward internationalism: Readings on cross-cultural communication* (pp. 117–142). Cambridge, MA: Newbury House.

Moran, R., & Harris, P. (Eds.) (1982). *Managing cultural synergy.* Houston, TX: Gulf.

Morgan, E., & Weigel, V. (1988). *Credits and credibility: Educating professionals for cul-tural sensitivity.* Paper presented at the Conference on Science and Technology for International Development, Myrtle Beach, South Carolina.

Morris, R. T. (1960). *The two-way mirror.* Minneapolis: University of Minnesota Press.

Morrison, A. M, & Von Glinow, M. A. (1990). Women and minorities in management. *American Psychologist, 45,* 200–207.

Nadler, B. N., Nadler, M. K., & Broome, B. J. (1985). Culture and the management of conflict situations. In W. B. Gudykunst, L. P. Stewart, & S. Ting-Toomey (Eds.), *Communication, culture, and organizational processes* (pp. 87–113). Beverly Hills, CA: Sage.

Nakane, C. (1974). *Japanese society.* Berkeley: University of California Press.

Nakane, C. (1984). The social system reflected in interpersonal relationship. In J. Condon & M. Sito (Eds.), *Intercultural encounters with Japan.* Tokyo: Simul.

Nakanishi, M. (1987). Perceptions of self-disclosure in initial interaction: A Japanese sample. *Human Communication Research, 13,* 305–318.

Natriello, G., McDill, E. L., & Pallas, A. M. (1990). *Schooling disadvantaged children: Racing against catastrophe.* New York: Teachers College Press.

Nierenberg, G. I., & Calero, H. H. (1971). *How to read a person like a book.* New York: Hawthorn.

Nieto, S. (1992). *Affirming diversity.* New York: Longman.

Nishyma, K. (1971). Interpersonal persuasion in a vertical society: The case of Japan. *Speech Monographs, 38,* 148–154.

Nixon, J. (1985). *A teacher's guide to multicultural education.* New York: Basil Blackwell.

Nomura, N., & Barnlund, D. (1983). Patterns of interpersonal criticism in Japan and the United States. *International Journal of Intercultural Relations, 7,* 1–8.

Oberg, K. (1960). Cultural shock: Adjustment to new cultural environments. *Practical Anthropology, 7,* 177–182.

Ogawa, D. (1979). Communication characteristics of Asian Americans in urban settings: The case of Honolulu Japanese. In M. K. Asante, E. Newmark, & C. A. Blake (Eds.), *Handbook of intercultural communication* (pp. 321–339). Beverly Hills, CA: Sage.

Okabe, R. (1983). Cultural assumptions of East and West. In W. B. Gudykunst (Ed.), *Intercultural communication theory* (pp. 21–44). Beverly Hills, CA: Sage.

Oliver, R. T. (1961). The rhetorical implications of Taoism. *Quarterly Journal of Speech, 47,* 27–35.

Oliver, R. T. (1962). *Culture and communication.* Springfield, IL: Thomas.

Park, M-S. (1979). *Communication styles in two different cultures: Korean and American.* Seoul, Korea: Han Shin.

Parker, W. M., Valley, M. M., & Geary, C. A. (1986). Acquiring cultural knowledge for counselors in training: A multi-faceted approach. *Counselor Education and Supervision, 26,* 61–71.

Parks, M. R. (1976, December). *Communication competence.* Paper presented at the meeting of the Speech Communication Association, San Francisco.

Patton, J. (1986). *Situated communication mismatches in the junior high classroom: A communication rules analysis.* Diss., Howard University.

Perelman, C. (1963). *The idea of justice and the problem of argument.* New York: Humanities Press.

Perry, W. G., Jr. (1970). *Forms of intellectual and ethical development in the college years.* New York: Holt, Rinehart and Winston.

Peterson, T. R. (1988). Reconstituting ethnocentrism: The American ethnic coalition and official English. *Howard Journal of Communications, 1,* 99–112.

Piaget, J. E. (1932). *The moral judgment of the child.* (M. Grabain, trans.) New York: Harcourt, Brace and World.

Phillips, G. M. (1983). A competent view of "competence." *Communication Education, 33*, 25–36.

Porter, R. E., & Samovar, L. (1982). Approaching intercultural communication. In L. A. Samovar & R. E. Porter (Eds.), *Intercultural communication: A reader* (pp. 26–42). Belmont, CA: Wadsworth.

Porter, R. E., & Samovar, L. A. (1994). An introduction to intercultural communication. In L. A. Samovar & R. E. Porter (Eds.), *Intercultural communication: A reader* (pp. 4-25). Belmont, CA: Wadsworth.

Pribram, K. H. (1949). *Conflicting patterns of thought.* Washington: Public Affairs Press.

Prosser, M. H. (Ed.) (1973). *Intercommunication among nations and people.* New York: Harper and Row.

Prosser, M. H. (1978) (Ed.). *The cultural dialogue: An introduction to intercultural communication.* Boston, MA: Houghton Mifflin.

Prosser, M. H. (1978). Intercultural communication theory and research: An overview of major constructs. In B. D. Ruben (Ed.), *Communication Yearbook, 2* (pp. 335–343). New Brunswick, NJ: Transaction.

Putnam, L. L., & Poole, M. S. (1987). Conflict and negotiation. In F. M. Jablin, L. L. Putnam, K. H. Roberts, & L. W. Porter (Eds.), *Handbook of organizational communication: An interdiscipline perspective* (pp. 549–599). Newbury Park, CA: Sage.

Pye, L. (1982). *Chinese commercial negotiation style.* Cambridge, MA: Oelgechlager, Gunn, and Hain.

Renwick, G. W. (1979). Evaluation: Some practical guidelines. In M. D. Pusch (Ed.), *Multicultural education: A cross cultural training approach* (pp. 104–204). La Grange Park, IL: Intercultural Network.

Rhinesmith, S. H. (1991). *Training and Development Journal,* 22–29.

Ricard, V. B. (1992). *Developing intercultural communication skills.* Malabar, FL: Krieger.

Rich, A. (1974). *Interracial communication.* New York: Harper and Row.

Ricoeur, P. (1976). *Interpretation theory: Discourse and the surplus of meaning.* Fort Worth: Texas University Press.

Ridge, A. (1993). A perspective of listening skills. In A. D. Wolvin & C. G. Coakley (Eds.), *Perspectives on listening.* (pp. 1–14). Norwood, NJ: Ablex.

Rifenbary, D. (1991). *An introduction to multicultural issues in career development.* Albuquerque, NM: University of New Mexico.

Roloff, M. E. (1981). *Interpersonal Communication: The social exchange approach.* Beverly Hills, CA: Sage.

Rosch, E. (1973). Natural categories. *Cognitive Psychology, 4*, 328–350.

Ross, R. (1980). Case study method. In D. S. Hoopes & P. Ventura (Eds.), *Intercultural sourcebook: Cross-cultural training methodologies* (pp. 142–143). Washington, DC: SIETAR.

Ruben, B. D. (1976). Assessing communication competency for intercultural adaptation. *Group and Organization Studies, 1*, 334–354.

Ruben, B. D. (1977). Guidelines for cross-cultural communication effectiveness. *Group and Organization Studies, 2*, 470–479.

Ruben, B. D. (1988). Human communication and cross-cultural effectiveness. In L. A. Samovar, & R. E. Porter (Eds.). *Intercultural communication: A reader.* Belmont, CA: Wadsworth.

Ruben, B. D. (1989). The study of cross-cultural competence: Traditions and contemporary issues. *International Journal of Intercultural Relations, 13,* 229–240.

Ruben, B. D., & Kealey, D. J. (1979). Behavioral assessment of communication competency and the prediction of cross-cultural adaptation. *International Journal of Intercultural Relations, 3,* 15–47.

Samovar, L. A., & Porter, R. E. (1988). Approaching intercultural communication. In L. A. Samovar & R. E. Porter (Eds.), *Intercultural communication: A reader* (pp. 15–30). Belmont, CA: Wadsworth.

Samovar, L. A., & Porter, R. E. (Eds.) (1994). *Intercultural communication: A reader.* Belmont, CA: Wadsworth.

Samovar, L. A., & Porter, R. E. (1995). *Communication between cultures.* Belmont, CA: Wadsworth.

Samovar, L. A., & Sanders, F. (1978). Language patterns of the prostitute: Some insights into a deviant subculture. *ETC: A review of general semantics, 34,* 34.

Saral, T. B. (1977a). Intercultural communication theory and research: An overview. In B. D. Ruben (Ed.), *Communication Yearbook 1* (pp. 389–396). New Brunswick, NJ: Transaction.

Saral, T. B. (1977b). Intercultural communication theory and research: An overview of challenge and opportunities. In D. Nimmo (Ed.), *Communication Yearbook 3* (pp. 395–406). New Brunswick, NJ: Transaction.

Schnapper, M. (1980). Culture simulation as a training tool. In D. S. Hoopes & P. Ventura (Eds.), *Intercultural sourcebook: Cross-cultural training methodologies* (pp. 7–10). Washington, DC: SIETAR.

Schneider, M. J. (1985). Verbal and nonverbal indices of the communicative performance and acculturation of Chinese immigrants. *International Journal of Intercultural Relations, 9,* 271–283.

Schutz, W. (1966). *The interpersonal underworld.* Palo Alto, CA: Science and Behavior Books.

Schwartz, S. (1990). Individualism-collectivism. *Journal of Cross-Cultural Psychology, 21,* 139–151.

Schwartz, S., & Sagiv. L. (1995). Identifying culture-specifics in the content and structure of values. *Journal of Cross-Cultural Psychology, 26,* 92–116.

Searle, W., & Ward, C. (1990). The prediction of psychological and sociocultural adjustment during cross-cultural transitions. *International Journal of Intercultural Relations, 14,* 449–463.

Seidel, G. (1981). Cross-cultural training procedures: Their theoretical framework and evaluation. In S. Bochner (Ed.), *The mediating person: Bridge between cultures.* Cambridge: Schenhman.

Settle, S. E. (1996). *A comparative narrative analysis of coverage of civil rights campaigns in Alabama by an African American and white Atlanta paper.* Unpublished dissertation, Howard University, May.

Sewell, W. H., & Davidsen, O. M. (1956). The adjustment of Scandinavian students. *Journal of Social Issues, 12,* 9–19.

Shiang, T. C. (1982). *A study of Chinese character.* Taipei: Shang Wu.

Shirts, G. (1973). *BAFA BAFA: A cross-cultural simulation.* Delmar, CA: Simile.

Shockley-Zalabak, P. (1994). *Understanding organizational communication.* White Plains, NY: Longman.

Short, B. (1988). Mandating a "mother tongue": Historical and political foundations of the English first movement. *Howard Journal of Communications, 1,* 86–98.

Shuter, R. (1993). On third-culture building. *Communication Yearbook, 16.* Newbury Park, CA: Sage, 429–436.

Silin, R. H. (1981). *Leadership and values: The organization of large-scale Taiwanese enterprise.* Cambridge, MA: Harvard University Press.

Singer, M. R. (1987). *Intercultural communication: A perceptual approach.* Englewood Cliffs, NJ: Prentice Hall.

Sitaram, K. S., & Cogdell, R. T. (1976). *Foundations of intercultural communication.* Columbus, OH: Bobbs-Merrill.

Sitaram, K. S., & Haapanen, L. W. (1979). The role of values in intercultural communication. In M. K. Asante & C. A. Blake (Eds.), *The handbook of intercultural communication* (pp. 147–160). Beverly Hills, CA: Sage.

Smalley, W. A. (1963). Culture shock, language shock, and the shock of self-discovery. *Practical Anthropology, 10,* 49–56.

Smith, A. (Ed.) (1966). *Communication and culture.* New York: Holt, Rinehart and Winston.

Smith, A. G. (1977). Research and theory in intercultural communication. In D. Hoopes et al. (Eds.), *Overview of intercultural education, training and research I.* Washington, DC: Society for Intercultural Education, Training and Research.

Smith, A. L. (1973). *Transracial communication.* Englewood Cliffs, NJ: Prentice Hall.

Smith, H. (1966). *Sensitivity to people.* New York: McGraw-Hill.

Smith, M. B. (1955). Some features of foreign student adjustment. *Journal of Higher Education, 26,* 231–241.

Smith, S., & Whitehead, G. (1984). Attributions for promotions and demotions in the United States and India. *Journal of Social Psychology, 30,* 526–537.

Snyder, M. (1974). Self-monitoring of expressive behavior. *Journal of Personality and Social Psychology, 30,* 528.

Snyder, M. (1979). Cognitive, behavioral, and interpersonal consequences of self-monitoring. In P. Pliner, K. R. Blankenstein, I. M. Spigel, T. Alloway, & L. Krames (Eds.), *Advances in the study of communication and affect: Perception of emotion in self and others* (pp. 181–201). New York: Plenum.

Sommer, R. (1969). *Personal space: The behavioral basis of design.* Englewood Cliffs, NJ: Prentice Hall.

Speicher, B. L. (1994). Interethnic conflict: Attribution and cultural ignorance. *Howard Journal of Communications, 5* (3). 195–213.

Spitzberg, B. H. (1988, November). *Progress and pitfalls in conceptualizing and researching intercultural communication competence.* Paper presented at the Speech Communication Association Conference, New Orleans, Louisiana.

Spitzberg, B. H. (1989). Issues in the development of a theory of interpersonal competence in intercultural context. *International Journal of Intercultural Relations, 13,* 241–268.

Spitzberg, B. H., & Cupach, W. R. (1984). *Interpersonal communication competence.* Beverly Hills, CA: Sage.

Starosta, W. J. (1971, Spring). United Nations: Agency for semantic consubstantiality. *Southern States Speech Journal.*

Starosta, W. J. (1973). Non-communication as game in international relations. In M. H.

Prosser and W. J. Starosta (Eds.), *Intercommunication among nations and peoples.* New York: Harper and Row.

Starosta, W. J. (1984). Intercultural rhetoric. In W. B. Gudykunst, Y. Y. Kim (Eds.), *Methods for intercultural communication* (pp. 229–238). Beverly Hills, CA: Sage.

Starosta, W. J. (1987). A little compulsion with our persuasion? "De Facto Coercion" in Mrs. Gandhi's family planning communication campaign. *Political Communication and Persuasion, 4,* 1987.

Starosta, W. J. (1990). Thinking through intercultural training assumptions in the aftermath. *International Journal of Intercultural Relations, 14,* 1–6.

Starosta, W. J. (1993). Re-centering culture in intercultural communication. *Arizona Communication Journal, 19,* 19–26.

Starosta, W. J., & Chaudhary, A. G. (1992). A case study of Satyagraha: Gandhi's 1939 salt march. *World Communication.*

Starosta, W. J. & Chaudhary, A. G. (1993, June). "I Can Wait 40 or 400 Years": Gandhian *Satyagraha* East and West, *International Philosophical Quarterly* , 163–172.

Starosta, W. J. & Hannon, S. W. (in press): The multilexicality of contemporary history: Recounted and enacted narratives of the Mohawk incident in Oka, Québec, *The International and Intercultural Communication Annual, 20.*

Starosta, W. J., & Olorunnisola, A. A. (1995, April). *A meta-model for third culture development.* Paper presented at the annual meeting of Eastern Communication Association, Pittsburgh, Pennsylvania.

Stauffer, A. (1982). Cultural synergy. In R. Moran & P. Harris (Eds.), *Managing cultural synergy.* Houston, TX: Gulf.

Sterba, R. L. A. (1978). Clandestine management in the imperial Chinese bureaucracy. *Academy of Management Review,* January, 69–78.

Stewart, E. C. (1972). *American cultural patterns: A cross-cultural perspective.* LaGrange Park, IL: Intercultural Network.

Stewart, E. C. (1978). Outline of intercultural communication. In F. L. Casmir (Ed.), *Intercultural and international communication* (pp. 265–344). Washington, DC: University Press of America.

Stewart, E. C. (1978). *American cultural patterns: A cross-cultural perspective.* Pittsburgh: Intercultural Communication Network.

Stewart, E. C., & Bennett, M. J. (1991). *American cultural patterns: A cross-cultural perspective.* Yarmouth, ME: Intercultural Press.

Stewart, E. C., & Buoyant, M. J. (1991). *American cultural patterns: A cross-cultural perspective.* Yarmouth, ME: Intercultural Press.

Stewart, J. (1983). Interpretive listening: An alternative to empathy. *Communication Education, 32,* 379–391.

Stewart, J. (Ed.). (1990). *Bridges, not walls: A book about interpersonal communication.* New York: McGraw-Hill.

Strack, S., & Lorr, M. (1990). Three approaches to interpersonal behavior and their common factors. *Journal of Personality Assessment, 54,* 782–790.

Streeton, P. (1975). The role of social science in development studies. *Development Digest, 14,* 51–58.

Sue, D. W. (1994). A model for cultural diversity training. In L. A. Samovar and R. E. Porter (Eds.), *Intercultural communication: A reader* (pp. 382–391). Belmont, CA: Wadworth.

Tannen, D. (1990). *You just don't understand: women and men in conversation.* New York: William Morrow.

Tapp, J. L., Kelman, H. C., Wrightsman, L. S., Triandis, H. C., & Coelho, G. V. (1974). Continuing concerns in cross-cultural ethics: A report. *International Journal of Psychology, 9,* 231–249.

Taylor, E. W. (1994). A learning model for becoming interculturally competent. *International Journal of Intercultural Relations, 18,* 389–408.

Templeton, F. (1966). Alienation and political participation: Some research findings. *Public Opinion Quarterly, 30,* 249–261.

Thayer, L. (1987). *On communication: Essays in understanding.* Norwood, NJ: Ablex.

Thiagarajan, S. & Steinwachs, B. (1990). *Barnga: A simulation game on cultural clashes.* Yarmouth, ME: Intercultural Press.

Thibaut, J. W, & Kelly, H. H. (1959). *The social psychology of groups.* New York: Wiley.

Thomas, L. T. (1994). Listening to intense messages: The role of arousal and affect in message content recognition. *Journal of the International Listening Association, 8,* 161–174.

Thomas, R. R. (1991). *Beyond race and gender.* New York: American Management Association.

Thorndyke, P. W., & Yekovich, F. R. (1981). An evaluation of alternative functional modes of narrative schema. *Journal of Verbal Learning and Verbal Behavior, 20,* 454–469.

Ting-Toomey, S. (1985). Toward a theory of conflict and culture. In W. B. Gudykunst, L. P. Stewart, & S. Ting-Toomey (Eds.), *Communication, culture, and organizational processes* (pp. 71–86). Beverly Hills, CA: Sage.

Ting-Toomey, S. (1988). Intercultural conflict style: A face-negotiation theory. In Y. Y. Kim & W. B. Gudykunst (Eds.), *Theories in intercultural communication* (pp. 213–235). Newbury Park, CA: Sage.

Ting-Toomey, S. (1994). Managing intercultural conflicts effectively. In L. A. Samovar & R. E. Porter (Eds.), *Intercultural communication: A reader* (360–372). Belmont, CA: Wadsworth.

Ting-Toomey, S., Trubisky, P., & Nishida, T. (1989, November). *An analysis of conflict styles in Japan and the United States.* Paper presented at the annual convention of the Speech Communication Association, San Francisco, California.

Torbiorn, I. (1982). *Living abroad: Personal adjustment and personnel policy in the overseas setting.* New York: Wiley.

Torrance, E. P. (1955). Some consequences of power differences on decision making in permanent and temporary three-man groups . In A. P. Hare, E. F. Borgatta, & R. F. Baises (Eds.), *Small groups: Studies in social interaction.* New York: Knopf.

Trager, G. L. (1958). Paralanguage: A first approximation. *Studies in Linguistics, 13,* 1–12.

Triandis, H. C. (1976). *Interpersonal behavior.* Monterey, CA: Brooks/Cole.

Triandis, H. C. (1977). Subjective culture and interpersonal relations across cultures. In L. Loeb-Adler (Ed.), Issues in cross-cultural research. *Annals of the New York Academy of Sciences, 285,* 418–434.

Triandis, H. C. (1977). Theoretical framework for evaluation of cross-cultural training effectiveness. *International Journal of Intercultural Relations, 1,* 195–213.

Turner, C. V. (1968). The Sinasina "Big Man" complex: A central culture theme. *Practical Anthropology, 15,* 16–23.

Tyler, V. L. (1978). Report of the working groups of the Second SCA Summer Conference on Intercultural Communication. In N. C. Asuncion-Lande (Ed.), *Ethical perspectives and critical issues in intercultural communication* (pp. 170–177). Falls Church, VA: SCA.

Tylor, E. B. (1958). *The origin of culture.* New York: Harper and Row.

Tylor, E. B. (1967). *The origin of culture.* New York: Harper and Row.

Vagas, M. F. (1986). *Louder than words: An introduction to nonverbal communication.* Ames: Iowa State University Press.

Valdivieso, R., & David, C. (1988). *Hispanics: Challenging issues for the 1990s.* Washington, DC: Population Trends and Public Policy.

Victor, D. A. (1992). *International business communication.* New York: Harper Collins.

Vinson, L. R., Johnson, C., & Hackman, M. Z. (1993). Explaining the effects of powerless language use on the evaluative listening process: A theory of implicit prototypes. *Journal of the International Listening Association, 7,* 35–53.

Waggenspack, B. M., & Hensley, W. E. (1989). Perception of the argumentativeness trait in interpersonal relationship situation. *Social Behavior and Personality, 17,* 111–120.

Ward, C., & Searly, W. (1991). The impact of value discrepancies and cultural identity on psychological and sociocultural adjustment of sojourners. *International Journal of Intercultural Relations, 15,* 209–226.

Warren, D., & Adler, P. (1977). An experiential approach to instruction in intercultural communication. *Communication Education, 26,* 128–134.

Wayne, M. S. (1970). Characteristic oral and written business communication problems of selected managerial trainees. *Journal of Business Communication, 16,* 43–48.

Weaver, G. (1978). *Crossing cultural barriers.* Dubuque, IA: Brown.

Weber, S. N. (1994). The need to be: The socio-cultural significance of black language. In L. A. Samovar and R. E. Porter (Eds.), *Intercultural communication: A reader* (pp. 221–226). Belmont, CA: Wadsworth.

Weeks, W. H., Pedersen, P. B., & Brislin, R. W. (1977) (Eds.). *A manual of structured experiences for cross-cultural learning.* Pittsburgh: SIETAR.

Weinstein, E. A. (1969). The development of interpersonal competence. In D. A. Goslin (Ed.), *Handbook of socialization theory and research* (pp. 753–775). Chicago: Rand McNally.

Wen, C. I. (1988). An investigation of Chinese national character: A value orientation perspective. In I. U. Lee and K. S. Yang (Eds.), *The Chinese character* (pp. 49–90). Taipei, Taiwan: Kwei Kwan.

Wheeless, E. W., & Duran, R. L. (1982). Gender orientation as a correlate of communicative competence. *Southern Speech Communication Journal, 48,* 51–64.

White, R. W. (1959). Motivation reconsidered: The concept of competence. *Psychological Review, 66,* 297–333.

Whorf, B. L. (1952). *Collected papers on metalinguistics.* DC: Department of State, Foreign Service Institute.

Wiemann, J. M. (1977). Explication and test of model of communication competence. *Human Communication Research, 3,* 195–213.

Wiener, M., & Mehrabian, A. (1968). *A language within language: Immediacy: A channel in verbal communication.* New York: Appleton-Century-Crofts.

Wilhelm, R. (1979). *Lectures on the I Ching: Constancy and change.* Princeton, NJ: Princeton University Press.

Williams, M. V. (1990). Managing work-place diversity. *Communication World*, January, 16–19.

Winikow, L. (1991). How women and minorities are reshaping corporate America. *Vital Speeches*, February 1, pp. 20–24.

Wishhard, W. (1990). The 21st century economy. In E. Cornish (Ed.), *The 1990s and Beyond* (pp. 131–136). Bethesda, MD: World Future Society.

Wolfson, K., & Norden, M. F. (1984). Measuring responses to filmed interpersonal conflict: A rules approach. In W. B. Gudykunst & Y. Y. Kim (Eds.), *Methods for intercultural research* (pp. 155–166). Beverly Hills, CA: Sage.

Wolfson, K., & Pearce, W. B. (1983). A cross-cultural comparison of the implications of self-disclosure on conversational logics. *Communication Quarterly, 31*, 249–256.

Wood, J. (1982). Communication and relational culture: Bases for the study of human relationships. *Communication Quarterly, 30*, 75–83.

Wood, J. W. (1994). Gender, communication, and culture. In L. A. Samovar and R. E. Porter (Eds.), *Intercultural communication: A reader* (pp. 155–164). Belmont, CA: Wadsworth.

Wozniak, T. (1991). Attracting and retaining the "Baby Bust" generation. *Journal of Compensation and Benefits,* March-April, 20–24.

Wright, A. (1970). *Experiential cross-cultural training.* Mimeo produced by Center for Research and Education, Estes Park, Colorado.

Wurzel, J. S. (1988). *Toward multiculturalism: A reader in multicultural education.* Yarmouth, ME: Intercultural Press.

Yang, H. J. (1978). *Communicative competence in Formosan sociable events: A participant observation study.* Dissertation Abstracts International, 39, 2622A.

Yang, K. S. (1982). "Yuan" and its functions in contemporary life. *Chinese Cultural Renaissance, 15*, 19–42.

Yeh, E., Chu, H., Klein, M., Alexander, A. & Miller, M. H. (1981). Psychiatric implications of cross-cultural education: Chinese students in the United States. In S. Bochner (Ed.), *The mediating person: Bridges between cultures,* (pp. 136–168). Boston, MA: Schenkman.

Yoshikawa, M. J. (1987). Cross-cultural adaptation and perceptual development. In Y. Y. Kim & W. B. Gudykunst (Eds.), *Cross-cultural adaptation* (pp. 140–148). London: Sage.

Yu, X. (1995). Conflict in a multicultural organization: An ethnographic attempt to discover work-related cultural assumptions between Chinese and American co-workers. *International Journal of Conflict Management, 6*, 211–232.

Yum, J. O. (1988). The impact of Confucianism on interpersonal relationships and communication patterns in East Asia. *Communication Monographs, 55*, 374–388.

Yum, J. O. (1987). Korean philosophy and communication. In D. L. Kincaid (Ed.), *Communication theory: Eastern and Western perspective* (pp. 71–86). New York: Academic Press.

Yum, J. O. (1987). The practice of uye-ri in interpersonal relationship. In D. L. Kincaid (Ed.), *Communication theory: Eastern and Western perspective* (pp. 87–100). New York: Academic Press.

Yum, J. O. (1988). The impact of Confucianism on interpersonal relationships and communication patterns in East Asia. *Communication Monographs, 55*, 374–388.

Yum, J. O. (1989). *Communication sensitivity and empathy in culturally diverse organizations.* Paper presented at the 75th Annual Conference of Speech Communication Association, San Francisco.

Zaharna, R. (1988). Self-shock and the intercultural challenge of identity. *The International Journal of Intercultural Relations.*

Zaharna, R. S. (1989). The double-binding challenge of identity. *International Journal of Intercultural Relations, 13*, 501–526.

Zaharna, R. S. (1991). The ontological function of interpersonal communication: A cross-cultural analysis of Americans and Palestinians. *Howard Journal of Communications, 3*, 87–98.

# Index